Butterworths Professional Dictionaries Series

DICTIONARY OF COMMERCIAL LAW

by

A. H. HUDSON, M.A., LL.B., Ph.D.

of Lincoln's Inn, Barrister
Professor of Common Law in the University of Liverpool

LONDON

BUTTERWORTHS

1983

England	Butterworth & Co (Publishers) Ltd, 88 Kingsway, LONDON WC2B 6AB
Australia	Butterworths Pty Ltd, SYDNEY, MELBOURNE, BRISBANE, ADELAIDE and PERTH
Canada	Butterworth & Co (Canada) Ltd, TORONTO Butterworth & Co (Western Canada) Ltd, VANCOUVER
New Zealand	Butterworths of New Zealand Ltd, WELLINGTON
Singapore	Butterworth & Co (Asia) Pte Ltd, SINGAPORE
South Africa	Butterworth Publishers (Pty) Ltd, DURBAN
U.S.A.	Mason Publishing Co, ST PAUL, Minnesota Butterworth Legal Publishers, SEATTLE, Washington; BOSTON, Massachusetts; and AUSTIN, Texas D & S Publishers, CLEARWATER, Florida

© Butterworth & Co (Publishers) Ltd 1983

Hudson, A. H.
  Dictionary of commercial law.
  1. Commercial law—England—Dictionaries
  I. Title
  344.206´7´0321 KD1627.5
  ISBN Hardcover 0 406 68159 7
        Softcover 0 406 68160 0

Printed by Billing Bookplan, Worcester
Photoset by Cotswold Typesetting Ltd, Gloucester

Preface

This dictionary is intended to provide within brief compass ready access to basic information relating to the terminology of most of the principal topics of both Commercial Law and Intellectual Property. As Commercial Law has no formal boundaries the selection of topics was largely based on that used for the current edition of the long-established student textbook, *Stevens and Borrie, Mercantile Law*. The Law of Contract and certain topics of commercial importance in the Law of Tort, such as Negligence and Interference with Goods, have been included since they may be relevant to problems arising over almost the whole field of Commercial Law. On the other hand, Company Law and Partnership, Taxation and Employment Law have been excluded, partly because they are ordinarily treated as independent subjects and partly because they are covered by other dictionaries in the series to which this belongs. Insurance Law (both Marine and non-Marine) has been excluded on the latter ground alone.

An attempt has been made to describe, rather than merely to define, the terms which are the subjects of the entries and the close interrelation of so many of the topics has required extensive cross-referencing. It is hoped that the work will be of use both as a work of reference and revision to students and others concerned with Commercial Law.

The advice and assistance of members of the staff of Messrs. Butterworths, which has been indispensable and invaluable in bringing this Dictionary to completion, especially in regard to the task of cross-referencing, is gratefully acknowledged.

Faculty of Law,
University of Liverpool
June 1983.

A. H. HUDSON

Publisher's Note

This Dictionary defines many words in ordinary everyday use which also have a specific legal meaning. Where it is important to a full appreciation of an entry that these words are understood in their legal context the cross-reference is indicated in the text by a dagger symbol (†). Statutes, cases and commercial law courts that are also the subject of their own entry are similarly distinguished.

It may be assumed that legal expressions and phrases used in the text are, as a general rule, separately defined at the appropriate place in the Dictionary.

A

Acceptance Credit. *See* BANKERS' COMMERCIAL CREDITS.

Acceptance for Honour Supra Protest. If a bill of exchange is dishonoured by non-acceptance and is not overdue (*see* MATURITY) and the holder has protested† the bill, any person not already liable on it, may with the holder's consent intervene and accept the bill for the honour of any party liable on it or for whom it is drawn. Where there is no express statement it is presumed to be for the honour of the drawer. This acceptance may be for the whole or part of the sum covered by the bill, should be written on it, should indicate it is for honour, and be signed by the acceptor for honour. Where a bill payable after sight† is accepted for honour its maturity is calculated from the noting† and not from the acceptance for honour. The acceptor for honour is taken to promise that on due presentment for payment he will pay the bill in accordance with his acceptance if the drawee does not do so when the bill has been presented to him and protested for non-payment and the acceptor for honour is notified of this. If the holder agrees to acceptance for honour this precludes his exercise of the right of recourse. (*See* PAYMENT FOR HONOUR SUPRA PROTEST). See the Bills of Exchange Act 1882, ss. 65, 66 and 67.

Acceptance in sale of goods. By the Sale of Goods Act 1979, s. 27 it is the duty of the buyer to accept and pay for goods in accordance with the contract of sale. By s. 11 (4) where a contract is not severable (e.g. not falling under s. 31 (2) where goods are to be delivered in instalments separately paid for) and the buyer has accepted the whole or part of the goods a breach of condition by the seller can only be treated as a breach of warranty, so on acceptance the buyer loses his right to reject the goods and can only sue for damages. By s. 35 a buyer is deemed to have accepted the goods when he tells the seller he has done so or when (subject to s. 34) the goods have been delivered to him and he does any act in relation to them inconsistent with the ownership of the seller or when after the lapse of a reasonable time he retains the goods without telling the seller he has rejected them. Prior to the Misrepresentation Act 1967 if the buyer sub-sold goods he was deemed to have accepted them even though he did not have an opportunity of examining them. The reference to s. 34 changes this for that section provides that when a buyer has not previously examined goods he is not deemed to have accepted them until he has had a

1

reasonable opportunity of examining them and, unless otherwise agreed, the seller is bound on request to give the buyer such an opportunity. Prima facie the goods should be examined at the place of delivery to the buyer. If the buyer, not having examined them, sub-sells and delivers goods which are defective and the seller had no reason to foresee this then the buyer will be taken to have accepted them because he will be treated as not having displaced the presumption that he had an opportunity to examine on delivery, *Saunt v Belcher* (1920) 26 Com Cas 115. In c.i.f. contracts there are separate rights of rejection for the shipping documents and the goods; acceptance of the documents is only conditional and does not preclude rejection of the goods: *Kwei Tek Chao v British Traders* [1954] 2 QB 459. If property has passed to the buyer and he is entitled to reject, the passing of property is only conditional. This explains why the buyer may still do acts inconsistent with a residual ownership in the seller. A sub-sale, with delivery, there having been an opportunity for the buyer to inspect, is a typical inconsistent act. What is an unreasonable period of time for retaining defective goods depends on the circumstances but the buyer is entitled to consider the position and make enquiries and tests, *Fisher, Reeves v Armour* [1920] 3 KB 614. Immediate rejection is not required unless, perhaps, the goods are perishable.

There can be no acceptance of goods which the seller is not entitled to sell, *Rowland v Divall* [1923] 2 KB 500.

Acceptance of a Bill of Exchange. This is defined by the Bills of Exchange Act 1882, s. 17 (1) as 'the signification by the drawee of his assent to the order of the drawer' to make the payment ordered. An acceptance is invalid unless it is written on the bill and signed by the drawee, his mere signature without additional words sufficing, and it must not express that the drawee will fulfil his promise otherwise than by the payment of money. When the time for payment comes, however, the holder may agree to take satisfaction in some other form. Acceptance may be effected before the bill has been signed by the drawer or is otherwise incomplete, when it is overdue or after it has been dishonoured by non-acceptance or dishonoured by non-payment. When a bill payable after sight† is dishonoured by non-acceptance and the drawee later accepts it the holder, if there is no agreement to the contrary, is entitled to have the bill accepted as at the date of the first presentment for acceptance. An acceptance may be general or qualified. A general acceptance assents without qualification to the order whereas a qualified acceptance departs from it. In particular an acceptance is qualified when it is conditional, making payment subject to some condition, or partial, that is for only part of the sum for which the bill is drawn, or local, to pay only at some particular place. An acceptance to pay at a particular place is general unless it expressly states the bill is not to be paid elsewhere. An acceptance may also be qualified as to time or if it is the acceptance of some but not all of the drawees. By s. 44 the holder may refuse to take a qualified acceptance and if he does not get an unqualified one he may treat the bill as dishonoured by non-acceptance. Where the holder takes a qualified acceptance the drawer or an indorser who has not expressly or impliedly authorised the taking or subsequently assented to it is discharged from liability on the bill but this does not apply to a partial acceptance for which due notice has been given. When there is partial acceptance of a foreign bill there must be protest for the balance. When the drawer or an indorser is given notice of a qualified acceptance and does not dissent within a reasonable time they will be taken to have assented.

Only in the case of acceptance for honour supra protest can a person other than the drawee accept a bill. Any person other than the drawee purporting to accept may incur the liabilities of an indorser under s. 56.

In certain cases presentment for acceptance of the bill by the holder to the drawee is required.

A bill of exchange cannot be drawn to be payable at a certain period after acceptance though it can be drawn payable at a certain period after sight: *Korea Exchange Bank v Debenhams* [1979] 1 Lloyd's Rep 548.

Acceptor of a Bill of Exchange. Normally the drawee writes his acceptance on a Bill of Exchange but he may be a person who intervenes to effect an acceptance for honour supra protest of a bill which has been dishonoured by non-acceptance. The Bills of Exchange Act 1882, s. 54 covering the liability of an acceptor other than one accepting for honour states that he is taken to promise to pay the bill according to the terms of his acceptance and is precluded from denying to a holder in due course the existence of the drawer, the genuineness of his signature and his capacity† and authority to draw the bill. In an order bill payable to the drawer's order the acceptor is precluded from denying the capacity of the drawer to indorse but not the genuineness or validity of the indorsement. In an order bill payable to someone other than the drawer, the acceptor may not deny the existence of the payee and his then capacity to indorse but may deny the genuineness or validity of his indorsement.

Accommodation Bill of Exchange. This is a bill of exchange where the party expressed to be primarily liable, the acceptor†, has not received value (*see* CONSIDERATION FOR A BILL OF EXCHANGE) for becoming party to the instrument and has merely lent his name to some other party to the instrument so that the other party may more easily effect negotiation of the instrument. The Bills of Exchange Act

1882, s. 59 (3) provides, by exception to the normal rules for payment in due course of a negotiable instrument, that when an accommodation bill is paid in due course by the party accommodated (the party to whom the acceptor lent his name) it is discharged. An accommodation bill is not any instrument carrying the name of an accommodation party but only one where the party expressed to be primarily liable is an accommodation party. Section 28 states that an accommodation party is one who has signed a bill as drawer, acceptor or indorser without receiving value for so doing but merely to lend his name to some other person. An accommodation party is liable to a holder for value, whether or not the holder knew him to be such when he took the instrument and, with greater reason, the accommodation party will be liable to a holder in due course.

By s. 89 these provisions apply with necessary modification to a promissory note. *See* PROMISSORY NOTE.

Accommodation Party. *See* ACCOMMODATION BILL OF EXCHANGE.

Accord and Satisfaction. *See* DISCHARGE OF CONTRACT BY AGREEMENT.

Account Payee Crossing. *See* CROSSED CHEQUE.

Account Stated. Acknowledgement of a debt upon which there arises an implied promise to pay. An example is an I.O.U. Since the promise is implied, not express, it is not a promissory note.

Act of Bankruptcy. Some circumstance, defined in bankruptcy legislation, indicating a debtor's unwillingness or inability to pay his debts. A creditor's bankruptcy petition must be grounded upon an act of bankruptcy committed within three months before the presentation of the petition.

By the Bankruptcy Act 1914, s. 1 (1) a debtor commits an act of bankruptcy in each of the following eight cases (in this context England includes Wales):

1. 'If in England or elsewhere he makes a conveyance or assignment of his property to a trustee or trustees for the benefit of his creditors generally.'

An assignment to one or more particular creditors is not an act of bankruptcy under this head nor is an assignment for the benefit of trade creditors only. It must be a conveyance of substantially all of a debtor's property to a trustee to represent all creditors.

A creditor who has acquiesced in such an assignment or recognised the title of the trustee cannot rely on it as an act of bankruptcy but if not bound by the assignment can rely on some other act. A creditor whose assent was obtained by fraud may rely on the assignment as may a creditor who assented to a proposed assignment but withdrew his assent before the execution of the deed.

2. 'If in England or elsewhere he makes a fraudulent conveyance, gift, delivery, or transfer of his property or any part thereof.'

For the purposes of this provision a transaction may be fraudulent if it tends to favour specific creditors contrary to the rules for distribution in bankruptcy, even if not made in bad faith though a transaction in bad faith will also suffice. Sale or mortgaging of property in the ordinary course of business will not necessarily be fraudulent but a conveyance in respect of a past debt will be, *Re Sinclair* (1884) 26 Ch D 319; though this will not be so if the transaction is partly in respect of a past debt and partly as a security for further advances to enable the debtor to carry on business, *Allen v Bonnett* (1870) 5 Ch App 577. Transfer from the debtor to a company under his control may also be fraudulent as tending to defeat or delay creditors, *Re Slobodinsky* [1903] 2 KB 517.

3. 'If in England or elsewhere he makes any conveyance or transfer of his property or any part thereof, or creates any charge thereon which would under this or any other Act be void as a fraudulent preference if he were adjudged bankrupt.' The concept of fradulent preference is also of importance in relation to distribution† of property amongst creditors since property so used may be recovered by the trustee in bankruptcy from its recipients for distribution amongst creditors of the bankrupt. Preference must be the 'dominant intention'. The word 'preference' implies free will so there will be no preference if it is shown that the transaction resulted from pressure from the creditor, including a threat to take legal proceedings or if the debtor mistakenly feared that proceedings would be taken, or if the debtor's object was to protect himself against criminal proceedings, or if the debtor desired to make recompense for a wrong.

4. 'If with intent to defeat or delay his creditors he does any of the following things, namely departs out of England, or being out of England remains out of England or departs from his dwelling-house, or otherwise absents himself, or begins to keep house.'

This creates five distinct acts of bankruptcy. Proof of intent is essential for all but it may be inferred from the circumstances. In the acts of departure and beginning to keep house intent must exist at the time of departure or commencement and three months are calculated from that point but the others are continuing acts where intent can exist at any point in the process and three months may be calculated from its termination. 'Keeping house' means refusing to see creditors when they call at reasonable hours.

5. 'If execution against him has been levied by seizure of his goods under process in any action in any court, or in any civil proceedings in the High Court, and the goods have been either sold or held by the sheriff for twenty-one days. Provided that where an interpleader summons has been taken out in regard to the goods seized, the time elapsing between the date at which such summons is taken out and the

date at which the proceedings on such summons are finally disposed of, settled or abandoned, shall not be taken into account in calculating such period of twenty-one days.'

It was held in *Re Dalton* [1963] Ch 336 that a sheriff 'holds' goods under this provision even though, after seizure, the debtor is allowed under a 'walking possession' agreement to trade in the goods seized provided any goods sold were replaced.

6. 'If he files in the court a declaration of his inability to pay his debts or presents a bankruptcy petition against himself.'

7. 'If a creditor has obtained a final judgment or final order against him for any amount, and execution thereon not having been stayed, has served on him in England, or, by leave of the court elsewhere, a bankruptcy notice under this Act, and he does not within ten days after service of the notice, in case the service is effected in England, and in case the service is effected elsewhere, then within the time limit in that behalf by the order giving leave to effect the service, either comply with the requirements of the notice or satisfy the court that he has a counterclaim, set-off or cross demand which equals or exceeds the amount of the judgment debt or the sum ordered to be paid, and which he could not set up in the action in which the judgment was obtained, or the proceedings in which the order was obtained.'

A bankruptcy notice must be in the form prescribed under the Bankruptcy Act 1914, s. 2. It must require the debtor to pay the judgment debt or sum ordered to be paid in accordance with the judgment or order or to secure or compound for it to the satisfaction of the creditor or the court and must state the consequences of non-compliance.

The period of ten days was substituted for the former period of seven days by the Insolvency Act 1976, s. 4. Bankruptcy notices are strictly construed. Any irregularity which might mislead or embarrass the debtor will render the notice void though purely formal defects may be corrected under the Bankruptcy Act 1914, s. 147 (1). This is the most frequently found act of bankruptcy.

8. 'If the debtor gives notice to any of his creditors that he has suspended, or that he is about to suspend, payment of his debts.'

The notice here need not be in writing and need not be given formally and deliberately. It may indicate merely a temporary suspension but must be unconditional. It may be given to a single creditor but must relate to a suspension in regard to creditors generally.

A further act of bankruptcy is included in the Bankruptcy Act 1914, s. 107 (4). If a judgment summons is taken out against a debtor, the court may, with the creditor's assent, instead of committing the debtor to prison make a receiving order against him. The debtor is deemed to have committed an act of bankruptcy at the time the order is made. This act will be rarely found since the Administration of Justice Act 1970 restricted imprisonment for debt.

When a criminal bankruptcy order is made against an offender under the Powers of Criminal Courts Act 1973, he is to be treated as having committed an act of bankruptcy on the date on which the order was made.

Where a person fails to make any payment he is required to make under an administration order it is provided by s. 11 of the Insolvency Act 1976 that the court may revoke the administration order and replace it by a receiving order. The person will be deemed to have committed an act of bankruptcy when the receiving order is made.

The acts of bankruptcy once provided for by the Administration of Justice Act 1965 and the Atttachment of Earnings Act 1971, under which an application for an administration order and the making of an order requiring a debtor to furnish a list of creditors for the making of an administration order constituted acts of bankruptcy, have been abolished by the Insolvency Act 1976.

Act of God. *See* COMMON CARRIER.

Actual authority of an agent. This comprises what the agent is explicitly or implicitly instructed to do by his principal. It need not be, though it frequently is, embodied in a contract. Formalities are not normally required. Thus appointment in writing is not required for an agent for a contract relating to land, though the contract itself requires to be evidenced in writing under the Statute of Frauds 1677 (now the Law of Property Act 1925, s. 40), *Heard v Pilley* (1869) 4 Ch App 548, but if the agent is to execute a deed or specialty his own appointment must be by deed, known as a power of attorney, to which Powers of Attorney Act 1971 applies. Section 1 governs the execution of the power, s. 2 abolishes requirements to deposit powers in court offices, s. 3 covers proof, s. 4 governs irrevocable powers given to the donee (agent) as a security and which are not to be revoked until the interest secured has ended, s. 5 protects donees and third parties unknowingly relying in good faith on a power which has been revoked, s. 6 additionally protects stock exchange transactions, s. 7 governs the execution of documents under a power of attorney and s. 10 provides that a general power in the form scheduled to the Act gives the donee power to do anything for the donor which he could lawfully do by attorney. Powers of attorney are interpreted more strictly than other written authority.

Actual authority may be express, when it is stated in the words spoken or written by the principal, perhaps raising problems of evidence or interpretation, or it may be implied, when the authority is inferred from the language used, as in respect of matters incidental to or necessarily connected with those mentioned, or is derived from the context of trade or professional custom ('customary authority'), or from the normal powers and duties of the agent's position or appointment ('usual authority'). Actual authority in its various forms is to be contrasted with apparent or ostensible authority where the principal does not instruct the agent but is responsible for an appearance of authority, on which he is held as liable as if it were actual, and with authority arising by operation of law, as in agency of necessity.

If there is ambiguity in actual authority the agent will not be liable if he acts on a reasonable interpretation, *Ireland v Livingston* (1872) LR 5 HL 395, and if he is acting within the authority the principal will be bound even though the agent is acting for his own ends, *Hambro v Burnand* [1904] 2 KB 10. An agent to sell does not necessarily have authority to receive payment, *Butwick v Grant* [1924] 2 KB 483, and an agent to receive payment does not necessarily have authority to take payment by cheque or means other than cash, *Williams v Evans* (1866) LR 1 QB 352, but if an unauthorised cheque or other negotiable instrument is honoured when taken by an agent for payment this will discharge the third party, *Bradford v Price* (1923) 92 LJB 871, being treated as equivalent to cash. Estate agents have no implied authority to receive deposits for a vendor from a prospective purchaser, *Sorrell v Finch* [1977] AC 728. 'Implied authority', 'customary authority' and 'usual authority' may also be relevant as sub-forms of apparent authority. *See also* USUAL AUTHORITY OF AN AGENT.

Ad idem. An abbreviated form of consensus ad idem.

Adjudication (Bankruptcy). This is the step in bankruptcy proceedings by which the court makes a debtor legally a bankrupt.

A debtor may at his own request be adjudged bankrupt at the time of the receiving order or at any later time. The court also has power on the application of any creditor or the official receiver to adjudge the debtor bankrupt on any of the following grounds.

1. A majority of the creditors at the first meeting or any adjournment resolve by ordinary resolution that the debtor be adjuged bankrupt.
2. The creditors pass no resolution.
3. The creditors do not meet or there is no quorum at the first meeting.
4. A composition† or scheme has not been approved within fourteen days after the public examination.
5. A composition or scheme is annulled by the court.
6. The debtor fails to pay an instalment due under a composition or scheme.
7. The debtor has improperly failed to make a statement of affairs.

8. The debtor has absconded.
9. The debtor does not intend to propose a composition or scheme.
10. The public examination has been adjourned sine die.
    An adjudication must be advertised in the *London Gazette* and a local paper.
    An adjudication may be annulled:
    (a) If the court thinks the debtor ought not to have been made bankrupt.
    (b) If the debts are paid in full or, if disputed, secured to the satisfaction of the court.
    (c) If a composition or scheme is accepted after adjudication and approved by the court.

Even when debts have been paid in full the court has discretion to refuse annulment, as when the debtor has committed bankruptcy offences. An unconditional release is not equivalent to payment in full. On annulment the property of the bankrupt will vest in him or a person appointed by the court. If the court makes no order after annulment on payment of a composition, the bankrupt's property revests in him.

Annulment must be advertised in the *London Gazette* and a local paper.

An important effect of adjudication is that the bankrupt's property will vest in the trustee in bankruptcy. A bankrupt also incurs a number of legal disabilities. He may not be elected to or act as a member of either House of Parliament or of any local authority or be appointed a justice of the peace. Disqualification from public office may continue for five years after discharge of the bankrupt unless a certificate† of misfortune is granted. He cannot practise as a solicitor nor without leave of the court can he act as a company director or as a receiver and manager for debenture holders.

If an undischarged bankrupt obtains credit of £50 or more without telling the creditor that he is bankrupt or trades under a name other than that under which he was bankrupted without disclosing the former name he is liable to imprisonment. The Bankruptcy Act 1914, Part VII sets out many other bankruptcy offences which may be committed either by bankrupts or by debtors against whom a receiving order has been made.

(See the Bankruptcy Act 1914, ss. 18 and 21.)

Administration in bankruptcy. The personal representative of a decreased debtor or any creditor whose debt would have sufficed for a bankruptcy petition if the debtor had been alive, may petition to have the estate administered in bankruptcy. The court cannot make an order until a personal representative has been appointed and it must be satisfied that there is no reasonable probability of the estate being sufficient for payment of the debts. Notice to the personal representative of the presentation of such a petition is equivalent to notice of an act of bankruptcy and after such notice no payment or transfer of property made by the personal representative will discharge him as against the official receiver or trustee in bankruptcy.

The official receiver becomes trustee, unless the creditors resolve to appoint a trustee. They may also appoint a committee of inspection. Funeral and testamentary expenses must be paid in priority to all other debts. Unliquidated damages in tort are provable by exception to the normal rules for proof of debts. The Bankruptcy Act 1914, s. 42 providing for the avoidance of certain settlements does not apply in the administration of a deceased debtor's estate in bankruptcy but fraudulent conveyances may be set aside under the Law of Property Act 1925, s. 172 (*see* SETTLEMENTS VOIDABLE IN BANKRUPTCY). See the Bankruptcy Act 1914, s. 130.

Administration order. In insolvency this is employed when judgment has been obtained against a debtor in a county court and he is unable to pay but his debts do not exceed £5000. The court, without putting the estate into bankruptcy may make an order for the payment of the debts by instalments or otherwise, in full or to such extent as appears practicable and subject to any conditions as to future earnings or income as the court thinks just. Where the debtor fails to make any payment the court may replace the administration order by a receiving order. The making of the administration order and the furnishing of lists of creditors are no longer acts of bankruptcy. (See County Courts Act 1959, ss. 148–156; Insolvency Act 1976, s. 13; County Courts (Administration Order Jurisdiction) Order 1981).

Advance freight. A payment of freight† by a shipper of goods to a shipowner in advance of the delivery of the goods to be carried. An agreement to make such a payment must be clearly shown and distinguished from an agreement for a loan. Even the use of the words 'advance freight' is not conclusive. There is an insurable interest in advance freight but not in a loan. Advance freight must be paid on the agreed date or at the start of the voyage. If the ship is lost after that date by excepted perils the shipper may not recover back the freight and, if it has not been paid, the shipowner may sue for it. The shipper may, however, recover it back if the voyage was not commenced within a reasonable time in a seaworthy† ship. Advance freight will not be payable on goods destroyed before the date of payment, *Weir v Girvin* [1900] 1 QB 45.

Advising bank. *See* BANKERS' COMMERCIAL CREDITS.

Agency. In law a relationship under which an intermediary, the agent, is empowered to enter into transactions, frequently contracts, on behalf of his principal with third parties, the principal and third party then being as bound by such a transaction as if they had entered into it directly. The agent normally does not acquire rights or incur liabilities on the transaction he has been instrumental in concluding. The agent's power to effect transactions is based upon authority either given to him by his principal, or which he is held out by the principal as having, or which the agent merely purported to possess but which is later ratified by the principal, or the necessity of the situation. (*See* ACTUAL AUTHORITY, EXPRESS AUTHORITY, IMPLIED AUTHORITY, APPARENT AUTHORITY, OSTENSIBLE AUTHORITY, USUAL AUTHORITY OF AN AGENT, RATIFICATION, AGENCY OF NECESSITY.) The law of agency deals with the rights and liabilities of principal and third party, principal and agent and agent and third party. (*See* REMUNERATION OF AGENT, INDEMNITY OF AGENT, AGENT, DUTIES OF, AGENT, LIABILITY OF, UNDISCLOSED PRINCIPAL, WARRANTY OF AUTHORITY, DELEGATUS NON POTEST DELEGARE.) In commerce the terms 'agent' and 'agency' are sometimes applied to sellers acting on their own behalf who do not put their suppliers in direct contractual relations with third parties.

The important capacity in agency is that of the principal. An agent of limited capacity (e.g. an infant) can be instrumental in concluding for a principal of full capacity any transaction into which the principal could enter personally and whilst a principal of limited capacity may with his capacity contract through an agent the principal cannot extend his capacity by employing an agent of full capacity. (*See* CAPACITY IN CONTRACT).

If a principal owes money to the third party and settles with the agent who fails to pay the third party, the principal will have to make a second payment to the third party: *Heald v Kenworthy* (1855) 10 Ex 739; *Irvine v Watson* (1880) 5 QBD 414; unless the third party has misled the principal into believing that settlement has been made with the agent: *Wyatt v Hertford* (1802) 3 East 147.

Agency of necessity. This arises when an agent or bailee holding another's property is faced with an emergency threatening the other's interest, as when perishables are likely to decay, and it is impossible to communicate with the owner. The holder may then, as agent of necessity, sell, raise money on the security of the property or incur expenses of preservation on behalf of the owner. The courts are reluctant to extend this and will be readier to find it as an extension of existing agency than where this did not pre-exist. *Springer v G.W.R.* [1921] 1 KB 257; *Sachs v Miklos* [1948] 2 KB 23; *Jebara v Ottoman Bank* [1927] 2 KB 254. Acceptance supra protest of a Bill of Exchange and salvage at sea are sometimes treated as types of agency of necessity. A deserted wife might at one time have been an agent of necessity of her husband but this was abolished by statute in 1970.

Agency, termination of agency. This may occur by act of the parties or operation of law. Fulfilment of the purpose of the agency, expiration of its time limit or mutual agreement may end it. In general a principal may at any time revoke the authority of an agent who will then cease to have actual authority, although if this revocation is not known to others the principal may become liable on the agent's continuing apparent authority. Similarly the agent may at any time renounce his authority, also ending his actual authority. Revocation and renunciation, though ending the agent's right to act, may amount to breach of contract by the party terminating. Whether or not the agent is a servant†, a term may be implied in the contract entitling him to reasonable notice. The principal may not revoke when the agent has 'an authority coupled with an interest', that is he has been given his authority as agent to collect money or secure property for himself, e.g. authority to sell goods and retain proceeds for himself in settlement of a debt due from the principal, *Raleigh v Atkinson* (1840) 6 M & W 670. The Powers of Attorney Act 1971, s. 4 applies this to powers of attorney and s. 5 protects both a donee (agent) and a third party who unknowingly and in good faith act on a power which has been revoked. Under operation of law the death of either party will end the agency. So also will insanity, but an insane principal may be liable on a continuing apparent authority, *Drew v Nunn* (1879) 4 QB 661. Cf. *Yonge v Toynbee* [1910] 1 KB 215 (which dealt with actual authority. This ended on insanity and the solicitor-agent who continued to act without knowing this was liable for breach of warranty of authority). Bankruptcy of the principal, but not necessarily that of the agent, will also determine the agency, as will supervening illegality and frustration of which death of a party is an example.

Agent. In law one who is empowered to enter into transactions, frequently contracts, with third parties on behalf of a principal, the principal and third party being as bound by such a transaction as if they had entered into it directly. *See* AGENCY. An agent must be distinguished from a servant, in law an employee who is part of his master's permanent organisation and over whose work the master has a right of detailed control and an independent contractor who is not part of his employer's permanent organisation and for whom the employer merely prescribes the ultimate objective of the work. Though servants and independent contractors may involve their employers in liability to third parties as by involving them in vicarious liability, this involvement is not the purpose of their employment as it is with agents. An employee may be simultaneously a servant or independent contractor and an agent, e.g. shop assistants, who are agents in making contracts of sale and servants in other aspects of their work. There are many sub-categories of agents. General and special agents, mentioned in older cases, are merely distinguished by the extent of their instructions and powers. Factors and brokers also appear in older cases and are included in mercantile agents covered by Factors Act 1889. Auctioneers, bankers, solicitors, partners, company directors, insurance brokers, freight forwarders and stockbrokers are examples of agents. In commerce the terms 'agent' and 'agency' are sometimes applied to sellers of goods who sell on their own behalf (e.g. when they hold a franchise for branded goods) and who do not put their suppliers in contractual relations with third parties.

Agent, duties of an agent to his principal. If the agency is gratuitous, not involving a contract between the parties, the agent will not be liable for total inaction but if he does commence performance he must show the care that a reasonably careful man of business would show in his own affairs, *Gomer v Pitt* (1922) 12 LlLR 115, unless he has professed to show a special skill when he must show the skill and care normally required of those possessing that skill. A contractual agent must carry out the principal's explicit instructions exactly, even if he thinks they are unwise. If they are ambiguous he will not be liable if he acts on a reasonable interpretation, *Ireland v Livingston* (1872) LR 5 HL 395. Terms may be implied from custom. He must not obey illegal and need not obey void instructions. He must show reasonable care, skill and diligence and, if he belongs to a profession, the care and skill appropriate to it. Agency is a relation of confidence hence the agent should perform his duties personally, not sub-delegating unless one of the exceptions to delegatus non potest delegare applies. Good faith is essential so he is not permitted even the possibility of conflict between duty and interest, *Boardman v Phipps* [1967] 2 AC 46, hence if he is employed to buy he must not sell his own goods to his principal even at a fair price, nor can he accept commission from the third party without full disclosure to and consent from his principal, *Fullwood v Hurley* [1927] 1 KB 498. A custom purporting to allow an agent to sell to his principal is bad, *Robinson v Mollett* (1875) LR 7 HL 802. He must make full disclosure before contracting with or accepting a gift from his principal. This duty may continue after the agency has ended, *Allison v Clayhills* (1908) 97 LT 709, as long as confidence continues. He must not make a secret profit from the agency and if he does he must account to the principal for it, even if the principal has not been named and even benefited from the agent's acts, *Boardman v Phipps*, but if the agent acted honestly he will still be entitled to remuneration, *Hippisley v Knee* [1905] 1 KB 1. If an agent takes a bribe the principal may dismiss the agent, avoid any contract with the third party even if the agent's conduct was not influenced by the bribe, hold the agent and third party jointly and severally liable in damages (*See* JOINT CONTRACTS), sue the agent either for damages or in quasi-contract for the bribe as money had and received to the principal's use, *Mahesan v Malaysia Government Officers Co-op Society* [1978] 2 All ER 405, and the guilty parties may be prosecuted under the Prevention of Corruption Acts 1906 and 1916. The agent is not a trustee of the profit or bribe for the principal so the latter cannot trace it into securities purchased by the agent, *Lister v Stubbs* (1890) 45 Ch D 1. (*See* TRACING). If the agent acquires confidential information as agent he must employ it only for the principal's benefit and not reveal it unless some public interest, e.g. suppression of crime, *Initial Services v Puterill* [1968] 1 QB 396, requires this. The agent must keep the property and money of the principal separate from his own, keep proper accounts and account to the principal for all money held or received for him, even on illegal transactions, unless the agency itself is illegal. If an agent acquires property in his own name for his principal he becomes a trustee of it. An agent is precluded by estoppel from asserting that either he or a third party has a better title to property he is holding as agent than his principal except that in regard to bailment he may assert a third party's title to subject matter if he has handed it to the third party or defends a claim for and with the authority of the third party.

Agent, liability of agent. If an agent acts for an identified principal or one whose existence is disclosed the general rule is that the agent takes neither rights nor liabilities on the transaction he has been instrumental in concluding but there are many exceptions. He may expressly agree to be liable jointly or alternatively with his principal, *International Rly v Niagara Parks* [1941] AC 328, and custom of trade may imply liability, *Anglo-Overseas v Titan Transport* [1959] 2 Lloyd's Rep 152. He will also be liable if he executes a deed in his own name, even though he describes himself as 'acting for and on behalf of' another. In regard to negotiable instruments he will not incur liability unless he signs but the Bills of Exchange Act 1882, s. 26 (1) provides that if he is to escape personal liability on a signature he must add 'representative' words making it clear that he is signing *as* agent, not merely 'descriptive' words which indicate that he is an agent or representative but do not make clear that he is signing in that capacity. A similar distinction applies to contracts in writing. If an agent signs without any qualification to his signature or merely adding descriptive words he will be prima facie personally liable, *Parker v Winlow* (1857) 7 E & B 942; *Universal Steam Navigation v McKelvie* [1923] AC 492 ('as agents' almost conclusive of agency); *The Swan* [1968] 1 Lloyd's Rep 5, but the strong presumption of personal liability from an unqualified or insufficiently qualified signature can be rebutted by clear indications of agency elsewhere in the document, *Gadd v Houghton* (1876) 1 Ex D 357, but not by parol evidence but such evidence may be used to show that by trade custom an agent who signs as agent may nevertheless in limited circumstances incur personal liability, *Hutchinson v Tatham* (1873) LR 8 CP 482. At one time there was a strong presumption that an agent who contracted on behalf of a foreign principal could alone sue or be sued to the exclusion of the principal (i.e. the agent was an agent in the commercial but not the legal sense. *See* AGENT). There is now no such presumption and the foreign character of the principal is merely one factor in determining whether an agent is to be liable jointly or in substitution for the principal, *Tehran-Europe v Belton* [1968] 2 QB 545. If an agent purports to contract on behalf of an unnamed, non-existent principal he will be liable and entitled on the contract, *Schmalz v Avery* (1851) 16 QB 655, unless the terms of the contract exclude this. He may also sue if he purported to act on behalf of a named non-existent principal if the third party continued with the transaction with knowledge of this or upon notice to the third party and provided he is not prejudiced. If the agent has purported to act on behalf of an unformed company under the European Communities Act 1972, s. 9 (2) he will be regarded as having contracted personally unless a contrary intention has been expressed in the contract.

For the rights and liabilities of an agent who contracts on behalf of an undisclosed principal, *see* UNDISCLOSED PRINCIPAL.

Agent, rights of an agent against his principal. These are to indemnity, remuneration and a lien. (*See* INDEMNITY; REMUNERATION; LIEN.)

Agreement to sell. *See* SALE OF GOODS.

Air consignment note. *See* CARRIAGE BY AIR; AIR WAYBILL.

Air waybill. *See* CARRIAGE BY AIR: AIR WAYBILL.

Allonge. Paper attached to a negotiable instrument upon which indorsements may be written. See the Bills of Exchange Act 1882, s. 32 (1).

Alteration of a negotiable instrument. This is normally a form of discharge of a negotiable instrument. The Bills of Exchange Act 1882, s. 64 provides that where a bill of exchange or an acceptance is materially altered without the assent of all parties liable on the bill, the bill is avoided except against a party who himself made, authorised or assented to the alteration and subsequent indorsers. If, however, a bill has been materially altered but this is not apparent and the bill comes into the hands of a holder in due course he may treat it as if it had not been altered and enforce payment of the original sum. Alterations to the date, the sum payable, time and place of payment, and, where a bill has been accepted generally the addition of a place of payment without the acceptor's assent are specified as material but the list is not exhaustive. In *Suffell v Bank of England* (1882) 9 QBD 555 at 568 it was said that any alteration is material which would 'alter the business effect of the instrument if used for any business purpose'. Also s. 78

provides that a crossing on a cheque is material and renders alteration unlawful except as authorised. Section 77 sets out a number of cases in which crossings may be added or altered. In addition the words 'Account payee' or 'account payee only' may by virtue of decided cases be added to a crossing. It is also possible by custom to 'open' a crossing so that the drawer may obtain cash for his cheque. A blank indorsement converting an order into a bearer instrument is not a material alteration. By s. 12 a date may be added, by s. 15 the name of a referee in case of need and by s. 34 a blank indorsement may be altered to a special. An accidental alteration is not material, *Hong Kong & Shanghai Bank v Lo Lee Shi* [1928] AC 181.

An acceptor† of a bill of exchange does not owe a duty to a later holder to ensure that the bill cannot easily be altered, *Scholfield v Lord Londesborough* [1896] AC 514, and the acceptor is only liable for the original sum but the drawer of a cheque does owe a duty to his bank not to draw his cheque so as to facilitate forgery, *London Joint Stock Bank v Macmillan and Arthur* [1918] AC 777, where gaps allowed the amount to be altered but this duty will not be broken if the alteration could not reasonably have been foreseen, *Slingsby v District Bank* [1932] 1 KB 544. Here the bankers could not debit the drawer's account and since the cheque had been discharged by material alteration could not rely on the protection given to a paying banker by ss. 60 and 80. It seems that any alteration to a banknote, even if not material in another instrument, will avoid it. *Leeds Bank v Walker* (1883) 11 QBD 84.

(See also the Bills of Exchange Act 1882, s. 89 applying these provisions to a promissory note).

By s. 79 (2) if a crossed cheque has had its crossing obliterated or imperceptibly altered a banker who in good faith and without negligence pays it in accordance with its appearance is protected from liability.

Analogous instruments. These are instruments which may or may not be negotiable instruments but resemble them sufficiently closely for the protection in respect of conversion of the paying banker and the collecting banker given by the Cheques Act 1957 primarily in respect of cheques to be extended to them. Section 1 (2) extends the protection of the paying banker to bankers drafts and 'to any document issued by a customer which though not a bill of exchange, is intended to enable a person to obtain payment from him of the sum mentioned in the document'. This would cover 'cheques' with impersonal payees and conditional instruments. Section 4 (2) extends the protection of the collecting banker not only to the categories covered by s. 1 (2) but also to certain Government orders for payment. Postal orders and money orders are covered by different legislation. For postal orders the Post Office Act 1953, s. 21 (3) (as amended by Post Office Act 1969, s. 76) gives protection to a banker collecting postal orders for 'a principal'. The banker is liable only to the principal, who in turn will be liable to the true owner if his title is defective. Money orders are covered by the Post Office Act 1969, s. 71. The collecting banker has no protection against liability in conversion to the true owner and if the Post Office finds that a money order was improperly collected by a banker it may withhold the amount from future payments to that banker who may similarly withhold the amount from later payments to the customer.

Ancillary credit businesses. The Consumer Credit Act 1974, s. 145 provides that these include any business in so far as it comprises or relates to credit brokerage, debt-adjusting, debt counselling, debt collecting or operating a credit reference agency. These businesses are subject to most of the licensing requirements of the Act, ss. 147–150, there are restrictions on brokerage fees, neither debtor–creditor agreements nor ancillary credit services may be canvassed off trade premises, they are subject to restrictions on seeking business similar to those for prospective creditors ss. 151–152, and their agreements are subject to the same requirements in regard to disclosure and formalities as regulated agreements, s. 156. By s. 146 barristers, solicitors, and certain owners, creditors and suppliers acting on their own behalf are excepted from s. 145.

Antecedent negotiations. The Consumer Credit Act 1974, s. 56 provides that these are any negotiations with the debtor or hirer conducted by the creditor or owner in relation to making any regulated agreement or conducted by a credit broker in relation to goods sold or to be sold to the creditor before becoming the subject matter of a debtor–creditor–supplier agreement or conducted by the supplier in relation to a transaction financed or to be financed by a debtor–creditor–supplier agreement. Negotiations are taken to begin when the negotiator and the debtor or hirer first get into communication (including through advertisement) and include any representations or other dealings between them. A relation of agency is deemed to exist between the creditor and the negotiator and this may not be excluded by contract. The creditor or owner will thus be liable for any misrepresentation made by the negotiator and any money given to the latter for the purposes of the agreement will be deemed to have been received by the creditor or owner.

Anticipatory breach. In contract this is where a party before the time for his performance declares he will not perform or disables himself from performance. *Hochster v De la Tour* (1853) 2 E & B 678; *Frost v Knight* (1872) LR 7 Ex 111. The other party may at once accept the breach and claim damages, or other relief or may keep the contract on foot to see if performance will be effected when the time arrives. In the latter case the contract remains in being for the benefit and burden of both parties so that if the party prospectively in breach would otherwise have been discharged by frustration he is still discharged despite his anticipatory breach, *Avery v Bowden* (1855) 5 E & B 714. *See* REMEDIES OF THE BUYER IN SALE OF GOODS; UNPAID SELLER.

Anticipatory credit. *See* BANKERS' COMMERCIAL CREDITS.

Anton Piller Order. So named from the case of *Anton Piller KG v Manufacturing Processes* [1976] Ch 55 this is an order of the court to a defendant to permit the plaintiff to enter the defendant's premises to inspect, remove or copy documents relating to an alleged infringement of intellectual property or alleged passing off. The defendant may also be ordered to deliver up or retain infringing articles. As the defendant is not present at the application, which may be made even before issue of writ, a very strong probability of infringement must be shown, with likelihood of serious harm to the plaintiff and a grave danger of evidence being suppressed. The facts that the plaintiff's solicitor must attend on the inspection, that the defendant must be allowed to consult his solicitor, and to apply to discharge the order, that the order does not authorise forced entry, and that the plaintiff must give an undertaking in damages distinguish the order from a search warrant. Failure to comply is contempt of court. The order is of importance in copyright and similar proceedings. A defendant may not refuse to comply with this order on the ground that to do so would involve self-incrimination or incrimination of his or her spouse but evidence so disclosed will not be admissible in proceedings for any related offence. Supreme Court Act 1981, s. 72.

Apparent authority of an agent. This arises when the agent has no actual authority but the principal either holds him out to third parties as being authorised or permits him to appear to them to be authorised. If third parties rely on the appearance the principal will be as liable as if it were actual. The apparent agent may have had no prior authority, or had authority which has ended or have had authority which he exceeded in the relevant transaction. Apparent authority is widely regarded as an application of estoppel, *Freeman & Lockyer v Buckhurst* [1964] 2 QB 480, and three ingredients are required: representation, reliance and a resulting alteration of position. The representation must be made by the principal or another agent qualified to make it, not by the apparent agent himself, *Farquharson v King* [1902] AC 325; *A–G Ceylon v Silva* [1953] AC 461. It may be made either in express words or by conduct, as by appointing the apparent agent to a position which usually carries certain authority, *Panorama v Fidelis Furnishing* [1971] 2 QB 711 (company secretary), *Summers v Solomon* (1857) 7 E & B 879 (shop manager) but must be of existing fact. Representation by conduct is sometimes termed implied apparent authority but must be distinguished from implied actual authority. (*See* IMPLIED AUTHORITY OF AN AGENT). The third party must have actual knowledge of the representation, *MacFisheries v Harrison* (1924) 93 LJKB 811 (third party did not read name over public house door), constructive knowledge not sufficing. The representation must have been made intentionally or, if made negligently, must be shown to be the 'proximate cause' of the loss suffered by the third party. It is uncertain whether *Hedley Byrne v Heller* [1964] AC 465 applies here but it may do. (*See* MISREPRESENTATION). The third party must have relied on the representation so that if he did not believe it or knew that it was untrue he cannot hold the principal liable, *Bloomenthal v Ford* [1897] AC 156; *Overbrook Estates v Glencombe Properties* [1974] 3 All ER 511. Where there are no unusual circumstances the third party will not be under a duty of inquiry but will be if he knows that there is a formal written authority, *Jacobs v Morris* [1902] 1 Ch 816, or where there are unusual circumstances or where the apparent agent is acting contrary to trade custom. Some dicta merely require that the third party should have changed his position in reliance on the representation, *Rama v Proved Tin* [1952] 2 QB 147, *Freeman & Lockyer v Buckhurst*, but others require he should have changed his position to his detriment, *Farquharson v King*, which appears more consistent with estoppel. Placing goods in another's possession does not of itself amount to a representation that the other is an agent for sale, *Farquharson v King*, *Central Newbury v Unity Finance* [1957] 1 QB 371. Some additional representation is required as in *Eastern Distributors v Goldring* [1957] 2 QB 600. If goods were entrusted to a dealer this was enough at common law to give him apparent authority to sell, *Pickering v Busk* (1812) 15 East 38, but not to pledge, raising problems in overseas trade. Hence legislation culminating in the Factors Act 1889 was passed, in part declaratory of the former law, to the effect that if goods or documents of title to them were left with the consent of the owner in the possession of a mercantile agent any sale, pledge or other disposition made by him when acting in the ordinary course of business of a mercantile agent was to be as valid as if he were expressly authorised by the owner, provided that the other party was acting in good faith and without notice. (*See* FACTORS ACT 1889.)

The anomalous case of *Watteau v Fenwick* [1893] 1 QB 346 is sometimes treated as a form of apparent authority. The agent was appointed manager of a public house but forbidden by the principal to purchase cigars although it was usual for such purchases to be made by managers. Hence there was no actual authority and strictly no apparent authority, since the manager was not held out as an agent, the third party being ignorant of the principal's existence. The case is sometimes regarded as a separate form of usual authority but may perhaps be best explained on the basis that the principal was liable for having created or permitted an appearance of ownership. (*See* USUAL AUTHORITY OF AN AGENT).

Appropriation of payments. At common law if a debtor owes several debts to one creditor and makes a payment insufficient to discharge all the debtor may unequivocally appropriate the payment when making it. If the debtor knowing of this right chooses not to exercise it, the creditor may appropriate, this being revocable until communicated to the debtor. Provided there is a genuine debt appropriation may be to a contract unenforceable for non-compliance with requirements of written evidence (*see* FORM IN CONTRACT) or because it is barred by the Limitation Act†, but the creditor must have some claim even if defective. It is not possible to appropriate to a contract void for illegality in contract. When there is a current account between the parties it is presumed under the rule in *Clayton's Case*† that monies are paid out in the order in which they were paid in. Under the Consumer Credit Act 1974, s. 81 the debtor may first appropriate but if he fails to do so and one or more of the agreements is hire purchase, conditional sale or a consumer hire agreement payment shall be appropriated proportionately among the agreements.

Arbitration. The legally effective adjudication of disputes otherwise than by the ordinary procedure of the courts. The arbitrator is often not a member of the judicial staff of the courts but on occasion may be. Arbitration frequently but not always depends on the agreement of the parties. Matters of criminal law and of status cannot be referred to arbitration. Arbitration may arise in many ways. Thus, in the High Court a case may be referred to a Circuit Judge as official referee's business either with the consent of the parties or if it involves accounts, prolonged investigation of documents or scientific or local investigations. The Judge of the Commercial Court with the consent of the Lord Chief Justice may act as an arbitrator in commercial disputes. Provision was made in 1973 for extended County Court arbitration, normally exercised by the registrar, primarily to deal with small consumer claims. This no longer requires an order of the court and can be employed despite objection from one of the parties. Rules of evidence need not apply and there are special provisions to limit costs. Many statutes provide for references either compulsorily or by consent, as in the case of industrial disputes. The Arbitration Act 1950 applies to statutory arbitrations, except in so far as it is excluded, as with industrial disputes. Commercial arbitrations normally arise by agreement out of court and are governed by the Arbitration Act 1950 as amended by the Arbitration Acts 1975 and 1979. *See* ARBITRATION: FOREIGN AND CONVENTION AWARDS.

Arbitration, appeals on law and preliminary point of law. The arbitrator's determination or 'award' was once subject to judicial review by the courts by means of a case stated on a point of law under s. 21 of the 1950 Act and through the jurisdiction to set aside or remit an award because of errors of fact or law on its face. These processes have been abolished by the Arbitration Act 1979 and replaced by an appeal on a point of law to the High Court and the determination of a preliminary point of law. For the appeal either all the parties must consent or the court must give leave. Leave is not to be given if there is a valid exclusion agreement or the appeal could not substantially affect the rights of one of the parties. Leave may be conditional. Where an award does not or does not sufficiently set out reasons the court, subject to conditions, may order the arbitrator to give reasons. The court may confirm, vary, set aside or remit an award. If it remits the arbitrator must make an award within three months. If the High Court certifies that the case relates to a question of law of general public importance or there is some other special reason and the High Court gives leave there may be an appeal to the Court of Appeal.

The determination of a preliminary point of law arising during the reference requires an application from one of the parties with the consent of either the arbitrator or umpire who has entered on the reference or the consent of all the other parties. It is excluded by a valid exclusion agreement. The High Court must be satisfied that the decision of the point might produce substantial savings in costs for the parties and that it is a point for which leave to appeal would have been given if an award had been made.

Both the appeal and the determination may be excluded by a valid exclusion agreement under ss. 3 and 4 of the Act. Such an agreement may relate to a particular award, awards under a particular reference or any other description of awards but it is not enough merely to purport to prohibit or restrict access to the High Court, or the making of a reasoned award or to restrict the jurisdiction of the High Court.

The power to exclude access to the court was to meet foreign reluctance to accept English arbitration hence this power is restricted for a 'domestic arbitration agreement'. This is one which does not provide for arbitration in a state other than the United Kingdom and to which no foreign national or resident or foreign or foreign-controlled body corporate is party. For a domestic agreement an exclusion agreement must be made after the commencement of an arbitration and such an agreement cannot exclude the jurisdiction of the court under s. 24 of the 1950 Act to intervene when the dispute involves a question whether a party has been guilty of fraud, though a non-domestic agreement may do so.

Moreover an exclusion agreement will be ineffective in regard to a claim involving the Admiralty jurisdiction or an insurance or commodity contract unless the exclusion agreement was made after the commencement of the arbitration or the question relates to a contract expressed to be governed by a law other than that of England and Wales. An exclusion agreement is of no effect in regard to a statutory arbitration referred to in s. 31 (1) of the 1950 Act.

The jurisdiction to correct slips under ss. 17 and 22 of the 1950 Act and to set an award aside for misconduct on the part of the arbitrator under s. 23 remains. Misconduct is, for example, hearing one side in the absence of the other or hearing witnesses in the absence of the parties.

An award may be enforced as a judgment or by action on the award or perhaps by attachment. The House of Lords have provided guidelines in *Pioneer Shipping v B.T.P.*, *The Nema* [1981] 3 WLR 292. See also the Supreme Court Act 1981, s. 148.

Arbitration, foreign and convention awards. Foreign awards may be enforced in this country under Part II of the Arbitration Act 1950 which gives effect to a Geneva Convention of 1927 or as Convention Awards under the Arbitration Act, 1975. This Act was passed to give effect to a New York Convention. If a party to a non-domestic agreement commences court proceedings these may be stayed. 'Domestic agreement' is defined as one which does not provide for arbitration in a state other than the United Kingdom, and to which no foreign national or resident or foreign or foreign-controlled body corporate is party. 'Convention awards' made in a state party to the New York Convention other than the United Kingdom are enforceable as court orders in accordance with the 1950 Act. Section 5 (2) of the 1975 Act specifies grounds on which enforcement may be refused. It may also be refused if the award deals with matters which may not be submitted to arbitration or if it is contrary to public policy. If a convention award is in part good it may be enforced to that extent. Where a convention award is also a foreign award under Part II of the 1950 Act the 1975 Act applies to the exclusion of the 1950 Act.

Under the State Immunity Act 1978 (*see* STATE IMMUNITY) a state is not immune from proceedings relating to arbitration when it has agreed in writing to submit to arbitration.

Arbitrator. Any person may be appointed as an arbitrator. An interest known to the parties is no bar. A submission† need not name an arbitrator. It is presumed that a reference is to a single arbitrator. If the parties fail to appoint or their appointee does not act, any party may serve the others with notice to concur in appointing and if they fail to do so within seven days the court may appoint. If the reference is to two arbitrators and one party fails to appoint the other may serve him with notice and if he fails to appoint within seven days the other may appoint his arbitrator to act as sole arbitrator but this may be set aside by the court. Under s. 6 of Arbitration Act 1979 there are similar provisions for appointment by the court after notice when a person not a party is empowered to and fails to appoint. This section also provides that when there is a reference to two arbitrators they may appoint an umpire at any time and shall do so forthwith if they cannot agree. He then enters on the whole reference in place of the arbitrators, having the same powers and duties as they had. The same section also provides that when there is a reference to three arbitrators, in the absence of contrary intention, the decision of any two is binding.

An arbitrator or umpire has many of the procedural powers of a judge and application can be made to the court for assistance when he has not, e.g. in respect of security for costs or a subpoena. An arbitrator may use his own expert knowledge, *Mediterranean & Eastern Export Co v Fortress Fabrics* [1948] 2 All ER 186. He may take sworn evidence and should observe the ordinary rules of evidence unless the parties have agreed to waive them, hence he should not call a witness without the consent of the parties, *Re Enoch* [1910] 1 KB 327. It was held in *Orion v Belfort* [1962] 2 Lloyd's Rep 257 that though the parties might waive rules of evidence and procedure they could not waive substantive law to have their dispute settled on a basis of 'equity' or 'fairness'. It seems, however, that such a clause if it only ousts technicalities and strict constructions may be valid, *Eagle Star v Yval* [1978] 1 Lloyd's Rep 357.

Arrival contracts. An alternative name for ex ship contracts.

Arrived ship. *See* VOYAGE CHARTERPARTY.

Assignments of contracts. The transfer of contractual rights considered as things or choses in action, a form of property, so that the assignee may sue the debtor or other party. Involuntary assignment occurs on death or bankruptcy. Historically, common law, apart from negotiable instruments, made very limited provision for voluntary assignment and hence statute allowed this in special cases such as insurance policies, bills of lading, patents and copyright. Then the Judicature Act 1873, s. 25 (6) re-enacted by the Law of Property Act 1925, s. 136 made general provision for the legal assignment of debts and other legal choses in action. Equity, however, freely allowed the assignment of equitable choses in action (those only enforceable in equity such as a share in a trust fund) and allowed the assignment of legal choses in action (those which could be enforced in the common law courts) provided the assignee when seeking to enforce it joined the assignor either as co-plaintiff or co-defendant to ensure that he would be bound by the proceedings. The division between legal and equitable assignment remains and if s. 136 is not satisfied the transaction may still take effect as an equitable assignment. Though s. 136 speaks of 'legal choses' in action it is settled that equitable choses may be assigned under it. If the requirements of the section are satisfied the assignee need not join the assignor when suing nor need the assignee show that he gave consideration. There must be notice in writing to the debtor, the assignment itself must be in writing and must be absolute and not by way of charge. This excludes conditional assignments, *Durham v Robertson* [1898] 1 QB 765, and assignments of part of a debt, *Williams v Atlantic Assurance* [1933] 1 KB 81, but not an outright assignment by way of mortgage with a provision for re-assignment on redemption, *Tancred v Delagoa Bay* (1889) 23 QBD 239. An assignment by way of charge entitles the assignee to payment out of a fund but does not transfer the fund to him. Assignments which are partial, conditional or by way of charge may be valid equitable assignments.

An equitable assignment may be very informal, a command, request, permission, provided the meaning is plain, *Brandt v Dunlop* [1905] AC 454, except that an assignment of an equitable interest or trust must be in writing signed by the assignor or his agent or by will, Law of Property Act 1925, s. 53 (1). When an equitable chose in action is assigned the assignor need not be joined in proceedings to enforce it; he need only be joined as co-plaintiff or co-defendant when there has been an equitable assignment of a legal chose in action. It is prudent for the assignee to give notice to the debtor in order to prevent payment to the assignor, and to secure priority over any subsequent assignments, *Dearle v Hall* (1828) 3 Russ 1, but notice is not essential to perfect the assignment as between assignor and assignee. Consideration is not necessary in a completed equitable assignment but is necessary if there is an agreement to assign in the future.

All assignments, whether legal or equitable are 'subject to equities' meaning that the debtor can raise against the assignee all defences (including set-off and counter claims arising out of the contract) which he could have raised against the assignor at the time he received notice of the assignment, *Business Computers v Anglo African Leasing* [1977] 2 All ER 741, except that if he does not rescind the contract he cannot raise against the assignee a claim for fraud in inducing the contract against the assignor, *Stoddart v Union Trust* [1912] 1 KB 181.

It was once said that 'a bare right to litigate' could not be assigned, but it now seems that an impersonal, as distinct from a personal, right to litigate may be assigned, or if a right is assignable, a right to litigate arising from it may be assigned, but an assignment that amounts to trafficking in litigation will be void for champerty, *Trendtex v Credit Suisse* (1981) *Times*, 27 October, HL.

Certain rights are unassignable such as some public service pensions, alimony and the benefit of contracts of a personal character or involving personal skill or confidence, *Kemp v Baerselman* [1906] 2 KB 604. If the contract to be assigned forbids assignment it seems that only clear language may nullify the transaction as between assignor and assignee but the prohibition will render it ineffective between assignee and debtor, *Helstan v Herts CC* [1978] 3 All ER 262.

It is not possible merely to assign the burden of a contract but this can in substance be achieved by novation, a new contract with a new party obliged (*see* PRIVITY OF CONTRACT). In impersonal (*British Waggon Co v Lea* (1880) 5 QBD 149), but not personal (*Robson and Sharpe v Drummond* (1831) 2 B & Ad 303), contracts a party may discharge his obligations by providing substitute performance.

Associated trade marks. *See* TRADE MARK INFRINGEMENT.

Attornment. Term applied to a case where an agent, bailee or debtor ceases to hold on behalf of the original principal bailor or creditor and transfers his liability to another.

Auctioneer. An agent to conduct an auction sale. He is not liable for breach of contract to prospective purchasers if a sale is not held or a lot withdrawn, *Harris v Nickerson* (1873) LR 8 QB 286 but he might be liable in deceit or for negligent misrepresentation. By the Unfair Contract Terms Act 1977†, s. 12 a buyer at an auction is not treated as buying as a consumer hence reasonable exclusion clauses will be valid against him. The auctioneer may sue for or receive the price even when the principal is disclosed and undertakes to give possession in return for the price. He must not delegate (*see* DELEGATUS NON POTEST DELEGARE). He should sell only for cash unless it is customary and reasonable to take a cheque but he may sue on a cheque for a deposit drawn in favour of himself, *Pollway v Abdullah* [1974] 2 All ER 381. He is liable to the principal for loss resulting from delivering goods without receiving the price and is responsible for storage. He has possession of the goods and a lien for charges and commission (*see* LIEN OF AGENT). This is said to extend to the proceeds which means that he can sue for the price, that the third party may not set up, to the extent of the lien, any defence or set off he may have against the principal and the auctioneer may use his claim to charges and commission by way of counterclaim or set off against the principal.

Auction sale. The Sale of Goods Act 1979, s. 57 provides that each lot is presumed to be the subject of a separate contract of sale; that such sale is complete when the auctioneer announces completion by the fall of the hammer or in other customary manner and that until then a bid may be retracted; that an auction may be notified as subject to a reserve or upset price; that a right to bid by or on behalf of the seller may be expressly reserved but if this is not done it is unlawful for a bid to be made by or on behalf of the seller or for the auctioneer to accept such a bid and the buyer may treat the sale as fraudulent. When the seller expressly reserves a right to bid either he or one other person on his behalf may bid. An announcement that an auction will be held is merely an invitation to treat. If the auction is not held a person attending cannot sue for breach of contract, *Harris v Nickerson* (1873) LR 8 QB 286, but if an auction is advertised as 'without reserve' the auctioneer must accept the highest bid, *Warlow v Harrison* (1858) 1 E & E 295, but otherwise he may reject any bid. If the sale is subject to reserve and the auctioneer mistakenly knocks down the goods before the reserve is reached the goods may be withdrawn, *McManus v Fortescue* [1907] 2 KB 1. An auctioneer who sells goods to which his principal has no title may be liable in conversion to the owner, *Consolidated Co v Curtis* [1892] 1 QB 495. If the sale was not obviously illegal the auctioneer can recover an indemnity from his principal but will be liable for breach of warranty of authority to the disappointed purchaser. An agreement between bidders to form a 'ring' or 'knock-out' to refrain from bidding to lower the price by the Auctions (Bidding Agreements) Act 1969 renders the sale voidable by the seller if one of the members is a dealer and, if the goods are not returned, the parties to the agreement are jointly and severally liable for any loss to the seller. The Act does not forbid a non-fraudulent agreement to buy on joint account. Criminal penalties are imposed by the Mock Auctions Act 1961 on mock auctions. By the Unfair Contract Terms Act 1977†, s. 12 the buyer at an auction is not treated as buying as a consumer and hence reasonable exclusion clauses will be valid against him.

Award. The decision of an arbitrator. *See* ARBITRATOR.

B

Back freight. A payment to the shipowner for expenses in protecting the goods when delivery cannot be made either because of the consignee's default, excepted peril or some other cause for which the shipowner is not responsible. He must then deal with the goods to the owner's advantage.

Back-to-back credit. *See* BANKERS' COMMERCIAL CREDITS.

Bailee. *See* BAILMENT.

Bailment. A delivery of goods by a deliveror, known as a 'bailor', to a deliveree, known as a 'bailee', upon a condition express or implied that they shall be returned to the bailor or dealt with according to his instructions when the purpose for which the bailment was made has been fulfilled. Many bailments are also contracts but this is not necessarily so. Common examples when goods are to be returned are loan, hire, deposit for storage, cleaning or repair and pledge or pawn and an example where goods are not to be returned is carriage. The bailee must return or deal with the identical goods bailed. The bailee must obtain possession of the goods and hence a person who merely gives permission (or a licence) to another to leave goods in or on his property does not incur the liabilities of a bailee, *Ashby v Tolhurst* [1937] 2 KB 242. If the bailment is for a fixed term only the bailee can sue third parties for interference with the goods (*see* TRESPASS TO GOODS: CONVERSION) but if it is a 'bailment at will' when the bailor can at any time call for the return of the goods both are said to have possession and either can sue. A bailee must take reasonable care of the goods in his possession and return them on proper demand, but if the bailee departs from the terms of the bailment as, e.g. by storing the goods in a place other than that agreed, he will be liable for loss or damage irrespective of negligence, unless he can show the loss would have happened in any event, *Lilley v Doubleday* (1881) 7 QBD 510. If a bailee sues a third party he may recover the whole value, accounting for any excess over the value of his interest to the bailor, *The Winkfield* [1902] P 42. An 'involuntary bailee' who has possession imposed on him without his consent is under no duty of care and has merely to refrain from deliberate damage, *Lethbridge v Phillips* (1819) 2 Stark 544, and under the conditions prescribed in the Unsolicited Goods and Services Act 1971, he may treat the goods as a gift to him.

Under stringent conditions a bailee may be an agent of necessity entitled to sell the bailor's goods when they are endangered and if goods are left with a bailee for an unduly long period the Disposal of Uncollected Goods Act 1952, now repealed and replaced by the Torts (Interference with Goods) Act 1977, s. 12, subject to notice or court order, gives the bailee a power of sale, giving a good title against the bailor but not against the true owner if the bailor is not that, and requiring the bailee to account to the bailor for the proceeds on the basis that the best method of sale was adopted but making deductions for expenses and accrued claims.

Bailor. *See* BAILMENT.

Banker and Customer for Bills of Exchange Act 1882 and Cheques Act 1957. The Bills of Exchange Act 1882, s. 2 merely provides that 'banker' 'includes a body of persons whether incorporated or not who carry on the business of banking'. The Banking Act 1979, s. 36 (2) provides that Parts I, II and III of that Act do not determine whether a person is a 'banker' for other than that Act so pre-1979 law continues for the 1882 and 1957 Acts—*United Dominions Trust v Kirkwood* [1966] 2 QB 431 indicates that the 'business of banking' requires that deposits should be accepted on current and deposit account, cheques and other items paid and collected for customers and that these should form a substantial part of the alleged banker's business. In addition, the banking community must have recognised that person or body as a banker. The banking business need not be the banker's primary business but the accounts must be available for payments generally and not merely for specific purposes. A 'customer' of a banker is one who has opened an account for however short a time, *Ladbrooke v Todd* (1914) 30 TLR 433; *Commissioners for Taxation v English, Scottish and Australian Bank* [1920] AC 683. If there is no account, or perhaps agreement to open an account, a long transaction of business will not make a person a customer, *Great Western Railway v London & County Bank* [1901] AC 414.

Bankers' commercial credits. Arrangements for securing the payment of the price† in export–import sale of goods. An importer will request a bank in his country (known as the 'issuing bank') to provide a credit for the payment. The issuing bank will then either advise the exporter itself or request a bank in the exporter's country (known as the 'correspondent bank') to make the credit available to the exporter, either by direct payment ('payment credit') or by accepting ('acceptance credit') bills of exchange drawn by him on the bank. (*See* ACCEPTANCE IN BILLS OF EXCHANGE). The correspondent bank (or issuing bank if it acts itself) secures control over the goods by taking from the seller the shipping documents of c.i.f. contracts, or the bill of lading in f.o.b. contracts. On reimbursement by the issuing bank, the correspondent bank will transmit the documents to it and the issuing bank in turn may allow the importer limited control of the documents under the terms of a trust letter or receipt to enable him to sell the goods and so reimburse the bank for the credit advanced by it, if he has not already provided funds. The credit is known as a 'revocable credit' if the issuing bank is entitled to withdraw it at any time and 'irrevocable' if it may not do so. It is known as a 'confirmed credit' if the correspondent bank adds its own undertaking to the seller to that of the issuing bank and 'unconfirmed' if it does not. At one time in this country the terms 'revocable' and 'unconfirmed' and 'irrevocable' and 'confirmed' were regarded as synonymous but the distinctions indicated are now well-established. The issuing bank is sometimes termed the 'originating' bank and the correspondent bank the 'intermediate' or 'advising' bank. The exporter in relation to the credit is known as the 'beneficiary'. The type of credit described is known as a 'documentary' credit in contrast to a 'clean' credit where documents relating to goods are not used. Credits may be transferable and divisible among beneficiaries. A 'back-to-back credit' is where one credit can be used as a security for further credits along a string of contracts, (a later buyer in the string makes his credit available to his seller to enable the latter to obtain a credit to pay his seller and so on). A 'revolving credit' is found when there is a standing credit for a series of transactions and as each transaction is paid off the credit is restored by the importer to its former limit. A 'Red clause' or 'anticipatory credit' or 'packing credit' is found when the seller is allowed to draw advances before the goods or documents are ready for delivery in order to obtain or prepare the goods. 'Red clauses' cover advances on the goods proper, 'Green clauses' advances on shipping and warehousing. They acquired these names because at one time they were printed in colour. Most credits are now acceptance credits, but at one time 'negotiation credits' were not uncommon, the exporter–seller drawing a bill of exchange on the importer–buyer and then negotiating it to the bank advancing the credit. (*See* NEGOTIATION OF NEGOTIABLE INSTRUMENTS). Most commercial credits now incorporate the Uniform Customs and Practice for Documentary Credits (U.C.P.) drawn up by the International Chamber of Commerce. These provide detailed regulation and a wide measure of international uniformity. Strict observance of the terms of the credit is required; any divergence between the terms of the credit and the documents tendered will entitle the bank to reject them, *Rayner v Hambro* [1943] 1 KB 37. If the seller makes a defective tender of documents he cannot later make a tender of correct documents to the buyer directly, *Soproma v Marine & Animal By-Products* [1966] 1 Lloyd's Rep 367. Credits when opened amount only to conditional not absolute payment; if the bank does not pay the buyer himself must, *Alan v El Nasr* [1972] 2 QB 189; *Man v*

Nigerian Sweets [1977] 2 Lloyd's Rep 50. A confirmed credit is a contract between the confirming correspondent bank and the seller; the buyer is not entitled to cancel it nor is the bank entitled to refuse payment because goods supplied under the underlying contract are defective, *Hamzeh Malas v British Imex* [1958] 2 QB 127. If fraud is proved (not merely alleged) it may be that a buyer could restrain the bank from making payment, *Discount Records v Barclays Bank* [1975] 1 All ER 1071. The buyer must provide the credit a reasonable time before the first day of the shipment period, *Sinason-Teicher Inter-American Grain v Oilcakes & Oilseeds* [1954] 3 All ER 468 and it must be available for use throughout the period, *Pavia v Thurmann-Nielsen* [1952] 2 QB 84 even if, as in f.o.b. contracts the buyer can choose the date within the period, *Ian Stach v Baker Bosley* [1958] 2 QB 130.

Bankers' draft. An instrument by which a branch of a bank orders another branch or its head office to make a payment. Since the bank's organisation is one corporate body the drawer and drawee are the same person, so the holder of the draft may by the Bills of Exchange Act 1882, s. 5 (2) treat the draft either as a bill of exchange or as a promissory note. Since bankers' drafts thus embody a bank's own obligation to pay they are treated as the equivalent of cash and purchased for use in transactions where a very reliable means of payment is required, as in the purchase of real property.

Bankruptcy. The process by which an individual or a partnership unable to pay their debts may be subjected to the status of being bankrupt, thus having their assets removed from their control and, perhaps with other assets treated as theirs, distributed to their creditors and by which they may ultimately be discharged from the status and from provable debts (*see* PROOF OF DEBTS). The chief legislative provisions are the Bankruptcy Act 1914, the Bankruptcy (Amendment) Act 1926, the Bankruptcy Rules 1952 and the Insolvency Act 1976. The liquidation of insolvent companies is separately regulated by the Companies Acts and Winding Up Rules, though some bankruptcy rules may be applicable in winding up.

In order that a court may make an adjudication of bankruptcy a 'debtor' must have committed an act of bankruptcy, manifesting an inability or unwillingness to pay debts. A 'debtor' is defined as including any person, whether a British subject or not, who, at the time when any act of bankruptcy was done or suffered, was either personally present in England or ordinarily resided or had a place of business in England or was carrying on business in England personally or by means of an agent or manager or was a member of a firm or partnership which carried on business in England. In this context England includes Wales. Since 1935 married women are fully subject to bankruptcy. So, too, are minors in respect of debts legally binding on them. Aliens also may be bankrupted but the rules regulating the presentation of a bankruptcy petition may in fact limit their liability. A deceased person cannot be made bankrupt on proceedings begun after his death but his estate may be subject to administration† in bankruptcy. Where a debtor dies after the presentation of the petition, proceedings may continue as if he were alive. Mentally disordered persons perhaps cannot commit an act of bankruptcy involving intent. They can be adjudged bankrupt before they come under the care of the Court of Protection but no subsequent bankruptcy can oust the powers of that court. It has, however, a discretion to apply property for the benefit both of creditors and of the mental patient. In the case of small bankruptcies the court may make either an order for summary administration or an administration order.

A petition may be presented by the debtor, a creditor or creditors to the court having jurisdiction. This may be either the High Court or the County Court depending on certain conditions as to the debtor's residence and carrying on of business.

The court will hear the petition and, if it does not dismiss it, will make a receiving order, constituting the Official Receiver the receiver of the debtor's property. The debtor will then attend a private interview with the Official Receiver and be instructed to prepare a statement of affairs. There will then come a first meeting of creidtors at which the debtor may make proposals for a composition† or scheme. The debtor may also have to undergo a public examination†. If the creditors do not accept a composition or scheme an adjudication in bankruptcy will be resolved on and a trustee in bankruptcy may be appointed. The debtor is now technically a bankrupt and his property will vest in the trustee who will distribute it. This will involve proof of debts, realisation of property divisible amongst creditors, including property used by the debtor to give a fraudulent preference which may also be subject to settlements voidable in bankruptcy. It may also involve disclaimer of onerous property. The trustee may be preceded by a special manager and be supervised by a committee of inspection. The concluding step is discharge of the bankrupt which may be on application or on qualification for automatic discharge. The discharge may be granted with a certificate of misfortune.

A possible alternative to bankruptcy proceedings is a deed of arrangement. In certain circumstances an order of criminal bank-ruptcy may be made against a convicted offender and an ordinary bankrupt or a debtor against whom a receiving order has been made may commit one or more bankruptcy offences. Apart from these the law of bankruptcy involves considerable control† over the property and person of the debtor and others.

Bankruptcy, control over the person and property of the debtor.
After a receiving order has been made the court may on the
application of the Official Receiver or the trustee in bankruptcy order
the debtor, his wife, any person known or suspected to possess any of
the debtor's property or to be indebted to him or any person deemed
capable of giving information about him to be examined on oath and
to produce documents in their possession. If they admit they hold
property of the debtor or are indebted to the debtor they may be
ordered to deliver it up or repay the debt. The debtor must give all
information and assistance that may reasonably be required by the
Official Receiver or trustee for the realisation and distribution of his
property. If he fails to do so he will be in contempt of court. The court
may on application order the re-direction of the debtor's letters.

The court may order the arrest of a debtor and the seizure of his
books, papers, money and goods if a bankruptcy notice has been issued
or if a bankruptcy petition has been filed and there is reason to believe
that the debtor has absconded or is about to abscond with a view to
avoiding payment, avoiding service of any petition, avoiding
appearance to a petition, avoiding an examination or delaying any
bankruptcy proceedings. The debtor may also be arrested if after
presentation of a petition there is reason to believe that he intends to
remove, conceal or destroy his papers or property, or if after service of
the petition he removes goods above £60 in value without leave of the
Official Receiver or trustee or if without good cause the debtor fails
to attend any examination ordered by the court. (See the Bankruptcy
Act 1914, ss. 22, 23, 24, 25 and the Insolvency Act 1976).

Bankruptcy Notice. *See* ACT OF BANKRUPTCY.

Bankruptcy of a partnership and partners. The rules relating to the
bankruptcy of an individual apply with variations to the bankruptcy
of a partnership. A receiving order may be made against a partnership
but it operates as an order against each partner. When such an order is
made the partners must submit a joint statement of the firm's affairs
and each partner must submit a statement of his own affairs.
Adjudication† is made against individuals by name and not against the
firm.

The first meeting of creditors is attended both by the joint creditors
of the firm and by the creditors of each partner's separate estate; the
trustee in bankruptcy appointed by the joint creditors is trustee for the
separate estates but each separate group of creditors is entitled to its
own committee of inspection.

Bankruptcy offences. These are largely contained in the Bankruptcy
Act 1914, Part VII, ss. 154–166 as amended by the Theft Act 1968.
Section 154 creates a large number of offences of fraudulent
misrepresentation or concealment of property or financial affairs

which may be committed either by a person against whom an adjudication† has been made or against whom a receiving order has been made. Section 155 renders it criminal for an undischarged bankrupt to obtain credit for more than £50 without disclosing his status or to trade in any name other than that under which he was bankrupted without revealing that name. Section 156 renders criminal the making of any gift, transfer or charge on property either by a person adjudged bankrupt or against whom a receiving order has been made with intent to defraud creditors. Section 157 deals with offences arising when a person adjudged bankrupt or against whom a receiving order has been made contributes to his losses by gambling or by rash and hazardous speculations. Section 158 covers offences committed when a debtor fails to keep proper accounts. Section 159 deals with the offence committed when a debtor absconds abroad with property. Section 161 provides for an order of court for a prosecution on a report by the Official Receiver or trustee in bankruptcy or on a representation by a creditor or member of the committee of inspection. Section 162 provides that discharge of the bankrupt or acceptance or approval of a composition or scheme of arrangement will not free a debtor from any criminal liability. Section 164 deals with the trial and punishment of offences, s. 165 with the duties of the Director of Public Prosecutions and s. 166 with evidence as to frauds by agents.

Certain offences once contained in Part VII of the Bankruptcy Act 1914 have been repealed and replaced by new offences created by ss. 15, 16 and 17 of the Theft Act 1968 which are of general application. These are offences of obtaining property by deception, obtaining a pecuniary advantage by deception and of false accounting.

Under the Companies Act 1948, ss. 187 and 367 it is an offence for an undischarged bankrupt without leave of the court to be a company director, to be directly or indirectly concerned in the management of a company, or to act as a receiver or manager for debenture holders.

Bankruptcy petition. This may be presented by the debtor or a creditor or creditors to the court having jurisdiction in the case. This will be the High Court where the debtor has carried on business or has resided in the London Bankruptcy District during the greater part of the six months before the presentation of the petition or for a longer period during that six months than in the district of any county court or when the debtor is not resident in England or when his residence cannot be ascertained. In any other case it is the county court (not within the London Bankruptcy District) within whose district the debtor has resided or carried on business for the greater part of the six months before the petition, preference being given to his 'business' rather than his 'residential' district.

For a creditor's petition the following five cumulative conditions must be satisfied under the Bankruptcy Act 1914, s. 4. (See the Bankruptcy Act 1914, ss. 98, 99, 100 and the Bankruptcy Rules 1952, r. 145).

1. The debt due to the creditor or the aggregate amount of debts due to creditors jointly petitioning must amount to £200 or more. The amount of £200 was substituted for the former amount of £50 by the Insolvency Act, 1976, s. 1 and Sch. 1, Part 1.

2. The debt must be liquidated and payable immediately or at a certain future time. The debt must have been liquidated before the act of bankruptcy on which the petition is founded and at the hearing the creditor must show that the debt existed both when the petition was presented and at the time of the hearing. *Re Debtors* (No. 669 of 1926) [1927] 1 Ch 19.

3. The act of bankruptcy on which the petition is grounded must have occurred within three months before the presentation of the petition.

4. The debtor is domiciled in England or has ordinarily resided in or had a dwelling house or place of business in England within a year before the presentation of the petition or has carried on business in England by a partner or agent.

   The references to 'business' do not apply to anyone who is domiciled, nor to a firm having its principal place of business, in Scotland or Northern Ireland.

5. If the petitioning creditor is secured he must in his petition either state that he is willing to give up his security for the benefit of creditors if the debtor is adjudged bankrupt or estimate its value, and in the latter case he may be admitted as a petitioning creditor to the extent of any balance. If he is the sole petitioning creditor the balance must exceed £200. If the petition states the debt incorrectly but the correct figure would have been sufficient a receiving order based on it will not be rescinded unless there are circumstances such as inadvertence to justify leave to amend the petition.

A creditor's petition must be verified by affidavit and served on the debtor. A creditor's petition may not be withdrawn, after presentment, without leave of the court.

If, on the hearing of a creditor's petition the court is not satisfied with the proof of the debt or the act of bankruptcy or of the service of the petition or is satisfied that for other 'sufficient cause' no receiving order ought to be made, the court may dismiss the petition. Examples of 'sufficient cause' are that the debtor's only asset is a life interest which will be forfeited on bankruptcy (*Re Otway* [1895] 1 QB 812), that there are no assets and no probability of any (*Re Betts* [1897] 1 QB 50; *Re Field* [1978] Ch 371), or that the petition was brought for the purpose of extortion (*Re Majory* [1955] Ch 600). When the act of bankruptcy relied on is non-compliance with a bankruptcy notice to pay, secure or compound a judgment debt the court may stay or dismiss the petition on the ground that an appeal is pending against the judgment and where the debtor appears and denies indebtedness the court may, instead of dismissing the petition, stay proceedings on it for the time necessary for trial of the disputed debt. If there is no reason for staying or dismissing the petition the court will make a receiving order.

A debtor's petition must allege that he is unable to pay his debts. The presentation is deemed an act of bankruptcy without any previous filing of a declaration of inability to pay his debts by the debtor and the court must forthwith make a receiving order. The petition cannot be withdrawn after presentment without leave. A criminal bankrupt cannot present a criminal bankruptcy petition against himself.

Normally a petition must be founded on an act of bankruptcy but the presentation of a debtor's petition will itself be such an act.

Bare boat charter. *See* CHARTERPARTY BY DEMISE.

Barter. This differs from sale of goods in that goods are exchanged for goods, not sold or agreed to be sold for a 'money consideration called the price'. If the consideration is partly money and partly goods it seems that it is sale (*Aldridge v Johnson* (1857) 7 E & B 885), as also if it is either money or goods (*South Australian Insurance Co v Randell* (1869) LR 3 PC 101). As in the case of contracts for work and materials† in contracts of barter terms as to merchantable quality†, fitness for purpose† and the like similar to those implied in sale by the Sale of Goods Act 1979 are now implied by the Supply of Goods and Services Act 1982.

Battle of the forms. A phrase descriptive of cases in the preliminaries to a contract (*see* OFFER AND ACCEPTANCE) where the parties exchange forms of offer and acceptance which contain mutually conflicting terms, it being for the court to determine which terms if any have overriding effect, applying the principle that a counter-offer is a rejection open for acceptance, but also that there is no contract if there is no consensus ad idem†. See *Butler Machine Tool Co v Ex-Cell-O Corp* [1979] 1 All ER 965.

Bearer bill or promissory note. The Bills of Exchange Act 1882, s. 2 provides that 'bearer' means the person in possession of a bill or note which is payable to bearer. This may include an unlawful holder such as a thief of such a bill. Section 8 (3) provides that an instrument is payable to bearer which is expressed to be so payable, or on which the only or last indorsement is an indorsement in blank. Section 7 (3) also

provides that where the payee is a fictitious or non-existing person†
the instrument may be treated as payable to bearer.

Berne Convention. *See* INTELLECTUAL PROPERTY, INTERNATIONAL
PROTECTION.

Bilateral contract. One consisting of an exchange of promises between
the parties and contrasted with a unilateral contract where a promise is
given for an act. *See also* SYNALLAGMATIC CONTRACT.

Bill of exchange. A form of negotiable instrument defined in the Bills
of Exchange Act 1882, s. 3 (1). 'A bill of exchange is an unconditional
order in writing, addressed by one person to another, signed by the
person giving it, requiring the person to whom it is addressed to pay
on demand or at a fixed or determinable future time, a sum certain in
money to or to the order of a specified person, or to bearer'. The
person drawing up and giving the order is known as the 'drawer', the
person to whom it is addressed is the drawee and the person to whom
payment is to be made is the payee. If the payee wishes to 'order'
payment to be made to someone else he does this by an indorsement,
which may be merely his signature†, this constituting an indorsement
in blank and making the instrument transferable by delivery, or in
addition to his signature it may name a specific indorsee thus
constituting a special indorsement, in which case the indorsee will
have to indorse again if he in his turn wishes to transfer the instrument.
Drawee and payee must be indicated with certainty. There may be
two or more drawees but not alternative or successive drawees. There
may be two or more joint or alternative payees or the bill may be
payable to one or some of several persons or to the holder of an office.
If the payee is a fictitious or non-existing person the bill may be treated
as payable to bearer. A bill may be drawn payable to or to the order of
the drawer or drawee but when drawer and drawee are the same
person or the drawee is a fictitious person or lacks capacity to contract,
the holder may treat the instrument either as a bill of exchange or as a
promissory note. The bill must be an order in imperative terms so that
there will be no doubt as to whether the drawee has fulfilled what was
required of him and it must not be conditional in the sense of payment
not being subject to the happening of some uncertain event. If it is
subject to such a condition the happening of the event will not cure the
document's invalidity as a bill. (*See* CONDITIONAL INSTRUMENTS). Bills
of exchange amount to a private currency amongst merchants and
their free circulation would be impeded if the fulfilment of conditions
had to be investigated. An order to pay out of a particular fund is
conditional since the fund might not be adequate but a general order
to pay coupled with an indication of a fund from which payment may
be made or the drawee reimburse himself or an indication of the
transaction giving rise to the bill is unconditional. A bill must not

order anything to be done other than the payment of money. A bill is not invalid because it is not dated, or it does not mention it was given for value or because it does not mention the place of drawing or payment. A date is presumed to be correct and a bill is not invalid merely because it is ante-dated, post-dated or dated on a Sunday. Section 14 of the Bills of Exchange Act 1882 as amended by s. 3 of the Banking and Financial Dealings Act 1971 makes provision for computation of time of payment of bills of exchange. A bill is payable on demand when it is stated to be so payable, when no time for payment is stated, or, as regards the acceptor or indorser of a bill which is accepted or indorsed when overdue, when it is thus accepted or indorsed. A bill is payable at a determinable future time when it is stated to be payable at a fixed period after its date or sight (i.e. exhibited to the drawee together with some indication from him of having seen it, such as acceptance) or at a fixed period after some event which is certain to happen even though the time of happening may be uncertain. When no date is mentioned in a bill stated to be payable at a fixed period after the date or the acceptance of a bill payable at a fixed period after sight† is undated any holder may insert the true date but if a wrong date is inserted in good faith or the bill comes into the hands of a holder in due course the date is taken to be true. When a bill contains words prohibiting transfer it is valid between the parties but not negotiable. A negotiable bill may be payable either to bearer or to order. It is payable to bearer if it is stated to be so or if the only or last indorsement is in blank. A bill is payable to order when it is stated to be payable to a particular person or to whoever he orders should receive payment or when it is stated to be payable to a particular person and does not forbid transfer. The sum payable by a bill is a sum† certain even though it is to be paid with interest, or by stated instalments or by stated instalments with the whole becoming due on default in an instalment or according to an indicated rate of exchange. Interest runs either from the date of the bill or, if undated, from the date of its issue. Where there is a discrepancy between words and figures for the sum payable, the amount in words is payable. The drawer of a bill and the indorsers are normally under a liability to guarantee payment by the drawee or acceptor†. The drawer and indorsers may exclude this liability by signing with words such as 'without recourse'. When there is dishonour of a bill because the draweee or acceptor refuse to accept or pay it the holder must normally give notice to the drawer or indorsers if he wishes to hold them to their liability but they may attach a waiver of need for such notice to their signatures. A document which is not valid as a bill may however be valid as an ordinary contract or as a promissory note.

(See the Bills of Exchange Act 1882, ss. 3–13 and 16 as amended).

One of the most frequently met forms of bill of exchange is the cheque defined in s. 73 as 'a bill of exchange drawn on a banker payable on demand'.

Bill of Lading. This document is a receipt acknowledging that goods have been loaded on a ship or received for shipment, a document of title which can be used as a symbol for transferring possession or property in the cargo whilst at sea and is good evidence of the contract of carriage but not the contract itself. The better view is that 'received for shipment' bills of lading, acknowledging that goods have been received by the carrier but not that they have been placed on board, through bills of lading and 'combined transport documents'† used in container traffic, are bills of lading for legal purposes. The Hague Rules, which incorporate many standard terms into most bills of lading and are scheduled to the Carriage of Goods by Sea Act 1971 apply by s. 1 (4) of the Act to 'a bill of lading or any similar document of title' as well as to non-negotiable receipts. A bill of lading stating that the goods are in good order and condition is said to be clean. If the bill notes defects it is 'claused'.

Bills of lading are often made out in triplicate, one copy being retained by the consignor, one going in the ship's papers and one being sent ahead to the consignee. If the bill is made out to bearer or the name of the consignee is left blank the consignee may transfer it by delivery. If it is made out to consignee or order, or to consignee or order or assigns he may transfer it by indorsement and delivery. If he indorses it in blank with his simple signature it may thereafter be transferred by mere delivery. If he indorses it in full by signing it and adding the name of the indorsee, together with the words 'or order', he in his turn will have to indorse, either in full or in blank to further transfer it. The holder may restrict further transfer by indorsing in full with the transferee's name but without the words 'or order'. A bill of lading is not a negotiable instrument since transfer to one who takes in good faith and for value will not in general give a better title than the transferor has, except (i) when an ordinary buyer of goods would get a better title and (ii) under the Sale of Goods Act 1979, s. 47 (2) such transfer may defeat wholly or partially a seller's lien or right of stoppage in transitu. Hence a bill of lading is described as 'semi-negotiable'. The Bills of Lading Act 1855, s. 1 provides that every consignee named in a bill or indorsee to whom property† in the goods has passed shall have the same rights and liabilities as if they were party to the contract in the bill. Whilst the shipowner may sue either the consignor, consignee or transferee, once the property has passed only the consignee or indorsee may sue the carrier, *The Albazero*; *The Albacruz* [1977] AC 774. A pledge of a bill does not pass the property so as to make the pledgee liable to pay the freight† unless he takes possession of the goods, *Sewell v Burdick* (1885) 10 App Cas 74. The bill of lading remains a document of title so long as the goods are in transit, *Barber v Meyerstein* (1870) LR 4 HL 317; *Barclays Bank v Customs and Excise* [1963] 1 Lloyd's Rep 81. As the bill of lading is evidence of the contract of carriage, not the contract itself, evidence may be given that the contract differed from the terms in the bill, *The Ardennes* [1951] 1 KB 55. The bill of lading may be preceded by the less formal mate's receipt† to be exchanged for the bill of lading.

Even if a ship is subject to a charterparty a bill of lading is usually found. If the charterer finds the cargo himself the bill is a receipt and document of title. The master or loading broker who signs the bill of lading usually does so as agent of the shipowner but may do so for the charterer when the latter puts the vessel for hire as a general ship or when there is a charterparty by demise, when the charterer has full control of the ship. If a charterparty provides that the master or broker shall be agent of the charterer this will not affect third parties who have no notice of this.

The master has no authority to sign a shipped bill of lading for goods not actually loaded and if he does so the shipowner or carrier (who may be a charterer) will not be liable to the shipper if they can rebut the prima facie evidence of loading raised by the master's signature. This applies to partial and total failure to load, but under the Bills of Lading Act 1855, s. 3 the master will be personally liable to a consignee or an indorsee of such a bill, which will be conclusive evidence against him, unless the holder received the bill knowing that the goods had not been shipped or the misrepresentation in the bill was caused by the fraud of the shipper, the holder or someone under whom the holder claims. The shipowner or carrier, though not liable to the original shipper, will be liable under Art. 4 of the Hague Rules, as scheduled to the Carriage of Goods by Sea Act 1971, to a transferee in good faith of the bill. The Rules are now incorporated in most bills of lading and cover very many of the rights and duties of the carrier.

The master should deliver the cargo to the consignee or assignee of the bill. If the bill was made in multiple copies and the different parts are in different hands the first transferee for value is entitled. If, without notice of conflicting claims, the master delivers to the first person to present a part the master will almost always be released from liability by the terms of the bill. If he knows of conflicting claims he should take out interpleader proceedings. If he delivers to a person not producing a bill of lading this will be fundamental breach but an indemnity taken from such a person will be enforced, *Sze Hai Tong v Rambler Cycle Co* [1959] AC 576.

Bills of Sale Acts 1878–1882. These were designed to prevent persons obtaining credit on the strength of goods in their possession but the title to which had been transferred to others, the Act of 1878 dealing with absolute transfers and the 1882 Act with those by way of mortgage or charge. The Acts strike at documents not transactions, not forbidding parol transfers of title but merely requiring that if transfers are in writing then certain formalities must be observed and documents registered under penalty of invalidity. The term 'bill of sale' is defined for both Acts in the 1878 Act, s. 4. It includes not only bills of sale properly so called (transfers of title, without possession) but also a wide variety of other documents with similar effect. The term does not include assignments for the benefit of creditors, marriage settlements, transfers of ships or shares in them (these are also termed 'bills of sale') transfers of goods in the ordinary course of trade, bills of lading or any document used in trade as proof of possession or control of, or authority for the possessor to transfer or receive, goods, nor agricultural charges on farming stock. Nor are pledge, hire purchase (*McEntire v Crossley Bros* [1895] AC 457), nor documents subsequent to and merely ancillary to oral transactions, such as mere receipts for money paid, within the Acts. In determining whether a document is within the Acts the court must look to the real nature and not the form of the transaction, so that what is apparently hire purchase may be an unregistered bill of sale, *North Central Wagon v Brailsford* [1962] 1 All ER 502. The Acts apply only to transactions relating to 'personal chattels', generally goods, including fixtures and growing crops if assigned separately from the land, and trade machinery but do not include leases of land, stocks, shares, contracts and other things or choses in action. Debentures granted by companies are, and securities given by friendly societies may be, excluded from the Acts. If an absolute bill of sale does not comply with the requirements of form and registration in the 1878 Act it is void as against the grantor's trustee in bankruptcy or assignee under an assignment for the benefit of creditors or execution creditors in so far as goods covered by the bill are in the possession or apparent possession of the grantor when these claims become effective. Mortgage or security bills of sale within the Act of 1882 are void, even as against the parties, if they do not follow the form scheduled to the Act, so that a covenant for repayment is void though the grantee may recover the principal as money lent. If the bill is in proper form but not attested or registered or does not truly state the consideration it is void against even the parties, so far as the chattels comprised in it are concerned, but covenants as to payment, interest and insurance remain valid. The form of the bill set out in the Act provides for an inventory of chattels covered by it and the bill is void against all except the grantor in respect of chattels not specifically described there.

Bill of Sale (Shipping). In the sense of the form of contract prescribed by the Merchant Shipping Act 1894 for the transfer of a British ship or share therein this is to be distinguished from documents similarly named within Bills of Sale Acts.

Bills in a set. This means that several copies of a bill of exchange are drawn. The Bills of Exchange Act 1882, s. 71 provides that if each part is numbered and contains a reference to the other parts (e.g. 'this first of exchange, this second, etc.') the whole of the parts form one bill. The acceptance† may be written on any part and should be written on one only but if the drawee accepts more than one and these accepted parts come into the hands of different holders in due course the acceptor is liable on each part as if it were a separate bill. When the holder of a set indorses two or more parts to different persons he is liable on each part and every indorser after him is liable on the part he indorsed as if it were a separate bill. When two or more parts are negotiated to different holders in due course the one whose title first accrues is as between these holders deemed to be the true owner of the bill, but this is not to affect the rights of a person who in due course accepts or pays the part first presented to him. If the acceptor of a bill drawn in a set pays it without requiring the part bearing the acceptance to be delivered up to him and when the bill matures that part is in the hands of a holder in due course the acceptor is liable to that holder. Subject to these rules when any part of a bill in a set is discharged by payment or by any other means of discharge the whole bill is discharged.

Blue Pencil Rule. *See* CONTRACTS IN RESTRAINT OF TRADE.

Book debts. Debts due to a creditor, treated as his property, a category of choses in action.

Bottomry Bond. A security for a loan binding a ship. Now obsolete, but some of the cases are relevant for agency of necessity.

Bribe. 'If a gift be made to a confidential agent with the view of inducing the agent to act in favour of the donor in relation to transactions between the donor and the agent's principal and that gift is secret as between the donor and the agent – that is to say, without the knowledge and consent of the principal – then the gift is a bribe . . . the court will not inquire into the donor's motive in giving the bribe, nor allow evidence to be gone into as to motive'. *Hovenden v Millhoff* (1900) 83 LT 41 at 43; *Industries and General Mortgage v Lewis* [1949] 2 All ER 573. *See* DUTIES OF AN AGENT TO HIS PRINCIPAL.

British ship. *See* REGISTRATION OF BRITISH SHIPS.

British shipowners. Those qualified to be the owners of British ships under s. 1 of the Merchant Shipping Act 1894, as amended, are British subjects and companies subject to and established under the law of a part of Her Majesty's Dominions and having their principal place of business in those Dominions. Since 1948 natural born British subjects have not enjoyed a preferred position. Most ships are now owned by incorporated companies. Foreigners may hold shares in such companies owning British ships but not shares in the ships themselves. For most vessels shipowners must undertake the process of registration of British ships if the ship is to be regarded as a British ship and an owner may be registered as an owner or joint-owner of one or more of the sixty-four shares into which the property in a British ship is divided. When a ship or a share in it is transferred on sale to a British owner the transaction must be embodied in a bill of sale as set out in the Merchant Shipping Act 1894 and the transferee must make a 'declaration of transfer', declaring his qualification to be a British shipowner. The bill of sale and declaration must then be produced to the registrar, who will register the transaction and will endorse the bill of sale. On sale to a non-British owner no bill of sale is required unless the ship is being sold outside the country of her port of registry. Such a sale may require a certificate of sale from the registrar at the port of registry. When ownership of a British ship or share therein is transmitted on death or bankruptcy the new owner, if qualified to be a British owner, should make and register a 'declaration of transmission'. If not so qualified the court may order on application a sale within a period of four weeks extendable to a year but if not thus sold the ship or share is subject to forefeiture. Possession of the ship or of the certificate of registry is prima facie evidence of ownership. The registered owners are prima facie liable to pay for repairs and necessaries but co-owners are not necessarily in partnership and, therefore, one co-owner is not necessarily an agent for his fellow-owners. (*See* BILL OF SALE (SHIPPING)).

Brokers. In older cases agents for the sale of goods who were not given possession of the goods (*see* FACTORS). Nowadays the term is also applied to many agents who do not deal in goods, such as stockbrokers and insurance brokers.

C

Cancellable agreements. *See* COOLING OFF PERIOD.

Cancellation of a negotiable instrument. The Bills of Exchange Act 1882, s. 63 provides that intentional and apparent cancellation of a bill of exchange by the holder or his agent amounts to discharge of a negotiable instrument. Any party liable may be discharged by the intentional cancellation of his name by the holder or his agent. Any indorser who would have had a right of recourse against the party discharged is also discharged. A cancellation made unintentionally, mistakenly or without the authority of the holder is inoperative but where an instrument appears to have been cancelled the burden of proving that the cancellation is inoperative lies on the party alleging this. The Act does not provide what form cancellation should take. By s. 89 these provisions apply to a promissory note.

Cancelling clause. *See* VOYAGE CHARTERPARTY and TIME CHARTERPARTY.

Capacity in contract. *See* CONTRACTUAL CAPACITY.

Capacity in relation to negotiable instruments. The Bills of Exchange Act 1882, s. 22 provides that capacity to incur liability as a party to a bill of exchange is co-extensive with capacity to contract. Ultra vires in relation to corporations is expressly preserved. An infant or minor under eighteen cannot incur liability on a bill of exchange, including a cheque, *Ex p Margrett, Re Soltykoff* [1891] 1 QB 413. This is so even if he misrepresents his age or purports to ratify it after full age or if it is given for necessaries, although in the last case he may be liable in contract or quasi-contract for the goods but not on the instrument. Nor may he be held liable on an instrument given during minority but post-dated to after majority, *Hutley v Peacock* (1913) 30 TLR 42. Section 22 further provides that where a bill is drawn or indorsed by an infant, minor or corporation having no capacity to incur liability on a bill the drawing or indorsement is not a total nullity but entitles the holder to trace his title through it so as to enforce the bill against any other party and receive payment of it.

By s. 89 these provisions apply to a promissory note. (*See* CONTRACTUAL CAPACITY).

Carriage by air: air waybill. All three forms of the Warsaw Convention (original, as amended at The Hague and as amended at Montreal) (*see* CARRIAGE BY AIR: CONVENTIONS AND LEGISLATION) make provision in the international air transport of goods for the issue of a document by the consignor containing prescribed particulars. The consignor may require the carrier to accept this document. The document required by the original Convention was an 'air consignment note'. Absence of or irregularity in such a document resulted in the carrier not being able to limit liability. (*See* CARRIAGE BY AIR: LIMITATION OF LIABILITY). The document was re-named an 'air waybill' by the amended Hague Convention. (Carriage by Air Act 1961). The contents required were reduced. It was to be in triplicate with one part marked 'for the carrier' and another 'for the consignee'. This was to accompany the cargo. The waybill was to contain details of the route. The consignor was responsible for accuracy and was required to indemnify the carrier for loss arising from inaccuracy or irregularity.

Absence of or irregularity in the waybill did not affect the validity of the contract but the carrier could not limit liability. The Montreal Protocol (Carriage by Air and Road Act 1979) makes changes. Any other suitable means of recording the contract may be used instead of a waybill but the carrier must, on request, give the consignor a receipt for the goods. The impossibility of using these substituted means on the route shall not entitle the carrier to refuse to accept the cargo. Non-compliance with the requirements of the waybills does not affect the contract and the carrier may limit his liability. By Article 34 of the Convention the documentary requirements (consignment notes and waybills) do not apply to carriage in extraordinary circumstances outside the normal scope of an air carrier's business.

It appears that the air waybill is neither a document of title nor a negotiable instrument. Article 15 of The Hague version of the Convention says that nothing in it is to prevent the issue of a negotiable air waybill but this does not appear in the Montreal version. The air waybill must contain necessary information for police and customs and have attached to it any necessary documents. The carrier need not check its sufficiency and the consignor is liable to the carrier for any loss caused by such insufficiency unless it results from the carrier's fault.

Carriage by air; baggage check. All three forms of the Warsaw Convention (original, as amended at The Hague and as amended at Montreal) (*see* CARRIAGE BY AIR: CONVENTIONS AND LEGISLATION) make provision for the issue in international air passenger transport of a baggage check and for the consequences of non-issue or issuing it in improper form. The original requirements (Carriage by Air Act 1932) were reduced by The Hague amendments (Carriage by Air Act 1961). This allowed the baggage check to be combined with the passenger ticket. (*See* CARRIAGE BY AIR: PASSENGER TICKET). Under the Montreal amendments (Carriage by Air and Road Act 1979) the Convention now refers to 'checked' luggage, not as formerly 'registered' luggage.

The baggage check may be combined or incorporated in the passenger ticket and should give the same route information but any other means of recording this information may be substituted. Non-compliance does not render the contract invalid. It is governed by the Convention and the carrier can still limit his liability. By Article 34 of the Convention the baggage check requirements do not apply to carriage in extraordinary circumstances outside the normal scope of an air carrier's business. (*See* CARRIAGE BY AIR: LIMITATION OF LIABILITY).

Carriage by air: combined carriage. When carriage is partly by air and partly by other means the Warsaw Convention applies only to the air carriage provided that it falls within its definition of international carriage. Terms relating to non-air carriage can be inserted in the air carriage document provided that the Convention is observed in regard to the air carriage. (*See* CARRIAGE BY AIR: CONVENTIONS AND LEGISLATION).

Carriage by air: conventions and legislation. International conventions to which effect has been given by statute embody codes applicable to international air transport. The principal convention is the Warsaw Convention 1929 to which effect was given by the Carriage by Air Act 1932. The Warsaw Convention was amended at The Hague in 1955 and the Carriage by Air Act 1961 enabled this country to ratify the Hague Protocol in 1967. The Carriage by Air (Supplementary Provisions) Act 1962 gives effect to the Guadalajara Convention 1961 dealing with sub-contracted carriage. The Carriage by Air and Road Act 1979 gives effect to the Montreal Protocols which further amend the Warsaw Convention as amended by The Hague and the Guadalajara Conventions. The conventions were intended to provide uniform rules of law applying irrespective of the nationality of airlines, passengers and cargo, but since the conventions and their amendments bind only countries acceding to them this has only been partially achieved. The unamended Warsaw Convention applies to flights to countries which have not accepted The Hague Protocol and the amended version to those which have. The Carriage by Air Act 1932 was repealed by the Act of 1961. The conventions and protocols are primarily applicable to 'international carriage' as defined but power was reserved by s. 10 of the 1961 Act to apply them to non-international carriage, i.e. internal flights or flights between this country and one which has not acceded to the conventions. This was done in this country in 1967 by the Carriage by Air Acts (Application of Provisions) Order 1967.

These conventions apply to all international carriage of persons, baggage or cargo by aircraft for reward and also to gratuitous carriage by aircraft performed by an air transport undertaking. 'International carriage' means all carriage in which 'the place of departure and the place of destination, whether or not there be a break in the carriage or a transhipment, are situated either within the territories of two High Contracting Parties or within the territory of a single High Contracting Party if there is an agreed stopping place within the territory of another State even if that State is not a High Contracting Party'. Carriage to be performed by a series of carriers will be regarded as one undivided carriage if the parties have treated it as a single operation and will still be international even if one or more of the separate contracts have to be performed wholly within one State.

The conventions prescribe the form of a passenger ticket, baggage ticket and air waybill (air consignment note under the unamended convention) and the effect of failure to provide these or to provide them in proper form.

The conventions also cover liability of the carrier, limitation of the carrier's liability, combined carriage and jurisdiction over claims (<i>see</i> CARRIAGE BY AIR: LIMITATION OF LIABILITY; CARRIAGE BY AIR: LIABILITY OF THE CARRIER; CARRIAGE BY AIR: COMBINED CARRIAGE; CARRIAGE BY AIR: COURTS AND PARTIES; CARRIAGE BY AIR: AIR WAYBILL; CARRIAGE BY AIR: BAGGAGE CHECK).

Carriage by air: courts and parties. An action for damages must be brought at the option of the plaintiff in the territory of one of the High Contracting Parties to the Warsaw Convention (<i>see</i> CARRIAGE BY AIR: CONVENTIONS AND LEGISLATION) before the court having jurisdiction either where the carrier is ordinarily resident or has his principal place of business or has an establishment by which the contract was made or at the place of destination. The Montreal Protocol adds that for death, injury or delay of a passenger or for destruction, loss, damage or delay of luggage the action may be brought in one of the above courts or in the territory of a High Contracting Party before a court within whose jurisdiction the carrier has an establishment if the passenger has his ordinary or permanent residence in that territory.

Where carriage is performed by successive carriers all forms of the Convention provide that each carrier who accepts passengers, baggage or cargo is subject to the Convention and is deemed to be a contracting party for his part of the carriage. A passenger can only sue the carrier performing the contract at the time when the accident or delay occurred except when the first carrier by express agreement assumes liability for the whole journey. In regard to baggage or cargo carried by successive carriers the passenger or consignor can sue the first carrier and the passenger or consignee can sue the last carrier and each may take action against the carrier in whose part of the journey the harm or delay took place. These carriers are jointly and severally liable to the passenger, consignor and consignee.

Carriage by air: goods: rights of consignor and consignee. All three forms of the Warsaw Convention (original, as amended at The Hague and as amended at Montreal) (*see* CARRIAGE BY AIR: CONVENTIONS AND LEGISLATION) make similar provision for these rights. Subject to his obligations under the contract of carriage the consignor may dispose of the cargo either by withdrawing it at the departure or destination aerodrome or at an intermediate landing or by calling for it to be delivered either at destination or in transit to a person other than the consignee or by requiring it to be returned to the departure aerodrome. In this the consignor must not prejudice the carrier or other consignors and must pay expenses. If it is impossible to carry out the consignor's orders the carrier must inform him forthwith. If the carrier obeys the consignor's orders without requiring production of the air waybill (*see* CARRIAGE BY AIR: AIR WAYBILL) delivered to the latter (or, the Montreal Protocol adds, the receipt for cargo given to him) he will be liable to any person lawfully in possession of the waybill (or receipt) but may recover against the consignor. The rights of the consignor cease when the rights of the consignee begin to operate on arrival but revive in the event of non-acceptance. On arrival, subject to contrary agreement, the carrier must give notice to the consignee. Except when the consignor has withdrawn the cargo the consignee is entitled to delivery on arrival on payment of dues and on complying with the conditions of carriage. The Hague Protocol adds that the consignee is entitled to delivery of the air waybill. If the carrier admits loss of the cargo or it is delayed more than seven days the consignee may enforce his contractual rights against the carrier.

Carriage by air: liability of carrier. All three forms of the Warsaw Convention (original, as amended at The Hague and as amended at Montreal) (*see* CARRIAGE BY AIR: CONVENTIONS AND LEGISLATION) make provision for the carriers' liability for death or personal injury to passengers, loss or damage to baggage or cargo and delay. In any event the carrier will not be liable if he can prove that he or his servants or agents took all necessary measures to avoid the harm or that it was impossible to do so. In the case of death or personal injury the carrier is only liable if it occurred on board or in embarking or disembarking. The Montreal Protocol adds that the carrier is not liable if it resulted from the passenger's state of health. Under the Hague Protocol it was provided that if it was proved that the harm was caused or contributed to by the negligence of the injured person the court might in accordance with its own law exonerate the carrier wholly or in part. The Montreal Protocol does not refer to the law of the court and is more specific, mentioning passengers, baggage and cargo and allowing partial or total exoneration not only for negligence but also for any wrongful act or omission causing or contributing to the harm on the part of the claimant or the person on whose behalf the claim is made. Also under the Montreal Protocol it is expressly provided that the carrier is not liable for damage to baggage resulting from inherent vice†. Under the Montreal Protocol the liability for baggage operates when the baggage is on board or being embarked or disembarked. Under The Hague Protocol baggage liability operates during 'carriage by air', defined as for cargo in all three protocols. This 'carriage' lasts as long as the goods are in the charge of the carrier, whether in an airport, on board, or, in a landing outside an airport, at any place whatever. This 'carriage' does not prima facie apply to carriage by land, sea or river outside an airport but if that external carriage takes place in performing an air carriage contract any damage is presumed to have taken place during air carriage. The Montreal Protocol expressly provides that the carrier is not to be liable for cargo damage resulting from inherent vice, defective packing by some person other than the carrier, act of war or armed conflict or act of public authority relating to the entry, exit or transit of the goods.

Any provision tending to relieve the carrier of liability or to fix lower financial limits for liability (*see* CARRIAGE BY AIR: LIMITATION OF LIABILITY), is null and void but this does not entail the nullity of the whole contract. Exclusion clauses are allowed by The Hague and Montreal Protocols in respect of inherent vice in cargo.

Under the original convention and The Hague Protocol it was provided that limitation of liability did not apply in respect of any intentional or reckless act done by the carrier or his servants or agents in the course of employment, but this does not appear in the Montreal Protocol. The original convention also provided a defence in respect of cargo if the harm was caused by negligent pilotage, navigation or handling of the aircraft and in all other respects the carrier and his servants took all necessary measures to avoid the harm. This defence does not appear in either The Hague or Montreal Protocols.

Carriage by air: limitation of liability. All three forms of the Warsaw Convention (original, as amended at The Hague and as amended at Montreal) (*see* CARRIAGE BY AIR: CONVENTIONS AND LEGISLATION) make provision for the carrier's liability (*see* CARRIAGE BY AIR: CARRIER'S LIABILITY) for injury, loss or damage to be subject to financial limits. For death or injury to a passenger in flight, embarking or disembarking liability was limited under the original convention to 125,000 gold francs. Under The Hague amendment this was increased to 250,000 gold francs. For cargo the limit has always been 250 gold francs per kilogram unless a special declaration was made and an increased charge was paid if required and for articles in the passenger's personal charge 5000 gold francs. The Carriage by Air and Road Act 1979, s. 4 provides for The Hague figures to be replaced by

16,600, 17 and 332 special drawing rights respectively. Under Articles 22 and 22A of the Montreal Protocol the limits will be 100,000 special drawing rights for death or injury to a passenger, 4,150 for delay to a passenger, and 1,000 for each passenger's baggage. It remains 17 special drawing rights for each kilogram of cargo unless a special declaration is made and any extra charge paid. If a servant or agent of the carrier is sued he may avail himself of these limits if he proves he was acting within the scope of his employment. If the carrier and his agents and servants are sued the total recoverable in respect of each victim or unit of loss shall not exceed the limit.

Time limits are also applicable. Any action for damages must be brought within two years of arrival. Receipt without complaint of baggage or cargo is prima facie evidence of correct performance. In the case of damage complaint must be made forthwith after discovery and in any event within seven days in the case of baggage and fourteen days in the case of cargo. Partial loss of contents of baggage is 'damage' for this period of notice, *Fothergill v Monarch Airlines* [1980] 3 WLR 809. For the 1961 Act and The Hague Protocol the Carriage by Air and Road Act 1979, s. 2 now expressly provides that partial loss and partial receipt are damage requiring this notice. In the case of delay complaint must be made within twenty-one days of receipt of the goods. All complaints must be in writing. These limits may be set aside if there is fraud by the carrier.

Any contractual provision relieving the carrier of liability or fixing limits lower than those in the appropriate version of the Convention is null but this does not entail nullity of the entire contract. Under the original Convention and The Hague Protocol irregularities in the passenger ticket (*see* CARRIAGE BY AIR: PASSENGER TICKET), air consignment note or air waybill (*see* CARRIAGE BY AIR: AIR WAYBILL) or in the baggage check (*see* CARRIAGE BY AIR: BAGGAGE CHECK) all resulted in the carrier being deprived of financial limitation on liability, but this is not the case under the Montreal Protocol scheduled to the Carriage by Air and Road Act 1979.

Carriage by air: passenger ticket. All three forms of the Warsaw Convention (original, as amended at The Hague and as amended at Montreal) (*see* CARRIAGE BY AIR: CONVENTIONS AND LEGISLATION) make provision for the issue in international air passenger transport of a ticket containing prescribed information and for the consequences of failing to issue it or issuing it in improper form. The original requirements (see Carriage by Air Act 1932, Schedule) were reduced by The Hague amendments (Carriage by Air Act 1961) but an individual ticket was still required. Under the Montreal amendments (Carriage by Air and Road Act 1979), points of departure, destination and agreed stopping places must still be mentioned but the ticket may be either individual or collective, any other means of recording the route information may be substituted for the ticket and there is no requirement of a notice that the ticket is subject to the Warsaw Convention. Non-compliance does not render the contract invalid. It is governed by the Convention and the carrier can still limit his liability. By Article 34 of the Convention the ticket requirements do not apply to carriage in extraordinary circumstances outside the normal scope of an air carrier's business. (*See* CARRIAGE BY AIR: LIMITATION OF LIABILITY).

Carriage by Railway Act 1972. This gives effect to the Convention Relating to the Liability of the Railway for Death of and Personal Injury to Passengers which is scheduled to the Act. This convention is supplemental to the first of two major conventions dealing with international rail traffic – the International Convention Concerning the Carriage of Passengers and Luggage by Rail (CIV) (known in the Act as the 'Railway Passenger Convention') and the International Convention Concerning the Carriage of Goods by Rail (CIM) (known in the Act as the 'Railway Freight Convention'). The two major conventions are not scheduled to the Act but s. 6 provides that no action of any kind relating to liability provided for in the conventions may be brought against a railway, its servants or its agents except in accordance with the conventions and s. 7 provides that where goods are carried in accordance with the Freight Convention the consignee shall not be entitled to enforce any right against the railway except in accordance with the convention. Moreover, when the consignee accepts the consignment note in respect of the goods prescribed by the convention, or purports to exercise any rights given him by the convention he shall then be treated as if he were a party to the contract of carriage from its formation, having all the rights and obligations conferred by the convention. Railway authorities in this country have used the tickets and consignment notes prescribed by the conventions for international traffic, thus incorporating the provisions of the appropriate convention into the contract of carriage. The Freight Convention requires the use of a consignment note with specified contents which must accompany the goods. It makes provision for the carriers' liability for loss, damage and delay to the goods, with certain exemptions from liability. Special provision is made for dangerous goods and certain other special consignments. Liability is limited both in respect of amount and time. The normal period of limitation is one year, but exceptionally may be two years.

Carriage of Goods by Road Act 1965. This gives statutory effect to the Convention on the Contract for the International Carriage of Goods by Road (CMR). It applies to every contract for the carriage of goods in road vehicles for reward when the place of taking over of the goods and the place of delivery are in two different countries, of which at least one is a contracting country, irrespective of the residence and nationality of the parties. It applies to state and government carriage but not to postal convention carriage, funerals and furniture removal, nor to carriage between the United Kingdom and the Republic of Ireland. The Contracting Parties agree not to vary the convention by special agreement except to make it inapplicable to frontier traffic or to authorise within their territories the use of consignment notes representing a title to goods. Where the road vehicle is carried over part of the journey by sea, rail, inland waterway or air and (except when performance becomes impossible) the goods are not unloaded the convention applies to the whole journey. If harm occurs merely through the use of the other means of transport the liability of the carrier is regulated by the law applicable to that other means. The carrier is responsible for his servants and agents. A consignment note must be made out in triplicate containing numerous prescribed particulars. The consignment note is not a document of title or a negotiable instrument. The first copy is for the sender, the second accompanies the goods and the third is kept by the carrier. The sender is responsible for loss to the carrier resulting from inadequacy or inaccuracy of many of these particulars but the carrier must check the note and the goods and packaging. The sender is responsible for loss caused by defective packing unless this was known to the carrier when he received the goods. The sender is responsible for Customs documents and other formalities. The sender may dispose of the goods whilst in transit until the second copy of the consignment note is delivered to the consignee; thereafter the consignee has the right and, by special entry on the note, may have it from the time when the note is drawn up. If the journey becomes impossible the carrier must seek instructions from the person entitled to dispose of the goods. If the consignee rejects the goods they must be disposed of according to the sender's instructions but the carrier may dispose of them without instructions if they are perishable, if their condition warrants this or the storage expenses would be disproportionately large. The carrier is liable for total or partial loss, damage or delay but not if this is caused by the wrongful act of the claimant or by his instructions not consequent on a wrongful act or neglect of the carrier, by inherent vice† or through circumstances which the carrier could not avoid and the consequences of which he was unable to prevent. The carrier is not relieved of liability because of the defective condition of the vehicle or the neglect or wrongful act of the person from whom he hired the vehicle but, in general, he is not liable for loss or damage arising from the use of open unsheltered vehicles when this use was agreed; lack of or defect in packing; handling, loading and unloading by the sender, the consignee and their agents; the nature of the goods rendering them vulnerable to harm; insufficiency of marks or numbers and the carriage of livestock. He must prove that refrigerated or similar vehicles were properly maintained. Non-delivery within thirty days of the agreed time limit or, if none, within sixty days of handing to the carrier is conclusive evidence of loss. The person entitled to claim may request to be notified if the goods are recovered within a year. The carrier will be liable for failure to collect 'cash on delivery'. The sender must tell the carrier of dangerous goods, otherwise the carrier may unload, destroy or render them harmless without compensation and claim expenses from the sender. The value of goods is fixed by the commodity exchange price or market price. In the absence of special declaration and surcharge compensation shall not exceed the amount of loss or 8.33 special drawing rights per kilogram (see Carriage by Air and Road Act 1979, s. 4). Five per cent interest is payable on compensation. Where there is an extra-contractual claim the carrier may avail himself of time limits in the Convention. In case of wilful misconduct or its equivalent neither the carrier nor his agents may avail themselves of limits on liability or any shifting of the burden of proof provided in Chapter IV of the Convention. The consignee must notify apparent damage to the carrier on delivery and non-apparent within seven days. Delay must be notified within twenty-one days. Proceedings must be taken either in a court or tribunal of an agreed contracting country or in the country where the defendant is ordinarily resident or has his principal place of business or where the branch where the contract was made is located or where the goods were taken over by the carrier or where the place of delivery is located. The period of limitation is one year or, in case of wilful default or its equivalent, three years starting from, in the case of partial loss or damage, the date of delivery, in the case of total loss from thirty days after the agreed time limit or, if none, sixty days from receipt by the carrier and in other cases from three months after the contract. If carriage is performed by successive road carriers each is responsible for the whole operation, the second and successive carriers becoming party to the contract by accepting the goods and the consignment note. Only the first or last successive carrier or the one in whose charge the goods were when lost or damaged may be sued singly but all may be sued together. A carrier who pays compensation under this may, subject to contrary agreement, recover against the other carriers who are in whole or part responsible for the loss or damage. Except for such an agreement between successive carriers, no contracting out is allowed. Any stipulation which would directly or indirectly derogate from the Convention is null and void but this does not involve the nullity of the rest of the contract. A benefit of insurance in favour of a carrier or any similar clause or a clause shifting the burden of proof will be null.

In *James Buchanan v Babco* [1978] AC 141 the House of Lords in holding carriers liable to excise duty on stolen whisky said that the English text was to be broadly interpreted to produce, if possible, conformity amongst contracting states but foreign decisions were not to be used. See *Thermo v Ferrimaster* [1981] 1 All ER 1142 for the position when a lorry is loaded on a ship.

Carriage of Goods by Sea Act 1971. The chaotic variety of provisions once found in bills of lading led to international agreement at The Hague in 1922 on many standard terms to be embodied in all bills of lading. These terms, known as the Hague Rules, were in their original form, scheduled to the Carriage of Goods by Sea Act 1924, which required that all outward bound bills of lading should carry a 'clause paramount' incorporating the Rules. Most other maritime nations passed similar legislation. Amendments to the Rules were agreed at Brussels in 1968 and the Carriage of Goods by Sea Act 1971 was passed to give effect to these, coming into force on 23 June 1977, and replacing the 1924 Act and its version of the Rules.

The Rules under the 1971 Act apply to the carriage of goods by sea from any port in Great Britain or Northern Ireland to any other port whether or not it is in Great Britain or Northern Ireland. 'Goods' within the Rules does not include livestock or deck cargo but the Act applies the Rules to their carriage. The Rules again apply where the bill of lading is issued in, or the port of shipment is in, another contracting state provided that the voyage is from a port in one state to a port in another state. The Rules also apply when the bill of lading expressly provides they are to do so and when a non-negotiable receipt similarly so provides. The Rules not only apply to bills of lading but to any similar document. They do not apply to charterparties but may be expressly incorporated in them. If bills are issued for cargo in a chartered ship the bills are subject to the Rules. The Rules apply to the coastal trade, its exclusion sanctioned by the 1924 Act no longer applying, and there is no longer need for a 'clause paramount'. The Rules do not apply when there is no agreement for the issue of a bill of lading or similar document nor to the carriage of particular goods, nor in the ordinary court of commerce, when the circumstances justify a special agreement. 'Carriage of goods' runs from loading to discharge and carriage before and after these events may be governed by terms to which the Rules do not apply.

The carrier is not absolutely bound to provide a seaworthy† ship but merely to use due diligence to make it so. If the voyage is in stages this obligation applies at the start of each stage. The carrier is liable for his servants† and independent contractors† in this. Breach of this obligation disentitles the carrier from relying on the many 'excepted perils' in the Act if mishap occurs. The carrier must properly and carefully load, handle, stow, carry, care for and discharge the goods. He will not be liable if the cargo is damaged by negligent management of the ship as distinct from the cargo. The carrier must also on demand from the shipper, issue a bill of lading showing the loading marks stamped on the goods to identify them, the number of packages or weight as furnished by the shipper and the apparent order and condition of the goods. The bill is prima facie evidence of this and is conclusive if transferred to a third party taking it in good faith. Unless written notice is given of loss or damage on delivery, or, if the harm is not apparent, within three days, removal of the goods will be prima facie evidence that they were as described in the bill of lading. Notice need not be given if the goods are subject to joint inspection. The period of limitation is one year, but British shipowners have agreed to extend it to two years.

The rules confer extensive exemptions from liability on the carrier. These apply to loss or damage resulting from the act, neglect or default of the master, mariner, pilot or servant of the carrier in the navigation of the ship, fire, unless caused by the actual fault or privity of the carrier, perils of the sea or navigable waters, Act of God†, act of war or public enemies, restraints of princes, seizure under legal process, quarantine, act or omission of the shipper or owner of the goods, his servants or agents, strikes, lock-outs, riots, the saving or attempting to save life at sea, wastage, inherent vice†, inadequate packing or marks and latent defects not discoverable by due diligence. The carrier is also not liable for loss arising from any other cause not involving his actual fault or privity or that of his servants or agents but the burden of proof is on the person claiming this protection.

Where the carrier is not exempt his liability was limited to 10,000 gold francs per package or unit or 30 francs per kilo of gross weight, whichever was the higher, unless the nature and value of the goods were declared and inserted in the bill of lading. Merchant Shipping Act 1981, s. 2 substitutes special drawing rights for gold francs, the figures being 666.67 and 2 units of account respectively. Where a container is used to consolidate packages, if the number of packages is stated in the bill of lading this is the number for this purpose. There is no limitation if the loss or damage was intentionally or recklessly caused by the carrier, but neither the carrier nor the ship will be liable if the nature or value of the goods is knowingly mis-stated by the shipper in the bill of lading. Deviation to save life and property and other reasonable deviation is allowed but unwarranted deviation prevents the shipowner relying on the excepted perils. Inflammable, explosive or dangerous goods shipped without the carrier's knowledge may be destroyed or rendered harmless without liability and even when shipped with his knowledge they may be similarly disposed of if they endanger ship or cargo, without liability, except to general average† if any. The carrier may surrender his rights and immunities and increase his responsibilities if this is embodied in the bill of lading, but, in general, his immunities cannot be increased and any contractual clause purporting to relieve him of statutory liability is void. A servant or agent of the carrier, but not an independent contractor, may avail himself of the carrier's defences under the Rules unless the servant or agent caused the harm or loss intentionally or recklessly.

Under the Unfair Contract Terms Act 1977 it is not possible by a contract term or notice to exclude liability in negligence for death or personal injury in any charterparty or contract for the carriage of goods by ship or hovercraft but certain other provisions of the Act do not extend to such contracts except in favour of a person dealing as a consumer. These include the subjection of terms excluding liability in negligence for harm other than death or personal injury to a test of reasonableness, provisions as to contractual liability and provisions as to miscellaneous contracts (e.g. work and materials). Where goods are carried by ship or hovercraft for only part of a journey or the means of transport is not specified but ship or hovercraft are not excluded, the position is the same except that the provisions of the Act apply with full force to miscellaneous contracts.

Carriage of Passengers by Road 1974 is designed to give effect to the Convention on the Contract for the International Carriage of Passengers and Luggage by Road which is scheduled to the Act. The Convention defines the scope of its application, defines persons for whom the carrier may be liable, prescribes transport documents both for passengers and luggage, and makes provision for the carriers' liability in respect of death and injury to passengers and loss of and damage to luggage. Provision is also made for claims and actions. The period of limitation for death and personal injury is three years from when the person suffering loss or injury would have had knowledge of it but may not exceed five years. Any contractual stipulation directly or indirectly contrary to the Convention is to be null and void but this is not to involve the nullity of the whole contract. The Carriage by Air and Road Act 1979, s. 4 provides that references to gold francs in the 1974 Act are to be replaced by references to special drawing rights.

Carriers Act 1830. *See* COMMON CARRIER.

Case stated. Either a procedure now abolished by the Arbitration Act 1979 for bringing an arbitration award before the court (*see* ARBITRATION), or a method of appealing on a point of law from a magistrates' court to the High Court or from the Crown Court to the High Court when the former has determined an appeal from a magistrates' court.

Caveat emptor. 'Buyer beware'. The original attitude of the common law was that it was for the buyer to protect himself in sale of goods. If he wished the seller to give undertakings as to title and quality of the goods it was for the buyer to bargain for express terms. In the nineteenth century the courts showed themselves ready to imply such terms unless the seller expressly or impliedly excluded them. This position achieved statutory form in the Sale of Goods Act 1893. After the 1939–45 War the courts developed the doctrine of the fundamental term or fundamental breach to curb exclusion clauses. The Supply of Goods (Implied Terms) Act 1973, s. 4 prevented most exclusion of terms as to title in sale of goods, merchantable quality, fitness for purpose, correspondence with description and terms in sale by sample in consumer sales and subjected exclusion clauses in other sales to a test of reasonableness. This was confirmed by the Unfair Contract Terms Act 1977† which in turn is adopted by the Sale of Goods Act 1979, s. 55. An auction sale cannot be a consumer transaction so that exclusion clauses may operate if reasonable. Exclusion is freely allowed in international supply contracts. The buyer also received protection under products liability, the Trade Descriptions Act† and the Fair Trading Act. Usage may imply terms as to quality. A comparable development took place in hire purchase marked by legislation in 1938, 1965 and the Consumer Credit Act 1974.

Since the terms as to merchantable quality and fitness for purpose implied by the Sale of Goods Act 1979, s. 14 are only implied when the seller sells in the course of a business, caveat emptor may still operate to some extent in private sales.

Certificate of misfortune (Bankruptcy). The Bankruptcy Act 1914, s. 26 (4) provides that the court in granting a discharge of the bankrupt may also grant a certificate to the effect that the bankruptcy was caused by misfortune without any misconduct on the bankrupt's part. This is in order to remove any statutory disqualification continuing after the discharge such as the period of five years disqualification from membership of Parliament, a local authority or appointment as a magistrate. Misfortune is strictly construed and such certificates are rarely granted, though there may be an appeal against refusal.

Certification trade mark. A trade mark† defined by the Trade Marks Act 1938, s. 37 as being 'adapted . . . to distinguish in the course of trade goods certified by any person in respect of origin, material, mode of manufacture, quality, accuracy or other characteristic from goods not so certified.' The proprietors of these marks may not trade in goods of the kind certified. The marks are usually owned by trade associations such as the Harris Tweed Association Ltd or the Stilton Cheese Makers' Association. See '*Stilton' Trade Mark* [1967] RPC 173. The proprietors must deposit in the Patent Office approved regulations for the use of their marks. These marks are registrable in Part A of the Register of Trade Marks and the rules for infringement are similar to those for ordinary trade marks. The Act makes special provision in s. 38 for Sheffield marks on metal goods the Cutler's Company being registered as proprietor of the word 'Sheffield' as a certification mark.

Cesser clause. *See* VOYAGE CHARTERPARTY and TIME CHARTERPARTY.

Champerty. Agreeing to conduct litigation for a share of property or damages recovered. Once both a crime and a tort, Criminal Law Act 1967, ss. 13 and 14 now provides that this is no longer so but also saves 'any rule of law' as to public policy or illegality in contract so that a champertous agreement is still a void contract. *See also* MAINTENANCE AND ASSIGNMENT OF CONTRACTS.

Charge. *See* MORTGAGE.

Charterparty. A contract for the hire of a ship. If the charterer undertakes the management of the ship, appointing and being responsible for the master and crew, it is known as a charterparty by demise, but in a simple charterparty the shipowner retains management of the vessel and crew. There may be a voyage charterparty to run for a voyage or voyages, a time charterparty to run for a fixed period or a mixed charterparty to run for a voyage or voyages within a fixed period. The word 'charterparty' derives from the fact that these contracts were once made in two copies on one sheet which was then divided along an indented line as a primitive protection against forgery – carta partita. Unlike the bill of lading, which is normally used for quantities of goods and not for the hire of a whole ship, the charterparty is the contract itself, not merely evidence of the contract, and hence it is more difficult to prove any alleged terms not included in the document. Charterparties are usually made on common forms known by code names, e.g. 'Gencon', 'Exxonvoy', but legislation does not impose requirements of content or form as the Carriage of Goods by Sea Act 1971 does for bills of lading. The Hague Rules, imposed by that Act on bills of lading, may be applied by agreement to charterparties.

It appears that the charterer's right to the use of the ship may be disregarded by one who buys the ship during the currency of the charter, even with notice of the charter, *Port Line v Ben Line* [1958] 2 QB 146, not following *Lord Strathcona SS Co v Dominion Coal Co* [1926] AC 108, though the charterer would have an action against the shipowner.

Charterparty by demise. Under such a charter, also known as 'net' or 'bare boat charter', the charterer undertakes full responsibility for control of the crew and the management of the vessel. The crew are his servants† and he is vicariously† liable for them; if salvage is earned the charterer and not the shipowner is entitled. The shipowner is not liable as carrier on bills of lading under any legislation governing them, nor is he liable for goods and services supplied to the ship during the charter. It may be a difficult question of fact whether a charterparty is by demise or not. The shipowner's only rights are to payment of the charter freight and return of the vessel when the charter has expired. Though a charterparty by demise may be for a voyage or voyages, in practice it is always for a period of time.

Cheque. The Bills of Exchange Act 1882, s. 73 defines a cheque as 'a bill of exchange drawn on a banker payable on demand'. It goes on to provide that except as otherwise provided in Part III of the Act (ss. 73–82 [the latter section now repealed and replaced by the Cheques Act 1957, s. 4]) the provisions of the Act applicable to a bill of exchange payable on demand apply to a cheque. In practice there is never an acceptance of a cheque by the drawee bank, *Bank of Baroda v Punjab National Bank* [1944] AC 176, so that rules relating to acceptance do not apply. As the drawer thus remains the party primarily liable, s. 74 provides that delay in making presentment for payment of a cheque does not wholly release the drawer as s. 45 provides in the case of ordinary demand bills. The drawer of a cheque is only released in the event of his bank failing during the delay and then only to the extent to which payment by the bank falls short of the full amount of the cheque. In the case of a crossed cheque a paying banker can be instructed to pay the amount of the cheque into another bank account or into an account with a particular banker. If a cheque is additionally crossed 'not negotiable' a transferee will not be able to obtain a better title than his transferor had. If a cheque is crossed 'account payee' or 'account payee only' a collecting banker is instructed to collect it for any account other than that of the payee only after stringent enquiry.

Cheques Act 1957. Prior to this Act it had been the practice to require the payee of a cheque paying it into his account to give an indorsement. This was believed to operate both as an indorsement and as a receipt, making it possible for the collecting banker to claim to be a holder in due course and thus true owner of the cheque, avoiding liability in conversion if the payee had no good title to the cheque, and entitled to sue on it if it was dishonoured by non-payment. It was also thought to give the paying banker the protection of the Bills of Exchange Act 1882, s. 60 which protected a banker paying in good faith and in the ordinary course of business on a forged indorsement on a cheque, if in fact the indorsement was forged. Checking the accuracy of indorsements led to much unproductive work and the Cheques Act 1957 was intended to eliminate the need for this as well as to effect other reforms. Section 1 protects a banker who pays in good faith and in the ordinary course of business a cheque, bankers' draft or mandate to pay which is not a bill of exchange (e.g. 'cheque' with an impersonal payee) if these instruments are unindorsed or irregularly indorsed and payment discharges the instrument. It is not clear whether the words 'absence of, or irregularity in, indorsement' cover the case of a forged indorsement (*see* FORGED AND UNAUTHORISED SIGNATURES ON BILLS OF EXCHANGE). If they do then s. 1 covers the same ground as the Bills of Exchange Act 1882, s. 60; if they do not, that section is still required for the protection of a banker paying on a forged indorsement. By a Resolution of the Committee of London Clearing Bankers in 1957 it was resolved to continue to require the indorsement of order instruments paid over the counter in cash. A banker failing to obtain such an indorsement might not be protected by s. 1 since he would not have acted 'in the ordinary course of business'. Indorsement is also still necessary when a cheque is negotiated to someone other than the original payee. The Bills of Exchange Act 1882, s. 80 as extended by the Cheques Act 1957, s. 5 may also protect payment on forged indorsements on crossed bankers' drafts and conditional instruments and the Stamp Act 1853, s. 19 may protect payments on forged indorsements on crossed (*see* CROSSED CHEQUES) or open bankers' drafts. The latter section originally gave protection in respect of payment on forged indorsements on cheques but in *Carpenters Co v British Mutual Banking Co* [1938] 1 KB 511 it was thought that the Stamp Act 1853, s. 19 had been impliedly repealed in relation to cheques by the Bills of Exchange Act 1882, s. 60. There seems to be much overlapping protection in these provisions. The Cheques Act 1957, s. 2 provides that a collecting banker who gives value for an order cheque will have the same right as if it had been indorsed in blank. This means that the collecting banker may become holder in due course of the cheque, as he might have done had the cheque been indorsed before the Act. He may thus both escape liability in conversion if the transferor did not have a good title and be entitled to sue on it if it is dishonoured. This section applies only to cheques, not to analogous instruments and only refers to the absence of, not to irregularity in, indorsement. Before the Cheques Act 1957, an indorsed cheque which appeared to have been paid could be used as evidence of payment, in effect a receipt. Section 3, pursuing the policy of making indorsement in many ways superfluous, makes an unindorsed cheque which appears to have been paid similarly evidence of payment. Section 4 protects a collecting banker, who in good faith and without negligence receives payment of cheques and certain analogous instruments (*see*

COLLECTING BANKER) and s. 5 extends the provisions of the Bills of Exchange Act 1882 relating to crossed cheques (ss. 76–81) to the analogous instruments covered by s. 4. Thus such crossed instruments must be paid to a banker and a paying banker acting in good faith and without negligence and a drawer may obtain the protection of s. 80. The crossing is a material part of the instrument and alteration will discharge it. (*See* ALTERATION OF A NEGOTIABLE INSTRUMENT). Section 6 (2) of the Act provides that the Act does not make negotiable any instrument which is otherwise not negotiable. It is not clear whether negotiable here means, as in the Bills of Exchange Act 1882, s. 8 (1) 'transferable' or as in s. 76 (2) (a crossed cheques provision) 'transferable with the full benefits of negotiability'. If the former, a banker who paid a conditional instrument which appeared to have been transferred would not receive any statutory protection if fulfilment of the condition, such as the provision of a receipt, could only have been effected by the original payee.

Chose in action. *See* THINGS IN ACTION.

Chose in possession. *See* THINGS IN ACTION.

C.I.F. Contracts. A form of sale of goods used in overseas trade. It names the port of destination and the price† quoted by the seller includes cost of the goods, insurance and freight. The seller must ship or buy afloat goods of the contract description. If they are unascertained goods he must normally give notice of appropriation. On or after shipment he must obtain a proper bill of lading and insurance policy. He performs the contract by transferring the shipping documents – bill of lading, insurance policy and invoice to the buyer on the 'prompt', the date fixed for payment. When payment is being made by banker's commercial credit the documents will in practice be transferred to a bank making payment. The special feature of the c.i.f. contract is the importance attached to the documents, *Smyth v Bailey* [1940] 3 All ER 60. If insurance is not effected the buyer may reject the goods even though they arrive safely, *Orient Co v Brekke and Howlid* [1913] 1 KB 531, but if proper documents (including a proper policy) are tendered the buyer must accept and pay for them even though the goods are lost, *Groom v Barber* [1915] 1 KB 316; *Manbre v Corn Products* [1919] 1 KB 198. It has been said that a c.i.f. contract is a sale of documents rather than goods but it may be rather a contract of sale of goods, to be performed by delivery of documents since a contract for the sale of specific goods c.i.f. is void if at the time of sale the goods had perished even though a policy relating to them was in existence, *Couturier v Hastie* (1856) 5 HLC 673. So also when a seller bought what he believed were goods afloat covered by regular documents and re-sold them it was held he did not fulfil the contract by handing over an apparently regular set of shipping documents when the goods had never existed, *Hindley v East India Produce Co* [1973] 2 Lloyd's Rep 515. There are separate rights to reject documents and goods if they are not in conformity with the contract, *Kwei Tek Chao v British Traders* [1954] 2 QB 459 (*see* REJECTION IN SALE OF GOODS), but if the buyer takes up without objection documents which do not conform he will be precluded from rejecting them later, *Panchaud v General Grain* [1970] 1 Lloyd's Rep 53. Since under the Sale of Goods Act 1979, s. 28 payment and delivery are concurrent conditions and delivery in a c.i.f. contract means delivery of shipping documents, the buyer (unless there is contrary agreement) cannot refuse to pay until he is able to examine the goods (*Clemens Horst v Biddle Bros* [1912] AC 18), s. 34 thus being excluded (*see* DELIVERY IN SALE OF GOODS). This does not exclude his right to reject the goods if they do not on arrival conform with the contract. Section 32 (1) providing that delivery to a carrier is prima facie delivery to the buyer, does not apply, nor does s. 32 (3) as there are always terms as to insurance, but s. 32 (2) requiring a seller to make a reasonable contract with a carrier, does apply. Property† normally passes on delivery of the shipping documents, *Comptoir D'Achat v Luis de Ridder, The Julia* [1949] AC 293, but in special circumstances this may be displaced, *The Albazero* [1977] AC 774. Risk† normally passes 'on shipment or as from shipment' (*Comptoir d'Achat v Luis de Ridder*), so that s. 20, linking property with risk, is displaced.

The bill of lading must normally be transferable, cover the voyage continuously over an agreed or customary route, state the goods are shipped and not merely received for shipment, be genuine in stating correct dates and not containing forgery, cover only the contract goods, be valid and effective and be 'clean', that is not contain any adverse comment on the good order or condition of the goods. The insurance policy must be assignable, legally effective (not an honour policy), cover only the contract goods continuously over the route and be usual in the trade or as specified in the contract. If it is usual or agreed the seller will not be in breach if it fails to cover other risks, e.g. war risks, *Groom v Barber* [1915] 1 KB 316. The invoice must at least enable the buyer to relate it to the contract but more detail may be required by the contract. The requirements as to documents may be modified by the contract, e.g. allowing a delivery order on the ship of a 'received for shipment' bill of lading or a certificate of insurance instead of a policy. The contract may also require other documents such as certificates of origin, quality, testing and the like. The contract may require the seller to give notice of appropriation of goods to the contract or to 'declare' a shipment within a given time and these documents may be added to the shipping documents. Such notice transforms hitherto unascertained goods into specific goods, and the seller is then bound to deliver those goods only in rendering performance, but does not transfer property.

There are many variants. C. & f. contracts are similar except the buyer arranges insurance. In 'c.i.f. and c.' contracts the additional c indicates the price, includes agent's commission and additional 'c and i' banker's interest and commission. Even though a contract is stated to be c.i.f. it may be found to be ex ship or arrival† if that is the real relation, *Comptoir d'Achat v Luis de Ridder*. True c.i.f. contracts are not used in carriage by air, *Morton-Norwich v Intergen* [1976] FSR 513. At one time export bans could not be pleaded as a ground of frustration in c.i.f. contracts since the seller could always purchase goods afloat to perform, *Vantol v Fairclough, Dodd* [1956] 3 All ER 750 but purchase afloat seems now rare so that such bans may now frustrate the contract, *Tradax v Andre* [1976] 1 Lloyd's Rep 416: *Czarnikow v Rolimpex* [1978] 2 All ER 1043. (Force majeure clauses).

When contracts cover a whole bulk shipment, goods under one of these contracts may be ascertained for passing† of property without being physically allocated and when the goods for that contract are ascertained by exhaustion there is no need for appropriation, *Karlshamm Oljefabriker v Eastport, The Elafi* [1982] 1 All ER 208.

A c.i.f. buyer who is unable to sue in contract because he is not holding the bill of lading may sue in negligence for damage to the cargo, *Shiffart und Kohlen v Chelsea Maritime, The Irene's Success* [1982] 1 All ER 218.

CIM. *See* PRIVATE CARRIER and CARRIAGE BY RAILWAY ACT 1972.

CIV. *See* PRIVATE CARRIER and CARRIAGE BY RAILWAY ACT 1972.

Civil Jurisdiction and Judgments Act 1982. *See* FOREIGN JUDGMENTS.

Claused bill of lading. *See* BILL OF LADING.

Clause paramount. *See* CARRIAGE OF GOODS BY SEA ACT 1971.

Clayton's Case. The rule in *Devaynes v Noble, Clayton's Case* (1816) 1 Mer 572 is a rebuttable presumption that monies are deemed to be paid out of a current account in the order in which they were paid in. This creates a problem where a banker has taken security for a current account overdraft and the customer creates a second mortgage on the same property. The banker cannot safely make further advances with notice of the second mortgage unless he is obliged to make the further advance. All non-obligatory further advances will be unsecured, all payments in will be appropriated to the advances secured by the mortgage until that is satisfied and the banker will be left with an unsecured overdraft. The banker should close the original account so that no payments in will be attributed to it and open a new account. A trustee who has mixed trust money with his own in a bank account cannot set up the rule in *Clayton's Case* against his beneficiary but will be presumed to have drawn on his own money. If he exhausts that the beneficiary is only entitled to the lowest sum to which the trust money was reduced unless payments in were appropriated to its replacement, *Re Hallett* (1880) 13 Ch D 696; *James Roscoe v Winder* [1915] 1 Ch 62. Where two claimants claim against an active account *Clayton's Case* applies between them otherwise they share *pari passu*. Where an innocent party has received trust money without consideration *Clayton's Case* applies.

Clean bill of lading. *See* BILL OF LADING.

Clean credit. *See* BANKERS' COMMERCIAL CREDITS.

CMR. *See* PRIVATE CARRIER and CARRIAGE OF GOODS BY ROAD ACT 1965.

Collateral contract. This is found where a contractual promise is made, the consideration for which is the making of a further contract, the dependent or collateral contract usually being preliminary to the main contract. Collateral contracts and the intent to form them must be proved strictly and should not conflict with the main contract. The device of the collateral contract may be used to escape the parol evidence rule when the collateral contract has not been embodied in the writing of the main contract; to evade formal requirements of writing (*see* FORM IN CONTRACT) as when undertakings not included in a note or memorandum in writing under the Law of Property Act 1925, s. 40 have been enforced as a contract collateral to the main contract evidenced by the note or memorandum; to circumvent privity of contract as where one party is taken to guarantee goods by a collateral contract if the other party will enter into a contract with a third party for the use of or purchase of those goods or to give a third party the benefit of exemption and exclusion clauses found in the main contract; or to overcome the normal consequences of illegality in contract as when the innocent party to a contract which is illegal as performed by the other may sue the other on a collateral contract that it should be performed legally. The warranty of authority given by a professed agent is also a collateral contract.

Collecting banker. One who obtains or 'collects' for the account of his customer (*see* BANKER AND CUSTOMER FOR BILLS OF EXCHANGE ACT 1882 AND CHEQUES ACT 1957) the proceeds of cheques and other instruments which the customer pays into the bank for the credit of his account. At common law if the customer had a defective title to the instrument the banker in collecting it would become liable in conversion to the true owner. This would be avoided if the banker could show that he had become a holder in due course and thus himself the true owner. The Cheques Act 1957†, s. 2 now facilitates this by providing that a collecting banker giving value for an unindorsed order cheque has the same right as if there were an indorsement on it. Statutory protection is given by the Cheques Act 1957, s. 4, re-enacting and extending the Bills of Exchange Act 1882, s. 82 (as amended by the Bills of Exchange

(Crossed Cheques) Act 1906) which only applied to crossed cheques. The Cheques Act 1957, s. 4 applies to the collection of cheques, crossed and uncrossed, any document issued by a customer of a banker which, though not a bill of exchange, is intended to enable a person to obtain payment from the banker (e.g. conditional orders and 'cheques' with impersonal payees), certain Government instruments for payment and bankers' drafts. The section provides that where a banker in good faith and without negligence receives payment for a customer of an instrument to which it applies or, having credited a customer's account with the amount of such an instrument, receives payment for himself and the customer has no title, or a defective title, to it, the banker does not incur any liability merely by receiving the payment. Numerous cases indicate the meaning of 'negligence' in this context, e.g. failure to take up proper references on opening the account. *Ladbroke v Todd* (1914) 30 TLR 433, collecting without proper enquiry for an employee a cheque originally payable to his employer, *Marquess of Bute v Barclays Bank* [1955] 1 QB 202, collecting an abnormally large number of cheques negotiated to a person other than the original payee ('third-party cheques') *Baker v Barclays Bank* [1955] 2 All ER 571, collecting cheques not consonant with the customer's business standing, *Nu-Stilo v Lloyds Bank Ltd* (1956) 77 JIB 239, collecting without proper inquiry for an account other than that of the payee a cheque crossed 'account payee' (*see* CROSSED CHEQUES).

Marfani v Midland Bank [1968] 1 WLR 956 shows that the courts will take account of changing banking practice and seems less stringent than earlier authorities. Section 4 (3) provides that a banker is not to be treated as negligent merely because he fails to concern himself with the absence of, or irregularity in, indorsement but this may not apply to unindorsed 'third party' cheques. By the Banking Act 1979, s. 47 the banker can now plead contributory negligence in reduction of his liability in any case where absence of negligence would be a defence under the Cheques Act 1957, s. 4.

Combined transport document. *See* THROUGH BILL OF LADING.

Committee of Inspection (Bankruptcy). This is elected from amongst creditors of a debtor at the first meeting of creditors or at some subsequent meeting to supervise the trustee in bankruptcy and the administration of the debtor's estate. There is no necessity to have such a committee. It should consist of three to five persons appointed by the creditors from amongst creditors qualified to vote at the meeting, or persons who hold or are to hold general proxies or powers of attorney from such creditors, but no one can vote until the creditor has proved his debt and his proof of debts has been admitted.

A committee member is in a fiduciary position and must not purchase any part of the estate or derive any profit from the bankruptcy without leave of the court. The committee acts by a majority present at a meeting which must be held at least monthly and a majority of all members forms a quorum. The committee may appoint the trustee in bankruptcy if the creditors resolve to leave the choice to it and may similarly fix his remuneration. The committee audits the books of the trustee and there are certain powers which the trustee can only exercise with the approval of the committee or, if there is none, the Department of Trade. These powers include power to carry on the debtor's business for beneficial winding up, to bring, defend or compromise actions and claims, to employ a solicitor or agent, to agree to accept future payment for property, to mortgage or pledge property, to pay debts, to refer disputes to arbitration and to divide in its existing form amongst creditors property not readily or advantageously saleable. Approval must not be general; it must be for specific transactions. The committee or the Department of Trade may also approve the appointment by the trustee of the bankrupt to carry on his trade for the benefit of the creditors and the making of an allowance to the bankrupt out of his property for the support of himself and his family or for services in winding up his estate. This allowance may be reduced by the court.

The trustee is under an overriding obligation to have regard in the administration of the estate to the wishes of the creditors expressed at a general meeting or by the committee of inspection. If they conflict the meeting prevails over the committee.

(See the Bankruptcy Act 1914, s. 20).

Common carrier. One who holds himself out as prepared to carry for reward goods or passengers or both and who, unlike the private carrier, does not reserve a general right to accept or reject prospective customers. The common carrier is under a duty to accept goods or passengers of the types he carries on the routes he follows subject to certain exceptions. For goods these are that the vehicle is full, that the goods are inadequately packed, that they are offered at an unreasonable time, that reasonable pre-payment of charges is refused, that the goods present an extraordinary risk or that they cannot be carried, e.g. because of unwieldy size or because their value is disproportionate to precautions the carrier can take. For passengers the exceptions are that the prospective passenger is not in a fit state to be carried, that there is no accommodation and that he has not tendered the proper fare. At common law a common carrier of goods was said to be 'an insurer', meaning that, subject to contrary agreement he is liable for loss or damage to the goods unless it resulted from an Act of God, an act of the Queen's enemies, inherent vice in the goods or inadequate packing. These exceptions do not avail the carrier if he contributes to their operation by his negligence. 'Act of God' means some operation of natural forces so unexpected in nature or extent of operation that no human foresight could be expected to foresee or guard against it, *Bridden v GNR* (1858) 28 LJ Ex 51 (snow); 'inherent vice' is some defect in the goods causing the harm, *Nugent v Smith* (1876) 1 CPD 423 (horse struggling during storm). The consignor must inform the carrier of any reason for special care or the carrier will not be liable for harm which otherwise might not have occurred, *Baldwin v L.C.D. Rly* (1882) 9 QBD 582 (wet rags spoilt in delayed journey. Carrier not liable because not told of their condition). The carrier's strict liability continues during transit and for a reasonable time thereafter. Then the carrier becomes a warehouseman, liable only for negligence, *Mitchell v L.Y.R.* (1875) LR 10 QB 256. The carrier's liability for delay to goods is not strict but only for negligence and a common carrier of passengers is only liable in negligence in any event.

The Carriers Act 1830 provides that by a displayed notice a common carrier may exclude liability for loss or damage to certain types of valuable goods worth more than £10 unless they are declared and an extra charge paid. Otherwise a common carrier cannot limit his liability by a notice as distinct from a ticket or other contractual transaction. The Unfair Contract Terms Act 1977† applies to contracts of carriage and is a much more important restraint on exclusion clauses. Since British Rail and most road hauliers are not now common carriers the 1830 Act is of small practical importance but may apply to the carriage of passengers' luggage on buses and coaches running as public service vehicles.

The carrier should follow his ordinary route, not necessarily the shortest, but without unnecessary deviation or delay. Misdelivery in breach of contract or when circumstances should have aroused suspicion will render the carrier liable not only in contract but for conversion. A consignor impliedly warrants both to a common and to a private carrier that the goods are fit to be carried with safety and if not, is liable even if he is not negligent in not knowing of or in not disclosing the danger, *Bamfield v Goole & Sheffield Co* [1910] 2 KB 94; *G.N.R. v L.E.P. Transport* [1922] 2 KB 742. At common law the common carrier has a particular lien on the goods he carries for his charges. This takes priority over an unpaid vendor's lien and stoppage in transitu. A carriers' general lien must arise from contract or binding usage.

Carriers by sea and air are never in practice now common carriers and even in land carriage they are rarely found.

Common law. In perhaps its most usual sense a body of judge-made law originally developed in the Courts of Exchequer, Common Pleas and King's Bench. It provided most of the basic rules of contract and tort and thus a substantial part of our commercial law in later centuries. Certain deficiencies in this common law, in particular the fact that it would not enforce uses (the modern trusts) and that its chief remedy was damages, to the exclusion of remedies akin to specific performance and injunction, led to the Lord Chancellor developing in the Court of Chancery a further body of judge-made law known as equity to supplement and correct the common law in these and other respects. From the seventeenth century it has been settled that when common law in this sense (often abbreviated to 'law') and equity conflict, equity is to prevail. Since the Judicature Acts 1873–75 a court will grant all legal (in the sense of common law) and all equitable remedies required by the case before it and this is sometimes spoken of as 'the fusion of law and equity'. The better opinion has been that there was merely a fusion of the courts and not of the substantive bodies of rules themselves since equitable remedies continue to be administered on principles different from those on which damages are awarded for the court has a wider discretion in granting equitable remedies. The Queen's Bench Division of the High Court of Justice, which has within it a Commercial Court and an Admiralty Court, represents the traditions and specialisms of the old common law courts, though it can grant all legal and equitable remedies required by a case before it. The Court of Chancery is now represented by the Chancery Division of the High Court. The Court of Chancery acquired a dominant role in property law and hence certain areas of law relating to commerce now fall within the sphere of the Chancery Division, such as company law and partnership, bankruptcy and patents (there is a Patents Court within the Division).

In a looser sense 'common law' is sometimes used to denote all judge-made law, both common law in the narrower sense above and equity, as contrasted with legislation. In a still wider sense 'common law' is sometimes employed to mean the Anglo-American legal tradition as contrasted with other legal traditions.

Common law lien. *See* POSSESSORY OR COMMON LAW LIEN.

Community Patent Convention. *See* INTELLECTUAL PROPERTY, INTERNATIONAL PROTECTION AND PATENTS, APPLICATIONS FOR.

Composition or Scheme (Bankruptcy). These are arrangements by which a debtor by making partial satisfaction of his debts may prevent the law of bankruptcy running its full course. In a composition he retains control of his assets whereas under a scheme of arrangement a trustee is appointed to control them. A composition or scheme may be accepted by creditors and approved by the court even after adjudication but normally it is dealt with at a meeting which may be the first meeting of creditors. The debtor must submit a proposal to the Official Receiver as soon as may be after the receiving order. The Official Receiver must summon a meeting of creditors, giving them a copy of the proposal and his report on it. This meeting must be held before the conclusion of the public examination and if the proposal is accepted by a majority in number and three-quarters in value of the creditors who have made proof of debts, the sanction of the court must then be obtained. This cannot be obtained until after the public examination is concluded. Approval cannot be given if the court is of the opinion that the proposal is not reasonable or that its terms are not calculated to benefit the general body of creditors or if it does not provide for prior payment of preferential debts. (*See* DISTRIBUTION OF PROPERTY AMONGST CREDITORS). If any of the facts disentitling a bankrupt to immediate discharge are present (*see* DISCHARGE OF THE BANKRUPT) the court may not approve the proposal, unless it provides reasonable security for a dividend of at least 25p in the £ on all provable unsecured debts. Released debts can be disregarded. Approval will not be refused because of the debtor's misconduct unless it is such as to make it contrary to public policy to give approval. Approval entails the discharging of the receiving order, the annulment of the adjudication and the reversion of the debtor's property to himself or a trustee under the scheme. Subject to the terms of the proposal the debtor is released from all liabilities from which he would have been released by discharge of the bankrupt. A composition or scheme binds all creditors in respect of their provable debts. A trustee under a scheme of arrangement is, as far as possible and subject to the scheme, in the same position as a trustee in bankruptcy. The court may annul a composition or scheme if it is not workable or the debtor does not fulfil his part in it. (See the Bankruptcy Act 1914, ss. 16, 17, 21).

Condition. This word has many meanings in contract and sale of goods. It may mean some event external to the contract upon which the existence of legal obligation is to depend (e.g. the approval of the subject matter by some third party, *Pym v Campbell* (1856) 6 E & B 370) known as a condition precedent, or some event upon the happening of which an existing contract is to end, known as a condition subsequent. It may also mean a term of a contract so important that if it is not fulfilled the other party may not only sue for damages but also elect to treat the contract as repudiated and not provide any further performance on his part. He may do this even though he has suffered no loss from the breach of condition. See the Sale of Goods Act 1979, s. 11 (3). In ss. 12–15 the Act implies a number of conditions as to title, correspondence with description, fitness for purpose, merchantable quality, and on sale by sample into the contracts it governs. Section 28 provides that payment of the price† and delivery† of the goods are concurrent conditions, that is to say that in the absence of contrary agreement, the seller must be ready and willing to deliver in exchange for the price and the buyer must be ready and willing to pay in exchange for the goods. 'Condition' in this sense is contrasted with warranty, a less important term, breach of which does not give the other party a right to treat the contract as repudiated but merely to sue for damages, s. 11 (3), and s. 53 (also allowing a breach of warranty to be set up in diminution or extinction of the price); s. 61 (1). Section 11 (2) provides that a party may, if he wishes, waive a breach of condition or elect to treat it as a breach of warranty, thus only seeking damages or reduction of price. Section 11 (4) further provides that where a contract is not severable (e.g. not falling under s. 31 (2) when goods are to be delivered in instalments paid for separately) and the buyer has accepted the goods or part of them the breach of a condition to be fulfilled by the seller can only be treated as a breach of warranty. 'Acceptance' here carries the same meaning as in s. 35 which provides that a buyer is deemed to have accepted goods either when he tells the seller he has done so, or when he does some act to them which is inconsistent with the ownership of the seller or when after the lapse of a reasonable time he keeps them without telling the seller he has rejected them. (*See* ACCEPTANCE IN SALE OF GOODS). The parties may expressly agree that a term is to be either a condition or a warranty but it is not enough for this merely to call a term 'a condition', *Schuler AG v Wickman* [1974] AC 235. The classification of terms into conditions and warranties has not always proved satisfactory and there may be innominate terms† breach of which may give rise either to a right to repudiate coupled with a claim for damages as with conditions, or merely to a claim for damages, as with warranties, depending on the seriousness of the particular breach. *Hong Kong Fir Shipping Co v Kawasaki Kisen Kaisha Ltd* [1962] 2 QB 26 (term as to ship being seaworthy). See also *The Mihalis Angelos* [1971] 1 QB 164; *Cehave v Bremer Handel* (*The Hansa Nord*) [1976] QB 44; *Reardon Smith v Hansen-Tangen* [1976] 1 WLR 989.

For some years conditions as terms of the contract were contrasted with the fundamental term or core of the contract. Liability for breach of condition could be excluded by exclusion clauses but not breach of the fundamental term or core of the contract. This rule of law for controlling exemption and exclusion clauses ended with the *Suisse Atlantique Case* [1967] 1 AC 361 where it was held that it was merely a rule of construction that exclusion clauses were not normally to be read as operating on fundamental terms. Since the comprehensive control of exclusion clauses provided by the Unfair Contract Terms Act 1977, the concept of the fundamental term and the associated concept of fundamental breach are not likely to be of importance.

Terms of the contract must also be carefully distinguished from representations made prior to the contract but not embodied in it. If such representations are deliberately or recklessly false they give rise to claims for deceit. If they are either negligently or innocently false remedies are provided by the Misrepresentation Act 1967.

Conditional indorsement. *See* INDORSEMENT OF A NEGOTIABLE INSTRUMENT.

Conditional instrument. This may superficially resemble a bill of exchange or a promissory note but the order for or promise of payment is expressed to be conditional upon the happening of an event which may or may not happen. Such an instrument cannot be a bill of exchange or promissory note (Bills of Exchange Act 1882, ss. 3 (1) and 83 (1)) and its defect will not be cured by the happening of the event (Bills of Exchange 1882, s. 11 (2)). Payment on an event which is bound to happen, even though the date when it will happen is uncertain, is not conditional. Payment expressed to be made only out of a particular fund is conditional since it may be uncertain whether the fund will be adequate but an order to pay coupled with a non-binding indication of the fund from which payment is to be made (e.g. cheque with indication of a particular account from which it may be paid) is not conditional nor is an instrument which states the transaction giving rise to the bill (Bills of Exchange Act 1882, s. 3 (3)). It is doubtful if a conditional instrument can be a negotiable instrument since the uncertainty attaching to the happening of the condition means that it cannot circulate with a speed and freedom akin to that of currency. It is because they are conditional in requiring a counter-signature before payment that it is generally thought that travellers' cheques are not negotiable. An instrument ordering the drawee bank to ensure on paying that a receipt form was signed was held not to be a cheque as the order to pay was not unconditional, *Bavins v London and South Western Bank* [1900] 1 QB 270. When the order to the drawee bank to pay was unconditional and the direction to complete the receipt form was addressed to the payee the instrument was held to be unconditional and a cheque, *Nathan v Ogdens* (1905) 94 LT 126. Whilst the essential order of a bill of exchange or cheque or the promise of a promissory note must be unconditional, bills and cheques may be accepted conditionally and bills, cheques and notes delivered and indorsed conditionally, though such conditional acceptance may not have the effects of a normal acceptance, a person paying an instrument need not ascertain whether a condition attached to indorsement has been fulfilled and the rights of a holder in due course will not be affected if a condition attached to delivery† had not been fulfilled.

Conditional sale. A contract for sale of goods where the property† is not to pass to the buyer until he has fulfilled the condition of paying the price which may be effected by instalments. See the Consumer Credit Act 1974, s. 189 which extends the concept to sales of land. Conditional sales to individuals† within the upper financial limit of

£5,000 are regulated by the Act as debtor–creditor–supplier agreements with 'restricted use' credit. The buyer is not a person who has 'agreed to buy' within the exception to nemo dat quod non habet contained in the Sale of Goods Act 1979, s. 25, and the Consumer Credit Act 1974, s. 86 restricts the powers of the seller on the death of the debtor and ss. 87–93, 129–136 on other events. The buyer is given a right of termination, ss. 99–103, except in respect of land.

Confidence. An action will lie for breach of an obligation of confidence if it can be shown that information was given to the defendant in circumstances entailing an obligation of confidence on his part and that improper use was made of the information. There may, but need not be, an express agreement; an obligation to treat the information as confidential may be implied from the circumstances as when an inventor discusses his plans with a possible developer, *Seager v Copydex* [1967] 1 WLR 923, or it may arise from an employment relationship since an employee is under an obligation not to make improper use of his employer's goodwill or trade secrets, *Robb v Green* [1895] 2 QB 315. A third party who acquires information which he knows or ought to know is confidential will be restrained from making use of it, and this may apply even to one who innocently acquires such information *Printers & Finishers Ltd v Holloway* [1965] RPC 239; *Fraser v Evans* [1969] 1 QB 349 at 361.

Remedies are damages and an injunction. There is now no need to show breach of contract or interference with property but it may be that an action for damages will only lie when the defendant knew or ought to have known of the confidence. Remedies will not be granted when it would be contrary to public policy† to do so, as when to enforce the confidence would conceal crime or other breach of the law, *Initial Services v Putterill* [1968] 1 QB 396, or where the alleged obligation is in unreasonable restraint of trade, as when it purports to bind a former employee for an unreasonably long time or over an unreasonably wide area in respect of goodwill or in respect of subject matter not properly a trade secret, *Empire Meat v Patrick* [1939] 2 All ER 85; *Morris v Saxelby* [1916] 1 AC 688. Remedies will also not be available if, though the information is confidential, the obligation is owed not to the plaintiff but to a third party, *Fraser v Evans* [1969] 1 QB 349.

Obligations of confidence are not confined to commercial matters. They may be used for example, to protect a lecturer's interest in his lectures, *Caird v Sime* (1887) 12 App Cas 326, and other material which for special reasons may not be the subject of a patent or copyright.

Confirmed credit. *See* BANKERS' COMMERCIAL CREDITS.

Confirming houses. Intermediaries in the export trade who act on behalf of overseas buyers, either purchasing goods and re-selling to the foreign buyer, thus acting as an agent in the commercial but not the legal sense, or concluding a contract between the home seller and the foreign buyer, thus acting as agents in the legal sense, but adding their own 'confirmation' or guarantee to the promise of the buyer. See *Sobell Industries v Cory Bros* [1955] 2 Lloyd's Rep 82; *Anglo-African Shipping v Mortner* [1962] 1 Lloyd's Rep 610.

Conflict of Laws (or Private International Law). This governs transactions involving a foreign element as where in a contract of sale the contract is made in one country to be performed in another. For commercial law the most important topics are the rules governing the choice of the proper law of contracts, the rules requiring matters of evidence and procedure, as distinct from substantive law to be dealt with by the lex fori, the rules governing the enforcement in this country of foreign judgments, the law governing sovereign, diplomatic and consular immunity and proof of foreign law (*see* FOREIGN LAW, PROOF OF).

Conflict of Laws for bills of exchange. The Bills of Exchange Act 1882, s. 72 provides rules which differ from ordinary rules for contract in referring most questions to be settled, not by the proper law, but by the law of the place where the contract is made or an act is done or to be done. Two exceptions are that when an instrument is issued outside the United Kingdom it will not be invalid merely because it is not stamped according to the law of the place of issue and where a bill of exchange, issued outside the United Kingdom, is formally correct according to United Kingdom law, it may be treated as valid for negotiation here even if it does not conform to the law of its place of issue. Section 72 (4) dealing with rates of exchange for foreign currencies has been repealed by the Administration of Justice Act 1977, s. 4. These rules apply to cheques and by the Bills of Exchange Act 1882, s. 89 to a promissory note.

Connected lender liability. This expression refers to the liability imposed by the Consumer Credit Act 1974, s. 75 on the creditor for breaches by the supplier under a debtor–creditor–supplier agreement. The creditor is jointly and severally liable with the supplier. (*See* JOINT CONTRACTS).

Consensus ad idem. 'Agreement in the same terms'. A phrase used to indicate that the parties to an agreement which may be a contract have reached that measure of agreement, in the same terms on the same subject matter, on which contractual obligation may be based.

Consideration. The law of simple or parol contract enforces not mere promises but bargains where there is some exchange of value, however minimal. A mere promise which does not stipulate some return from the promisee must be by deed or specialty if it is to be enforceable. Consideration is the return for which the offeror bargains. It has been defined as 'the price for which the promise of the other is bought', *Dunlop v Selfridge* [1915] AC 847 at 855, and in terms of benefit and detriment in *Currie v Misa* (1875) LR 10 Ex 153 where it was said that 'A valuable consideration in the sense of the law may consist either in some right, interest, profit or benefit accruing to one party or some forebearance, detriment, loss or responsibility given, suffered or undertaken by the other'. The Sale of Goods Act 1979, s. 2 (1) speaks of 'a money consideration, called the price', the payment or promise of payment of the price being a benefit to the seller, a detriment to the buyer. The detailed rules of consideration may all be derived from the concept of bargain. Thus 'consideration may be executed (where the promise is given for an act, e.g. payment of money), or executory (where the promise is given for a promise in return, e.g. promise of payment of money) but must not be past' (where the promise is given in respect of some unbargained benefit to the promisor in the past). An offeror may bargain for an executed act in the future or for a promise to be fulfilled in the future but cannot bargain for past conduct. There is one real and one apparent exception to the rule that past consideration is no consideration. The Bills of Exchange Act 1882, s. 27 (1) (b) provides that 'an antecedent debt or liability' may be valuable consideration for a bill of exchange. (*See* CONSIDERATION FOR A BILL OF EXCHANGE). This is a real exception. The apparent exception is where an offeror requests an act for which payment might be expected but does not mention a specific sum. If, after the act requested has been done, the offeror promises payment in respect of it, the promise will be regarded, not as made in respect of past consideration, but rather as a definition of the payment impliedly promised in the original request and hence made in respect of an executed consideration, *Lampleigh v Brathwait* (1615) Hob 105; *Re Casey's Patents, Stewart v Casey* [1892] 1 Ch 104. Another rule, associated with the doctrine of privity of contract, is that 'consideration must move from the promisee'. This again reflects bargain, for if the promisee suing the offeror has not provided consideration he is not truly a party to a bargain and it is still the case that a non-party is attempting to sue if a third party has purported to provide consideration and either the promisee or the third party attempt to sue the offeror. Consideration need not 'move to the promisor' but on his instructions its benefit may be given to a third party. Valid consideration in contract is often described, as in *Currie v Misa* as 'valuable' consideration, which does not mean that it need have economic value, still less be an adequate economic return for the promise, 'valuable' merely being used in contrast to the 'good' consideration of family affection which may be effective in trusts but not in contract, though the word 'good' is also sometimes confusingly used to indicate a consideration valid in contract.

Bargain also appears in the rule that 'consideration must be "real" or "sufficient" (synonyms) but need not be adequate'. If a party is obtaining in return for his promise an act or the promise of an act to which he is not already entitled, either at general law or by existing contract that suffices, there being no need for it to be a fair economic return for the promise, that being left to the bargain of the parties, *Chappel v Nestlé* [1960] AC 87 at 114; *Haigh v Brooks* (1839) 10 Ad & El 309 (worthless paper enough). So if a party in return for a promise merely does his public duty, *Collins v Godefroy* (1831) 1 B & Ad 950 (appear as witness) or private duty, *Stilk v Myrick* (1809) 2 Camp 317 (perform contract of service) to the promisee or gives up a claim known to be worthless, *Wade v Simeon* (1846) 2 CB 548, there is no consideration but if he does anything more, *England v Davidson* (1840) 11 Ad & El 856; *Glasbrook v Glamorgan C.C.* [1925] AC 270 (police do more than strict duty) or if a doubtful claim is compromised, *Miles v N.Z. Alford Estate* (1886) 32 Ch D 266 there will be. A promise to perform a contract with a third party may be consideration since it involves losing the possibility of discharging the first contract otherwise than by performance (*see* DISCHARGE OF CONTRACT BY AGREEMENT), *Shadwell v Shadwell* (1860) 9 CBNS 159; *Scotson v Pegg* (1861) 6 H & N 295; *New Zealand Shipping v Satterthwaite* [1975] AC 154. These rules find special application in the rule in *Pinnel's Case* (1602) 5 Co Rep 117a or *Foakes v Beer* (1884) 9 App Cas 605, that payment of a lesser sum of money will not discharge an obligation to pay a greater but if there is any variation in the time or method of payment of the lesser sum which can be interpreted as a benefit to the creditor (in *Pinnel's Case* 'a horse, a hawk or a robe, etc.' for the balance were mentioned), and not as extra indulgence to the debtor, *Vanbergen v St Edmund's Properties* [1933] 2 KB 223, this will be consideration for a full discharge. Merely paying a smaller sum by cheque instead of cash is not sufficient alteration to provide consideration, *D. & C. Builders v Rees* [1966] 2 QB 617. The operation of the rule in *Pinnel's Case* or *Foakes v Beer* has been minimised by the rule in *Hightrees House*† ([1947] KB 130) or promissory or equitable estoppel which under certain conditions restrains a promisor from resiling from a promise even though no consideration is given for it. This is linked to variation and waiver of contract which raise related problems. If payment of a lesser sum or sums is made by a debtor in fulfilling a composition with creditors or by a third party and is accepted by the creditor, this will be binding since it would be a fraud on fellow creditors or the third party for any creditor to seek to recover the full amount, *Hirachand Punamchand v Temple* [1911] 2 KB 330.

In quasi-contract 'total failure of consideration' means failure of performance, not of the promise of performance.

Consideration for a bill of exchange may be any consideration sufficient for a simple contract and an antecedent debt or liability, whether the bill is payable on demand or at a future time. This is an exception to the rules of past consideration. When consideration has been given at any time for a bill the holder is deemed to be a holder for valuable consideration as against the acceptor and all parties who became parties prior to such time. This is an exception to the rules of privity of contract. When a holder has a lien on a bill he is a holder for value to the extent of the lien. Every party whose signature† appears on a bill is presumed to have become a party for consideration. (See the Bills of Exchange Act 1882, ss. 27 and 30 and s. 89 applying these to a promissory note).

Consular immunity. Under the Consular Relations Act 1968 consular officers are not civilly liable in respect of acts done in carrying out consular functions except when they have not contracted expressly or impliedly as agents of their sending state or when they are sued for damage caused to a third party by a vehicle, vessel or aircraft in an accident in the United Kingdom. There are certain exceptions from taxation and privileges may be waived. Privileges are not accorded to consular employees, service staff and families who carry on any private gainful occupation in the United Kingdom.

Consumer Credit Act 1974. This requires that traders concerned with the provision of consumer credit should be licensed under a system administered by the Director-General of Fair Trading†. If they are not they commit an offence, s. 39, and their agreements are, generally, unenforceable, ss. 40, 148, 149. There is also machinery for the protection of debtors when agreements are enforceable. The Act replaces legislation relating to hire-purchase, pawnbrokers (*see* PAWN OR PLEDGE), moneylenders (*see* MONEYLENDERS ACTS). The Bills of Sale Acts 1878–1882† and the Hire Purchase Act 1964, Part III are not altered. The Act embodies general principles stated in new terminology, detailed regulation being left to statutory instruments. It does not facilitate chattel mortgages, nor alter the basic concept of hire-purchase, nor deal except marginally, with implied terms, nor affect third party rights such as the exceptions to nemo dat quod non habet nor amend the Fair Trading Act 1973. Part I of the Consumer Credit Act 1974 deals with the powers and duties of the Director-General of Fair Trading, Part II deals with transactions covered by or excluded from the Act, including consumer credit agreements, regulated agreements, personal credit agreements, running account credit, fixed sum credit, restricted use credit, unrestricted use credit, debtor–creditor–supplier agreements, debtor–creditor agreements, credit token agreements, consumer hire agreements, exempt agreements, small agreements, multiple agreements and linked transactions. Part III deals with licensing of credit and hire businesses, specifying in s. 21 businesses requiring a licence, providing in s. 22 for a standard licence and a group licence and then covering the issue, renewal, variation, suspension and revocation of licences. Any regulated agreement (other than a non-commercial agreement) made by an unlicensed trader is to be unenforceable unless the Director-General makes a validating order, s. 40, and unlicensed trading is an offence, s. 39.

Part IV regulates advertising and canvassing. In particular the sending of credit circulars to minors and the sending of unsolicited credit-tokens to anyone is prohibited, ss. 50, 51. Part V of the Act deals with entry into credit or hire agreements covering preliminaries such as disclosure of information, antecedent negotiations and withdrawal from a prospective agreement, the form, content and execution of an agreement, notice of cancellation rights, acceptance of credit tokens and cancellation of certain agreements within a cooling off period†. Part VI deals with matters arising during the currency of credit or hire agreements such as the liability of a creditor for breaches by a supplier, duties to give notice and information, appropriation of payments, variations of agreements and liability for the misuse of credit tokens or credit facilities. Part VII deals with default and termination of agreements, providing for default notices, restricting remedies for default and specifying the effect of premature payment† by the debtor. Part VIII deals with security, making provision for the form and content of securities, ineffective securities, duties to give information, the realisation of securities and prevention of evasion of the Act by the use of securities. It then provides for pledge or pawn, for restrictions on negotiable instruments used as securities and the enforcement of land mortgages. Part IX deals with judicial control, covering enforcement orders on infringement and death, extension of time by time orders, protection orders, hire and hire purchase agreements and extortionate credit bargains. Part X deals with ancillary credit businesses, their regulation by licensing, control of their advertisements, canvassing and formation of agreements, also making special provision for credit reference agencies. Part XI provides for the enforcement of the Act and Part XII is supplemental, dealing with procedural matters, subordinate legislation and interpretation of the Act, s. 188 and Schedule 2 containing illustrations of the use of the new terminology in the Act, though if there is conflict the illustrations are to yield to the other provisions of the Act.

Consumer credit agreement. Consumer Credit Act 1974, s. 8, provides that such an agreement is a personal credit agreement by which the creditor provides the debtor with credit not exceeding £5,000. Such an agreement is a regulated agreement within the Act, unless it is an exempt agreement within s. 16. There are many sub-classes of consumer credit agreements depending on the type of credit, such as running account credit, fixed sum credit, restricted use credit and unrestricted use credit agreements. They are also categorised as debtor–creditor–supplier agreements, debtor–creditor agreements, credit token agreements, small agreements, multiple agreements and non-commercial agreements. The other principal form of regulated agreement other than a consumer credit agreement is the consumer hire agreement.

Consumer Hire Agreement. The Consumer Credit Act 1974, s. 15 provides that this is an agreement made by a person with an individual, the hirer, for the bailment of goods provided that (a) it is not a hire purchase agreement, (b) it is capable of subsisting for more than three months, and (c) it does not require payments in excess of £5,000. Such an agreement is a regulated agreement within the Act unless it is an exempt agreement.

Contract. In English law the term 'contract' is applied to two anomalous cases, contracts by deed or specialty and contracts of record, where liability depends not on agreement or the appearance of agreement but on the employment of formalities. Most contracts are, however, simple or parol contracts where liability is founded on the objective appearance of agreement and most of contract law is directed to regulating these. Their formation is dealt with under offer and acceptance, intent to create legal relations, contractual capacity and consideration, which latter head embodies the principle that the law of simple contract has been directed to enforcing bargains, where there is an exchange of value, however small, rather than mere promises not forming part of a bargain. Such gratuitous promises must be made by deed to be legally effective. In general no special formalities are required for simple contracts but exceptional cases are dealt with in form in contract. The relative importance of the various terms of a contract is indicated by classifying them as conditions, warranties and innominate terms. Exemption and exclusion clauses, which are designed to relieve a party of what otherwise might be his liabilities, have been controlled by a number of judicial devices and by the Unfair Contract Terms Act 1977†. Vitiating factors which may render an apparent contract wholly or partially invalid include mistake, misrepresentation, illegality, duress, and undue influence. Discharge terminating the liabilities of the parties, may come about by performance (*see* DISCHARGE OF CONTRACT BY PERFORMANCE), breach (*see* DISCHARGE OF CONTRACT BY BREACH; FRUSTRATION) or impossibility of performance or agreement (*see* DISCHARGE BY AGREEMENT). Parties who may take rights or incur liabilities are defined by privity of contract and its exceptions together with assignment. Breach may be remedied by damages (*see* DAMAGES IN CONTRACT), specific performance and injunction.

Contracts in restraint of trade. The courts have long regarded contracts in unreasonable restraint of trade as void contracts as being contrary to public policy. The chief classes of such contracts are those between the vendor and purchaser of a business directed to preventing the vendor destroying the goodwill he has sold and those between an employer and employee, designed to preserve the employer's goodwill and trade secrets after the employee has left the employment. Any contractual restraint which is wider in geographical area or in activity restrained or longer in time than is necessary to preserve the interest which may be protected is invalid. The wider the area, the longer the period and the greater the range of activity prohibited, the stronger the presumption of invalidity but worldwide and lifelong restraints have been upheld on the sale of a worldwide business, *Nordenfelt v Maxim Nordenfelt* [1894] AC 535, or termination of a confidential appointment, *Fitch v Dewes* [1921] 2 AC 158. The courts have tended to favour vendor-purchaser restraints in contrast to employer–employee restraints which may be affected by inequality of bargaining power, *Mason v Provident Clothing* [1913] AC 724. In *Esso v Harper's Garage* [1968] AC 269 it was pointed out that it must first be asked whether a restriction is so wide as to be prima facie void and, if so, whether it can be justified as reasonable. Under the first question many types of restraint such as sole agency agreements, tied public houses and negative covenants in leases and sales of land have regularly been regarded as valid. Vendor–purchaser and employer–employee covenants of the classic type are handled under the second question, together with contracts of the type in *Harper's Case* under which a garage company was closely tied to a petrol supplier. Reasonableness is to be considered as at the time when the contract was made. Restraints arising from membership of trade associations and restrictions accepted by distributors of goods, as in *Harper's Case*, are subject to similar tests but the latter two types of restraint are now handled under the restrictive trade practices legislation (*see* RESTRICTIVE TRADE PRACTICES). Where a restraint is excessive the court will not sever the excess and enforce the residue if this involves re-drafting the contract and writing in words not already there but it will effect severance if this can be done applying the 'blue pencil rule' and merely deleting words or clauses referring to the excessive area, period or activity, *Goldsoll v Goldman* [1915] 1 Ch 292. It will be more ready to do this in vendor–purchaser than in employer–employee restraints, *Attwood v Lamont* [1920] 3 KB 571.

Contracts of Record. These are enforced as contracts because they have been embodied in the records of a Court of Record, e.g. judgments. Their enforceability depends on form not agreement.

Contractual capacity. Certain persons cannot be bound by the full range of contracts into which a natural person of full age and capacity may enter. These include infants or minors, corporations, the mentally disordered and drunkards.

Infants or minors (synonyms) were formerly those under twenty-one but the Family Law Reform Act 1969 reduced the age of majority to eighteen. They may be bound by contracts for necessaries, defined in the Sale of Goods Act 1979, s. 3 (3) as goods 'suitable to the condition in life of the minor . . . and to his actual requirements at the time of sale and delivery'. Luxuries are excluded but luxurious articles of utility may come within the category, *Chapple v Cooper* (1844) 13 M & W 252. There is no liability for goods if the infant is already supplied with them. The better opinion, supported by the Sale of Goods Act 1979, s. 3 (2), is that an infant is only liable to pay a reasonable price for necessaries actually delivered and is not liable on an executory contract or to pay a contractual price hence his liability appears to be not contractual but in quasi-contract. An infant may be bound by beneficial contracts of education and service, whether executory or not, *Roberts v Gray* [1913] 1 KB 520. Whether such a contract is beneficial depends on the whole of its terms, *Clements v L.N.W.R.* [1894] 2 QB 482; *De Francesco v Barnum* (1890) 45 Ch D 430. An infant may enter into a voidable contract relating to property of a permanent nature, such as land or shares. If he does not avoid it either before or a reasonable time after, attaining majority, he will be fully bound by it, *Edwards v Carter* [1893] AC 360. An infant is not bound by a trading contract, made to carry on his trade or business, *Cowern v Nield* [1912] 2 KB 419; *Mercantile Union v Ball* [1937] 2 KB 498. The Infants Relief Act 1874, s. 1 provides that all contracts whether specialty or simple contracts made by infants for the repayment of money lent or to be lent, for goods supplied or to be supplied other than necessaries and all accounts stated† with infants are 'absolutely void'. Despite these words it appears that an adult party to such contracts is bound, that goods obtained by an infant under such a contract may be retained by him, as property passes on delivery, *Stocks v Wilson* [1913] 2 KB 235, and that money paid by an infant under such a contract can only be recovered by him if there is total failure of consideration, *Valentine v Canali* (1889) 24 QBD 166. 'Contracts for goods' includes barter. If money is lent for necessaries the loan cannot be recovered but if the money is spent on necessaries the lender will be given by subrogation the same rights against the infant as the supplier of necessaries. An infant cannot be liable on a negotiable instrument even if given for necessaries, *Re Soltykoff* [1891] 1 QB 413, but the supplier may sue on the underlying contract. The Betting and Loans (Infants) Act 1890 renders void any promise by a person of full age to repay money borrowed in his minority, together with any associated negotiable instruments. If an adult guarantees an infants' debt, the guarantee being dependent on the void debt is itself void, *Coutts v Browne-Lecky* [1947] KB 104, but it is otherwise if the adult gives an indemnity, *Yeoman Credit v Latter* [1961] 2 All ER 294. (*See* FORM IN CONTRACT). The Infants Relief Act 1874, s. 2 avoids any fresh promise after full age to pay any debt contracted during infancy and any ratification (but not fresh promise) after full age of any contract entered into during infancy. 'Ratification' here implies mere confirmation, 'fresh promise' a new contract, covering the old. Although infants are generally liable in tort they are not liable for torts directly connected with contracts upon which they cannot be sued, *Jennings v Rundall* (1799) 8 TR 335 (over-riding hired mare) but may be liable for torts independent of such contracts, *Burnard v Haggis* (1863) 14 CBNS 45 (injuring hired horse by prohibited jumping). An infant is not liable in deceit† for inducing a contract not binding upon him by misrepresenting his age but he may come under an equitable obligation to restore property or the actual money, if in his possession, obtained under such a contract, *Leslie v Sheill* [1914] 3 KB 607.

A corporation is an artificial person, a corporation sole being an office, treated as a legal person independently of its holders, a corporation aggregate a group treated as a legal person independently of its members. If a corporation is created by royal charter and enters into a contract foreign to its purposes, this will be valid but may give grounds for forfeiting the charter. If it is formed by or under statute (e.g. a company under the Companies Act 1948 entering a contract outside the objects clause of its memorandum) the contract is ultra vires 'beyond the powers' null and void and cannot be ratified by the company, *Ashbury v Riche* (1875) LR 7 HL 653, but the European Communities Act 1972, s. 9 (1) provides for liability to other parties acting in good faith in respect of acts decided upon by the directors. If a contract is not ultra vires the company but merely beyond the powers of the directors it may be validated by ratification by the company. The mentally ill and, it seems, drunkards are liable for necessaries just as infants; Sale of Goods Act 1979, s. 3. They are also bound by their contracts unless they did not know what they were doing and this was known to the other party, in which case the contract is voidable at the incapacitated person's option, *Imperial Loan v Stone* [1892] 1 QB 599.

An unincorporated body is not a competent contracting party but persons who act for it may be personally liable or under agency. For foreign sovereigns and states, diplomats and consuls *see* CONFLICT OF LAWS, STATE IMMUNITY; DIPLOMATIC IMMUNITY; CONSULAR IMMUNITY.

Contra proferentem. A principle of construction that words in a contract or other transaction, e.g. exemption and exclusion clauses, are in case of doubt to be construed against a party who has included them for his own advantage.

Contributory negligence. This defence applies when a plaintiff contributes to the harm that befalls him or his property by lack of proper care for safety. Unlike the tort of negligence there is no need for a legal duty of care. Before the Law Reform (Contributory Negligence) Act 1945 this defence barred all recovery in tort in non-maritime cases but that Act now requires the court to assess the damages the plaintiff would have recovered but for his contributory negligence, then to assess the percentage by which his lack of care contributed to his loss and then to reduce the original amount of damages by that percentage. The court does not intervene unless there is at least 10 per cent of contributory negligence, *Johnson v Tennant* (1954), unreported, 19 November, CA. In maritime cases apportionment of damages always applied and the position under the Maritime Conventions Act 1911, resembles the post-1945 non-maritime law. The defendant must plead the defence, *Fookes v Slaytor* [1978] 1 WLR 1293, and he bears the burden of proof of it, *Owens v Brimmell* [1977] QB 859. The defence applies to many torts besides negligence but not to deceit nor, under the Torts (Interference with Goods) Act 1977, s. 11, to conversion. The Banking Act 1979, s. 47, however, provides that it may apply to the liability in conversion of a collecting banker for handling cheques and other instruments under the Cheques Act 1957, s. 4. It is doubtful how far the defence applies to liability in contract but it may apply when contractual and tortious duties of care co-exist, *De Meza v Apple* [1974] 1 Lloyd's Rep 508. In such a case it may only apply if the claim is in tort, *Sole v Hallt* [1973] QB 574. Contributory negligence may be negatived in whole or in part if the plaintiff was acting in 'the agony of the moment', that is in a dilemma produced by the defendant, *Jones v Boyce* (1816) 1 Stark 493; *The Bywell Castle* (1879) 4 PD 219; *Sayers v Harlow* [1958] 1 WLR 623. Passengers will not have their claims reduced because of the contributory negligence of those in charge of their ship or vehicle (*Mills v Armstrong, The Bernina* (1880) 13 App Cas 1). Children (*Yachuk v Blais* [1949] AC 386); the elderly (*Daly v Liverpool Corporation* [1939] 2 All ER 142); and workers (*Caswell v Powell Duffryn* [1940] AC 152); may have their contributory negligence judged by lenient standards but the relaxation for workers may only apply to actions for breach of statutory duty; *Staveley Iron Co v Jones* [1956] AC 627. Disobedience by an employee is not necessarily contributory negligence; *Westwood v Post Office* [1974] AC 1.

Convention award. *See* ARBITRATION: FOREIGN AND CONVENTION AWARDS.

Conversion. One of the torts now grouped together as wrongful interference with goods†. Conversion, also known as trover, is any intentional act involving a wrongful denial of the plaintiff's title to goods. By the Torts (Interference with Goods) Act 1977, s. 11 mere denial of title is not now enough but this, if malicious, may be trade libel (also known as slander of title). Conversion is to be contrasted with trespass to goods which is direct interference with the plaintiff's possession of goods without asserting title to them, as by moving them without permission, *Fouldes v Willoughby* (1841) 8 M & W 540. The two torts may co-exist when there is interference with possession which implies denial of title. Although conversion protects title the plaintiff must show that at the time of the act complained of he had either possession or an immediate right to possession of the goods. The latter would avail a bailor when the goods were in the possession of a bailee under a bailment at will. If the goods were subject to a bailment for a fixed term the bailor would have an action on the case for harm to his reversionary interest. A bailee may sue for conversion of the goods bailed, *The Winkfield* [1902] P 42. In a bailment at will either bailor or bailee may sue. A bailee must account to the bailor for any excess in damages over the value of his own interest. Examples of acts constituting conversion when they imply wrongful denial of the plaintiff's title are the taking, using, altering, destroying, mis-delivering, receiving, and the selling and delivering of chattels. In some cases, e.g. altering, it may be a question of degree whether there is conversion. Sale without delivery is void and not conversion except in market overt when a good title will pass to an innocent purchaser. Handling, such as transport and warehousing, which does not imply a dealing with title, is not conversion if done in good faith. The 1977 Act, s. 2, having abolished detinue, provides that conversion now lies for loss and destruction of goods which a bailee allows to happen in breach of duty and s. 11 provides that receiving a pledge is conversion if the delivery of the goods is conversion. Proof of a demand for the goods by the plaintiff and an unconditional refusal by the defendant is good evidence of conversion, but it is otherwise if the refusal is subject to a reasonable condition, such as proof of title, *Alexander v Southey* (1821) 5 B & Ald 247. If goods are put into a person's possession without his consent this is not conversion on his part. He is termed an 'involuntary bailee' and will not be liable for negligent harm but must not wilfully harm them, *Lethbridge v Phillips* (1819) 2 Stark 544. He will not be liable if he takes reasonable but unsuccessful steps to return them, *Elvin & Powell v Plummer Roddis* (1933) 50 TLR 158, but will be if he acts unreasonably, as by signing a delivery order and so facilitating another's dishonest acquisition of the goods, *Hiort v Bott* (1874) LR 9 Ex 86. The Unsolicited Goods and Services Act 1971 provides, subject to conditions, that an involuntary bailee may treat the goods as a gift after six months or after thirty days notice to the sender if he does not retake them. When lost goods are found the owner's claim prevails. If the owner does not claim and the goods are found in a place of unrestricted public access the finder will be entitled as against the occupier but not if the goods were in or attached to the land or the occupier manifested an intent that, despite public access, he would control objects lost, nor if the land was private, *Parker v B.A.B.* [1982] 1 All ER 834. Under s. 10 of the 1977 Act a co-owner commits conversion if he wrongfully destroys the goods or disposes or purports to dispose of the entire property in the goods. Under s. 8 it is now always a defence to show that some third party has a better title than the plaintiff and s. 7 provides that where there is double liability, as where there are claims by a finder of goods and the true owner, a plaintiff such as the finder who is unjustly enriched must account to other claimants and they must ultimately reimburse the defendant if he has paid in damages more than the value of the goods. By s. 6 improvements made in good faith to the goods are to be taken into account in assessing damages. By s. 3 when goods are wrongfully detained the court may order specific delivery, either with or as an alternative to damages and by s. 4 it may grant interim possession by way of interlocutory relief. By s. 5 when a plaintiff's claim for damages is assessed as full compensation and is paid his title is extinguished. It seems that plaintiffs with limited titles, such as bailees, may recover the full value of the goods but must then account for any excess over the value of their interest.

Good faith and due care are in general no defence in conversion, *Hollins v Fowler* (1875) LR 7 HL 757; *Consolidated Co v Curtis* [1892] 1 QB 495. There are a number of statutory and common law qualifications to this strict liability. They include the protection of a bona fide purchaser of goods in market overt or from a mercantile agent under the Factors Act 1889† or under s. 23 (voidable title), s. 24 (seller in possession) and s. 25 (buyer in possession after sale) of the Sale of Goods Act 1979 or of a car subject to hire purchase under the Hire Purchase Act 1964, Part III. Other examples are when the plaintiff is estopped by his representation or negligence from asserting his title, the protection of a collecting banker under s. 4 of the Cheques Act 1957 and the exemption of a carrier or warehouseman whose dealings do not imply any transacting with title. When there are successive acts of conversion of the same goods the Limitation Act 1980, s. 3 provides that time in respect of the series runs from the first act and extinguishes title. Hence when time has run the original owner may not re-take the goods. The 1977 Act, s. 11 provides that contributory negligence is not a defence to conversion but by the Banking Act 1979, s. 47 it may be a defence to the liability of a collecting banker in respect of cheques and other instruments under the Cheques Act 1957, s. 4. Re-taking or recaption of converted chattels is a remedy by way of self-help. Reasonable force may be used against the first taker and any third party who has not acquired a good title. It is doubtful how far it is permissible to take the goods from the property of an innocent third party.

Cooling off period. The Consumer Credit Act 1974, s. 67 provides that a regulated agreement is a cancellable agreement if oral representations were made in the presence of the debtor or hirer during antecedent negotiations and the debtor signed the agreement at some place other than certain trade premises. Agreements relating to land and agreements excluded from the documentation provisions of the Act, that is non-commercial agreements, certain small agreements and overdrafts are not cancellable. By s. 68 the 'cooling off period' lasts from the execution of the agreement and for five clear days from the receipt of a copy of the agreement under s. 63 or notice under s. 64. If the creditor is under no obligation to send a copy or notice then the 'cooling off period' lasts for fourteen days from the execution of the agreement. Even if the agreement is cancelled the debtor or hirer remains liable for goods supplied to meet an emergency or which have been incorporated by himself or his relative in other goods under a debtor–creditor–supplier agreement for restricted use credit. Section 70 provides for the recovery of money paid by the debtor or hirer, s. 71 for the repayment of credit advances to the debtor, providing that if repayment is made within a month of cancellation or before the first instalment is due, no interest is payable and s. 72 deals with the return of goods upon cancellation and s. 73 with the return of goods given in part exchange.

Copyright. In the Copyright Act 1956, s. 1 (1) this is defined 'in relation to a work' as 'the exclusive right, . . . , to do, and to authorise other persons to do, certain acts in relation to that work in the United Kingdom and in any other country to which the relevant provision of [the] Act extends'. The 'acts' which may be done or authorised 'are those acts which . . . are designated as the acts restricted by the copyright in a work of that description'.

Copyright in this sense extends to literary, dramatic, musical, artistic works, sound recordings, cinematograph films, television and sound broadcasts. (*See* COPYRIGHT; LITERARY, DRAMATIC, MUSICAL AND ARTISTIC WORKS and COPYRIGHT; SOUND RECORDINGS, FILMS AND BROADCASTS). The 'acts restricted' are, broadly, the making of copies of the work and publishing them. Such copyright is to be distinguished from 'design copyright' in a registered design† under the Registered Designs Act 1949 which is primarily intended for ornamental patterns and features of mass-produced articles. Unlike ordinary copyright, 'design copyright' requires formalities of registration for acquisition and will be infringed by any closely resembling article whether or not there has been copying, whereas ordinary copyright is only infringed by deliberate copying. Ordinary artistic copyright as well as a claim to 'design copyright' may co-exist in respect of the same article. If the person entitled elects to rely on copyright as distinct from 'design copyright', then the Design Copyright Act 1968 limits protection to fifteen years instead of the longer periods available under copyright.

Copyright in the ordinary sense is given inter alia to those who are 'qualified persons' as defined in the 1956 Act. This expression covers British subjects, British protected persons, citizens of the Republic of Ireland and persons domiciled or resident in the United Kingdom or in other countries to which the relevant provision extends. Thus copyright often does not depend on where the work originated but upon the person claiming it. Provision was made to extend the Act to the Isle of Man, Channel Islands, colonies and dependencies or for applying it to countries which by convention give similar treatment to works protected in this country. For this purpose some countries require the work to be marked © with the copyright owner's name and date of publication. (*See* INTELLECTUAL PROPERTY: INTERNATIONAL PROTECTION). Copyright may be extended to the works of international organisations such as the U.N. There is Crown copyright in Government works. In addition to being a 'qualified person' a claimant must satisfy other conditions which vary with the subject matter.

Subject to contrary agreement the author of original literary, dramatic, musical and artistic works is normally entitled to the copyright. If the work is made in the course of the author's employment under a contract of service or apprenticeship the employer is normally the person entitled, but if the author is employed by a newspaper, magazine or periodical the employer–proprietor is only entitled to the copyright for publication in newspapers and the like; in other respects the author has the copyright. Where a photograph, portrait or engraving is commissioned for money or money's worth the person commissioning it is entitled to the copyright, but the negative or plate may remain the property of the photographer or artist. The 'maker' owns the copyright in a sound recording, unless it was commissioned, the 'maker' being the owner when the first record was produced. The copyright in a cinematograph film also belongs to the 'maker' who is 'the person by whom the arrangements necessary for the making of the film are undertaken'. Copyright in broadcasts belongs to the B.B.C. and I.T.A. Publishers are given a twenty-five year period of copyright in the typography of editions.

A work is presumed to be copyright and the plaintiff to be the owner unless these are put in issue by the defence. When an author's name appears on a work, he is presumed to be the author and owner of the copyright. If no author but a publisher is named he is presumed to be the owner. If the author is dead or the work is pseudonymous or anonymous it is for the defence to prove that the work is not original and to disprove allegations as to first publication. The defence must also disprove certain statements on record labels at the time of issue.

Copyright may be assigned, bequeathed or transmitted by operation of law. Assignment, which must be in writing, may be present or future, partial or total. Licences may be granted, binding on successors in title unless they purchased in good faith without notice. An assignee and an exclusive licensee may sue for infringement. A change in the ownership of an original work does not necessarily carry with it copyright but a bequest of an unpublished work is presumed to do so.

The Unfair Contract Terms Act 1977† has only limited application so far as a contract relates to the creation, transfer or termination of any right in a copyright. There can be no copyright in immoral, scandalous, obscene or libellous works but there may be copyright in a work which itself infringes copyright. There is no copyright in an idea (this may be protected by confidence or its written expression protected by copyright), nor in a live performance nor in a lecture (though these may be protected either by confidence† (*Caird v Sime* (1887) 12 App Cas 326) or in the case of performances, by the criminal law under the Dramatic & Musical Performers Protection Act 1958 and the Performers Protection Act 1963. Nor is there copyright in the mere title, style, plot or characters of a book nor in advertising slogans (though these may be protected under passing off†).

There may be multiple, or overlapping copyrights, subject to different periods, e.g. in a record and in music and in words on it.

Copyright, exemptions. A wide variety of dealings with literary, dramatic, musical and artistic works are exempted from the restrictions of copyright. These include any fair dealing with literary dramatic or musical work for research or private study, for criticism or review and for reporting current events in a newspaper or periodical if suitably acknowledged, or by broadcasting or in a film. Reproduction for judicial proceedings or law reports is exempt as is recitation by one person in public of a literary or dramatic work suitably acknowledged. So also is the inclusion, subject to conditions, of a short passage in a collection for schools. Where under assignment or licence a work may be broadcast it may be recorded or filmed provided the reproductions are destroyed within twenty-eight days of first use for broadcasting. Use of copyright material by teachers or in examination papers is exempted. Somewhat similar exemptions apply to artistic works. Painting, drawing, making an engraving of or photographing or filming or televising a sculpture or work of artistic craftsmanship on permanent view to the public or a work of architecture is exempt. An artistic work may be included in the background of a film or television broadcast. Reconstruction of a building is not infringement, neither is the reproduction of his work by the author of an artistic work (in which he may not own the copyright) provided he does not repeat or imitate the main design. Special exemptions cover copying by certain libraries. Making an object in three dimensions will not infringe copyright in a work of two dimensions if the object would not appear to persons who are not experts to be a reproduction. Where musical records have been made or imported for retail sale any manufacturer can make records for the same purpose on giving notice and paying a royalty fixed under the Copyright Act 1956. (*See* COPYRIGHT, LITERARY, DRAMATIC, MUSICAL AND ARTISTIC WORKS and COPYRIGHT IN SOUND RECORDINGS, FILMS AND BROADCASTS).

Copyright in sound recording, films and broadcasts. For records the 'acts restricted' are making a record embodying the recording, causing the recording to be heard in public or broadcasting it. Causing it to be heard in public in a residential hotel or holiday camp (unless a charge is made for admission to where it is heard) or in certain non-profit making clubs (unless a charge is made and not applied to the purposes of the club) is not infringement. Copyright in records is lost if they are issued to the public without a label on the records or container giving the year of first publication. For films (including sound track) the 'acts restricted' are making a copy of the film, causing it to be seen or heard in public, broadcasting it or transmitting it through a diffusion service. In both records and films the copyright belongs to the 'maker' as defined by the Act. Copyright in television and sound broadcasts, when made in this country or another country to which the Copyright Act 1956 extends, belongs to the B.B.C. or I.T.A. The 'acts restricted' are in regard to visual images making, not for private purposes, a film or copy of a film (not a still); in regard to sound, making a recording not for private purposes; causing such images or sounds to be seen or heard in public by a paying audience or re-broadcasting them. The Copyright Act 1956 (Amendment) Act 1982 makes it an offence to be in possession by way of trade of an infringing recording or film.

Copyright lasts for fifty years from the end of the year when the recording or film was first published or the broadcast first made. For news films and others registrable under Part II of the Films Act 1960 the period runs from the year of registration. When copyright in a film has expired to show it in public does not infringe copyright in the work on which it was based. News films may be shown fifty years after the events depicted. Repetition of a broadcast does not increase length of copyright.

In many presentations to the public there may be multiple or overlapping copyrights subject to different periods and in different ownership.

Copyright, literary, dramatic, musical and artistic works. Copyright exists in every published original literary, dramatic or musical work if the author was a 'qualified person' (*see* COPYRIGHT) for a substantial part of the time when it was made. It need not possess merit and the requirement of originality for published and unpublished works is minimal. 'Copyright Acts are not concerned with the originality of ideas, but with the expression of thought, and, in the case of "literary work", with the expression of thought in print or writing. The originality which is required relates to the expression of the thought. But the Copyright Act 1956 does not require that the expression must be in an original or novel form, but that the work must not be copied from another work – that it should originate from the author', *University of London Press v University Tutorial Press* [1916] 2 Ch 601 (examination papers). The Act itself specifies that 'literary work' includes 'any written table or compilation'. Hence directories and anthologies are protected except where there is no real skill or judgment in preparing them as in a selection of non-copyright tables to be included in a diary, *Cramp v Smythson* [1944] AC 329.

Copyright subsists in a published original literary, dramatic or musical work if it was first published in the United Kingdom or a country to which the relevant section of the Copyright Act 1956 extends, or the author was a 'qualified person' when the work was first published or was dead but a 'qualified person' immediately before his death.

Such a work is published if reproductions of the work or edition have been issued to the public. Performance is not publication nor is the issue of records, the exhibition of an artistic work, construction of a work of architecture or the issue of photographs or engravings of a work of architecture or of a sculpture. A publication which is merely colourable and not intended to satisfy the reasonable needs of the public is to be disregarded except so far as it amounts to infringement. No account is taken of unauthorised publication.

The 'acts restricted' by copyright in a literary, dramatic or musical work are reproducing the work in any material form, publishing the work, performing the work in public, broadcasting it, transmitting it to subscribers on a diffusion service, making an 'adaptation' of it and also publishing such an 'adaptation' in any of the ways specified. 'Adaptation' means turning a non-dramatic into a dramatic work or vice versa, translating a work, converting it into picture strip form or arranging or transcribing a musical work. Arranging or transcribing requires deliberation but sub-conscious copying may perhaps take place, *Francis Day and Hunter v Bron* [1963] Ch 587. Importation, sale and other dealings with offending articles also constitute infringement. A parody does not necessarily infringe, *Joy Music v Sunday Pictorial* [1960] 2 QB 60.

Copyright in literary, dramatic and musical works lasts for fifty years after the calendar year in which the author died, but if, before his death, the work had not been published, performed in public, offered for sale as records or broadcast, the period does not begin until the end of the year when one of these was first done to the work or to an adaptation of it. 'Dramatic work' includes a choreographic work or entertainment in dumb show if reduced to writing in the form in which it is to be presented but does not include a cinematograph film, as distinct from its script or scenario.

'Artistic works' include paintings, sculptures, drawings, engravings and photographs, irrespective of artistic quality; 'drawings' covering diagrams, maps, charts or plans; works of architecture including models for buildings; and other works of artistic craftsmanship. This last does not cover a suite of furniture, *George Hensher v Restawhile* [1976] AC 64 but engineering drawings may be artistic works, *L.B. (Plastics) Ltd v Swish Products* [1977] FSR 87.

Copyright subsists in published and unpublished artistic works on a similar basis to that for literary, dramatic and musical works, the duration being fifty years from the year of the author's death, but in the case of an engraving not published before death time runs from first publication, and for a photograph time runs in any event from first publication.

The 'acts restricted' are reproducing the work in any material form, publishing it, including it in a television broadcast and causing such a broadcast to be transmitted on a diffusion service. In a picture of a well-known subject copyright consists in the choice of viewpoint, balance of foreground, features in middle ground, *Krisarts v Briarfine* [1977] FSR 557.

Copyright, remedies. Remedies for infringement of copyright are damages and injunction. Instead of damages an account of profits may be claimed. The delivery up of infringing copies or plates may be claimed and damages for those sold. Damages cannot be claimed against an innocent infringer but additional damages may be awarded for flagrancy or benefit. An injunction will not be granted in respect of an infringing building after construction has started. The Customs may be required to prohibit the import of infringing copies. False attribution of ownership of a copyright work or passing off an altered artistic work as unaltered gives rise to damages. Deliberate infringement of copyright is a summary offence, as is unauthorised recording, filming and broadcasting of live performances under the Dramatic and Musical Performers Protection Act 1958, and the Performers Protection Act, 1963.

Crown copyright will not in practice be enforced in respect of legislation.

Since 1978 state immunity has not fully applied to copyright actions and the Unfair Contract Terms Act 1977† has only limited application so far as a contract relates to copyright. (*See* INTELLECTUAL PROPERTY, INTERNATIONAL PROTECTION).

Correspondence with description in sale of goods. Sale of Goods Act 1979, s. 13 provides that where there is a contract for the sale of goods by description there is an implied condition that the goods will correspond with the description. In sale by sample as well as by description, the bulk must correspond both with sample and description. A sale of goods may be a sale by description even though the goods, exposed for sale or hire, are selected by the buyer. 'The term "sale of goods by description" must apply to all cases where the purchaser has not seen the goods, but is relying on the description alone', *Varley v Whipp* [1900] 1 QB 513 at 516. All sales of future or unascertained goods must be sales by description, *Travers v Longel* (1947) 64 TLR 150 at 153. A thing may be 'sold by description, though it is specific, so long as it is sold not merely as the specific thing, but as a thing corresponding to a description', e.g. woollen undergarments, *Grant v Australian Knitting Mills* [1936] AC 85 at 100. All sales except sales 'as the specific thing' may be sales by description. Not all words of an apparently descriptive character used prior to a sale may be part of the 'description' requiring correspondence, *Harrison v Knowles & Foster* [1918] 1 KB 608; *Oscar Chess v Williams* [1957] 1 WLR 370. They may be mere representations and not part of the contract. It has been said that words may only form 'the description' when they have been employed to identify the goods, *Ashington Piggeries v Christopher Hill* [1972] AC 441. In commodity sales of unascertained goods very strict compliance with description has been required, *Arcos v Ronaasen* [1933] AC 470; *Re Moore and Landauer* [1921] 2 KB 519. Doubt as to these was expressed in *Reardon Smith Lines v Hansen Tangen* [1976] 1 WLR 989 but it was also said that there may be a distinction between commercial commodity sales of unascertained goods where a very strict standard is required and other sales where it may be more relaxed.

Under the Unfair Contract Terms Act 1977†, s. 6 liability under s. 13 of the Sale of Goods Act cannot be excluded or restricted by any contract terms as against anyone dealing as a consumer and against others an exclusion clause will only be effective in so far as it is reasonable, but s. 26 allows exclusion in international supply contracts. The Sale of Goods Act 1979, s. 13, unlike the terms as to merchantable quality and fitness for purpose implied by s. 14, is not limited to sales 'in the course of a business' and hence may apply to private sales.

Correspondent Bank. *See* BANKERS' COMMERCIAL CREDITS.

County Court Arbitration. Provision was made in 1973 for an extended county court arbitral jurisdiction, normally exercised by the registrar, primarily to deal with small consumer claims. This no longer requires an order of the court and can be employed despite objection from a party. The reference may be rescinded if the case involves difficult questions of fact or law or fraud or both parties have agreed that it should go to full trial. The reference may also be set aside if the subject matter, circumstances of the parties or the interests of any other person make arbitration inappropriate. The hearing is to be informal, strict rules of evidence are not to apply and the registrar can adopt any procedure he considers fair to the parties. Though arbitrations will usually be heard by the registrar he may refer the case for hearing by a judge or another arbitrator. Parties may recover limited costs.

Course of dealing. A regularly followed mode of transacting business between individuals as distinct from custom and usage applicable throughout a trade, profession or locality. A consistent course of dealing may allow a court to imply or incorporate terms into a contract, *Spurling v Bradshaw* [1956] 2 All ER 121; *McCutcheon v MacBrayne* [1964] 1 All ER 430; *British Crane Hire Corp v Ipswich Plant Hire Ltd* [1974] 1 All ER 1059.

Covenant. *See* DEED.

Credit. The Consumer Credit Act 1974, s. 9, provides that this includes a cash loan and any form of financial accommodation and, if provided in foreign currency, its sterling equivalent. In hire purchase the owner of the goods is deemed to provide fixed sum credit to the amount of the total purchase price, less the deposit and the total charge for credit. In assessing the amount of credit for the purposes of the Act any charge for credit, such as interest, is to be left out of the account, even though time is allowed for payment. Credit may be 'running account' or 'fixed sum', s. 10. The former is a facility under a personal credit agreement under which the debtor may receive from time to time cash, goods and services (or any of them) to such an amount or value that, taking into account any repayments he may make, the credit limit (if any) is not exceeded. Examples are bank overdrafts, credit cards and shop budget accounts. Any other form of credit is 'fixed-sum credit'. Running-account credit is regulated by the Act if the credit limit does not exceed £5,000. Section 10 (3) (b) contains anti-evasion provisions designed to prevent running-account agreements being taken out of the scope of the Act by the fixing of unduly high credit limits, including a provision that an agreement will still be within the Act, despite a limit exceeding £5,000, if it is not probable when it is made that the debit balance will exceed £5,000. By s. 171 (1) the parties may agree that s. 10 is not to apply and then it will be for the debtor to prove that in fact it should. Credit may also be 'restricted-use' or 'unrestricted-use'. By s. 11 the former is a regulated consumer credit agreement which is to finance either a transaction between the creditor and debtor or to finance a transaction between the debtor and a supplier other than the creditor or to refinance any indebtedness of the debtor, provided that the debtor is required to use the credit for these purposes. Any other credit, even if it contemplates a particular use, is 'unrestricted use credit'.

Credit broker. *See* CREDIT BROKERAGE.

Credit brokerage. The Consumer Credit Act 1974, s. 145 provides that this means the effecting of introductions† of individuals† to persons carrying on consumer credit business or businesses which relate to consumer credit agreements other than certain exempt agreements or who make unregulated agreements which would be regulated agreements if the proper law were that of part of the United Kingdom. Credit brokerage is an ancillary credit business and subject to the provisions of the Act common to these.

Credit reference agency. The Consumer Credit Act 1974, s. 145 provides that this is a person carrying on a business comprising the furnishing of persons with information relevant to the financial standing of individuals†, the information being collected for this purpose. It is an anciliary credit business and subject to the provisions of the Act common to these. Section 157 imposes a duty on a creditor, owner or negotiator on prescribed request in writing from the debtor or hirer to reveal the credit reference agency from which information was acquired, s 158 requires the agency to disclose filed information on written request and fee from an individual and to give him a copy of this information relating to him and s. 159 enables him to require the correction of wrong information. Section 160 provides an alternative procedure for business consumers (partnerships and other unincorporated bodies).

Credit sale. A contract for sale of goods where the property† passes to the buyer on or before delivery but payment of the price is postponed and may be effected by instalments. See the Consumer Credit Act 1974, s. 189. Credit sales to individuals† within the upper financial limit of £5,000 are regulated by the Act as debtor–creditor–supplier agreements with 'restricted use' credit. Unlike hire purchase and conditional sale there is no statutory right of termination and the creditor has no right to retake possession if the debtor falls into arrears. Hence protection orders, time orders and similar protection does not apply to credit sales.

Credit token agreements. Consumer Credit Act 1974, s. 14, provides that a credit token is a card, check, voucher, stamp, coupon, form, booklet or other document or thing given to an individual† by a person carrying on a consumer credit business who undertakes that on production of the token he will supply cash, goods and services (or any of them) or that if the token is produced to a third party who supplies cash, goods or services (or any of them) he, the issuer, will pay the third party for them in return for payment from the individual recipient of the token. Cash point cards issued by banks are included, since the use of the token to operate a machine amounts to production, as are credit cards. A credit token agreement is a regulated agreement for the provision of credit in connection with the use of the token. In addition to the general requirements of the Consumer Credit Act 1974 credit token agreements are subject to a special prohibition on sending unsolicited tokens, s. 51, special cancellation and copy provisions, ss. 63, 64, 70, 85, special provisions in s. 66 that the recipient is not to be liable for improper use until he has accepted the token, a limitation, by s. 84, of the recipient's liability for improper use to £30, except when the user obtained the token with the recipient's consent, special provision by the same section for complete protection when notice of loss is given to the issuer and special provisions for documentation, s. 179.

Criminal bankruptcy. This was introduced by the Criminal Justice Act 1972 and is now governed by the Powers of Criminal Courts Act 1973. The purpose is to make the assets of offenders available to compensate their victims for loss or damage but not for personal injury. When a person is convicted in the Crown Court and it appears that loss or damage has been suffered to an amount exceeding £15,000 by persons whose identity is known to the court a criminal bankruptcy order may be made. The order is regarded as an act of bankruptcy and any identified person named in the order or the Director of Public Prosecutions, acting as Official Petitioner, may present a criminal bankruptcy petition but the offender may not present his own petition. The petition must be presented in the High Court but may be transferred to another court. A creditor's petition must be presented within three months of the order but extended time may be allowed to the Official Petitioner. When a receiving order is made the duties of the debtor will follow the general pattern of ordinary bankruptcy but a liquidated petitioner's debt of £200 need not be proved, nor need the petitioner disclose any security or prove the domicile of the debtor. The Official Receiver must be the trustee in bankruptcy. Powers additional to those in ordinary bankruptcy are given for the recovery and realisation of assets. In the case of a deceased offender there may be administration in bankruptcy but the Official Receiver must be the trustee. A copy of the criminal bankruptcy order is sufficient evidence of the debt unless it is shown that the loss or damage is greater or less or was not caused by the offence but this does not allow proof that the offender did not commit the offences in question. If ordinary bankruptcy proceedings are in progress when a criminal bankruptcy order is made they may be set aside on the application of the Official Petitioner. There is no appeal against a criminal bankruptcy order but the order may be rescinded or amended on appeal against conviction for the offence in respect of which the order was made. Criminal bankruptcy is additional to any method of dealing with an offender other than the making of a compensation order, to which it is an alternative.

Crossed cheques. A crossing is an instruction to a banker to pay a cheque into a bank account or into a specified person's bank account. This is a safeguard against dishonest handling since such cheques can be traced with ease to the recipient account.

The Bills of Exchange Act 1882, s. 76 provides that where the cheque carries on its face the words 'and company' or any abbreviation of them between parallel transverse lines or two parallel lines, in either case with or without the words 'not negotiable', it is crossed generally and should be paid to a banker. Where the crossings bear the name of a banker with or without 'not negotiable' the cheque is crossed specially and should be paid to that banker. Special crossings need not have the parallel lines. The words 'not negotiable' need not be within the lines. By s. 77 a cheque may be crossed by the drawer or the holder; the holder may convert a general into a special crossing and may add 'Not negotiable'. Where a cheque is crossed specially the banker to whom it is specially crossed may cross it specially to another banker who is to act as agent to collect the proceeds. A collecting banker may cross a cheque specially to himself. A crossing is a material part of a cheque and by s. 78 it is unlawful to obliterate, add to or alter it except as authorised by the Act. (*See* ALTERATION OF NEGOTIABLE INSTRUMENT). The practice of 'opening a crossing' so that a cheque with a printed crossing may be paid in cash depends on custom and the 'a/c payee' crossing depends on case law. By s. 81 when a cheque is crossed 'not negotiable' it is still transferable but only subject† to equities. An 'account payee' crossing requires the collecting banker to make stringent inquiries before collecting the proceeds of the cheque for any account other than that of the named payee. There may be rare circumstances where the collecting banker is exempt from making inquiries in such a case, as when he collects the cheque for another banker who is an agent for collection, *Importers Co v Westminster Bank* [1927] 2 KB 297. By s. 80 when a drawee banker pays a crossed cheque in accordance with the general or special crossing to a banker, that paying banker and, if the cheque has come into the hands of the payee, the drawer, are deemed to be in the same position as if payment had been made to the true owner and thus usually free of liability. The Cheques Act 1957, s. 5 (re-enacting the Revenue Act 1883, s. 17 and the Bills of Exchange Act (1882) Amendment Act 1932) extends the crossed cheques provisions of the Bills of Exchange Act 1882 to all those analogous instruments mentioned in s. 4 (b) (c) and (d), i.e. mandates to a banker to pay which are not bills of exchange, e.g. 'cheques' with impersonal payees, certain Government instruments and bankers' drafts.

By the Bills of Exchange Act 1882, s. 79 (2) if a crossing has been obliterated or imperceptibly altered a banker who pays the instrument in good faith and without negligence in accordance with its appearance is protected from liability.

Crossing of Cheque. *See* CROSSED CHEQUE.

Custom and usage. Where the parties to a contract must be taken to have known of a local or trade custom applicable to the contract, the court will interpret the contract subject to the custom, thus giving words special meanings, e.g. 'baker's dozen', and even adding terms to the contract, the parties being assumed to have impliedly agreed that the custom should apply to the contract. Such a custom must be certain, reasonable, generally accepted in the trade, profession or locality and must not contradict the express terms of the contract as that would show an intent to exclude the custom. The custom may be of recent origin. *Produce Brokers v Olympia Oil & Cake Mill* [1916] 1 AC 314; *Re Sutro* [1917] 2 KB 348. *See* COURSE OF DEALING.

Customary authority of an agent. *See* ACTUAL AUTHORITY OF AN AGENT, IMPLIED AUTHORITY OF AN AGENT.

D

Damages. Monetary compensation for the infringement of a right. In tort their basic purpose is to put the injured party in the same position as if the tort had not been committed whilst in contract it is to place him in the same position as if the contract had been performed. Aggravated damages may be awarded in tort in compensation for outrageous conduct by the defendant, and exemplary damages which are punitive rather than compensatory, if aggravated damages do not suffice, in respect of oppressive or unconstitutional conduct by officials, or when the tort is calculated to provide a profit for the wrongdoer greater than compensatory damages or if statute allows them, *Cassell v Broome* [1972] AC 1027. In most torts the plaintiff can recover in respect of all consequences of the tort which are within the broad range of the reasonably foreseeable, *The Wagon Mound* [1961] AC 388; *Stewart v West African Terminals* [1964] 2 Lloyd's Rep 371. In some torts, such as deceit, he may recover for all direct consequences, *Doyle v Olby* [1969] 2 QB 158. Consequences outside the limits of foresight or directness are too remote and will not be covered by damages.

The rules of remoteness in contract are stated in *Hadley v Baxendale* (1854) 9 Ex 341. Damages are available for such results of breach as (1) 'may be considered either arising naturally, i.e. according to the usual course of things, from such breach of contract itself' or (2) 'such as may reasonably be supposed to have been in the contemplation of both parties at the time they made the contract as the probable result of breach of it'. These rules have been refined in a number of further cases, notably *Victoria Laundry v Newman Industries* [1949] 2 KB 528 and *Koufos v Czarnikow, The Heron II* [1969] 1 AC 350. Under rule (1) if the consequences of the breach could ordinarily have been foreseen by the defendant when he entered into the contract there is no need to show that this likelihood was specially drawn to his attention, but under rule (2) if the consequences arise from exceptional circumstances associated with the contract the defendant will not be liable in damages for these unless he was given information enabling him to foresee them. In *Hadley v Baxendale* a carrier was not liable for the stoppage of a factory resulting from delay in carrying a mill shaft since he did not know it was so vital and in *Victoria Laundry v Newman Industries* the defendants who failed to deliver machinery were not liable for the plaintiff's loss of exceptionally lucrative but unnotified contracts. When damages cannot be recovered for an unforeseeable exceptional loss which actually occurred, there may be recovery for foreseeable ordinary loss which did not occur, *Cory Bros v Thames Ironworks* (1868) LR 3 QB 181.

In *Koufos v Czarnikow*, *The Heron II*, a delay in carriage case, a difference between tort and contract was said to be that in contract recovery is possible for loss which, when contracting, was not unlikely to result from breach or which was of a high degree of probability whereas in tort recovery was available for loss which was reasonably foreseeable as likely to happen even in the most unusual case unless the risk was so small that a reasonable man would be justified in ignoring it, wider recovery being possible in tort because in contract if one party wishes to extend liability this can be drawn to the other's attention whereas this cannot be done in tort.

Damages in tort are always unliquidated, to be assessed by the court, whereas in contract they may be either unliquidated, to be assessed by the court under *Hadley v Baxendale*, or liquidated, that is agreed in advance by the parties. This may be done even if it is difficult to estimate the likely loss, *Dunlop v New Garage* [1915] AC 79, but such a sum must be a genuine pre-estimate. If it is not, but is exorbitant or excessive so as to deter a party from breach it will be a penalty and not recoverable, damages then being assessed as unliquidated. It is not conclusive that the parties have designated an agreed sum either a penalty or liquidated damages. The court will look to the substance.

In both contract and tort damages may be merely nominal when a party's rights have been infringed but he has not suffered substantial loss.

In both contract and tort a plaintiff should take reasonable steps to mitigate his loss and will not be able to recover damages for any loss which might have been avoided by mitigation, *Brace v Calder* [1895] 2 QB 253. He is not obliged to take steps which might injure his commercial reputation, *Finlay v Kwik Hoo Tong* [1929] 1 KB 400. He is not obliged to mitigate if he does not accept a discharging breach, *White & Carter (Councils) Ltd v McGregor* [1962] AC 413. (*See* DISCHARGE OF CONTRACT BY BREACH).

If an award of damages is in respect of lost earnings an estimated deduction must be made in respect of the tax that would have been incurred, *B.T.C. v Gourley* [1956] AC 185; *Parsons v B.N.M.* [1964] 1 QB 95.

If a contract allows alternative methods of performance damages will be assessed on the basis that the defendant would have chosen the method which involves the least liability in damages, *Laverack v Woods* [1967] 1 QB 278.

Damages may be awarded in a foreign currency, *Miliangos v Frank* [1976] AC 443.

Days of grace. Until the Banking and Financial Dealings Act 1971 it was provided by the Bills of Exchange Act 1882, s. 14 (1) that for all bills of exchange not payable on demand, that is, for all bills payable at the end of a period of time, three days, known as days of grace, were to be added to the period, unless the instrument provided otherwise. These extra days were historically a matter of favour but became obligatory unless excluded. They were abolished by the Banking and Financial Dealings Act 1971, s. 3.

Dead freight. When a charterer fails to load a full and complete cargo his liability in damages in respect of the empty space is styled 'dead freight'.

Debenture certificate. *See* DEBENTURE WARRANT.

Debenture warrant. A debenture is a document, normally one of a series, evidencing a loan to a company and either transferable on a register by a separate document of transfer as with shares covered by a share certificate or in bearer form transferable by delivery as with shares covered by a share warrant. Such a debenture warrant will normally carry coupons to be detached and returned to the company in exchange for interest when the company advertises payment is available. Debenture warrants are a form of negotiable instrument, *Edelstein v Schuler* [1902] 2 KB 144.

Debt-adjusting. The Consumer Credit Act 1974, s. 145 provides that in relation to consumer credit agreements or consumer hire agreements this means negotiating with the creditor or owner on behalf of the debtor or hirer for the discharge of a debt or taking over in return for payment by the debtor or hirer his obligation to discharge a debt or any similar activity in liquidating debts. Debt-adjusting is an ancillary credit business and subject to the provisions of the Act common to these.

Debt-collecting. The Consumer Credit Act 1974, s. 145 provides that this is the taking of steps to procure payment of debts under consumer credit agreements, or consumer hire agreements. It is an ancillary credit business and subject to the provisions of the Act common to these.

Debt-counselling. The Consumer Credit Act 1974, s. 145 provides that this is the giving of advice to debtors or hirers about the liquidation of debts due under consumer credit agreements or consumer hire agreements. It is an ancillary credit business and subject to the provisions of the Act common to these.

Debtor–creditor agreement. The Consumer Credit Act 1974, s. 13 provides that such an agreement is a regulated consumer credit agreement which *either* involves 'restricted-use' credit to finance a transaction between the debtor and a supplier other than the creditor but is not made under pre-existing arrangements or in contemplation of future arrangements between the creditor and the supplier *or* is a 'restricted-use' credit agreement to refinance any indebtedness of the debtor *or* is an 'unrestricted use' credit agreement which is not made by the creditor under pre-existing arrangements with a supplier knowing that the credit is to be used for a transaction between the debtor and a supplier. The third sub-category covers overdrafts and personal loans. Any regulated consumer credit agreement which is not a debtor–creditor agreement is a debtor–creditor–supplier agreement. The distinction is important because it is an offence to canvas debtor–creditor agreements off trade premises, s. 49, disclosure requirements may vary, cancellation of a debtor–creditor–supplier agreement extends to the agreement for the supply of goods and there are special provisions for their return and deposit, ss. 19, 69, and if the debtor in a debtor–creditor–supplier agreement has a claim against the suppliers for misrepresentation or breach he has a similar claim against the creditor, ss. 56, 75.

Debtor–creditor–supplier agreement. Consumer Credit Act 1974, s. 12 provides that such an agreement is a regulated consumer credit agreement which either involves 'restricted-use' credit to finance a transaction between the debtor and the creditor or 'restricted-use' credit to finance a transaction between the debtor and a supplier than the creditor or an 'unrestricted-use' credit agreement which is made by the creditor under pre-existing arrangements between himself and a supplier in the knowledge that the credit is to be used to finace a transaction between the debtor and the supplier. A debtor–creditor–supplier agreement may involve only two parties and the first sub-category above covers hire purchase, credit sale and conditional sale both when the retailer himself advances the credit and when the retailer sells the goods to a finance house which in its turn provides credit to the debtor. Any regulated consumer credit agreement which is not a debtor–creditor–supplier agreement is a debtor–creditor agreement. See that entry for the implications of the distinction.

Deceit. *See* MISREPRESENTATION.

Deed. A document signed, sealed and delivered by the obligor, who undertakes liabilities under it. A general requirement of signature for deeds came in the Law of Property Act 1925, s. 73. For sealing there is now no need for wax or embossing. It suffices if a party signs intending to execute a document which indicates a place for a seal, *First National Securities v Jones* [1978] 2 All ER 221. Delivery is any dealing with the document which indicates that the obligor intends it to take effect as a deed. It need not necessarily be actual delivery to the obligee. If the document is delivered so that it is not to take effect until some condition has been fulfilled it is known as an escrow. Gratuitous promises, i.e. not made for consideration, will be legally enforceable if embodied in a deed. The period of limitation for deeds is twelve years as against the six years for simple or parol contracts. Promises in a deed are referred to as covenants. A lease for more than three years must be under seal if it is to take full legal effect.

Deeds of arrangement. By these debtors seek to avoid even the partial application of the law of bankruptcy to their affairs in return for part payment of their debts. Unlike a composition† or scheme of arrangement which involves the partial operation of the bankruptcy law, a deed of arrangement will only bind assenting creditors. A deed of arrangement is a contract and hence subject to the general rules of contract. Any secret preference given to or bargained for by a creditor will allow others to withdraw.

If these agreements fall within the definition of a 'deed of arrangement' in the Deeds of Arrangement Act 1914 they must comply with the Act to be valid. The Act defines a deed of arrangement as any instrument, under seal or not, made for the benefit of creditors generally or made by an insolvent debtor for the benefit of any three or more creditors. It may be an assignment of property, a deed or agreement for a composition and, where creditors obtain any control over the property or business of the debtor, a deed of inspectorship, letter of licence or agreement for carrying on or winding up the business. Such a document will be void unless it is registered with the Department of Trade within seven days after execution and stamped. If the deed affects land it must also be registered as a land charge or it will be void against a purchaser of the land. A deed for the benefit of creditors generally will also be void unless assented to by a majority in number and value within twenty-one days of registration. Within a further seven days the trustee must file a statutory declaration of compliance. Within seven days of the filing the trustee must give security unless a majority in number and value of the creditors dispense with it otherwise the court may declare the deed void or appoint a new trustee.

A conveyance or assignment for the benefit of creditors generally is an act of bankruptcy available for three months to a non-assenting creditor, but if he is served with notice of the deed by the trustee this is reduced to one month. The trustee should not act under a deed for three months unless all creditors have assented, for if the debtor is bankrupted the trustee would have to account for all dealings under the doctrine of 'relation back'. If the deed is void the trustee must account for all dealings even if a bankruptcy petition is presented after three months from the execution of the deed. Where, however, a deed is void because the proper majority did not assent or, in the case of a deed for the benefit of three or more creditors, because the debtor was insolvent at the time of execution and the deed was not properly registered and is not otherwise void, if a receiving order is made on a bankruptcy petition presented more than three months after the execution of the deed, the trustee under the deed is not liable to account for the debtor's property if he proves he did not know and had no reason to suspect the deed was void.

A trustee under a deed of arrangement must account annually to the Department of Trade and every six months to the creditors, a majority in number and value of whom can demand an audit during the administration or within twelve months of final accounts.

Default notices. The Consumer Credit Act 1974 allows a creditor or owner freedom to sue for payments due but by s. 87 if he wishes, because the debtor or hirer is in default, to terminate the agreement, demand earlier payment, recover possession of land or goods or treat any of the debtor's rights as terminated, restricted or deferred, the creditor must give at least seven days notice in prescribed form specifying the breach, what may be done to remedy it and, if that is not possible, what compensation is required. If remedy or compensation are provided the breach is treated as never having happened, s. 89. By s. 86 the creditor or owner on the death of the debtor or hirer cannot do any of the acts mentioned in s. 87 if the agreement is fully secured and if it is unsecured or partially secured then only with an order of the court. Section 76 requires not less than seven days notice for demanding earlier payment, recovery of possession of land or goods or termination or restriction or deferment of a debtor's rights when this is done under a term of the agreement. Section 98 requires similar length of notice for termination of agreements in non-default cases.

Defensive trade mark. *See* TRADE MARK INFRINGEMENT.

Del credere agent. An agent for sale who undertakes to his principal, the seller, that the third party buyer will pay the price but does not otherwise guarantee the due performance of the contract. A contract of such agency is not a contract of guarantee within the Statute of Frauds 1677, s. 4 and does not require to be evidenced in writing. Such agency is now not frequently found being replaced by confirming houses, bankers commercial credits, export credit guarantees and other methods of ensuring payment of the price.

Delegatus non potest delegare. 'A delegate is not himself able to delegate'. This expresses the rule that an agent must normally act personally and not appoint a sub-agent to perform his duties. There are exceptions when custom and usage allow delegation, where proper performance requires delegation and where there is an express or implied agreement to allow delegation, *De Bussche v Alt* (1878) 8 Ch D

286. Purely ministerial functions, not involving confidence or discretion may be delegated and unforeseen circumstances may also allow delegation. Even when a sub-agent may be appointed there will normally be no privity between him and the principal—the sub-agent will be liable to and entitled against the agent alone, *Calico Printers v Barclays Bank* (1931) 145 LT 51, where sub-agents were not liable to the principal for failing to insure goods. This case was decided before *Donoghue v Stevenson* [1932] AC 562, and it may be that in such a case the sub-agent would now be liable to the principal in negligence, *Gilchrist Watt v York* [1970] 3 All ER 825. If clear proof is given, privity of contract between principal and sub-agent may be established with consequent direct rights and liabilities. Even without privity a sub-agent who knows that he is so employed owes a duty of good faith to the principal and will be liable for any secret profit he makes, *Powell v Evan Jones* [1905] 1 KB 11.

Deliverable state. The Sale of Goods Act 1979, s. 61 (5) provides that 'goods† are in a deliverable state within the meaning of this Act when they are in such a state that the buyer would under the contract be bound to take delivery† of them'. This concept is required by s. 18, rr. 1, 2, 3 and 5 on the passing of property† and by s. 29 (5) which, in the absence of contrary agreement, makes the seller responsible for the expenses of putting goods into a deliverable state. 'It depends on the actual state of the goods at the time of the contract and the state in which they are to be delivered by the terms of the contract', *Underwood v Burgh Castle Brick and Cement* [1922] 1 KB 343 (engine sold f.o.r. still affixed to concrete bed at time of contract not then in a deliverable state). It appears goods may be defective but still in a deliverable state.

Delivery in sale of goods. By the Sale of Goods Act 1979, s. 27 delivery is a duty of the seller and s. 61 defines it as 'voluntary transfer of possession from one person to another'. Such transfer may be actual or constructive. The latter occurs where there is attornment by a bailee originally holding for one party agreeing (s. 29 (4)) to hold for another or a seller after sale agrees to hold the goods as bailee for the buyer or a buyer, holding goods before the sale as a bailee, afterwards holds in his own right. The transfer of a document of title such as a bill of lading may effect delivery as in c.i.f. contracts and delivery to the buyer's agent is delivery to the buyer himself. Transfer of a means of control, such as a key to a warehouse, may also be delivery. Delivery to a carrier for transit to the buyer is prima facie delivery to the buyer (s. 32 (1)). Although by s. 10 time of payment is not treated as a condition, time of delivery has been so regarded so that trifling delay entitles the buyer to reject, *Bowes v Shand* (1877) 2 App Cas 455 (*See* REJECTION IN SALE OF GOODS). The buyer may waive strict compliance with time of delivery, but if he wishes to reinstate it as fundamental he must give the seller reasonable notice, *Charles Rickards v Oppenhaim* [1950] 1 KB 616, unless it is clear that in any event the seller could not comply, *Ets Chainbaux v Harbormaster* [1955] 1 Lloyd's Rep 303. Waiver must be clear and unequivocal and waiver of one term is not necessarily waiver of a related term, *Finagrain v Krue* [1976] 2 Lloyd's Rep 508. Section 28 provides that unless otherwise agreed delivery and payment are concurrent conditions, that is the seller must be ready and willing to deliver and the buyer to pay. Section 29 opens by providing that whether it is for the seller to send or the buyer to take the goods depends on the contract but, if there is no express or implied term, the place of delivery is the sellers' place of business if he has one, otherwise his residence, except that if the contract is for specific goods which the parties know are at a particular place, it is that place. Demand or tender of delivery may be ineffective unless made at a reasonable hour. What is reasonable is a question of fact. Unless otherwise agreed the expenses of putting goods into a deliverable state† fall on the seller.

Section 30 deals with delivery of wrong quantity. If too little is delivered the buyer may reject but if he accepts he must pay at the contract rate; if too much, he may accept the contract goods and reject the rest or may reject or accept the whole; if he accepts the whole he must pay for the balance at the contract rate. Where the seller delivers the contract goods mixed with goods of a different description, the buyer may accept the contract goods and reject the rest or he may reject the whole. These provisions are subject to any usage, special agreement or course of dealing between the parties. Section 31 provides that unless otherwise agreed a buyer is not obliged to take delivery in instalments. Where goods are to be delivered by instalments separately paid for and the seller makes one or more defective deliveries or the buyer fails to pay for one or more instalments it is a question in each case depending on the contract and the circumstances whether the breach is a repudiation of the whole contract (i.e. amounting to a breach of condition) or whether it is a severable breach giving rise to a right to compensation but not to treat the whole as repudiated (i.e. amounting to a breach of warranty). A trivial failure late in the performance of a long contract will be far less serious than a grave failure early in performance, *Maple Flock v Universal Furniture* [1934] 1 KB 148, where it was said that regard should be had not only to the quantitative aspect of the breach but also the probability of repetition, *Robert A. Munro v Meyer* [1930] 2 KB 312. Section 32 provides that delivery to a carrier for carriage to the buyer is prima facie delivery to the buyer. The buyer need not have named the carrier. The seller must make a proper contract with the carrier and if he fails to do so the buyer may either refuse to treat the delivery as made to himself or hold the seller liable in damages, *Thomas Young v Hobson* (1949) 65 TLR 365 (goods sent at owner's not company's risk). When goods are sent by sea and it is usual to insure the seller must give the buyer notice to enable him to insure. If the seller fails to do so, the goods are at his risk whilst at sea. This applies to f.o.b. contracts, *Wimble v Rosenberg* [1913] 3 KB 743. Section 33 provides that where the seller agrees to deliver goods at his own risk at a place other than where they were sold the buyer must (unless otherwise agreed) take the risk of any deterioration necessarily incident to the transit. The seller may, however, be liable if the goods are not in a fit state to endure the voyage or journey and they decay *because of this initial unfitness*. *Mash & Murrell v Emanuel* [1961] 1 All ER 485 (rvsd. on facts [1962] 1 All ER 77n); *Kemp v Tolland* [1956] 2 Lloyd's Rep 681; but see *Cordova v Victor* [1966] 1 WLR 793, *Oleificio Zucchi v Northern Sales* [1965] 2 Lloyd's Rep 496 at 518; and *Crowther v Shannon* [1975] 1 WLR 30. *See* FITNESS FOR PURPOSE.

Delivery of a bill of exchange or promissory note. The Bills of Exchange Act 1882, s. 2 defines this as the 'transfer of possession, actual or constructive, from one person to another'. Constructive transfer takes place from one principal to another when an agent holding an instrument on behalf of one principal attorns and so agrees to hold it on behalf of the other. It also takes place when a transferor with the authority of the transferee, puts an instrument into the post for transmission to the transferee. There is no transfer of possession whilst the instrument remains with the transferor's agent but there will be when it is handed to the transferee's agent. Section 21 provides that every contract on a bill of exchange 'whether it be the drawer's, the acceptor's or an indorser's, is incomplete and revocable, until delivery of the instrument in order to give effect thereto'. Section 84 provides that 'a promissory note is inchoate and incomplete until delivery' to the payee or bearer. The first delivery of a complete bill or note to a holder is known as issue.

Demand. A bill of exchange or promissory note is payable on demand when it is expressed to be payable on demand, at sight† or on presentation (to the drawee or maker) or in which no time for payment is mentioned. A cheque is a bill of exchange drawn on a banker payable on demand. (Bills of Exchange Act 1882, ss. 10 and 73). A bank note is a form of promissory note payable on demand. See also s. 36 (3) which provides that a demand bill is overdue when it appears to have been in circulation for an unreasonable time and s. 86 requiring presentment for payment† of a demand note after negotiation, but also providing that a demand note is not overdue† merely because it appears that a reasonable time for presenting it for payment has elapsed since issue†. Section 60 protects a paying banker who pays a demand bill (in effect, cheque) drawn on him when the indorsement is forged. Section 45 (2) requires presentment for payment of a demand bill within a reasonable time after issue to make the drawer liable on the right of recourse and within a reasonable time after indorsement to render the indorser similarly liable.

De minimis non curat lex. 'The law does not concern itself with very trifling matters'. One of the principal applications of this maxim in commercial law is that very trifling departures from description in sale of goods (*see* CORRESPONDENCE WITH DESCRIPTION) or trifling excess or deficiency in quantity (*see* DELIVERY IN SALE OF GOODS) will not be treated as a breach of contract. The difference must be microscopic. Compare *Wilensko Slaski v Fenwick* [1938] 3 All ER 429 (1 per cent not de minimis) and *Shipton Anderson v Weil* [1912] 1 KB 574 (1 lb in 100 tons de minimis). See also *Margaronis Navigation Agency v Henry W. Peabody* [1965] 1 QB 300 (application a question of fact depending on circumstances of case). The maxim does not apply to bankers' commercial credits unless they are subject to the Uniform Customs and Practice for Documentary Credits (U.C.P.).

Demurrage. *See* VOYAGE CHARTERPARTY.

Design copyright. *See* REGISTERED DESIGNS.

Diplomatic immunity. It was once the general rule that foreign diplomats enjoyed immunity in United Kingdom courts unless this was waived. The Diplomatic Privileges Act 1964 now embodies many further exceptions. Diplomats proper are immune in civil and criminal law except in real actions relating to immovables other than mission land, in proceedings on succession on death and in actions relating to non-official professional or commercial activities in the United Kingdom, and are exempt from taxes and enforcement proceedings. Administrative and technical staff, if non-permanently resident aliens, are immune in criminal law but not in civil law for non-official acts and are exempt from taxes and enforcement proceedings. Domestic and service staff, if non-permanently resident aliens, are liable in civil and criminal law for non-official acts and have a limited fiscal exemption. Private servants, if non-permanently resident aliens, are also allowed such a limited exemption but other immunities are at the discretion of the receiving State. Immunity begins on entry and ceases on leaving the United Kingdom. If the employment ends but the person remains in this country then it ceases after a reasonable period to leave the country but continues in force in respect of acts done whilst in post.

Director-General of Fair Trading. The office of Director-General was established by the Fair Trading Act 1973 and many of his functions are specified in that Act. He must collect and process information concerning commercial activities relating to the supply of goods and services in the United Kingdom to discover practices which may harmfully affect the interests of consumers and must also investigate monopoly situations and uncompetitive practices. He must inform and assist the Secretary of State in regard to these. Under Part II of the Act the Director is, together with the Secretary of State or other appropriate Minister, one of those who may refer 'consumer trade practices' to the Consumer Protection Advisory Committee. Some references may be made by him with a proposal for a recommendation to the Secretary of State that an order be made modifying or forbidding certain practices. Under Part III of the Act, where it appears that a person is engaging in conduct detrimental to consumers the Director must seek to obtain written assurances to desist and if this proves unavailing, he must take proceedings before the Restrictive Practices Court†. Under Parts IV and V of the Act, dealing with monopolies and mergers, he may require information as to monopoly situations and either the Director or the Secretary of State or the Secretary of State together with other Ministers may make monopoly references to the Monopolies and Mergers Commission† whether for factual investigation or in order to have prohibitory orders made. The Director cannot himself make merger references to the Commission but he must obtain information about cases which might be referred and make recommendations to the Secretary of State. Where the Commission reports in a monopoly or merger case the Director must, if asked by the appropriate Minister, consult with the parties to obtain undertakings from them. If these are not given or not observed he must advise the Minister as to the exercise of his powers. Part IX of the Fair Trading Act 1973 also transferred to the Director the functions of the former Registrar of Restrictive Trading Agreements under the Restrictive Trade Practices Act 1956 (as amended in 1968) and the Resale Prices Act 1964. The Director must now investigate, register and bring such agreements before the Restrictive Practices Court, this function now being governed by the Restrictive Practices Acts 1976 and 1977 and the Resale Prices Act 1976. Under the Competition Act 1980 he must refer to the Monopolies Commission practices tending to distort competition. Under Part XII of the 1973 Act he must make annual and other reports, publish advice and information to consumers and encourage trade associations to prepare codes of practice for consumer protection.

Discharge of a negotiable instrument. This means that the contractual obligations embodied in an instrument have come to an end either by performance, that is payment in due course or in some other way provided for by law such as renunciation†, cancellation†, alteration†, or the acceptor becoming holder of the instrument. (See the Bills of Exchange Act 1882, ss. 59–64 and s. 89.) The discharge of the instrument as a whole must be distinguished from the discharge of individual parties as when only their signatures are cancelled and they and subsequent indorsers are discharged or the discharge of a drawer and indorsers on the failure of a holder to give proper notice of dishonour.

Discharge of contract. This covers the ways in which the parties or one or some of them may be released from their obligations. There may be discharge of contract by performance, discharge of contract by breach, discharge of contract by agreement or by frustration (also called impossibility of performance). *See also* DISCHARGE OF NEGOTIABLE INSTRUMENTS.

Discharge of contract by agreement. This will release parties from their obligations to perform. In all cases discharge may be effected by deed or specialty. A contract by deed may be discharged by a parol or simple contract, *Berry v Berry* [1929] 2 KB 316. When a simple contract is wholly or partially executory on both sides each party's agreement to relinquish his claim to further performance is the required consideration for the other's agreement to relinquish his claim, but when one party has wholly performed his obligation then the other must either be released by deed or else there must be an 'accord and satisfaction', the 'accord' being the agreement to release and the 'satisfaction' being fresh consideration for that promise. That fresh consideration may itself be an executory promise but it will discharge the original contract, *British Russian Gazette v Associated Newspapers* [1933] 2 KB 616.

If a contract is unenforceable unless evidenced in writing (*see* FORM IN CONTRACT) an attempt merely to vary or modify the original contract which is not itself evidenced in writing will be wholly ineffective and the original can be enforced unvaried but the original contract can be wholly discharged by a new contract not evidenced in writing even though the new contract is intended not merely to discharge but also to replace the original and is ineffective for this second purpose because of the lack of written evidence, *Morris v Baron* [1918] AC 1.

If a party agrees without consideration to waive the strict performance of his contractual rights he will not be entitled to insist on his original rights without giving the other party a reasonable opportunity to restore the position, *Panoutsos v Raymond Hadley* [1917] 2 KB 473; *Charles Rickards v Oppenhaim* [1950] 1 KB 616. This is associated with, if not an example of promissory estoppel or the rule in *Hightrees House*. The rule in *Pinnel's Case* (1602) 5 Co Rep 117a or *Foakes v Beer* (1884) 9 App Cas 605 which has been so limited in scope by promissory estoppel (*see* CONSIDERATION) is itself a special case of accord and satisfaction. *See also* DISCHARGE OF NEGOTIABLE INSTRUMENTS.

Discharge of contract by breach. Following certain types of breach of contract the party not in breach has a choice or election. He may accept the breach, treat the contract as discharged or terminated, make no further performance on his part, resist any action by the party in breach and sue for a quantum meruit or damages. This termination of the contract was once referred to as rescission but in *Johnson v Agnew* [1980] AC 367, 373, it was said that it differs from recission for e.g. misrepresentation, in that termination for breach operates for the future and does not result in a contract being treated as never having existed. When termination takes place an arbitration clause may remain in force, *Heyman v Darwins* [1942] AC 356. A party electing to discharge the contract must inform the other without unreasonable delay and the choice is final, *Scarf v Jardine* (1882) 7 App Cas 345. Alternatively the party not in breach may not accept the breach but affirm the contract, treating it as continuing fully in existence, provide performance in so far as he has a substantial or legitimate interest in doing so, and in so far as he can do so without the co-operation of the other party, then sue for the value of the performance, *White & Carter (Councils) Ltd v McGregor* [1962] AC 413. This qualifies the normal rule that a plaintiff should mitigate his loss (*See* DAMAGES).

Whether a breach permits election to terminate depends on a number of factors. One is the order in which the parties are to provide performance. The performance of one may be a condition precedent to that of the other, hence if it is not provided the other may terminate. Again performance from each may be concurrent conditions so that both must be ready and willing to perform, hence if one is not, the other may terminate (e.g. in sale of goods the obligation of the buyer to pay and the seller to deliver). Another approach is to classify contractual promises as dependent, as in concurrent conditions, or independent when failure on the part of one will not allow the other to terminate, (e.g. covenants of a tenant to pay rent and landlord to repair in a lease, *Taylor v Webb* [1937] 2 KB 283). There is no general rule for classification. It depends primarily on the agreement of the parties and on the construction of the terms of the contract, subject to some special cases covered by precedent. Usually promises are treated as dependent and if performance is to be provided at the same time this will indicate concurrence. Yet another factor is whether the contract is an 'entire contract', where a lump sum of money is to be paid for a performance, when any imperfection in performance will allow the other to terminate, *Cutter v Powell* (1795) 6 TR 320, or whether the contract is divisible, in which case only serious breach will permit termination. Whether a contract is entire or not depends on the agreement and its construction but most contracts are divisible. Lastly if one party has committed a breach of condition as distinct from a breach of warranty, or, in the case of an innominate term, a breach equivalent to a breach of condition going to the root of the contract, either by refusal to perform or by disabling himself from performing, the other may terminate. When a party repudiates or disables himself before the time for performance this is anticipatory breach. Instalment contracts raise special problems. The Sale of Goods Act 1979, s. 31 provides that it is a question depending on the facts and in *Maple Flock v Universal Furniture* [1934] 1 KB 148 it was said that regard should be had not only to the quantity involved in the breach but also to the probability of repetition.

If a party relies on an inadequate ground to purport to terminate he may, if he discovers that a sufficient ground existed, rely on that provided that he does not delay unreasonably in doing so, *Panchaud v Etablissements General Grain* [1970] 1 Lloyd's Rep 53 or otherwise prejudice the other party. A party cannot terminate even if there is serious breach if he has accepted a substantial benefit under the contract or waived the breach. The Apportionment Act 1870 which provides that certain periodic payments are deemed to accrue from day to day may be relevant but it is doubtful if a party in breach can rely on the Act.

Discharge of contract by performance. The normal rule is that a party must perform precisely and exactly. It is not enough that he has provided an equivalent or more valuable substitute, *Legh v Lillie* (1860) 6 H & N 165 nor, subject to frustration and the terms of the contract (*see* EXEMPTION AND EXCLUSION CLAUSES; UNFAIR CONTRACT TERMS ACT 1977) is it normally an answer to say that a party has tried his best if he did not fulfil his promise. Contracts for professional services will, however, be construed as requiring due care rather than the necessary achievement of a given result. Where the personal abilities of a party are required for performance he must perform personally but in impersonal contracts he may provide performance through others, *Robson & Sharpe v Drummond* (1831) 2B & Ad 303, *British Waggon Co v Lea* (1880) 5 QBD 149. Where alternative performances are available the party who is to act first, subject to contrary agreement, chooses, *Reed v Kilburn Co-operative Society* (1875) LR 10 QB 264.

In some exceptional cases a party who has not provided exact performance may recover in respect of what he has provided. These are (1) Where there is not an entire contract but a divisible contract and some of the obligations have been fulfilled (*see* DISCHARGE OF CONTRACT BY BREACH); (2) Where the other party has prevented performance. Here either damages or quantum meruit are available; (3) Where partial performance has been freely accepted by the other party in circumstances which permit a new contract to pay for it to be implied; *Sumpter v Hedges* [1898] 1 QB 673; (4) Where there has been substantial performance with only trifling variation from that promised, *Dakin v Lee* [1916] 1 KB 566; *Hoenig v Issacs* [1952] 2 All ER 176; (5) Where he is in breach of a warranty as distinct from a condition.

At common law time for performance was of the essence so that any delay was a breach allowing the other party to terminate (*see* DISCHARGE OF CONTRACT BY BREACH). Equity relaxed this for contracts relating to land, (see Law of Property Act 1925, s. 41). Time will continue to be of the essence, even in such contracts as well as others, if the contract provides to that effect, if the nature of the subject matter, e.g. short leases or reversions, requires it or if the party not in delay makes it of the essence by giving notice requiring performance within a reasonable time. Time, unless unimportant, is normally of the essence in commercial contracts. A seller's date for delivery of goods is of the essence, *Reuter v Sala* (1879) 4 CPD 239, but by the Sale of Goods Act 1979, s. 10 time for payment is not of the essence unless otherwise agreed. Time for fulfilment of conditions precedent is of the essence but if no time is provided this must take place within a reasonable time as must other performance for which time is not fixed. The Bills of Exchange Act 1882, ss. 41 and 45 provides that bills of exchange must be presented for acceptance or payment within a specified time (*see* PRESENTMENT FOR PAYMENT OF A BILL OF EXCHANGE OR PROMISSORY NOTE and PRESENTMENT FOR ACCEPTANCE) and the Sale of Goods Act 1979, s. 29 (5) makes similar provision for delivery in sale of goods.

If a party makes a valid tender of performance (e.g. proffers delivery of goods) other than payment and the tender is rejected this discharges the party tendering and he may recover damages. A party making a rejected tender of payment must continue ready and willing to pay and, if he is sued, pay into court so that costs will be borne by the other. For a valid tender of payment the debtor must seek out the creditor and actually produce the money unless the creditor waives production, the money being in legal tender and the exact amount due must be proffered unless the debtor waives any claim to change. Any special terms of the contract must be observed.

Discharge of the bankrupt. This is an order of the court granting the bankrupt a release and freeing him from the status of bankruptcy. He may continue liable to disabilities in respect of holding public office for five years after discharge unless he is also granted a certificate of misfortune. Discharge may be obtained either under the Bankruptcy Act 1914, s. 26 as amended by the Bankruptcy (Amendment) Act 1926 or automatically or on the application of the Official Receiver under the Insolvency Act 1976, ss. 7 and 8.

Under the Bankruptcy Acts a bankrupt may apply at any time after adjudication for discharge. The application must be heard in open court after the conclusion of the public examination. The trustee in bankruptcy, the Official Receiver and the creditors may all oppose discharge. The court will take account of a report by the Official Receiver and has a discretion to grant or refuse a discharge. This may be absolute and unconditional or conditional, in being subject to conditions as to future income or after-acquired property or suspensive, in being stayed for a period of time, or both conditional and suspensive.

Where the bankrupt has committed a bankruptcy offence or any other offence connected with his bankruptcy or where any of the twelve facts mentioned below are proved the court cannot grant an unconditional discharge but must either refuse a discharge, suspend it for a period, suspend it until the bankrupt has paid 50p in the £ or grant it subject to the bankrupt consenting to judgment being entered against him for any part of the provable debts, the judgment to be satisfied out of future earnings or after-acquired property. The court may also impose any other conditions it could under its general powers.

The twelve facts requiring the refusal of an immediate unconditional discharge are:

1. The assets are not equal to 50p in the £ unless the bankrupt is not responsible for this.
2. Proper account books have not been kept for the three years before the bankruptcy.
3. The debtor continued to trade knowing he was insolvent.
4. He contracted a debt provable in bankruptcy without any reasonable expectation (which he must prove) of being able to pay it.
5. He fails to explain satisfactorily any loss or deficiency of assets.
6. He contributed to his bankruptcy by rash speculations, unjustifiable extravagance, gambling or culpable neglect of business.
7. He has put creditors to unnecessary expense by a frivolous defence to an action brought against him.
8. He contributed to his bankruptcy by bringing a frivolous action.
9. Within three months before the receiving order when unable to pay his debts as they fell due he gave an undue preference to any creditor.
10. Within three months before the receiving order he incurred liabilities to make his assets equal to 50p in the £.
11. He has on a previous occasion been bankrupted or made a composition or arrangement with creditors (*see* COMPOSITION OR SCHEME).
12. He has been guilty of fraud or a fraudulent breach of trust.

The Bankruptcy Act 1914, s. 27 provides that the making of an ante-nuptial settlement which is unjustifiable having regard to the state of the settlor's affairs when it was made or the making of any covenant on marriage to settle after-acquired property on his wife or children when the settlement or covenant was made to defeat or delay creditors, is equivalent to fraud for the purposes of the rules relating to discharge.

Two further methods of discharge are available under the Insolvency Act 1976. Under s. 7 if the court makes an order that the public examination is concluded or may be dispensed with it may also make an order that the debtor is in any event to be discharged five years after adjudication. This order may be rescinded on the application of the Official Receiver or the trustee before the expiry of the five years. This is 'automatic' discharge. Section 8 provides for discharge on the application of the Official Receiver when the debtor has not applied for discharge and the adjudication has not been annulled and no order for automatic discharge was made or, if made, has been rescinded. The application must be made in the sixth year after adjudication and the court may grant the application unconditionally, conditionally or suspensively or refuse it. Suspension may be for a period or until the debtor pays a dividend of not less than 50p in the £. It may be a condition that the bankrupt submit to judgment for any balance not satisfied at discharge, the balance to be paid out of future earnings or after-acquired property.

The effect of discharge is to release the bankrupt (but not his partner or co-trustee or surety) from every debt provable in bankruptcy (*see* PROOF OF DEBTS) except:

1. A debt on a recognisance or due to the Crown or for a revenue offence or on a bail bond. He may, however, be discharged if the Treasury consents in writing.
2. A debt resulting from fraud or a fraudulent breach of trust.
3. Liabilities under an affiliation order except to such extent as the court expressly orders.

After discharge the bankrupt is still under a duty to assist the trustee in the realisation and distribution of property and may be committed for contempt if he fails to do so.

Disclaimer of onerous property. This is a notification by a trustee in bankruptcy of his refusal to accept the ownership of onerous property. It may be land burdened with onerous covenants, shares or stock in companies, unprofitable contracts or any other property that is not saleable or readily saleable because it binds its possessor to the performance of an onerous act, or the payment of money.

A disclaimer must be in writing and signed by the trustee. It need not be by deed. It must take place within twelve months after the appointment of the trustee or, if he does not know of the property within that year, then within twelve months of his acquiring that knowledge. If the property consists of leaseholds the trustee must obtain leave of the court, unless there is an order for summary administration†, or the trustee serves the lessor with notice of intent to disclaim and the lessor does not within seven days require the matter to be brought before the court or where the property has been sub-let or mortgaged the trustee serves the lessor and sub-lessee or mortgagee with notice of intent to disclaim and none within fourteen days require the matter to be brought before the court.

A person interested in property or a contract may make written application to the trustee, requiring him to decide whether he will disclaim or not. If the trustee does not do so within twenty-eight days the right is lost and he becomes personally liable for the property or is regarded as having adopted the contract.

The effect of the disclaimer is to release the bankrupt and the estate from any liability in respect of the property from the date of the disclaimer and to discharge the trustee from personal liability, notwithstanding any previous acts of ownership but will not release the trustee from liability to pay rates for any period of voluntary occupation of property.

Persons who suffer loss as a result of the disclaimer may, if they have an interest in disclaimed property, apply to the court for an order vesting it in themselves. If the person is an underlessee or mortgagee of a lease the order will make that person either subject to the bankrupt's liabilities in respect of the property or subject to the liabilities of an assignee of the bankrupt's interest. If the underlessee or mortgagee declines to take a vesting order on the terms offered by the court they are to be excluded from all interest in the property. In any case, a loss caused by the disclaimer is a provable debt.

Any person who is, against the trustee, entitled to the benefit or subject to the burden of a contract with the bankrupt may apply to the court for its rescission and the court may rescind on terms it thinks equitable. Damages may be awarded to or against either party, and may be a provable debt for the person making the application.

(See the Bankruptcy Act 1914, s. 54).

Discount. Transferring a negotiable instrument for immediate payment of less than its face value to a discounter who may hold it until maturity.

Dishonour by non-acceptance. The Bills of Exchange Act 1882, s. 43 provides that a bill of exchange is dishonoured by non-acceptance when there is proper presentment for acceptance and acceptance is refused or cannot be obtained or when presentment for acceptance is excused and the bill is not accepted. Subject to the Act when a bill is dishonoured by non-acceptance the holder has an immediate right of recourse against the drawer and indorsers and it is not necessary for him to make presentment for payment. By s. 44 a holder may refuse a qualified acceptance and treat the bill as dishonoured.

Dishonour by non-payment. The Bills of Exchange Act 1882, s. 47 provides that a bill of exchange is dishonoured by non-payment when there is proper presentment for payment and payment is refused or cannot be obtained or presentment for payment is excused and the bill is overdue (*see* MATURITY) and unpaid. Subject to the Act, when an instrument is dishonoured by non-payment the holder has an immediate right of recourse against the drawer and indorsers. (See also the Bills of Exchange Act 1882, s. 89 applying this to a promissory note.)

Disposal of Uncollected Goods Act 1952. This, now repealed and replaced by the Torts (Interference with Goods) Act 1977 gave certain bailees (*see* BAILMENT) a right, subject to conditions, to sell goods not collected by the bailor.

Distribution of property amongst creditors (Bankruptcy). The duty of the trustee in bankruptcy is to pay certain costs and charges and then, after he has investigated and admitted proof of debts from creditors, to pay them in accordance with certain priorities laid down by law.

The Bankruptcy Rules 1952, r. 115 provide that assets remaining after paying the proper expenses of preserving, realising and getting in the debtor's assets shall, subject to any order of the court, be applied to paying first various costs and charges in accordance with their priority in the list. Each head is to be paid in full before anything is paid on a succeeding head. Heads include the actual expenses of the Official Receiver, petitioning creditor's deposit, remuneration of the special manager, an allowance made to the debtor by the Official Receiver, disbursements by the trustee in bankruptcy, allowance to the debtor by the trustee, and the trustee's remuneration.

The trustee must then pay certain categories of preferential debts. Thus claims against officers of savings banks under the Trustee Savings Bank Act 1969, s. 72 and against officers of friendly societies under the Friendly Societies Act 1974, s 59 are to be paid in priority to all other debts. So also under the Bankruptcy Act 1914, s. 130 (6) are the funeral expenses of a deceased debtor when the estate is subject to administration in bankruptcy. Similar provision is made by the Deeds of Arrangement Act 1914, s. 21 for the expenses of a trustee of such a deed which is avoided by the bankruptcy of the debtor. These are sometimes called pre-preferential debts. Thereafter come certain preferential debts specified in the Bankruptcy Act 1914, s. 33 (1). They include rates for the year before the receiving order, a year's assessed taxes and the wages or salary of any clerk or servant, workman or labourer not exceeding £800 for services within four months before the order. This latter includes various payments under Employment Protection (Consolidation) Act 1978, ss. 121–127 such as guarantee payments, medical suspension payments, payment for time off for union duties and for seeking work and protective award payments. The Insolvency Act 1976 raised the amount to £800. Lenders of money to pay salaries or wages do not themselves become preferred creditors if the money is so used, contrary to the position in company winding up. The Employment Protection (Consolidation) Act 1978 provides that employees may claim against the Secretary of State who is subrogated to their claims against the debtor. Accrued holiday remuneration is also included. Social security, pension contributions and redundancy fund contributions payable during the year before the receiving order are also preferential. Preferential debts rank equally between themselves and must be paid in full unless the assets are insufficient, when they are to abate in equal proportions. No composition† or scheme will be approved by the court which does not provide for payment in priority of these debts.

A landlord has no priority for rent over other creditors unless he has distrained. If he distrains within three months before the bankruptcy he must pay the preferential creditors out of the proceeds. If he thus suffers loss, he acquires the same priority as those he has paid. If he distrains after the commencement of the bankruptcy he can do so for six months' rent accrued prior to adjudication and distress is not available for rent payable after the date of the distress. If he does not recover the full rent he can prove as an ordinary creditor. If the trustee remains in possession without making a disclaimer of onerous property the landlord may distrain for rent due after adjudication. A landlord may take action for possession following forfeiture of the lease for non-payment of rent without leave.

If there have been mutual debts, credits or dealings between the bankrupt and a creditor a balance must be struck and that only claimed or paid but a creditor cannot claim the benefit of any set-off when he had notice of an available act of bankruptcy when he gave credit. These rules cannot be excluded by agreement.

A secured creditor may either rely on his security and not prove or surrender his security and prove for the whole debt or realise it and prove for any deficit or assess its value and prove for any deficit. In this last case the trustee may redeem the security at the assessed value or the creditor may require him to elect to redeem within six months. The trustee if dissatisfied with the valuation may demand a sale and the creditor may with leave of the court amend the valuation. If a creditor omits to state in his proof that he is secured, the security must be surrendered to the trustee for the benefit of creditors unless the court allows amendment. A secured creditor is one who holds a mortgage, charge or lien on the property of the debtor. It does not include one secured by guarantee or by a security over the property of a third person.

All ordinary debts proved in the bankruptcy are payable pari passu but there are six types of deferred or postponed debts which are only paid when all other creditors have been paid in full. These include claims by moneylenders and other creditors to interest in excess of five per cent, debts within s. 3 of the Partnership Act 1890 such as loans at interest varying with profits, money lent by a spouse for use in the other's business, claims by trustees of settlements avoided by a trustee in bankruptcy (*see* SETTLEMENTS VOIDABLE IN BANKRUPTCY) and claims by joint creditors of an insolvent partner which are postponed until claims by separate creditors have been paid.

After all debts within s. 33 of the Bankruptcy Act 1914 have been paid any surplus is first to be applied in paying four per cent interest on the debts. The claim of the trustee of an avoided settlement is not, but deferred interest is, a debt for this purpose. If after all costs, expenses and debts have been paid in full with interest there is any surplus s. 69 provides that that surplus is to go to the bankrupt.

The estate of the bankrupt is distributed to creditors as dividends. There may be one or more dividends and the timetable in the Act and the Rules may be varied. Due notice must be given. In a small bankruptcy with summary administration there should, if possible, be only one dividend paid within six months. A trustee may not be sued for a dividend but the court may order him to make payment.

(See also the Bankruptcy Act 1914, ss. 30–35 and ss. 62–69; Sch. II, rr. 10–18; Bankruptcy (Amendment) Act 1926, s. 11).

Dividend warrant. This normally takes the form of a cheque drawn by a company in favour of a shareholder. It has been queried whether the expression as used in the Bills of Exchange Act 1882, s. 95 (allowing crossing†) and s. 97 (saving special custom) also covers interest warrants, whether for interest on Government securities or company debentures, but in *Slingsby v Westminster Bank* [1931] 1 KB 173 it was said it did. The statutory protection for the collecting banker in s. 4 of the Cheques Act 1957 and its extension to crossing by s. 5 are sufficiently wide to include interest warrants for the payment of interest on Government and other securities and s. 97 of the 1882 Act does preserve a custom relating to dividend warrants under which only one of several payees may indorse. (*See* INDORSEMENT). It is not clear whether this custom applies to interest warrants.

Documentary credit. *See* BANKERS' COMMERCIAL CREDITS.

Documents of title. The Factors Act 1889, s. 1 (4) provides that this 'shall include any bill of lading, dock warrant, warehousekeeper's certificate, and warrant or order for the delivery of goods and any other document used in the ordinary course of business as proof of the possession and control of goods, or authorising or purporting to authorise, either by endorsement or delivery, the possessor of the document to transfer or receive goods thereby represented'. The most important example is the bill of lading. Transfer of such documents with the appropriate intent will transfer possession and ownership of the goods they represent. In c.i.f. contracts 'delivery' is constituted by delivery of the documents. (*See* DELIVERY IN SALE OF GOODS). An air way bill†, and a mate's receipt† are not documents of title. Documents of title are not in general bills of sale, being excluded from that category by the Bills of Sale Act 1878. A car log book is not a document of title, *Beverley v Oakley* [1982] RTR 417.

Domestic arbitration agreement. *See* ARBITRATION: APPEAL ON LAW AND PRELIMINARY POINT OF LAW and ARBITRATION, FOREIGN AND CONVENTION AWARDS.

Drawee. In a bill of exchange or cheque the party to whom the order to make payment is addressed. By the Bills of Exchange Act 1882, s. 6 the drawee must be named or indicated with reasonable certainty and a bill may be addressed to two or more drawees, whether they are partners or not, but not to two drawees in the alternative or to two or more in succession. By acceptance the drawee may become the acceptor and hence the party primarily liable on the bill. Only the drawee may accept except in acceptance for honour supra protest. A cheque is in practice never accepted by the drawee bank, *Bank of Baroda v Punjab National Bank* [1944] AC 176, hence the drawer remains the person primarily liable on a cheque. The acceptance of a bearer cheque would be an infringement of the Bank Charter Act 1844, ss. 11 and 28. By the Bills of Exchange Act 1882, s. 5 (2) when the drawer and drawee are the same person (as in a bankers' draft) or where the drawee is a fictitious person or a person not having capacity to contract (e.g. a minor), the holder may treat the instrument either as a bill of exchange or as a promissory note. There is no authority on a fictitious drawee but on analogy with a fictitious or non-existing person as payee it would seem to cover a case where the drawer did not intend the named drawee to make payment. By s. 41 (2) presentment for acceptance is excused when the drawee is fictitious or lacks capacity to contract by bill, by s. 46 (2) presentment for payment is excused when the drawee is fictitious, and by s. 50 (2) notice of dishonour need not be given to the drawer where drawer and drawee are the same person or where the drawee is fictitious or lacks capacity to contract and need not be given to an indorser when the drawee is fictitious or lacks capacity to contract and the indorser knew this when he indorsed the bill. By s. 53

it is provided that in England and Wales, as distinct from Scotland, a bill of exchange does not operate as an assignment of funds which are in the hands of the drawee to pay the bill and, therefore, a drawee who does not accept a bill is not liable on it.

Drawer. For a bill of exchange this is the party who draws up or formulates the unconditional order which is an essential feature of a bill. Unless a drawer takes advantage of the Bills of Exchange Act 1882, s. 16 to add stipulations negativing or limiting his liability (e.g. 'without recourse', 'sans recours') he is, in effect, a guarantor of the party from whom payment is primarily expected, the drawee or acceptor, and the holder of the bill has a right of recourse against the drawer to enforce this, provided the proper steps of notice of dishonour are taken when dishonour by non-acceptance or dishonour by non-payment occur. By s. 57 (1) the holder may recover from the drawer who, in turn, may recover against the acceptor when there is one. By s. 55 the drawer of a bill impliedly undertakes by drawing it that on proper presentment it shall be accepted and paid according to its terms and that he will compensate the holder and any indorser who is compelled to pay it provided the necessary steps on dishonour have been taken and is precluded from denying to a holder in due course the existence of the payee and his capacity at that time to give an indorsement. By s. 5 a bill may be drawn payable to or to the order of the drawer or to or to the order of the drawee. Where drawer and drawee are the same person, as in bankers' drafts, the holder may, as he chooses, treat the instrument as either a bill or as a promissory note.

Duress. As a vitiating factor in contract this means the use or threat of the use of unlawful force, either tortious or criminal, to procure a contract, certainly rendering it voidable and perhaps void. Duress of goods does not suffice for this. Duress is limited in scope and the use of improper pressure in procuring a contract more frequently falls within the wider equitable doctrine of undue influence.

E

E.C.G.D. *See* EXPORT CREDIT GUARANTEES.

E.E.C. Competition Law. Article 85 of the Treaty of Rome (which by the European Communities Act 1972 is part of English law) prohibits all agreements, decisions and concerted practices of undertakings which may affect trade between member States and which are intended to or do distort competition within the Common Market. The Article refers in particular to the fixing of prices and trading conditions, limits on production, markets, technical development and investment, the sharing of markets or supplies, the application of dissimilar terms to similar transactions placing traders at a competitive disadvantage and the addition of supplementary obligations to contracts which have no connection with the subject of the contract. Any prohibited agreements or decisions are automatically void. The prohibition may be declared not applicable to agreements, decisions or categories of them between undertakings or concerted practices which improve the production and distribution of goods or promote technical or economic progress, whilst allowing consumers a fair share of the benefits, and which do not impose unnecessary restrictions or facilitate the elimination of competition in respect of a substantial part of the products. Article 86 prohibits abuse by one or more undertakings of 'a dominant position within the Common Market' in so far as it affects trade between member States. This Article also refers to the particular types of restrictive practices specified in Article 85 (1).

Agreements, decisions and practices within Article 85 (1) must be notified to the Commission. There is no need to notify (a) agreements to which only undertakings within one member State are parties and which do not affect imports or exports, (b) agreements to which only two undertakings are parties and which restrict resale prices or patents, designs, trade marks and similar industrial property rights, (c) standardization and joint research agreements.

The Commission has wide investigatory powers. A party who wishes to be certain that an agreement is not prohibited may obtain a 'negative clearance' from the Commission.

The Commission has used powers under Article 85 to grant block exemptions to certain categories of agreements. These include exclusive agency agreements, exclusive dealing agreements, co-operation agreements, specialisation agreements and agreements of minor importance. To be valid a restrictive practice must satisfy both EEC and municipal legislation. The Restrictive Trade Practices Act 1976, s. 5 makes it clear that English law prohibiting restrictive trade practices continues to apply in principle notwithstanding that an agreement may be exempt under EEC law, but in order to avoid conflict the Restrictive Practices Court† may decline or postpone the exercise of its powers having regard to Article 85 or exemptions granted under it and by s. 21 the Director-General of Fair Trading may similarly refrain from taking proceedings. (*See also* AGENCY, CONTRACT, REGISTERED DESIGNS, PATENTS, TRADE MARKS, RESALE PRICE MAINTENANCE for English law on these topics.)

Emblements. Crops produced by annual labour, e.g. potatoes, cabbages, as distinct from the perennial produce, e.g. trees. Emblements are sometimes also called fructus industriales and are always goods†, whether sold severed or to be severed from the ground and whether or not they are to grow further after sale. Perennial produce if sold standing so as to gain further growth after sale may be both goods for the purposes of the Sale of Goods Act as being 'things forming part of the land which are agreed to be severed . . . under the contract of sale' and an interest in land coming under the evidential requirements of s. 40 of the Law of Property Act 1925, *Marshall v Green* (1875) 1 CPD 35. There are special rules for hops, where each successive crop is fructus industriales and other crops which take a year to mature and then last for a number of seasons. The first crop is emblements.

Employment and indemnity clause. *See* TIME CHARTERPARTY.

Entire contract. *See* DISCHARGE OF CONTRACT BY PERFORMANCE and DISCHARGE OF CONTRACT BY BREACH.

Equitable estoppel. Once used as an alternative description for promissory estoppel or the rule in *Hightrees House*. It is no longer so used since it was pointed out in *Re Vandervells Trust* [1974] Ch 269, (rvsd. on other grounds), ibid. that estoppel in equity included both promissory and proprietary estoppel, though in *Crabb v Arun D.C.* [1976] Ch 179 this further distinction was not thought helpful.

Equitable lien. A form of real security created by equity giving a right to have specific property allocated to the payment of specific liabilities, and, unlike the common law or possessory lien not dependent on the party entitled to the lien having possession of the property subject to the lien. The term is normally used of rights arising by operation of law rather than by specific agreement, the latter being known as charges. Instances of equitable liens are that of the unpaid vendor of land who has allowed the purchaser to go into possession, that of the purchaser of land who has paid the price but not received possession and the right of a partner on dissolution to have the firm's assets applied in payment of its liabilities. The holder may enforce the security by applying to the court for equitable remedies such as an offer for sale or appointment of a receiver.

Equities. In regard to negotiable instruments and assignment of contract this means defects in a transferor's title. *See* SUBJECT TO EQUITIES.

Equity. A body of judge-made law originally developed by the Lord Chancellor in the Court of Chancery to supplement and correct the original common law. This it did by enforcing new rights, e.g. uses and trusts, developing new remedies, e.g. specific performance and injunctions and creating new procedures, e.g. discovery. Until the Restoration equity was a relatively flexible amelioration of the common law, but thereafter it developed into a body of rules, almost, if not quite, as technical as the common law, though some of its original flexibility remained in the broad principle that equitable remedies are discretionary. This dicretion does not give wide freedom to judges granting these remedies but must be exercised in accordance with guiding precedents whose general effects have since the eighteenth century been summed up in a number of maxims of equity such as 'equity looks to substance not form', 'where the equities are equal the law prevails,' 'he who seeks equity must do equity', 'he who comes to equity must come with clean hands', 'delay defeats equity' and 'equity does nothing in vain'. Since the seventeenth century in the event of conflict equity prevails over common law. Since the Judicature Acts 1873–75 all courts grant all common law and equitable remedies required by the case before them but, though this is referred to as 'the fusion of law and equity' the better opinion has been that it was a fusion of courts and administration rather than of the substantive bodies of rules since equitable remedies continue to be granted on a discretionary basis which differs from the common law. The traditions and specialisms of the Court of Chancery are now represented by the Chancery Division of the High Court of Justice. Since the Court of Chancery acquired a dominant role in property law certain areas of law relating to commerce now fall within the sphere of the Division such as company law and partnership, bankruptcy and patents (there is a Patents Court within the Division).

Estate agents. Agents who advertise and negotiate the sale and letting of land and houses. Normally an estate agent is not obliged to take any steps to dispose of property but is entitled to commission on its sale, *Luxor v Cooper* [1941] AC 108. He is not entitled to the ordinary indemnity of an agent since his commission is regarded as covering his expenses. Since in the lengthy process of negotiating the sale of land or houses their client-principals may decide to withdraw and so prevent them earning commission, estate agents have devised many formulae intended to entitle them to commission on some event earlier than the execution of a binding contract of sale. Whilst this can be done by clear and unequivocal language the courts presume strongly that commission is only payable on a concluded sale. If an agent is appointed 'sole agent' he will be entitled to payment if another agent sells but not if the principal sells himself, *Bentall, Horsley & Baldry v Vicary* [1931] 1 KB 253, but if the agent is given 'the sole right to sell' he can claim even if the principal sells. An estate agent does not have implied authority to accept deposit money on behalf of the vendor, *Sorrell v Finch* [1977] AC 728. The Estate Agents Act 1979 makes provision for the regulation of the profession.

Estoppel. A rule of evidence by which a party is precluded in the case of common law estoppel from departing from some allegation of fact which he made to the other party and upon which the other party acted to his detriment and in the case of promissory estoppel (sometimes called equitable estoppel) is precluded from resiling, perhaps temporarily, from some promise, even without consideration, made to the other. The representor or promisor must intend the other to rely on his declaration. The principle of estoppel underlies certain rules governing exceptions to nemo dat quod non habet and ostensible or apparent authority of an agent.

European Patent Convention. *See* INTELLECTUAL PROPERTY, INTERNATIONAL PROTECTION and PATENTS, APPLICATIONS FOR.

Exchange control. Legislation, principally the Exchange Control Act 1947, which sought to protect the economy by restricting a variety of financial dealings with an international element. These controls were withdrawn in October 1979.

Execution creditors (Bankruptcy). When execution has issued against the land, goods or debts of a bankrupt the execution creditor is not entitled to retain the 'benefit of the execution or attachment' unless it is completed by either the seizure and sale of goods or seizure or appointment of a receiver over the land or the receipt of the debt. This completion must take place before the receiving order and before the execution creditor has notice of a petition or available act of bankruptcy. In relation to goods 'the benefit of the execution' refers to the charge on the goods acquired by issue of the writ and not any money actually received by the creditor in satisfaction of his debt. Moreover if before sale or completion of an execution notice is served on the sheriff that a receiving order has been made against the debtor, the sheriff must on request hand over the goods and any money received in partial satisfaction to the trustee in bankruptcy or the Official Receiver.

When the sheriff seizes goods for a judgment of more than £250, he must deduct expenses and keep the balance for fourteen days; if during that time he has notice of a bankruptcy petition and a receiving order is made upon it or any other petition of which the sheriff has notice he must pay the balance to the Official Receiver or trustee who are entitled as against the execution creditor.

Exempt agreement. The Consumer Credit Act 1974, s. 16, provides that this includes certain consumer credit agreements made by building societies, local authorities, and, if specified by statutory instrument, insurance companies, friendly societies, employers' or workers' organisations, charities, land improvement companies and certain other corporate bodies and secured on land. It also includes agreements in which the number of payments or the charge for credit does not exceed a number or rate fixed by statutory instrument or agreements connected with countries outside the United Kingdom if specified by statutory instrument. Similarly hiring agreements for gas, water, electricity meters and post office equipment may be exempted. Since exempt agreements are not regulated as consumer credit agreements, s. 8, nor consumer hire agreements, s. 15, they escape almost all control by the Act except judicial control relating to extortionate credit bargains. Small agreements within s. 17 and non-commercial agreements within s. 189 enjoy certain partial exemption and under s. 74 bank overdrafts may be exempted from most of the requirements as to formalities.

Exemption and exclusion clauses. Clauses, often found in standard form contracts, designed to exclude or exempt a party from liability he would otherwise incur for non-fulfilment of the undertakings of a contract. The courts sought to restrict their operation by various means. In the ticket† cases reasonable notice of the terms is required if they are to be incorporated by a notice or unsigned document. Any misrepresentation as to the scope of clauses will also prevent their operation, *Curtis v Chemical Cleaning* [1951] 1 KB 805. Under the contra proferentem rule the language of such clauses is interpreted strictly against a party relying on them. At one time the devices of 'fundamental breach' or 'breach of a fundamental term' were regarded as rules of law that exemption clauses were inoperative when there was serious departure from the basic obligations of the contract but the House of Lords in *Suisse Atlantique* [1967] 1 AC 371 and in *Photo Productions v Securicor* [1980] 2 All ER 556 held that there was merely a rule of construction that exemption clauses should be interpreted as normally intended not to apply to such breaches but that a sufficiently widely drawn clause could even then give protection.

Exemption clauses may not exclude liability for fraud, *Pearson v Dublin Corporation* [1907] AC 351, and the Misrepresentation Act 1967, s. 3 (as amended by the Unfair Contract Terms Act 1977, s. 8) subjects to a requirement of reasonableness clauses seeking to restrict liability or remedies for misrepresentation prior to a contract. Many statutes nullified exclusion clauses in particular classes of contract. The complex provisions of the Unfair Contract Terms Act 1977 more generally deprives certain classes of exemption clause of all effect and subjects others to a requirement of reasonableness if they are to be operative. (*See* UNFAIR CONTRACT TERMS ACT 1977). Delegated legislation made in 1976 under the Fair Trading Act 1973, Part II, prohibits the inclusion of void exemption and exclusion clauses, lest they discourage parties from asserting their rights. A clause which limits liability will not be construed as strictly as one which excludes it: *Ailsa Craig v Malvern* [1983] 1 All ER 101. Some exemption clauses are regarded by the courts as indicating the party who is to insure against loss, hence a stevedore, who might appear to have been debarred by the rules of privity† from relying on such clauses in a contract of carriage by sea has been held entitled to do so by a collateral contract; *New Zealand Shipping v Satterthwaite* [1975] AC 154.

Existing goods. The Sale of Goods Act 1979, s. 5 (1) defines these as 'goods† owned or possessed by the seller' and contrasts them with future goods†.

Export credit guarantees. These are arrangements provided by a Government department (export credit guarantee department— E.C.G.D.) to insure exporters against certain commercial and political risks of non-payment. They do not cover risks which can be covered by ordinary commercial insurance.

Export–import licences in sale of goods. In the absence of agreement by the parties it is the duty of the buyer to obtain licences in ex works contracts. In ex ship contracts it is for the buyer to obtain an import licence and for the seller to obtain an export licence. The same is only presumptively the case in f.o.b. and c.i.f. contracts, *Pound v Hardy* [1956] AC 588. If the duty to obtain the licence is absolute a party who fails to obtain it will be in breach of contract but if the duty is merely to use his best endeavours and his best efforts fail then the contract is discharged by frustration. Frequently the matter is covered by a force majeure clause.

Ex ship contracts. A form of sale of goods used in overseas trade. 'The seller has to cause delivery to be made to the buyer from a ship which has arrived at the port of delivery and has reached a place therein, which is usual for delivery of goods of the kind in question. The seller has, therefore, to pay the freight, or otherwise to release the shipowner's lien and to furnish the buyer with an effectual direction to the ship to deliver. Till this is done the buyer is not bound to pay for the goods.' *Yangtze Insurance Association v Lukmanjee* [1918] AC 585 at 589. The buyer is in no way concerned with the shipping of the goods, shipping documents do not represent the goods as in c.i.f. contracts and the seller must deliver the actual goods. The Sale of Goods Act 1979, s. 32 which makes delivery to a carrier prima facie delivery to the buyer, which requires the seller to make a proper contract on behalf of the buyer and requires notice in some cases to the buyer to enable him to insure has no application to ex ship contracts. Property† and risk† pass to the buyer on delivery to him. Even though a contract is described as a c.i.f. contract it may be found to be an ex ship contract if its terms are in accord with the latter type, *Comptoir D'Achat v Luis de Ridder, The Julia* [1949] AC 293. Ex ship contracts are also termed 'arrival contracts'.

Extortionate credit bargains. The Consumer Credit Act 1974, s. 137 provides that a court may re-open such a bargain to do justice. This may be done on application by the debtor or surety or at the instance of the debtor or surety in proceedings to enforce the agreement or in other proceedings where the amount is relevant. The power exists in respect of credit agreements as defined in s. 137. Thus it does not apply to a consumer hire agreement but does apply to all consumer credit agreements even though they are small agreements or exempt agreements. By s. 138 a bargain is extortionate if it requires the debtor or a relative to make payments (whether unconditionally or not) which are grossly exorbitant or otherwise grossly contravenes the ordinary principles of fair dealing. The court must take into account prevailing interest rates, age, experience, business capacity, financial pressure and its nature in regard to the debtor and in regard to the creditor, the degree of risk, taking account of any security, his relationship to the debtor and whether or not a colourable cash price was quoted for goods or services. The court may also consider in relation to a linked† transaction how far it was required for the protection of debtor or creditor. The court may also take account of associated transactions. By s. 139 an order re-opening the transaction to relieve a debtor or surety of any sum in excess of that fairly and reasonably due may not alter the effect of any judgment but may direct accounts to be taken, set aside in whole or part any obligation on debtor or surety, require the creditor to repay in whole or part any sum paid under the bargain or a related agreement by the debtor or surety, whether to the creditor or to another, direct the return to the surety of any property provided as security or alter the terms of the credit agreement or any security instrument.

Ex turpi causa non oritur actio. 'Out of an evil cause no action arises'. This maxim embodies the rules that no action can be brought on a contract tainted with illegality (*see* ILLEGALITY IN CONTRACT), and that in tort one tortfeasor cannot sue for harm inherently associated with an illegal joint enterprise, *N.C.B. v England* [1954] AC 403; *Ashton v Turner* [1981] 1 QB 137.

Ex works. A form of sale of goods where the buyer takes delivery† at the seller's works, factory or warehouse. Usually property† and risk† will pass at delivery† since the goods will often be unascertained goods only ascertained at delivery but if goods were appropriated to the contract before delivery then these might pass earlier as they might do in the sale of specific goods. (*See* PASSING OF PROPERTY).

F

Factors. In older cases agents for the sale of goods who were given possession of the goods. (*See* BROKERS.) Nowadays the term is also applied to firms who purchase and collect book† debts. The Factors Act 1889, though using the term 'factor' in its title, in fact applies to a specially defined class of mercantile agents.

Factors Act 1889. Placing goods† in the possession of another does not of itself give him apparent authority to sell them. Placing them in the hands of a trading agent might be enough for sale, *Pickering v Busk* (1812) 15 East 38, but not for apparent authority to pledge or otherwise dispose of them. As this raised problems in overseas trade, legislation was passed, in part declaratory of the common law, culminating in the Factors Act 1889, to the effect that if goods or documents of title to them, were with the consent of the owner in the possession of a mercantile agent any sale, pledge or other disposition made by him when acting in the ordinary course of business of a mercantile agent was to be as valid as if the agent were expressly authorised by the owner, provided the other party was acting in good faith and without notice. A mercantile agent is defined as one 'having in the customary course of his business as such agent authority either to sell goods or to consign goods for the purposes of sale, or to buy goods or to raise money on the security of goods' (Factors Act 1889, s. 1 (1); Sale of Goods Act 1979, s. 26). Although a person can be a mercantile agent for one transaction only, or have one principal only, *Lowther v Harris* [1927] 1 KB 393, it must be in the 'customary course' of the type of agency he is conducting to do one of the four matters specified in the definition, hence if he is a servant, shop assistant, carrier, warehouseman or merely acting as a friend of the owner of the goods to make enquiries, *Budberg v Jerwood* (1934) 51 TLR 99, he will not be a mercantile agent. It may be difficult to distinguish a mercantile agent from a buyer on sale or return, *Weiner v Harris* [1910] 1 KB 285; *Weiner v Gill* [1906] 2 KB 574, but important, because in the case of the buyer the contract between the seller and buyer on sale or return may preclude the third party obtaining title whereas this will not be so with the agent. In *Weiner v Harris* the so-called buyer could never obtain property† in the goods hence he was held to be an agent, in contrast to *Weiner v Gill*. The fact that the agent also has an independent business will not prevent him being a mercantile agent,

Weiner v Harris, but if the goods came into his possession before he became a mercantile agent his later agency will not bring him within the Factors Act unless the owner consents afresh to his holding the goods in his new character, *Heap v Motorists Advisory Agency* [1923] 1 KB 577. The agent must have possession of the goods as mercantile agent not as a bailee (e.g. hire purchaser, borrower), *Staffs Motor v British Wagon* [1934] 2 KB 305; *Astley v Miller* [1968] 2 All ER 36. The owner of the goods may himself be the agent as in *Lloyds Bank v Bank of America* [1938] 2 KB 147 where the plaintiffs released pledged documents of title to the owner, a mercantile agent, who dishonestly pledged them to the defendants. Held that when rights of ownership were divided between two or more persons consent to the possession of the agent might be given, as it was here, by both or all of these persons, including the agent himself. Goods may be in the possession of the agent with the consent of the owner even if the agent had been guilty of criminal dishonesty in obtaining possession, *Folkes v King* [1923] 1 KB 282; *Pearson v Rose & Young* [1951] 1 KB 275. Consent is presumed, s. 2 (4). The disposition to the third party must be in the ordinary course of business of a mercantile agent, not necessarily of the particular type of agent in question. In *Oppenheimer v Attenborough* [1908] 1 KB 221 the plaintiff diamond merchant handed diamonds to the broker agent to show possible buyers. The agent dishonestly pledged the gems, evidence being given that it was not customary in the diamond trade for brokers to pledge stones. Held this was still in the ordinary course of business which required that the transaction should be in 'business hours, at a proper place of business and in other respects in the ordinary way in which a mercantile agent would act, so that there is nothing to lead the [third party] to believe that anything is being done wrong . . .' The third party must prove that he acted in good faith and without notice of the agent's lack of authority. Notice appears to mean actual knowledge, but such knowledge may be inferred from the circumstances of the case as when goods are pledged at an unusual rate of interest, *Janesich v Attenborough* (1910) 102 LT 605.

The withdrawal of the owner's consent to possession is not to affect bona fide third parties acting without knowing of it. A pledge of documents of title is a pledge of the goods they cover. When a mercantile agent pledges goods or documents for an antecedent debt the pledgee acquires no rights other than those the agent already had to the goods or documents. The consideration given by a third party may be cash, negotiable instruments or other goods or documents or consideration but when goods are pledged by an agent for a consideration other than cash the pledgee acquires no greater rights than the value of the consideration. Mercantile agents may act through clerks and other intermediaries. Sections 8 and 9 of the 1889

Act governing sales by sellers remaining in possession and buyers who have obtained possession of goods cover almost the same ground as ss. 24 and 25 of the Sale of Goods Act 1979. (*See* NEMO DAT QUOD NON HABET) and s. 10 covers that covered by s. 47 (2) of the latter Act. (*See* UNPAID SELLER).

Fair Trading Act 1973. This Act was designed to promote freedom of competition and consumer protection. It created the office of Director-General of Fair Trading, transferred to it the functions of the Registrar of Restrictive Trade Practices and imposed on its holder many functions to achieve the ends of the Act. It also created the Consumer Protection Advisory Committee to report and recommend, renamed the Monopolies Commission as the Monopolies and Mergers Commission (*see* MONOPOLIES and MERGERS) and these and the law of restrictive trade practices were substantially amended and re-stated. Under Part II of the Act a Minister or the Director-General may, subject to certain restrictions, refer to the Consumer Protection Advisory Committee to report on the question whether a consumer trade practice adversely affects consumers in the United Kingdom and under s. 17 this may be done with a proposal that there should be a recommendation for prohibitory delegated legislation. This procedure was used in 1976 to prohibit the inclusion of void exemption and exclusion clauses in transactions lest they mislead parties as to their rights and in 1977 to prohibit advertisements which represented a trade sale to be a private sale so that a party might suppose that certain statutory implied terms in sale of goods were not incorporated. Under Part III when it appears to the Director that a person in carrying on business has persisted in conduct detrimental or unfair to consumers the Director is to attempt to obtain written assurances that he will desist. If these are refused or, if given, broken, the Director may apply to the Restrictive Practices Court† for a court order. Part IV deals with the functions of the Director and the Monopolies and Mergers Commission in regard to Monopolies Situations and Uncompetitive Practices. Part V deals with Mergers, Part VI with references to the Commission other than Monopoly and Mergers references, such as references relating to practices resulting from or supporting monopolies or which are uncompetitive and Part VII contains provisions relating to references to the Consumer Protection Advisory Committee or the Commission, covering procedure of investigations and matters relating to reports and their publication. Part VIII contains additional provisions relating to references to the Commission, commencing with a definition of 'public interest' and then providing for a wide range of procedural matters, many relating to reports. Parts IX and X amending the Restrictive Trade Practices Acts 1956 and 1968 and extending them to agreements for services have, with the exception of s. 94, transferring the functions of the Registrar of Restrictive Trade Practices to the Director-General, been repealed and re-enacted in the Restrictive Trade Practices Act 1976. Part XI provides for the regulation of pyramid selling and Part XII contains a number of supplementary provisions, many of a procedural nature.

F.A.S. contracts. (Free alongside ship). A form of sale of goods used in overseas trade. It names the port where the ship is to be loaded and is a variant of f.o.b. contracts in that it specifies an earlier point of delivery†. The seller is not party to the contract of carriage and the buyer arranges shipping. The seller must bear the expenses of putting the goods alongside the ship on the quay, within reach of the ship's tackle or so that land apparatus can load them. If the ship cannot moor the goods may have to be placed in lighters alongside. The expenses of loading are borne by the buyer but the seller may undertake the additional duty of ensuring the goods are loaded. Goods so sold are normally unascertained goods†. Property† and risk† will thus normally pass on unconditional appropriation to the contract (*see* PASSING OF PROPERTY), that is, when the goods are delivered alongside.

Fictitious or non-existing person in relation to bills of exchange. Many provisions of the Bills of Exchange Act 1882 make use of these concepts. Section 5 provides that where the drawee of a bill of exchange is fictitious the holder may treat the instrument as a bill of exchange or promissory note. Section 7 provides that where the payee is fictitious or non-existing the bill may be treated as a bearer bill. Section 41 excuses presentment for acceptance when the drawee is fictitious and s. 46 similarly excuses presentment for payment. These concepts have been most fully considered in relation to the fictitious payee. Any indorsement purporting to be made by such a payee must be a forged or unauthorised signature†. On general rules it would be a nullity and a holder of the instrument could not sue the drawer or acceptor since the forgery would break the chain of title. Since the instrument can be treated as payable to bearer the indorsement can be ignored and prior parties can be held liable. It has been held that a payee is fictitious or non-existing for this purpose when the creator of the instrument, usually the drawer, does not intend him to receive payment. This is so even though an existing person may bear the payee's name. As payee, the payee is fictitious, *Bank of England v Vagliano Bros* [1891] AC 107; *Clutton v Attenborough* [1897] AC 90. If, however, the creator of the instrument, usually the drawer, intends the payee to receive payment but is deceived as to the reasons for making payment the payee is not fictitious, the bill is not a bearer bill and a forged indorsement will break the chain of title, *Vinden v Hughes* [1905] 1 KB 795; *North & South Wales Bank v Macbeth* [1908] AC 137.

An alteration to the name of a real payee will not make him fictitious, *Goldman v Cox* (1924) 40 TLR 744. A fictitious person must be distinguished from a real person using an assumed name. Section 23 provides that where a person signs a bill in a trade or assumed name he is liable as if he had signed it in his own name.

Fieri facias. *See* FI. FA,

Fi. Fa. An abbreviation for fieri facias, a writ of execution used to enforce judgments. *See* WRITS OF EXECUTION AND SALE OF GOODS. The Sheriff is directed to seize enough of the execution debtor's goods to make up the amount specified in the writ.

First meeting of creditors (bankruptcy). The Bankruptcy Act 1914, s. 13 provides that as soon as may be after the making of a receiving order against a debtor a general meeting of his creditors (referred to in the Act as the first meeting of creditors) shall be held to consider whether a composition† or scheme of arrangement should be accepted or whether the creditors should pass a resolution upon which there may be an adjudication by the court. The first meeting is usually the most important and is often the last. The meeting may be adjourned or any particular question may be left to a later meeting. The debtor must attend to be examined and give information required by the meeting. If adjudication is resolved upon the meeting may appoint a trustee in bankruptcy and a committee of inspection. The Official Receiver or his nominee takes the chair at the first meeting but the chairman of subsequent meetings is elected by the meeting.

(*See* the Bankruptcy Act 1914, s. 13).

Fitness for purpose. The Sale of Goods Act 1979, s. 14 opens by providing that except for the two conditions as to merchantable quality and fitness for purpose implied in contracts for sale of goods by that section, terms implied by usage, terms implied by s. 15 in sale by sample and terms implied by any other enactment there is no implied term as to quality or fitness for purpose in sale of goods. The Sale of Goods Act 1893, s. 14 (1) implied a condition as to fitness for purpose but this was amended by the Supply of Goods (Implied Terms) Act 1973 in regard to the sellers' business involvement, the buyers' reliance on the sellers' skill and judgment, the purpose itself and a proviso relating to patent or trade names. The sub-section was further amended by the Consumer Credit Act 1974 to include references to instalment payments and a credit broker. These amendments have been embodied in the 1979 Act and hence authorities on the 1893 sub-section must be used with care.

The Sale of Goods Act 1979, s. 14 (3) provides that where the seller sells goods in the course of a business and the buyer expressly or by implication makes known to the seller or, where the price† is wholly or partly payable by instalments and the goods were previously sold by a credit broker to the seller, to that credit broker, any particular purpose for which the goods are being bought, there is an implied condition that the goods supplied are reasonably fit for that purpose, whether or not it is a purpose for which such goods are commonly supplied, except when it is shown that the buyer does not rely or that it is unreasonable for him to rely, on the skill or judgment of the seller or credit broker.

The term does not apply to private sales but does cover not only goods sold but also goods 'supplied' in performance or purported performance of the contract, *Geddling v Marsh* [1920] 1 KB 668 (returnable drink bottle), *Chapronière v Mason* (1905) 21 TLR 633 (stone in bun), *Wilson v Rickett, Cockerell* [1954] 1 QB 598 (detonator in fuel). It covers goods which can only be used for one purpose, *Priest v Last* [1903] 2 KB 148 (hot water bottle), and covers both manufactured and non-manufactured goods, *Frost v Aylesbury Dairy* [1905] 1 KB 608 (milk). Once the buyer shows the seller knew the purpose, reliance by the buyer will be presumed unless rebutted by the seller. There may be reliance even though both parties operate in the same commodity market and even though the buyer intends to check the goods, *Kendall v Lillico* [1969] 2 AC 31. Partial reliance may be enough, *Cammell Laird v Manganese Bronze* [1934] AC 402. The term will not be implied when the buyer fails to reveal peculiarities on his side rendering the goods unfit which could not have been contemplated by the seller, *Griffiths v Peter Conway* [1939] 1 All ER 685 (allergy to tweed) but will be implied if the seller is on notice that there may be special requirements, *Manchester Liners v Rea* [1922] 2 AC 74 (coal for named ship). If a buyer orders goods by a patent or trade name there may not be reliance on the seller. The sellers' liability is strict and extends to hidden defects not discoverable with care, skill and judgment, *Frost v Aylesbury Dairy*, *Kendall v Lillico*, but the goods need not be absolutely fit but only reasonably so, *Bartlett v Sydney Marcus* [1965] 1 WLR 1013 (secondhand car needing repairs). It has been held that when perishable goods must undergo a journey or voyage they should be reasonably fit to withstand deterioration during transit *Mash & Murrell v Emanuel* [1961] 1 All ER 485 (rvsd. on facts [1962] 1 All ER 77n); *Kemp v Tolland* [1956] 2 Lloyd's Rep 681 but language in recent cases raises doubts as to whether fitness for purpose implies durability at least in the case of non-perishables, *Crowther v Shannon* [1975] 1 WLR 30. Under the Unfair Contract Terms Act 1977†, s. 6 liability under s. 14 cannot be excluded or restricted by any contract term as against anyone dealing as a consumer and as against others an exclusion clause will only be effective so far as it is reasonable, but s. 26 allows exclusion in international supply contracts.

Fixed or determinable future time for bills of exchange and promissory notes. A bill or note is not invalid because it is not dated, Bills of Exchange Act 1882, s. 3 (4). Where it is dated or an acceptance or indorsement is dated that date is presumed to be correct until proved otherwise. A bill or note is not invalid because it is ante-dated, post-dated or dated on a Sunday (s. 13). Where an instrument payable at a period after date is issued undated or where the acceptance of a bill payable at a fixed period after sight† is undated any holder may insert the date of issue or acceptance and is to be paid accordingly. If the holder in good faith mistakenly inserts a wrong date or in any case where a wrong date is inserted and the bill comes into the hands of a holder in due course the bill is not avoided but operates as if the date inserted was correct (s. 12). Where an instrument is expressed to be payable on demand, at sight or on presentation or when no time for payment is mentioned it is payable on demand. If it is not payable on demand the due date is calculated under ss. 14 and 92. Section 14 (1) originally made provision for the obligatory addition of three days of grace to any period for the maturing of an instrument. Days of grace have been abolished by the Banking and Financial Dealings Act 1971. If the instrument is to be paid at a fixed period after date, after sight, or after the happening of a specified event, the day from which the time is to begin to run is excluded and the day of payment is included. Where the instrument is payable at a fixed period after sight, the time runs from the date of acceptance or noting† or protesting†. By the Banking and Financial Dealings Act 1971 an instrument is due and payable on the last day of the time fixed but if that is a non-business day then on the next succeeding business day. The Bills of Exchange Act 1882, s. 92 (as amended by the Banking and Financial Dealings Act 1971) provides that 'non-business days' mean Sunday, Saturday, Good Friday, Christmas Day, Bank Holidays or a day appointed by Royal Proclamation as a public fast or thanksgiving day. Any other day is a business day. Section 92 also provides that where by the Act the time for doing an act is less than three days 'non-business days' are excluded. The whole of the business hours of the day of payment are available to make payment, *Kennedy v Thomas* [1894] 2 QB 759. A bill cannot be drawn payable at a period 'after acceptance', this not being read as synonymous with 'after sight', *Korea Exchange Bank v Debenhams* [1979] 1 Lloyd's Rep 548 and a bill or note cannot be drawn payable 'on or before' a specified date, *Williamson v Rider* [1973] 1 QB 89.

Fixed sum credit. *See* CREDIT.

Fixtures. Goods† which have been so attached to land as to become in law part of it. If the article is permanently affixed it will be presumed that it is a fixture but this may be rebutted by showing that the affixation has been for the better use of the goods as goods rather than for the better use of the building or land, *Leigh v Taylor* [1902] AC 157. There are complex rules as to entitlement to fixtures as between landlord and tenant, vendor and puchaser, etc. A sale of tenant's fixtures has been held to be neither a sale of goods nor of land, *Thomas v Jennings* (1896) 66 LJQB 5 unless the seller undertook to sever.

F.O.B. contracts. (Free on board). A form of sale of goods used in overseas trade. It names the port or ports of loading. There are many variants but a common feature is that it is for the seller to bear all charges and expenses up to loading the goods on board an effective ship to be nominated by the buyer. 'Effective' means that the ship must be capable of taking the cargo within the contract time. Later expenses of carriage and insurance are for the buyer. In *Pyrene v Scindia* [1954] 2 QB 402 at 424 three types were distinguished. In the first or 'classic' type (*Wimble v Rosenberg* [1913] 3 KB 743) the seller should 'procure a bill of lading in terms usual in the trade . . . the seller is a party to the contract of carriage at least until he takes out the bill of lading in the buyer's name'. In the second the seller is asked to make arrangements for shipping and perhaps to take the bill of lading in his own name, obtaining payment when he transfers it to the buyer as in c.i.f. contracts. In the third the shipping arrangements are made by the buyer or his forwarding agent and the seller, on the goods being loaded, obtains a mate's receipt† which he hands to the buyer or his agent for them to obtain the bill of lading. The distinction between the first and second is that in the latter the seller, as an additional duty, arranges for shipping. Distinctions between the first and third are that in the first the seller does and in the third he does not make a contract with the carrier and in the first but not in the third he holds, and may be bound to procure, a bill of lading. The third may now be the form most often used. Additional duties in relation to carriage and insurance may be placed on the seller so that the contract may resemble a c.i.f. contract but the ultimate cost of these in an f.o.b. contract falls on the buyer whereas it is the converse in a c.i.f. contract. Variation in these charges is for the benefit or loss of buyer in an f.o.b. contract and for the seller in c.i.f. The f.o.b. form is so flexible that a contract may be f.o.b. although it does not mention f.o.b. and refers to calculations on a c.i.f. basis, *Carlos Federspiel v Twigg* [1957] 1 Lloyd's Rep 240; *The Parchim* [1918] AC 157. Under an f.o.b. contract the seller must actually ship goods or cause them to be shipped; he cannot, as in a c.i.f. contract, tender documents covering goods already afloat or appropriate to the contract a cargo which was not initially loaded in fulfilment of the contract.

Risk and property normally pass on shipment when the goods cross the ship's rail (*see* RISK IN SALE OF GOODS and PASSING OF PROPERTY IN SALE OF GOODS). Risk will pass on shipment even though property does not then pass, e.g. because the right of disposal has been reserved. It may be that in strictness risk passes when the seller's duties are completed and so if the contract were on 'f.o.b. and stowed' terms where the seller is also responsible for stowage, risk would pass when stowing is completed. Risk may be on the buyer before shipment when that has been delayed by his fault. Risk may remain on the seller after shipment when he fails to make a reasonable contract of carriage in accordance with the Sale of Goods Act 1979, s. 32 (2), if it is his duty to arrange carriage, or if he fails to give notice to enable the buyer to insure under s. 33 (3) or if he fails to load goods fit to endure the voyage (*see* FITNESS FOR PURPOSE).

F.o.b. may be merely a basis for calculating export values for customs purposes and not refer to delivery. In American usage (Uniform Commercial Code 2-319 (1)) 'f.o.b. named place of shipment' corresponds to the English and Commonwealth usage whilst 'f.o.b. named place of destination' corresponds to ex ship or arrival contracts. In carriage by air the term f.o.b. airport, analogous to the shipping contract, is now found.

Force and fear. A term of Scots Law used in the Bills of Exchange Act 1882 and corresponding to duress in English law.

Force majeure. A concept of Continental law resembling frustration. Though force majeure is not a concept of English law the term is often applied to clauses in contracts making express provision for circumstances impeding performance.

F.O.R. contract (Free on rail). A form of sale of goods where the seller undertakes to hand the goods to the railway carrier at a named place of departure. The seller bears all expenses to that point. In the f.o.t. variant (free on truck) the seller bears expenses to the loading on the rail vehicle. The normal rules as to delivery† in sale of goods, passing of property† in sale of goods and risk† apply unless expressly or implicitly varied.

Foreign award. *See* ARBITRATION: FOREIGN AND CONVENTION AWARDS.

Foreign bill. *See* INLAND AND FOREIGN BILLS AND NOTES.

Foreign judgments. These may be enforced either under legislation or at common law. The principal statutes are the Foreign Judgments (Reciprocal Enforcement) Act 1933 and the Civil Jurisdiction and Judgments Act 1982. Under the 1933 Act judgments of superior courts in foreign and Commonwealth countries, which accord reciprocity to United Kingdom judgments, may be registered as of right and enforced as if they had been given in the registering court on the date of registration and will carry interest provided they were made within the preceding six years. Judgments in inferior tribunals may be registered since 1982. The Act must have been applied to the foreign country by Order in Council, the judgment had (until the 1982 Act) to be final and conclusive between the parties and for a sum of money, not being for taxes, fine or penalty. The registration will be set aside on application if the judgment was not one to which the Act applies, the court delivering it had no jurisdiction, the judgment was obtained by fraud on the court, its enforcement would be contrary to public policy, the defendant did not receive proper notice and did not appear and the rights under the judgment are not vested in the person registering. Mere technical defects will not result in the registration being set aside but it may be if the matter was already the subject of a final but earlier judgment. Earlier Acts, the Judgments Extension Act 1868 and the Administration of Justice Act 1920, provided for the registration of Scottish, Northern Irish and Commonwealth judgments. The 1933 Act will eventually supersede the 1920 Act as the former is extended to further countries. Special provision has been made by the European Communities (Enforcement of Community Judgments) Order 1972 for the registration and enforcement of the judgments of tribunals of the E.E.C. but this does not apply to courts of member States which are covered by the Civil Jurisdiction and Judgments Act 1982. A foreign judgment which may be registered under the 1933 Act may not be enforced by action at common law but otherwise a final foreign, Commonwealth or colonial judgment having jurisdiction will be treated here as conclusive of any matter of fact or law decided by it provided it was (if in personam) for a definite sum and may be enforced by action provided it does not conflict with public policy or natural justice, or was not obtained by fraud. In actions in personam (merely binding the parties) the foreign court will be treated as having jurisdiction when the defendant was present in the foreign country when the action began or submitted to the jurisdiction. The mere possession of property in that country is not sufficient. In actions in rem (determining status and binding everyone) jurisdiction belongs to the courts where the property is located but English courts would not enforce foreign judgments relating to immovables (land) until the 1982 Act s. 30 abrogated this rule.

The fraud of the plaintiff in obtaining judgment may be pleaded in defence even though this was raised in the original proceedings and an English court will grant an injunction restraining the enforcement of a foreign judgment obtained by fraud or breach of contract.

Foreign arbitral awards may also be enforced under the provisions of either the Arbitration Act 1950 or the Arbitration Act 1975 (*see* ARBITRATION). The State Immunity Act 1978 (*see* STATE IMMUNITY) and the Protection of Trading Interests Act 1980 contain provisions for the enforcement of foreign judgments.

The complex Civil Jurisdiction and Judgments Act 1982 now makes provision for the enforcement of judgments both within the United Kingdom and when delivered in the courts of E.E.C. countries. Part I of the Act is designed to give effect to two

Conventions regulating the enforcement of judgments of the courts of member countries throughout the E.E.C. in civil and commercial matters, but there are exceptions, including arbitration and bankruptcy. Under the Conventions jurisdiction of a court is largely based on domicile in the Continental sense of habitual residence, ss. 41–46. There are some more detailed rules which differ from the established English rules. Part II of the Act provides for enforcement of Scottish and Northern Irish judgments but, though independent of the Conventions is made subject to them, s. 16 (4). Some foreign judgments against States may be recognised and enforced, s. 31, foreign judgments entitled to recognition and enforcement will bar proceedings for the same matter in the U.K., s. 34, the 1933 Act is extended to judgments of inferior tribunals, interim judgments and some arbitration awards, s. 35, and the Protection of Trading Interests Act 1980† is amended in respect of multiple awards of damages, s. 38.

Foreign Law, proof of. Under the European Communities Act 1972, s. 3, the law of the E.E.C. is judicially noticed by English courts but law foreign to England and Wales, including Scots and Irish law and the law of member States of the E.E.C., which is to be applied by English courts in a conflict of laws case must be proved, as a fact, by the evidence of a competent witness who need not be a practitioner in the country in question. Foreign law proved in previous cases may, on notice, be cited from reports without an expert's evidence, Civil Evidence Act 1972, s. 4. Scots' civil and Northern Irish law need not be proved in the House of Lords. In the absence of proof to the contrary, foreign law is presumed to be the same as English law. Foreign law, though fact, is determined by the judge, not the jury, when there is jury trial.

Forged and unauthorised signatures on bills of exchange or promissory notes. The Bills of Exchange Act 1882, s. 24 provides that subject to other provisions of the Act a forged or unauthorised signature is wholly inoperative and no right to retain an instrument or give a discharge or enforce payment can be acquired through or under that signature unless the party against whom it is sought to retain or enforce payment of the instrument is precluded from setting up the forgery or want of authority. Thus if the signature of the drawer is forged to a cheque the payee cannot sue the apparent drawer and if the drawee banker pays the cheque he cannot debit the purported drawer's account. If an indorsement is forged the holder can sue any indorsers up to that indorsement (and the forger) but cannot sue prior parties. There are, however, numerous qualifications to the general rule. An unauthorised signature may be subject to ratification. A forged signature cannot be ratified by the party whose signature it purports to be but he may be bound by an estoppel and liable if he represents the signature to be genuine to the detriment of another acting on the representation or if he remains silent when there is a duty to reveal the forgery, *Leach v Buchanan* (1802) 4 Esp 226; *Greenwood v Martins Bank* [1933] AC 51, *Brown v Westminster Bank* [1964] 2 Lloyd's Rep 187. A bank by paying a cheque does not impliedly represent the drawer's signature to be genuine so as to be precluded from recovering back the money paid, *National Westminster v Barclays Bank* [1975] QB 654.

By s. 54 (2) an acceptor may not deny the genuineness of the drawer's signature and by s. 55 (2) (b) an indorser may similarly not deny the genuineness of the drawer's signature. The warranties of a transferor by delivery under s. 58 may also preclude the transferor from setting up a forgery. When the payee is a fictitious or non-existent person, s. 7 (3) provides the instrument may be treated as payable to bearer and a forged indorsement thus ignored. If the forgery took place in a foreign country where title can be transmitted through a forgery then under the rules for conflict of laws in s. 72 the forgery may be ignored. Section 60 protects a banker who pays in good faith and in the ordinary course of business a cheque on a forged indorsement and the Cheques Act 1957, ss. 1 and 4 provide protection for paying bankers and collecting bankers handling cheques when indorsements are absent or irregular. It is not clear whether these latter sections cover forgery of indorsements.

Form in contract. Gratuitous promises made for no consideration and leases for more than three years must be by deed or specialty. For less than three years there are no formal requirements for leases, but contracts to grant a lease for any period must be evidenced in writing. In general a simple or parol contract requires no special form but may be made by word of mouth, conduct or in writing. By exception certain contracts must be in writing and will be null if not so made. They include negotiable instruments (see the Bills of Exchange Act 1882, s. 3) and bills of sale (see the Bills of Sale (Amendment) Act 1882 and sales of ships (also known as bills of sale)) (*see* the Merchant Shipping Act 1894, s. 24) as also mortgages of ships (ibid., s. 31). With other contracts failure to provide writing or prescribed form may result either in penalties or in restrictions on enforcement. These include policies of life and marine insurance and regulated consumer credit agreements within the Consumer Credit Act 1974, s. 65.

The Statute of Frauds 1677 originally required that a wide range of contracts should be 'evidenced in writing' if they were to be enforceable. Section 17, governing sale of goods of the value of £10 and upwards was re-enacted as the Sale of Goods Act 1893, s. 4; part of the Statute of Frauds, s. 4 governing contracts for the sale or other disposition of land or any interest therein was re-enacted as the Law of Property Act 1925, s. 40. The Statute of Frauds in effect protected fraud by allowing the unscrupulous to raise a technical defence of lack of writing so the Law Reform (Enforcement of Contracts) Act 1954 repealed the Sale of Goods Act 1893, s. 4 and the Statute of Frauds, s. 4, except in so far as it governed contracts 'to answer for the debt, default or miscarriage of another', that is, contracts of guarantee. Now only these and contracts relating to land require Statute of Fraud type evidence but authorities on the repealed provisions may still guide on the form of the evidence.

It became the policy of the courts to restrict the operation of the Statute of Frauds and a narrow meaning was given to contracts of guarantee. They were confined to agreements which were conditional upon a principal debtor failing to pay but if a promisor undertakes a sole responsibility which is not conditional on another's failure this was a contract of indemnity and not within the statute, *Mountstephen v Lakeman* (1874) LR 7 HL 17. Even if there is a promise to answer for another this is not within the Statute if it is part of a larger transaction such as del credere agency nor is a promise made, not to a creditor, but to the debtor, *Eastwood v Kenyon* (1840) 11 Ad & El 438 but a promise to pay damages in tort if the tortfeasor does not may be within the Statute and require writing, *Kirkham v Marter* (1819) 2 B & Ald 613. Contracts for the sale or other disposition of land do not include contracts for the sale of standing fructus industriales (annual produce) but may include sale of standing fructus naturales (perennial produce such as trees) if they are to derive further benefit from the land after the contract, *Marshall v Green* (1875) 1 CPD 35. The 'note or memorandum in writing' need not have been prepared as such and it suffices if it comes into existence before proceedings commence, *Farr, Smith v Messrs* [1928] 1 KB 397. It may be composed of several documents if a sufficient express or implied cross-reference can be shown, *Long v Millar* (1879) 4 CPD 450. It must name or identify the parties, the subject matter and state the material terms. In guarantees it need not state the consideration, Mercantile Law Amendment Act 1856. An omitted material term may be waived by a plaintiff for whose benefit it exists or taken into account with the memorandum contents for a defendant benefited by it, *North v Loomes* [1919] 1 Ch 378; *Scott v Bradley* [1971] 1 Ch 850. It seems a 'subject to contract' document will not suffice, *Tiverton v Wearwell* [1975] Ch 146 but cf. *Daulia v Four Millbank Nominees* [1978] Ch 231. The memorandum must be signed by 'the party to be charged', the defendant, but the signature need not be a subscription or handwritten. It may be printed and appear in any position provided it is intended to authenticate the whole document, *Caton v Caton* (1867) LR 2 HL 127. Signature may be by a duly authorised agent.

A contract not sufficiently evidenced may be enforced if the defendant does not plead the absence of writing, it may be used as a defence to justify the retention of money paid under it, *Monnickendam v Leanse* (1923) 39 TLR 445, and if a plaintiff can show a sufficient act of part performance unequivocally referable to the type of contract in question the court may grant specific performance, *Maddison v Alderson* (1883) 8 App Cas 467; *Rawlinson v Ames* [1925] Ch 96. Payment of money with other circumstances may be unequivocal, *Steadman v Steadman* [1976] AC 536 but cf. *Re Gonin* [1979] Ch 16. Part performance is confined to contracts relating to land. Since contracts within the Statute of Frauds, s. 4 and the Law of Property Act, s. 40 which are insufficiently evidenced may have so many legal effects they are not termed void or voidable but unenforceable contracts as not being enforceable by a direct action for damages.

Bodies corporate once had to contract under their common seal, subject to a number of exceptions. The requirements and the need for exceptions were abolished by the Corporate Bodies' Contracts Act 1960 and they now contract as natural persons as do companies within the Companies Act 1948 by s. 32.

Forwarding agent. An agent who arranges for the transport of goods. *See* FREIGHT FORWARDER.

Fraudulent preference. The Bankruptcy Act 1914, s. 44 (1) as amended by Companies Act 1947, s. 115 provides that if a person who is unable to pay his debts as they fall due within six months before the presentation of a bankruptcy petition upon which an adjudication of bankruptcy is made against him, with a view to prefer a creditor or any surety for the debt due to that creditor, transfers property to the creditor, pays the debt or allows his property to be taken for the debt, then he has made a fraudulent preference which is void against the trustee in bankruptcy, to whom the creditor must return the money or property. The rights of bona fide purchasers for value without notice are preserved so that the preference might be described as voidable.

Preference must be the 'dominant intention' of the transaction and 'with a view to prefer' means with the intention of preferring but intention may be inferred from the circumstances. The word 'preference' implies an act freely done and hence facts showing that the debtor was acting under pressure may prevent a transaction falling into this category. Thus a threat of legal proceedings, *Ex p Taylor* (1886) 18 QBD 295; an anxiety to ward off criminal proceedings *Sharp v Jackson* [1899] AC 419, or even a desire to make good a wrong, *Ex p Lake* [1901] 1 QB 710, have all prevented a transaction being regarded as a preference.

A fraudulent preference may be an act of bankrupcy under the Bankruptcy Act 1914, s. 1 and the making of an 'undue preference' by a bankrupt is a ground for refusing an unconditional discharge of the bankrupt under s. 26. 'Undue preference' is a wider concept than fraudulent preference but even in the latter there is no necessity to prove fraud in the ordinary legal sense of deceit, its chief features being a voluntary decision by the debtor to depart from the rules for the distribution of his assets with intent to favour one or more creditors.

Freight. Payment to a shipowner for the carriage of cargo. Unless otherwise agreed it is not payable until the voyage is completed and the cargo delivered except when non-delivery results from the fault of the shipper alone. Even when non-delivery results from an excepted peril the shipowner is not entitled to freight nor, in the absence of contrary agreement, if the goods delivered are for business purposes different from those shipped, *Asfar v Blundell* [1896] 1 QB 123, but is payable if goods are merely damaged though the shipper would have a cross-claim in respect of the damage. A claim in respect of short delivery of cargo cannot be set up as a defence or set-off to a claim for freight, *Aries Tanker Corp v Total Transport* [1977] 1 WLR 185 but an equitable set off in respect of time may be, *The Teno* [1977] 2 Lloyd's Rep 289.

If the shipowner abandons the vessel without intending to re-take possession, even under stress of weather, the cargo owner may treat the contract as at an end and not pay freight even if the cargo is later salved. The shipowner is not barred from claiming freight on the ground that he has overloaded in breach of safety legislation, *St. John Shipping v Rank* [1957] 1 QB 267. The shipper of goods is primarily liable to pay freight but the Bills of Lading Act 1855 imposes on consignees named in the bill of lading and indorsees of the bill to whom property in the goods passes a similar liability so that the shipowner may sue any of these. *See also* ADVANCE FREIGHT, BACK FREIGHT, DEAD FREIGHT, LUMP SUM FREIGHT and FREIGHT PRO RATA.

Freight forwarder. An agent who arranges for the transport of goods. *See* FORWARDING AGENT.

Freight pro rata. Freight paid for the carriage of goods by sea when the contract has been performed in part only and there has been a voluntary acceptance of part of the goods or of the goods at a point short of their agreed destination. This gives rise to an implied contract to pay for the carriage effected. Where because of war a voyage was cut short because continuance would have been illegal no freight was recoverable because no fresh agreement by the cargo owners to pay freight pro rata could be inferred from their taking the cargo, *St Enoch Shipping v Phosphate Mining* [1916] 2 KB 624.

Fructus industriales. *See* FORM IN CONTRACT.

Fructus naturales. *See* FORM IN CONTRACT.

Frustration. This means that a contract is discharged by supervening impossibility of performance. Modern law starts with *Taylor v*

Caldwell (1863) 3 B & S 826 (destruction by fire of hired building) holding that when the performance of a contract depends on the continued existence of a particular person, place or thing a term might be implied that if they ceased to exist the contract would be discharged and the parties released. To these grounds were added supervening illegality, where a contract originally legal becomes illegal, *Baily v De Crespigny* (1869) LR 4 QB 180 and 'frustration of the adventure' when some purpose accepted by both the parties as fundamental to the contract ceases to be possible, e.g. Coronation procession cannot be viewed from a hired room because of the King's illness, *Krell v Henry* [1903] 2 KB 740. Explanations other than the implied term, such as that the court imposes the just solution, have been advanced, *Denny, Mott & Dickson v Fraser* [1944] AC 265.

The death, serious illness, call-up or internment of parties to contracts to perform services have all been held to frustrate them. Extra delay or expense in fulfilling a contract, even if substantial, will not frustrate it, *Tsakiroglon v Noblee & Thorl* [1962] AC 93; *Davis Contractors v Fareham U.D.C.* [1956] AC 696, unless they are so great as to render continued performance radically different from what the parties had originally contemplated, *Metropolitan Water Board v Dick Kerr* [1918] AC 119. A party cannot claim to be discharged by self-induced frustration, a hindering event for which he is responsible, *Maritime National Fish v Ocean Trawlers* [1935] AC 524. It is doubtful how far negligent conduct can amount to this and the burden of proof that it is self-induced rests on the party alleging it, *Joseph Constantine v Imperial Smelting Corp* [1942] AC 154. A frustrating circumstance must be accepted by both parties as fundamental to the contract, *Blackburn Bobbin v Allen* [1918] 2 KB 467, CA (assumed continuance of supply of timber not common to both, hence no frustration). It appears that a lease or a contract for the sale of land can be frustrated, *National Carriers v Panalpina* [1981] 1 All ER 161.

Law Reform (Frustrated Contracts) Act 1943 provides that when a contract governed by English law (*see* CONFLICT OF LAWS) has become impossible of performance or otherwise frustrated all sums paid or payable before discharge are recoverable or cease to be payable, the court having a discretion to make an allowance up to the amounts of these sums for expenses incurred by a party. Where one party has 'obtained a valuable benefit' before discharge the court may order the party benefited to pay a reasonable sum not exceeding the benefit. The Act binds the Crown but may be excluded by the contract. It does not apply to voyage charterparties, contracts of insurance, contracts for sale of goods to which the Sale of Goods Act 1979, s. 7 applies or any contract for the sale of specific goods which is frustrated by the goods perishing.

Fundamental breach. *See* EXEMPTION AND EXCLUSION CLAUSES.
Fundamental term. *See* EXEMPTION AND EXCLUSION CLAUSES.
Future goods. The Sale of Goods Act 1979, s. 61 (1) defines these as
'goods† to be manufactured or acquired by the seller after the making
of the contract of sale'. Section 5 (1) contrasts them with existing
goods, owned or possessed by the seller. Section 5 (2) provides that
there may be a contract for the sale of goods, the seller's acquisition of
which depends on a contingency and s. 5 (3) provides that a purported
present sale (passing property†) of future goods (see s. 2 (4) and (5))
takes effect as an agreement to sell, that is, to transfer property when it
is acquired. Goods may be both future and specific goods, as when the
parties agree upon the sale of particular goods to be acquired by the
seller.

G

Garnishee order. This directs a person who owes money to a judgment debtor to make payment, not to the judgment debtor but to the judgment creditor.

Gateway. *See* RESALE PRICE MAINTENANCE and RESTRICTIVE TRADE PRACTICES.

General acceptance of a bill of exchange. *See* ACCEPTANCE OF A BILL OF EXCHANGE.

General agent. *See* AGENT.

General average. This is maritime loss caused by or directly consequential on a general average act which occurs when any extraordinary sacrifice or expenditure is voluntarily and reasonably made or incurred to preserve property imperilled in a common adventure. The loss must be borne rateably by all interested making general average contributions. Examples are the jettisoning of cargo to save the ship and perhaps other cargo, voluntary stranding to avoid wreck and the expenses of putting into a port of refuge for preservation of ship and cargo. A general average sacrifice must be made to avoid a real danger common to all interests, some sacrifice must be essential, it must be voluntary, it must be a real sacrifice and not merely the abandonment of something of no value and the danger must not have arisen through such fault on the part of the person seeking contribution as might have involved him in legal liability. The ship, cargo or some part of them must have been saved if there is to be contribution. The owners of the ship, the freight and the cargo who have benefited from the sacrifice must contribute but the wages and effects of seamen and passengers' luggage are not required to do so. An owner of cargo who has had to make a general average contribution may sue the owners of a ship whose negligence created the peril, *Morrison SS Co Ltd v Greystoke Castle* [1947] AC 265. Contributions are calculated by average adjusters according to the law of the place of delivery. The York-Antwerp Rules which are designed to create uniform international practice are almost always embodied in charterparties and bills of lading.

General crossing. *See* CROSSED CHEQUE.

General lien. *See* POSSESSORY OR COMMON LAW LIEN.

Genus numquam perit. 'The type of goods never perishes'. A contract for the sale of purely generic goods can never be discharged by frustration when goods which the seller intended to supply in performance are lost or become unobtainable. *Blackburn Bobbin v Allen* [1918] 2 KB 467, CA. The type never perishes and the seller should obtain substitutes. If, however, generic goods are to come from a defined source agreed by the parties as basic to the contract and the source fails, e.g. crops to be grown on specified land, there may be frustration, *Howell v Coupland* (1876) LR I QBD 258, CA.

Good faith. The Bills of Exchange Act 1882, s. 90 provides that for the purposes of the Act a thing is deemed to be done in good faith where it is in fact done honestly, whether it is done negligently or not. See *Raphael v Bank of England* (1855) 17 CB 161. Section 30 (2) further provides that every holder is presumed to be a holder in due course but if it is proved that acceptance, issue or negotiation is affected with fraud, duress, force and fear or illegality the burden of proof is shifted unless and until the holder proves that value (*see* CONSIDERATION FOR A BILL OF EXCHANGE) in good faith has been given subsequently to the alleged fraud or illegality.

Goods. Defined in the Sale of Goods Act 1979, s. 61 (1) as including 'all personal chattels other than things in action and money'; 'in particular "goods" includes emblements, industrial growing crops† and things attached to or forming part of the land which are agreed to be severed before sale or under the contract of sale.' The concluding words will cover not only rock, sand, gravel and soil but also fixtures, chattels so attached to the land as to become part of it. Section 61 (1) also provides that goods may be 'future goods' 'to be manufactured or acquired by the seller after the making of the contract of sale', or 'specific goods' 'identified or agreed on at the time a contract of sale is made'. Goods may be both 'future' and 'specific' as where the parties agree upon the sale of particular goods to be acquired by the seller. Goods may also be 'ascertained', as when they are subsequently appropriated to the contract, or 'unascertained goods' as where they are agreed to be sold merely by description or when an unsevered part of a larger whole, such as a cargo of wheat, is agreed to be sold. Whether goods are 'specific', 'ascertained' or 'unascertained' is important for the operation of the rules for the passing of property contained in ss. 16–19 of the Act. Section 5 contrasts 'existing goods, owned or possessed by the seller', with 'future goods' defined as in s. 61 (1). It also provides that there may be a contract for the sale of goods, the acquisition of which by the seller depends on a contingency and that where a contract purports to make a present sale of future goods it operates as an agreement to sell. Section 6 provides that where there is a contract for the sale of specific goods which, unknown to the seller, have ceased to exist the contract is void and s. 7 provides that where there is an agreement for the sale of specific goods and later the goods, without seller's or buyer's fault perish before the risk† has passed to the buyer the contract is avoided. Section 6 is regarded as an application of common mistake† to sale of goods (see *Couturier v Hastie* (1856) 5 HLC 673) and s. 7 an application of frustration. These sections may be subject to agreement to the contrary under s. 55. Where goods never existed a defendant was taken to have impliedly promised that they had, *McRae v Commonwealth Disposals Commission* (1951) 84 CLR 377. When part of an indivisible parcel of goods was stolen the whole was regarded as perished, *Barrow, Lane & Ballard v Philip Phillips* [1929] 1 KB 574 but where part of a crop failed, frustration applied to the failed part and the grower was obliged to offer the balance to the buyer, *Sainsbury v Street* [1972] 1 WLR 834.

Water, oil and gas appear capable of being 'goods' but it is more doubtful if electricity or mechanical power are 'goods'.

Green clause. *See* BANKERS' COMMERCIAL CREDITS.

Group licence. The Consumer Credit Act 1974, s. 22 provides that this is one of the two forms of licence required for carrying on consumer credit or consumer hire business by anyone other than a local authority or body corporate authorised by statute to carry on the business. The other form of licence is the standard licence. The Director-General of Fair Trading† is only to issue a group licence if he is satisfied that the public interest is better served by it than by requiring individual applications from members of the group. In practice it is used for professions, such as solicitors, where consumer credit business is subsidiary to other work. Group licences may be issued for an indefinite period and may not authorise the canvassing of debtor–creditor–supplier agreements off business premises. For other matters relating to licences and the effects of unlicensed trading, *see* STANDARD LICENCE.

Guadalajara Convention. *See* CARRIAGE BY AIR: CONVENTIONS AND LEGISLATION.

Guarantee (or suretyship). A form of personal† security under which a guarantor or surety undertakes by contract to a creditor to answer for the debt, default or miscarriage of another, the debtor, if the debtor does not fulfil his obligations. Liability in tort as well as contract may be guaranteed. Unless given by deed, a guarantee requires consideration but giving credit to the debtor suffices. Under the Statute of Frauds 1677, s. 4 a guarantee must be evidenced by a note or memorandum in writing, signed by the party to be held liable, (*see* FORM IN CONTRACT) if it is to be enforceable by an action for damages. The memorandum need not state the consideration (Mercantile Law Amendment Act 1856, s. 3) and writing is not required if the contract is part of a larger transaction, *Fitzgerald v Dressler* (1860) 7 CBNS 374. A guarantee, as being dependent on the non-fulfilment of a principal obligation, is to be distinguished from an indemnity by which the indemnifier promises he will save the creditor from loss, whatever may or may not be the debtor's liability. An indemnity does not require written evidence. If the principal obligation is void any guarantee of it is void also, *Coutts v Browne-Lecky* [1947] KB 104, but an indemnity covering the same ground as a void contract may be valid, *Yeoman Credit v Latter* [1961] 2 All ER 294. A guarantee is not normally a contract uberrimae fidei hence the creditor is not under a duty to disclose to the surety matters relating to the debtor which might influence his decision to undertake the suretyship but some fidelity bonds (guaranteeing the honesty of employees) may involve such a duty, *L.G.O. v Holloway* [1912] 2 KB 72.

The surety is liable for the amount for which he engaged himself, which may be the whole or part of the debt. If he is a joint surety (*see* JOINT AND SEVERAL CONTRACTS) he may be sued for the whole amount for which the sureties are liable but will have a right of contribution against his co-sureties. It is a question of construction whether a guarantee covers one transaction or is to continue for many until revoked. Although the surety only becomes liable on the debtor's default, he cannot insist that the creditor sue the debtor first, though he can call upon the creditor to sue the debtor and, if the surety is sued, he can rely on any set-off the debtor may have against the creditor. The surety is not bound by any decision as between the creditor and debtor and his liability will have to be established in separate proceedings.

After having paid the debt the surety has the following rights at common law. As against the principal debtor he can recover the amount of the debt with interest and enforce all rights the creditor enjoyed. As against the creditor he may claim all judgments, securities, set-offs and priorities related to the debt and use the creditor's name in all proceedings (Mercantile Law Amendment Act 1856, s. 5). If he is surety for only part, his claims here will be only partial. As against co-sureties he can claim contribution if he has paid more than his proper share.

The surety is discharged if the principal debt is paid (*see* DISCHARGE BY PERFORMANCE) or is discharged by frustration and on the following special grounds; if the creditor alters the terms of the debt or contract guaranteed without the surety's consent but acceptance by the creditor of wrongful repudiation by the debtor is not such alteration, *Moschi v L.E.P.* [1973] AC 331; if the creditor by binding contract, not reserving his rights against the surety, gives extra time to the debtor but not by mere forebearance to sue; if the creditor gives up any security or takes a new one in place of an old; any negligence of the creditor in dealing with the debtor or misuse of securities by the creditor so as to prejudice the rights of the surety; whilst an absolute discharge of the debtor releases the surety a covenant by the creditor not to sue, coupled with a reservation of rights against the surety will not release him; release of one or more joint sureties releases all but a surety who has contracted severally (*see* JOINT AND SEVERAL CONTRACTS) is only discharged if the discharge of another prejudices his claims to contribution; death of a surety, if the consideration is divisible, will discharge a continuing guarantee but the death of one co-surety will not release his fellows; if the guarantee was conditional on another also becoming a surety and this fails, the guarantee fails also; if an indivisible consideration is given for a continuing guarantee then it cannot be revoked but if it is divisible the guarantee may be revoked by notice; a continuing guarantee of a partnership firm is revoked by any change in the constitution of the firm. Neither discharge in bankruptcy of the debtor nor the acceptance of an arrangement (*see* DEEDS OF ARRANGEMENT) by his creditors releases sureties for his debts. The creditor may prove in the surety's bankruptcy but the surety may not prove in that of the debtor unless he has paid the debt or the creditor has agreed not to sue whilst reserving rights against the surety. The Consumer Credit Act 1974, ss. 105–113 protect sureties for transactions within the Act. The sections cover formalities, information, power to make rules relating to realisation of securities and evasion of the Act by means of a security is prevented.

H

Hadley v Baxendale. *See* DAMAGES.

Hague Rules. *See* CARRIAGE OF GOODS BY SEA ACT 1971.

Hague-Visby Rules. The amended form of the Hague Rules now applied to most bills of lading by the Carriage of Goods by Sea Act 1971 (in force June 1977). The Merchant Shipping Act 1981 now substitutes special drawing rights for gold francs in measures of limitation of liability in the Rules.

Hallmarking of articles of gold, silver and platinum by an assay office to indicate the fineness of the metal is governed by Hallmarking Act 1973.

Hamburg Rules. Proposed uniform rules to be applied to bills of lading, replacing the Hague-Visby Rules which are now operative under the Carriage of Goods by Sea Act 1971 (in force June 1977). The Hamburg Rules would considerably reduce the carriers' present protection against liability.

Hightrees House. *See* PROMISSORY ESTOPPEL.

Hire Purchase. A bailment of hire, also giving the hirer an option of purchase when he has paid a prescribed number of instalments of hire. This form was adopted for what were in substance instalment purchases of goods to reduce or eliminate the risk of the hirer giving a third party a good title to the goods under exceptions to nemo dat quod non habet which would have been present with credit sale and conditional sale, *Helby v Matthews* [1895] AC 471, and to evade the obstacles to chattel mortgages presented by the Bills of Sale Acts 1878–82†, *McEntire v Crossley Bros* [1895] AC 457. Hire Purchase contracts are usually standard form contracts of great complexity but since 1938 statute has intervened to regulate some of their incidents. The Consumer Credit Act 1974, s. 189 defines hire purchase and these contracts are regulated by the Act if they are within the upper financial limit of £5,000 and the hirer is an individual. They are debtor–creditor–supplier agreements for 'restricted use' credit. Prior to the Act it was usual to refer to the parties as 'the owner' and 'the hirer' but now the Act terms them 'the creditor' and 'the debtor'.

Dealers may provide their customers with credit for hire purchase but often the dealer will sell the goods to a finance company with which the customer makes the contract of hire purchase. The dealer often enters into a 'recourse agreement' with the finance house, which is a guarantee or indemnity in respect of the customer's liability, or agrees to repurchase if the customer defaults. An owner of goods may sell them to a dealer and receive them back on hire purchase terms, either from the retailer or a finance company. If all intend this to be security for a loan it falls within the Bills of Sale Act 1882 but if one party regards it as genuine hire purchase it does not. (*Polsky v S. & A. Services* [1951] 1 All ER 185; *Snook v London & West Riding* [1967] 2 QB 786.) The Supply of Goods (Implied Terms) Act 1967, ss. 8–11 implies in hire purchase terms as to title, description, fitness, quality and sample similar to those in sale of goods. Dealers may be liable on a collateral contract if they warrant the goods to induce the customer to enter into hire purchase with a finance company, *Andrews v Hopkinson* [1957] 1 QB 229. At common law the dealer is not usually an agent of the finance company, *Mercantile Credit v Hamblin* [1965] 2 QB 242, but it is otherwise under the Consumer Credit Act 1974, ss. 56, 57 (receiving notice of withdrawal), s. 69 (notice of cancellation) and s. 102 (rescission). As a regulated agreement within the Act hire purchase must comply with numerous requirements as to form, disclosure and copies ss. 55, 60–65 and when made off trade premises may be cancellable ss. 67–73. (*See* COOLING OFF PERIOD). When a creditor wishes to terminate a contract for breach or under its terms he must serve a default notice or similar notice on the debtor, ss. 76, 87–89, 98. Hire purchase contracts often contain minimum payment clauses operative on premature termination. If this is for breach and the sum is excessive it is a penalty†, *Bridge v Campbell Discount* [1962] AC 600, and may be so even if there is termination without breach. If the minimum payment clause is not applied and the breach is repudiatory the creditor may recover his full loss, *Yeoman Credit v Waragowski* [1961] 1 WLR 1124, but if non-repudiatory then only arrears, damages for negligent harm and costs may be recovered, *Financings v Baldock* [1963] 2 QB 104. Under the 1974 Act, ss. 99, 100 the debtor may terminate at any time on giving notice, returning the goods and paying the smallest of either the minimum payment clause or the amount bringing payments to half the hire purchase price or the creditor's loss. Under ss. 94, 95 the debtor may make premature payment, receiving a rebate of interest. If one third of the hire purchase price has been paid or tendered the creditor can recover possession of the goods only by court order unless the debtor consents or has transferred them to third parties or has abandoned them, s. 90. In proceedings the court may make a time order or a return order or a transfer order, ss. 129, 133. Guarantors should be joined in the case.

Hire Purchase Act 1964, Part III. Complex statutory provisions, now re-enacted as the Consumer Credit Act, 1974, Sch. 4, to ensure that a 'private purchaser' in good faith of a motor vehicle which is subject to a hire-purchase agreement or a conditional sale agreement obtains a good title to the vehicle by exception to the principle nemo dat quod non habet. The 'private purchaser' is contrasted with the 'trade or finance purchaser, a motor dealer or finance house'. These latter are not protected since they can obtain information through H.P.I. (Hire Purchase Information), a trade organisation. The private purchaser may take the vehicle either on sale, conditional sale or hire purchase. Even if the hire-purchase or conditional sale agreement has been determined the former hirer or conditional buyer can give a good title but the protection does not apply if the vehicle has been let out on an ordinary contract of hiring, if it has been stolen from, and not disposed of, by the original hirer or conditional buyer or if the first private purchaser of the car acted in bad faith. In this last case no subsequent purchaser in good faith can acquire title.

Holder in due course of a bill of exchange or promissory note. The Bills of Exchange Act 1882, s. 29 provides that a holder in due course is a holder who has taken an instrument complete and regular on the face of it, before it was overdue†, without notice of dishonour if it had been dishonoured, in good† faith, for value (*see* CONSIDERATION FOR A BILL OF EXCHANGE) and without notice, at the time of the negotiation† of the instrument to him of any defect in the title of the person who negotiated it to him. A person's title is defective when he obtained an instrument or an acceptance by fraud, duress, force and fear† or other unlawful means or for an illegal consideration or negotiates it in breach of faith or fraud. A holder (whether for value or not) who derives title from a holder in due course and is not party to any fraud or illegality affecting the instrument has the rights of a holder in due course. By s. 30 (2) every holder is presumed to be a holder in due course but the presumption is reversed once it is proved in an action that the acceptance, issue or negotiation of an instrument is affected by fraud, duress, force and fear or illegality. By s. 38 (2) a holder in due course holds the instrument free of any defect of title in prior parties as well as from mere personal defences amongst prior parties (e.g. lack of notice of dishonour) and may enforce payment against all parties liable on the instrument. He thus obtains the full benefits of negotiability. A named payee cannot be a holder in due course, *Jones v Waring & Gillow* [1926] AC 670. A transferee of an inchoate instrument again could not be a holder in due course but absence of an acceptance does not make a bill incomplete or irregular, *National Park Bank v Berrgren* (1914) 110 LT 907. It is not essential to be a holder in due course in order to be able to sue on an instrument and a holder with an unimpeachable title may fail to be a holder in due course because of some apparent irregularity, such as a discrepancy between a payee's name and indorsement, which does not affect title, *Arab Bank v Ross* [1972] 2 QB 216. Where a drawer drew and discounted† a bill and received it back from the discounter, a holder in due course, it was held the drawer could sue, *Jade International v Robert Nicholas* [1978] QB 917. The fact that the negotiation of a bill is known or suspected to amount to a fraudulent preference in bankruptcy will not necessarily prevent a transferee being a holder in due course, *Osterreichische Landerbank v S'Elite* [1980] 2 All ER 651. There are, however, some defects or qualification to title which even a holder in due course cannot completely override. These include State immunity, forged† and unauthorised signatures on bills of exchange, infancy and corporate ultra vires (*see* CAPACITY IN RELATION TO NEGOTIABLE INSTRUMENTS) though title may be traced through such parties, the exclusion of liability by signing sans recours (*see* RIGHT OF RECOURSE) and signatures in respect of which the defence of non est factum can be pleaded. In many of these cases though one or more parties may be exempt from liability the holder in due course may well be able to sue other parties to the instrument.

The transfer of an instrument for less than full value will not of itself prevent the transferee from being a holder in due course but transfer at a considerable undervalue may be regarded as evidence of a suspicion of defective title and thus bar acquisition of the status, *Jones v Gordon* (1887) 2 App Cas at 632; *Dailey v Defries* (1863) 11 WLR 376. Conversely the fact that full value was given will be evidence supporting good faith, *Raphael v Bank of England* (1855) 17 CB 161.

Holder of a bill of exchange or promissory note. The Bills of Exchange Act 1882, s. 2 provides that 'holder' means the payee or indorsee of a bill or note who is in possession of it, or the bearer thereof. Possession may be actual or constructive. The latter is found when the instrument is held by an agent on behalf of his principal as holder. Special types of holder are the holder for value who has given consideration for the instrument or is entitled to the benefit of previous consideration but may not be entitled to the full benefits of negotiability since the instrument may be irregular in form or overdue and the holder in due course who is entitled to these full benefits. A holder is to be distinguished from the possessor of an instrument which is not in its terms payable to him, such as a person who takes an order bill or promissory note without a necessary indorsement. By s. 31 (4) such a person acquires whatever title his transferor had in the bill and the right to demand the requisite indorsement. If, however, between acquiring possession and obtaining the indorsement the possessor learns of some defect in his transferor's title, the instrument will be subject to this defect after the indorsement and the possessor will not become a holder in due course, *Whistler v Forster* (1863) 14 CBNS 248. The Cheques Act 1957†, s. 2 however provides that if a banker takes an unindorsed order cheque for value (*see* CONSIDERATION

FOR A BILL OF EXCHANGE) the banker will have the same rights as if the cheque carries an indorsement and, therefore, the banker could at once become a holder in due course of the cheque.

By s. 30 (2) every holder is presumed to be a holder in due course but if in an action it is proved that acceptance, issue†, or negotiation† is affected with fraud, duress†, or force and fear†, or illegality the burden of proof is shifted until the holder proves that value (*see* CONSIDERATION FOR A BILL OF EXCHANGE) in good faith was given for the instrument subsequent to the alleged fraud or illegality.

By s. 38 (1) any holder may sue on an instrument in his own name and by s. 38 (3) if his title is defective and he negotiates the instrument to a holder in due course the latter obtains a good title. Moreover, if payment in due course is made to a holder the person making it gets a valid discharge. By s. 28 a holder for value may sue an accommodation party† whether or not he was known to be such when the instrument was transferred.

I

Illegality in contract. Certain contracts are vitiated either because their formation or their purpose infringe either statute or common law, including public policy. Some, such as wagering contracts and restrictive trade practices are rendered void by statute. (*See* VOID CONTRACTS). Others, such as contracts ousting the jurisdiction of the courts, prejudicing the status of marriage and contracts in restraint of trade are void at common law. Other types of contracts are rendered illegal by statute or are so at common law. The latter include contracts to commit crimes and torts, contracts that are sexually immoral, that prejudice public safety and the foreign relations of this country, that prejudice the administration of justice or promote corruption or that are intended to defraud the revenue. The consequences of such illegality are more serious than if a contract is merely void.

If the formation of a contract is illegal then, even if one or both of the parties are acting in good faith in ignorance of the law, it is utterly void, no action lies on it and any property transferred is irrecoverable unless a cause of action can be made out, e.g. in bailment, which does not require disclosure of the illegality, *Amar Singh v Kulubaya* [1964] AC 142; *Bowmakers v Barnet Instruments* [1945] KB 65; or unless one of the exceptions to in pari delicto potior est condito defendentis operates. Subsequent dependent transactions are void. The same consequences follow if a contract is on its face valid but to the knowledge of both parties is to be employed for an illegal purpose. It seems from *Singh v Ali* [1960] AC 167 and *Belvoir v Stapleton* [1971] 1 QB 210 that property† in goods may pass under such contracts.

When the formation of a contract is not illegal but only the mode of performance or exploitation adopted by one of the parties then he suffers the consequences set out above but the rights of the innocent party are not affected, except in respect of action after learning of the illegality. Apart from this, normal remedies, e.g. damages, are available to him, property transferred may be recovered by him and any collateral contract by which the guilty party undertook to perform legally may be enforced, *Strongman v Sincock* [1955] 2 QB 525.

Where a contract is obviously illegal the court will refuse to enforce it even though the illegality is not pleaded. Where a contract is apparently legal, evidence of facts showing an illegal purpose cannot be given unless these facts have been pleaded but if in the course of a trial facts are proven which show that the contract had an illegal purpose the court will refuse to enforce it.

When a contract is void, as distinct from illegal, at common law it cannot be enforced in so far as it contravenes public policy but money paid or property transferred under it is recoverable, subsequent transactions are not necessarily void, if the contract is valid by a foreign proper law it is enforceable in England and lawful promises may be severed from unlawful and the lawful enforced under the blue pencil rule.

Implied authority of an agent. A term which has been used with varying meanings both by courts and writers. It may be a form of actual authority, when it will cover matters to be derived by inference from the express authority given by the principal, that is matters which though not mentioned are necessary or incidental to those mentioned or are derived from a context of trade or professional custom ('customary authority') or from the normal powers and duties of the agent's position ('usual authority'). The term may also be used as a synonym for apparent authority (e.g. *Brooks v Hassall* (1883) 49 LT 569) and the factors of custom and appointment may be relevant to determining the scope and nature of apparent authority. Implied actual authority and apparent authority may be closely related and not easily distinguished, *Hely-Hutchinson v Brayhead* [1968] 1 QB 549.

Impossibility of performance. *See* FRUSTRATION.

Inchoate instruments in relation to negotiable instruments. The typical example of such an instrument is the blank cheque. The Bills of Exchange Act 1882, s. 20 provides that where a signature† on blank paper is delivered by the signer to be converted into a bill of exchange it operates as presumptive authority to fill it up as a bill for any amount, using the signature for that of the drawer, acceptor, or indorser, and when there is an omission in a bill the person in possession is presumed to have authority to complete it as he thinks fit. If such a completed instrument is to be enforced against anyone who became a party to it before completion it must be filled up within a reasonable time and strictly in accordance with authority given. If, however, there is negotiation of such an instrument to a holder in due course he may enforce it as if it had been completed in time and with authority even if this was not so. Originally s. 20 required that the paper should be stamped but references to stamping were repealed by the Finance Act 1970 (*see* STAMP DUTIES FOR BILLS OF EXCHANGE AND PROMISSORY NOTES). It is essential for these provisions to operate that the inchoate instrument should have been 'delivered' i.e., physically transferred, with intent to be completed as a negotiable instrument. If it was handed over for safe keeping, *Smith v Prosser* [1907] 2 KB 735, or stolen, *Baxendale v Bennett* (1878) 3 QBD 525, and then improperly completed the signer will not be liable even to a holder in due course. The named payee of a negotiable instrument cannot be its holder in due course, *Jones v Waring & Gillow* [1926] AC 670, but such a payee may rely on the doctrine of estoppel against the signer provided the payee has taken the instrument to his detriment on a representation from the signer, *Lloyds Bank v Cooke* [1907] 1 KB 794. This estoppel only applies if the incomplete instrument was intended to be negotiable. If this was not so because it had been crossed with a 'not negotiable' crossing then there will not be estoppel to help the payee, *Wilson and Meeson v Pickering* [1946] KB 422. See also the Bills of Exchange Act 1882, s. 12 allowing for the insertion of dates into undated bills and acceptances. By s. 89 these provisions so far as applicable, are applied to a promissory note.

Indemnity. *See* GUARANTEE.

Indemnity of an agent. Every agent whether gratuitous or contractual in the absence of contrary agreement is entitled to be reimbursed by his principal all expenses lawfully incurred whilst acting within his actual, implied or customary authority, when acting as an agent of necessity or when ratification operates. He may be entitled even when acting unlawfully, provided he did not know of the illegality, as when an auctioneer was liable in conversion for selling property† to which his principal had no title, *Adamson v Jarvis* (1827) 4 Bing 66, or under a reasonable mistake. He is not entitled in respect of unratified unauthorised acts or which are manifestly or to his knowledge unlawful, nor for expenses resulting from his own default, negligence or insolvency nor for payments in respect of any agreement avoided by the Gaming Act 1845. (See the Gaming Act 1892). (*See* WAGERING CONTRACTS). Many office and professional expenses are regarded as covered by commission if earned (e.g. advertising by estate agents) and hence not subject to indemnity. (*See* REMUNERATION OF AGENT).

Independent contractor. *See* AGENT and |VICARIOUS LIABILITY.

Individual. The Consumer Credit Act 1974, s. 189 implicitly provides that this means a natural person or a partnership firm or unincorporated body, not entirely composed of bodies corporate. Hence it excludes companies and other bodies corporate. 'Person' does include companies.

Indorsee. A person to whom a bill of exchange or promissory note is specially indorsed either by the payee or a subsequent indorser. *See* INDORSEMENT.

Indorsement in blank. *See* INDORSEMENT OF A NEGOTIABLE INSTRUMENT.

Indorsement of a negotiable instrument. By the Bills of Exchange Act 1882, s. 31 this is the procedure required to effect a negotiation of an order bill or promissory note. An indorsement must be written on the instrument itself and be signed by the indorser. His simple signature† suffices. An indorsement written on an 'allonge' (additional paper attached to the instrument) or on a copy in a country where copies are recognised is deemed to be written on the bill. A partial indorsement, either of part of the sum or of the instrument to two or more indorsees severally is not permitted. When an instrument is payable to two or more payees who are not partners all must indorse unless one has authority to act for the others. Where the payee or indorsee of an instrument is wrongly designated or his name misspelt he should indorse in that incorrect form adding, in practice, his correct name. Where there are two or more indorsements they are assumed to have been made in the order in which they appear. Indorsements may be in blank, special, restrictive or conditional. Indorsement in blank consists of the simple signature of the indorser and specifies no indorsee. The instrument becomes payable to bearer but any person may convert the blank indorsement into a special indorsement by writing in the name of an indorsee. The provisions of the Act relating to a payee apply to an indorsee under a special indorsement. Where an instrument has been indorsed conditionally the condition may be ignored by the payer and payment to the indorsee is valid whether the condition has been fulfilled or not. An indorsement is restrictive, which prohibits further negotiation or which merely gives authority to deal with the instrument for a particular purpose, e.g. collect the amount for the indorser, but is not a transfer of ownership. A restrictive indorsement entitles the indorsee to receive payment of the instrument and sue any party his indorser could have sued but no power to transfer otherwise than it expressly authorises him to exercise. When there is such power, all later indorsees take with the same rights and liabilities as the first indorsee under the restrictive indorsement. (See the Bills of Exchange Act 1882, ss. 31–35). By s. 60 a banker who in good faith and in the ordinary course of business pays a cheque drawn on him on a forged indorsement is protected from liability in conversion. The Cheques Act 1957† was intended to eliminate indorsement when a payee paid a cheque into his own bank account and provides in ss. 1 and 4 that a banker who pays or collects a cheque or certain analogous instruments is not to incur liability merely because of the absence of or irregularity in the indorsement. Section 2 provides that a banker who takes an unindorsed order cheque for value has the same rights as if it had been indorsed and could therefore take immediately as a holder in due course. This constitutes an exception to the Bills of Exchange Act 1882, s. 31 (4) which gives limited rights to the transferee of an unindorsed order cheque. Section 3 provides that an unindorsed order cheque which appears to have been paid by the drawee banker is evidence of the receipt by the payee of the amount of the cheque. In practice an indorsement is usually written on the back of an instrument but it may be written on the face, *Young v Glover* (1857) 3 Jur (NS) QB 637. These provisions apply under the Bills of Exchange Act 1882, s. 89 to a promissory note.

By a resolution of the Committee of London Clearing Bankers 1957 it was decided to continue to require indorsement of cheques and other instruments paid in cash over the counter even though this is no longer necessary under the Cheques Act 1957. It seems that if a paying banker failed to demand such an indorsement he would not be protected by s. 1 of the Act since he would not have acted 'in the ordinary course of business', a pre-condition of protection.

Indorser. The holder of an order bill who writes his signature† on it in order to effect a negotiation of it. The Bills of Exchange Act 1882, s. 55 (2) provides that an indorser by indorsing an instrument is taken to undertake that on proper presentment for acceptance and presentment for payment it will be accepted and paid and that if there is dishonour by non-acceptance or dishonour by non-payment he will compensate the holder or a later indorser who is compelled to pay it, provide that the requisite proceedings on dishonour are taken. (*See* NOTICE OF DISHONOUR). The indorser, having used the instrument as a substitute for money is taken to have in effect guaranteed payment by the acceptor, drawee or drawer of a bill or the maker of a promissory note. Moreover an indorser may not deny to a holder in due course the genuineness and regularity of the drawer's signature and all previous indorsements nor may he deny to his immediate or a later indorsee that the instrument was valid at the time of his indorsement and that he had a good title to it. Section 56 provides that where a person signs a bill otherwise than as drawer or acceptor he incurs the liability of an indorser to a holder in due course. Such a person, signing a negotiable instrument without intending to effect a negotiation of it thus becomes in effect a guarantor of it and is sometimes known as a 'quasi-indorser'. By s. 89 these provisions apply to a promissory note. By s. 16 an indorser may exclude his liabilities by adding to his signature words such as 'without recourse' or 'sans recours'.

Industrial growing crops. A term added to the definition of goods† in the Sale of Goods Act when the Act was extended to Scotland, but not a term of Scots Law. It may be wider than emblements and include crops such as grass and clover.

Infant. *See* CONTRACTUAL CAPACITY.

Inherent vice. *See* COMMON CARRIER.

Injunction. An order of the court directing a person to undertake or to desist from some course of conduct. The former are known as mandatory, the latter as prohibitory injunctions. A quia timet injunction may be obtained to prevent an apprehended wrong and an interlocutory injunction may be obtained to prevent one party seriously prejudicing the other pending final judgment in an action between them. Final injunctions may be granted by such a final judgment. As they are remedies developed by equity injunctions are discretionary and the plaintiff must satisfy the court that his conduct has been equitable, and that damages are not an adequate remedy. Injunctions may be granted to restrain breaches of contract, including express negative terms in contracts of employment but not when to do so would be in effect to grant specific performance of the employment contract.

Injurious Falsehood. *See* TRADE LIBEL.

Inland and foreign bills of exchange and promissory notes. The Bills of Exchange Act 1882, s. 4 provides that an inland bill of exchange is one which purports to be both drawn and payable within the British Islands or drawn within the British Islands on a resident. Any other bill is a foreign bill. Unless the contrary appears a holder may treat a bill as an inland bill. 'British Islands' means the United Kingdom, the Isle of Man and the Channel Islands. By s. 83 (4) a promissory note which is or purports to be both made and payable within the British Islands is an inland note and any other is a foreign note. Section 51 (2) provides that where a foreign bill is dishonoured by non-acceptance it must be protested† and where a foreign bill not dishonoured by non-acceptance is dishonoured by non-payment it must similarly be protested. Such protest is by s. 89 not necessary for a foreign note dishonoured by non-payment. A bill which has been protested for non-acceptance may later be protested for non-payment. If a foreign instrument is not protested in accordance with s. 51(2) the drawer and indorsers are released from liability under the right of recourse. Protest is optional in the case of an inland instrument but proper notice of dishonour must still be given to preserve the rights of the holder.

Innominate term. A term of a contract which cannot initially be classified as either a condition, breach of which gives a right to repudiate as well as damages, or a warranty, a less important term, breach of which is remedied by damages and not repudiation. Breach of an innominate term may either give rise to a right to repudiate and damages, as with breach of condition, or merely to damages, as with breach of warranty, depending on the seriousness of the breach which actually occurs. See *Hong Kong Fir Shipping Co v Kawasaki Kisen Kaisha Ltd* [1962] 2 QB 26.

In pari delicto potior est conditio defendentis. ('In equal fault the position of the defendant is the stronger'). This expresses the general rule that when money has been paid or property transferred in pursuance of an illegal contract where the parties are equally at fault it cannot be recovered by the transferor. Exceptions to the rule are when the illegal purpose has not been even partially carried out, *Taylor v Bowers* (1876) 1 QBD 291, when one party was led to contract by fraud or strong pressure, *Reynell v Sprye* (1852) 1 De GM & G 660, when the party receiving the money or property is under some fiduciary duty to the other and when the illegality arose from the infringement of statute passed for the protection of a class to which the transferor belongs. (*See* ILLEGALITY IN CONTRACT).

Intellectual property. A comprehensive term covering copyright patents, trade marks and analagous rights founded on confidence† and pasing off†.

Intellectual property, international protection. The United Kingdom is party to a number of Conventions under which British subjects may obtain protection for their intellectual property in foreign countries in return for similar protection for the property of subjects of other States party to these Conventions. For copyright there is the Berne Convention of 1886, as revised in 1908, 1948, 1967, and 1971. This gives protection on a basis of equality amongst member States. There is also the Universal Copyright Convention 1952 which is less stringent than the Berne Convention but to which both the U.S.A. and U.S.S.R. are parties. The symbol © together with the name of the copyright owner and date of first publication is necessary for U.C.C. protection but not under the Berne Convention. For patents there is the Paris Convention on Industrial Property as revised in 1900, 1911, 1925, 1934, 1958 and 1967 which facilitates access for foreigners to the municipal systems of member States. Similarly the European Patent Convention 1973 provides a unified system for awarding patents in member States party to the Convention through the European Patent Office in Munich. An applicant receives a number of separate national patents. The Community Patent Convention 1975 is designed eventually to provide a single patent throughout the E.E.C. The Patent Co-operation Treaty 1970 (effective 1978) is designed to facilitate applications in many countries for their municipal patents by providing a unified procedure and does not produce a supranational patent. Trade marks come within the Paris Convention on Industrial Property 1883, facilitating municipal applications, and this country is not party to the Madrid Agreement of 1891 on international registration.

A United Nations organ, the World Intellectual Property Organisation, administers the Berne Convention, the Paris Convention and the Patent Cooperation Treaty whilst U.N.E.S.C.O. administers the Universal Copyright Convention.

Intent to create legal relations. An essential ingredient in the formation of a contract. In social and domestic agreements it will be presumed that there is no intent to create legal relations, whereas in business and professional agreements the contrary will be presumed. These presumptions may be rebutted. A business agreement may be deprived of legal effect if it is stated to be 'binding in honour only', *Rose and Frank v Crompton* [1925] AC 445. Clear language must be used to do this. 'Ex gratia' was not sufficiently clear, *Edwards v Skyways Ltd* [1964] 1 All ER 449. The words 'subject to contract' are widely used to exclude intent to create legal relations especially in agreements preliminary to contracts for the sale of land, *Chillingworth v Esche* [1924] 1 Ch 97, but an agreement described as 'provisional' was held fully binding in *Branca v Cobarro* [1947] KB 854. Whilst it is possible to deprive an agreement of all legal effect and also to make a tribunal other than the courts final on any dispute of fact arising under an agreement having legal effect it is not permissible, on grounds of public policy to oust the jurisdiction of the courts over matters of law arising under such an agreement, except in so far as this is allowed by the Arbitration Act, 1979. (*See* ARBITRATION: APPEAL ON LAW AND PRELIMINARY POINT OF LAW) *Lee v Showmen's Guild* [1952] 2 QB 329; *Baker v Jones* [1954] 2 All ER 553.

Lack of intent to create legal relations may be inferred from informality when, as in the case of sale of land, formality might be expected: *Clifton v Palumbo* [1944] 2 All ER 497.

Inter absentes. 'Between persons not present'. Used in mistake in contract to describe persons not dealing face to face.

Interest Warrant. *See* DIVIDEND WARRANT.

Interference with goods. The Torts (Interference with Goods) Act 1977, s. 1 introduced the comprehensive descriptions of 'wrongful interference' or 'wrongful interference with goods' for the torts of conversion, trespass to goods, negligence resulting in harm to goods and any other tort in so far as it results in damage to goods or an interest in goods. The last category may cover harm to the reversionary interest under a bailment for a fixed term and perhaps trade libel. The Act (s. 2) also abolished detinue which lay for the wrongful retention of goods but in substitution provides that conversion now lies for loss and destruction of goods which a bailee allows to happen in breach of duty. The Act in ss. 3 and 4 provides for judgment for specific delivery with or as an alternative to damages and for interlocutory relief when goods are wrongfully detained. In ss. 5–11 the Act sets out law relating to the extinction of a plaintiff's title on payment of damages, allowance for improvement of goods, double liability, competing rights to goods, concurrent actions and co-ownership in relation to the torts it covers. Section 11 provides that a mere denial of another's title to goods is not conversion (but if malicious it may be trade libel), that receiving a pledge is conversion if the delivery is conversion and that contributory negligence is not a defence to conversion. This last has been amended by the Banking Act 1979, s. 47 to allow the defence in respect of the handling of cheques and other instruments by a collecting banker within the Cheques Act 1957, s. 4. The 1977 Act in s. 12 provides a power of sale for bailees in respect of uncollected goods and s. 13 permits the court to authorise the sale of goods held by a bailee. Section 14 excludes money and choses in action from 'goods' for the purposes of the Act but when a chose in action is represented by a document such as a negotiable instrument or insurance policy damages for conversion of the document will include the value of the underlying right.

Intermediary bank. *See* BANKERS' COMMERCIAL CREDITS.

International Carriage of Perishable Footstuffs Act 1976 enables the United Kingdom to be a party to the A.P.T. Agreement to establish common standards for refrigerated and similar vehicles.

International supply contract. *See* PROPER LAW and UNFAIR CONTRACT TERMS ACT 1977.

Interpleader. When a person holds property to which he makes no claim himself but to which others make conflicting claims the possessor may take out an interpleader summons for the court to determine these claims. If possession was transferred to one of the claimants without such authority and his claim proved defective then even though the transfer was in good faith and with due care the transferor would be liable in conversion to one with a better title.

Inter praesentes. 'Between persons present'. Used in mistake in contract to describe persons dealing face-to-face.

Invitation to treat. An indication or declaration from a person that he is willing to receive offers† from others, which if they are accepted by him will ripen into contracts. Many invitations to treat may resemble offers and the only distinction is the intention with which the declaration was made. On the basis of commercial convenience the courts have indicated that certain types of declaration will be taken to be invitations. Thus an advertisement that an auction sale will be held, *Harris v Nickerson* (1873) LR 8 QB 286 and the auctioneer's request for bids, Sale of Goods Act 1979, s. 57 (2), are invitations but an announcement that an auction is without reserve is an offer, *Warlow v Harrison* (1859) 1 E & E 309. Goods displayed in shop windows or self-service shelves with prices attached are invitations so that the shopkeeper can refuse to sell, *Pharmaceutical Society v Boots Cash Chemists* [1953] 1 QB 401, so also the advertisement of goods in a catalogue, *Grainger v Gough* [1896] AC 325, since otherwise the advertiser might be overwhelmed by numerous acceptances, and requests for tenders, *Spencer v Harding* (1870) LR 5 CP 561. If an advertisement offers a prize or reward for an act it may, however, be treated as an offer, *Carlill v Carbolic Smoke Ball Co* [1893] 1 QB 256.

I.O.U. This is evidence of an account stated which is an admission of a debt upon which arises an implied promise to pay. As such it is not a negotiable instrument but if express promissory words of payment are added it may be a promissory note and in that case negotiable, *Brooks v Elkins* (1836) 2 M & W 74.

Irrevocable credit. *See* BANKERS' COMMERCIAL CREDITS.

Issue of a bill of exchange or promissory note. This is defined in the Bills of Exchange Act 1882, s. 2 as meaning 'the first delivery of a bill or note, complete in form to a person who takes it as holder'.

Issuing bank. *See* BANKERS' COMMERCIAL CREDITS.

J

Joint and several contracts. A joint contractual promise is found when two or more persons, e.g. partners, are treated as making one single promise to the other party or parties to the contract or as receiving such a promise. Where two or more persons jointly contract with the other party or parties but each joint contractor also individually contracts with the other party or parties there is joint and several liability.

Each joint promisor is liable in full on the promise but if judgment is enforced against him alone he may normally recover contribution from his fellows. All joint contractors should normally be sued together and one or all (but not some) joint contractors may be sued. If one joint contractor is sued alone an unsatisfied judgment against him no longer bars proceedings against his fellows, Civil Liability Act 1978, ss. 3 and 7, and only a satisfied judgment against a joint and several contractor discharges his fellows. The liability of a joint debtor (except in partnership) and the rights of a joint creditor pass by survivorship to his co-contractors but a several debt or claim binds or benefits the party's estate.

Release by the creditor of one joint or joint and several debtor releases all and a release by or payment to one joint creditor discharges the whole debt.

A defence available to one joint or joint and several debtor will benefit his fellows if it goes to the substance of the debt and is not merely personal to himself and, conversely, a defence against one joint or joint and several creditor, which is not merely personal to himself, will avail against the other co-creditors.

L

Laydays. *See* VOYAGE CHARTERPARTY.

Laytime. *See* VOYAGE CHARTERPARTY.

Legal tender. Sums of different types of money to which a creditor may not take objection if they are proffered in settlement of a debt. Bank of England notes and gold coins are legal tender for any amount, silver or cupro-nickel coins exceeding ten new pence for any amount up to £10 and similar coins of ten new pence or under for up to £5 whereas bronze coins are legal tender up to twenty new pence. The Currency and Bank Notes Act, 1954, s. 1; Coinage Act 1971, s. 2.

Letter of credit. A synonym for a bankers' commercial credit.

Lex actus. Law of the country with which a transaction is most closely connected. *See* PROPER LAW.

Lex fori. In a contract case in conflict of laws the essential validity of the contract is governed by the proper law but evidence, procedure and remedies governed by the lex fori, the local law of the court, which will effect the classification. If the lapse of a foreign period of limitation bars the right it may be given effect as part of the proper law but not if it merely bars the remedy for then it would be procedural and ignored. Priorities of creditors and enforcement of judgments are procedural. Remoteness of damage in contract, i.e. the range of consequences for which damages will be awarded, is substantive, *D'Almeida Aravjo v Becker* [1953] 2 QB 329 whereas measure of damages, i.e. quantification, is procedural. Whilst interest on a debt is for the proper law it may be that interest on damages is procedural, *Miliangos v Frank (No. 2)* [1977] QB 489 but see *Helmsing Schiffharts v Malta Drydocks* [1977] 2 Lloyd's Rep 444. Damages may be awarded in a foreign currency, *Milangos v Frank* [1976] AC 443.

Lex loci actus or contractus. The law of the country in which an act is done or contract made. *See* PROPER LAW; CONFLICT OF LAWS FOR BILLS OF EXCHANGE.

Lex situs. The law of the country where property is located. *See* PROPER LAW.

Lex loci solutionis. The law of the country where a contract is performed or debt paid. *See* PROPER LAW.

Lien. A form of real security, normally arising by operation of law and not by agreement for its creation, giving the party entitled to it, some right against property of the other party, to enable the former to make good some claim against the latter which may or may not be associated with that property. There are three major, and dissimilar, forms of lien, possessory or common law liens, equitable liens and maritime liens.

Lien of agent. The lien entitles the agent to retain possession of the principal's goods until claims for indemnity and remuneration have been settled and is normally a particular lien. Either by agreement or custom an agent may have a general lien. Many classes of agents, e.g. solicitors and bankers, have a general lien by custom. The agent must have obtained possession lawfully and there must be no agreement or special purpose inconsistent with the lien. It is lost by waiver or by parting with possession of the goods. A sub-agent without privity may have a limited lien over the principal's property. *See* DELEGATUS NON POTEST DELEGARE. With privity a sub-agent has normal rights of lien.

Limitation. Rules of law to ensure that stale claims are not litigated, now largely embodied in the Limitation Act 1980. Thus in simple contract and in tort (except personal injuries) actions must be commenced within six years of the cause of action accruing. In tort and contract involving personal injuries the period is three years subject to a discretion in the court. In actions on deeds (specialty contracts) and for land the period is twelve years. There are special provisions for conversion†. For rent the period is six years. Time is extended in favour of persons under disability (mental patients, infants). Fraud, concealment or mistake misleading the plaintiff may prevent time running and acknowledgment or part-payment by the defendant may re-start its running. Arbitration is covered; s. 34 makes provision for it to be commenced by notice, whereas ordinary actions are commenced by issue of the writ. Many statutes, e.g. Carriage of Goods by Sea Act 1971 contain their own periods of limitation. By s. 39 these are not affected by the Act.

Limitation of a shipowner's liability. Under the Merchant Shipping Act 1894, ss. 502 and 503 and the Merchant Shipping (Liability of Shipowners and Others) Act 1958, s. 3 the 'owner' of a British ship is wholly or partially protected against liability for loss or damage to goods which occurs without actual fault or privity on his part. The word 'owner' covers 'any charterer and any person interested in or in the possession of the ship and, in particular, any manager or operator of the ship'. Masters and crew may also be protected. There is no liability for loss or damage by fire even when caused by the ship being unseaworthy, but the shipowner must prove absence of privity or fault. A corporate body such as a commercial company may be liable for the fault or privity of its central or governing management, *Lennards Carrying Co v Asiatic Petroleum Co* [1915] AC 705, but no owner is liable merely for the fault or privity of his employees. When gold, silver, jewels or watches are lost or damaged by dishonest taking there is again no liability without actual privity or fault unless the owner or master had been given on shipment a notice of nature and value.

Liability is subject to financial limits in the following cases when the misfortune has occurred without actual privity or fault whether the ship is British or foreign. These cases are when loss of life or personal injury occurs to any person carried on the ship, when damage happens to any goods on board and when loss of life or injury is caused to any person not on board or loss or damage happens to any property not on board or any rights are infringed by improper navigation or by any person in loading, carrying or discharging cargo or in embarking, carrying or disembarking passengers. Failure to warn the master as to use of radar may be 'actual fault', *The Lady Gwendolen* [1965] P 294, as will failure to warn of special difficulties in the handling of the ship which might not be obvious to a competent master, *Standard Oil v Clan Line* [1924] AC 100, and hence limitation will not be available in such cases.

The financial limit for liability for loss of life or personal injury (with or without damage to vessels or goods) was an aggregate amount equivalent to 3,100 gold francs per ton of the ship. For a ship under 300 tons the sum was and is multiplied by 300. For damage to vessels or goods (with or without loss of life or injury) the limit was an amount not exceeding 1,000 gold francs per ton. If there are claims in respect of both death and personal injury and harm to vessels and goods exceeding the fund for the ship the claims for loss of life and injury were entitled to 2,100 francs per ton and the balance of claims for loss of life and injury and the claims for vessels and goods ranked equally against the remaining 1,000 gold francs per ton, *The Victoria* (1888) 13 PD 125. Limits of liability apply to the aggregate of such liabilities which are incurred on any distinct occasion. The fault of one part owner does not prevent another from limiting liability and a master who is also owner may limit, *The Annie Hay* [1968] 1 All ER 657. Merchant Shipping Act 1981, s. 1 substitutes special drawing rights for gold francs, 3,100 and 1,000 francs being now 206.67 and 66.67 special drawing rights.

Liquidated damages. *See* DAMAGES.

Lump sum freight. A sum paid for the hire of a ship for one entire service. If the whole cargo is lost no freight† is earned but if a substantial portion is delivered and the rest is lost through excepted perils the whole freight will be recoverable even though the ship itself does not arrive.

Linked transactions. The Consumer Credit Act 1974, s. 19 provides that these arise when a transaction is entered into by a debtor, hirer or relative of his which is not part of a principal regulated agreement, actual or prospective, but is *either* entered into in compliance with a term in the principal agreement *or* the principal agreement is a debtor–creditor–supplier agreement and a subsidiary agreement is to be financed by the main agreement *or* the other party is a creditor, owner of goods, his associate, a person represented by a credit broker who has also taken part in antecedent negotiations for the principal agreement or a person who knew or contemplated that the principal agreement would be made and suggested the subsidiary transaction to the debtor, hirer or his relative in order to induce the creditor or owner to enter into the principal agreement or for some purpose connected with the principal agreement or, where the principal agreement is a 'restricted-use' credit agreement, for a purpose related to a transaction financed by the principal agreement.

A guarantee or suretyship or an indemnity is not a linked transaction.

A linked transaction entered into before the making of the principal agreement has no effect until the latter agreement is made.

If a party withdraws from a prospective principal agreement, s. 57, or cancels or is discharged from an actual one, ss. 69, 70, 96, then any linked transaction is similarly invalidated.

Loss leader. *See* RESALE PRICE MAINTENANCE.

Loss of negotiable instrument. Where a bill of exchange or promissory note has been lost before it is overdue (*see* MATURITY), the holder may apply to the drawer in the case of a bill or the maker of a promissory note for another instrument to the same effect, giving security, if required, to indemnify the drawer or maker against all claims if the lost instrument is found. In any action on a bill or note the court or a judge may order that the loss shall not be set up provided that an indemnity is given against the claims of any other person on the instrument. No duplicate of an acceptance or indorsement may be demanded (see the Bills of Exchange Act 1882, ss. 69, 70 and 89, and Common Law Procedure Act 1854, s. 78 which makes similar provision for other negotiable instruments). When an instrument has been destroyed and not lost, action may be brought on it on proof of destruction, *Hong Kong and Shanghai Bank v Lo Lee Shi* [1928] AC 181.

M

Maintenance. Improper interference in the litigation of another person. Once both a crime and a tort, the Criminal Law Act 1967, ss. 13 and 14 now provides this is no longer so but also saves 'any rule of law' as to public policy or illegality in contract so that an agreement tainted by maintenance is still a void contract. (*See also* CHAMPERTY and ASSIGNMENT OF CONTRACTS).

Maker of a promissory note. The person who makes the unconditional promise in writing to pay at a fixed or determinable future time a sum certain in money which is the essential feature of a promissory note: Bills of Exchange Act 1882, s. 83 (1). By s. 89 (2) the maker of a note is taken to correspond to the acceptor of a bill of exchange when applying the provisions of the Act relating to bills of exchange to promissory notes. Thus the maker is the party primarily liable on a note. By s. 88 the maker of a note by making it is taken to engage to pay it according to its tenor and is precluded from denying to a holder in due course the existence of the payee. By s. 85 a promissory note may be made by two or more makers and they may be liable jointly or jointly and severally. This may affect selection amongst the makers as defendants to an action on the note and perhaps survival of liability but since the Civil Liability Act 1978 judgment recovered against one joint contractor does not release the others. This removes one important difference between the two forms of liability. (*See* JOINT AND SEVERAL CONTRACTS.)

Mareva Injunction. So named from the case of *Mareva Compania Naviera SA v International Bulk Carriers* [1975] 2 Lloyd's Rep 509 this is an injunction to restrain a defendant from removing assets from the jurisdiction so as to defeat enforcement of a judgment by a successful plaintiff. It will not be granted merely because the defendant is foreign, *Third Chandris v Unimarine* [1979] 2 All ER 972. In *The Siskina* [1979] AC 210 the House of Lords held that the plaintiff must show a good arguable case that he has a cause of action within the jurisdiction but this has been qualified by the Civil Jurisdiction and Judgments Act 1982 which applies to civil and commercial proceedings (excluding wills, insolvency, arbitration, revenue, customs, administrative or matrimonial matters) and is designed to give effect to a Convention on Enforcement of Judgments amongst E.E.C. Countries. By s. 25 interim relief, including a *Mareva* injunction, may be granted if the court thinks it expedient, if proceedings have been commenced in another contracting state or a part of the United Kingdom where the High Court has no jurisdiction and the proceedings fall within the scope of the Convention. By the Supreme Court Act 1981, s. 37, the court may grant a *Mareva* injunction whether or not the defendant is domiciled, present or resident within the jurisdiction. The injunction does not affect other security rights in the defendant's property and will normally allow the use of the assets for ordinary business and domestic purposes, *The Cretan Harmony* [1978] 1 Lloyd's Rep 425. There must also be a real risk that if the injunction is not granted the defendant will not satisfy the judgment, *Establissement Esefka v Central Bank of Nigeria* [1979] 1 Lloyd's Rep 445, and an injunction will not be allowed to restrain the freedom of action of third parties: *Galaxia Maritime SA v Mineralimportexport, The Eleftherios* [1982] 1 All ER 796.

Maritime lien. This right attaches to property, usually a ship, as a result of some liability incurred in connection with a maritime adventure. Unlike a common law lien it does not depend upon possession of the property but follows the property, binding it in the hands of successive transferees even if they purchase in good faith and for value, *The Bold Buccleugh* (1851) 7 Moo PC 267. It is enforced by arrest and sale (unless security is given) ordered by the Admiralty Court. Such liens include that of the salvor for salvage, of seamen for their wages, of the master for wages and disbursements and the lien for damage caused in a collision over the ship responsible for the collision. A lien takes priority over mortgages of a ship. The lien of a later salvor is preferred to that of an earlier salvor and to an earlier damage lien, (e.g. for collision) since the later salvor has saved the property for the benefit of the earlier liens, *The Inna* [1938] P 148, but a later damage lien takes precedence over an earlier salvage lien, *The Veritas* [1901] P 304. Amongst damage liens a party who has obtained judgment has priority over those who have only commenced proceedings but otherwise such liens rank equally amongst themselves even if the collisions did not occur at the same time, *The Stream Fisher* [1927] P 73. As between damage liens and contractual liens it seems that normally damage liens take priority over prior contractual liens because those holding the contractual liens voluntarily chose to be involved with the ship and, in the case of the master and seamen, may have been responsible for the damage. Amongst contractual liens the later the lien the higher the priority, but the seamen's lien for wages takes precedence over the master's for wages and disbursements. Prior maritime liens (e.g. for salvage) take priority over a shiprepairer's possessory lien for repairs, *The Russland* (1924) 130 LT 763, but the repairer's lien takes priority over any subsequent maritime liens (e.g. for seamen's wages) created whilst the vessel is in his hands.

Liens remain inchoate until they are enforced by Admiralty proceedings in rem against the ship over which they are claimed. Many other claims are enforced by these proceedings, e.g. towage, and these are said to give rise to statutory liens which follow the vessel into the hands of successive transferees, except, unlike maritime liens proper, a bona fide purchaser for value. Prior maritime liens take priority over statutory liens.

Market overt. An exception to nemo dat quod non habet, the rule that a seller with a defective title cannot confer a better one on his buyer, Sale of Goods Act 1979, s. 22 provides that when goods are sold in market overt, according to market custom, a buyer in good faith and without notice of the sellers' defective title acquires a good title. The market must be public and legally constituted either by statute, charter or prescription. By custom all shops in the City of London are market overt. The sale must be open and between sunrise and sunset, *Reid v Commissioner for Police* [1973] QB 551. A sale to a trader is not covered, *Ardath Tobacco Co v Ocker* (1931) 47 TLR 177 nor is a sale by sample since the whole transaction must take place in the market, *Crane v London Dock Co* (1864) 33 LJQB 224. Market overt does not operate in Scotland or Wales.

Mate's receipt. An acknowledgment that goods have been shipped which is issued prior to the bill of lading, is less formal than the bill of lading and exchanged for it. A bill of lading may be issued without production of the mate's receipt if those issuing the bill do not know of any conflicting interest. If the bill and the receipt get into different hands, delivery must be made to the holder of the bill. The receipt is not normally a document of title but may be so by local custom, *Kum v Wah Tat Bank Ltd* [1971] 1 Lloyd's Rep 439, if it does not contain terms inconsistent with that character.

Maturity of a negotiable instrument. This means the time at which the instrument is payable. A demand instrument is always mature until in the case of a bill of exchange it appears to have been in circulation for an unreasonable time since issue, but this does not apply to a promissory note. (Bills of Exchange Act 1882, ss. 36 (3), 86 (3)). A time instrument is mature on the last day of the period of time specified. By s. 45 there should be presentment for payment on that day unless delay or non-presentment is excused under s. 46. For demand instruments presentment for payment should be made within a reasonable time. When maturity has passed an instrument is 'overdue' and can only be transferred subject to equities.

Mercantile agent. *See* FACTORS ACT 1889.

Merchandise Marks Acts 1862–1953, now repealed and replaced by the Trade Descriptions Acts 1968–1972† rendered criminal the misleading use of trade marks and trade descriptions and provided for the implication, unless excluded, of a warranty that marks and descriptions were genuine, thus providing a civil remedy.

Merchantable quality. The Sale of Goods Act 1979, s. 14 opens by providing that except for the two conditions as to merchantable quality and fitness for purpose implied in contracts for sale of goods by that section, terms implied by usage, terms implied by s. 15 in sale by sample and terms implied by any other enactment there is no implied term as to quality or fitness for purpose in sale of goods: Sale of Goods Act 1893, s. 14 (2) implied a condition as to merchantable quality but this was amended by the Supply of Goods (Implied Term) Act 1973 which removed the requirement that the sale should be by description, amended the circumstances in which the condition would not be implied and introduced a definition of 'merchantable quality'. These amendments have been embodied in the 1979 Act and hence authorities on the 1893 sub-section must be used with care. The new definition in s. 14 (6) provides that 'goods of any kind are of merchantable quality . . . if they are as fit for the purpose or purposes for which goods of that kind are commonly bought as it is reasonable to expect having regard to any description applied to them, the price (if relevant) and all the other relevant circumstances'. To be merchantable goods need not be 'of good, or fair or average quality'. They may be of inferior or even bad quality, taking into account price, description and other circumstances, *Taylor v Combined Buyers* [1924] NZLR 627 at 645; *Brown v Craiks* [1970] 1 All ER 823. They may be secondhand, *Bartlett v Sydney Marcus* [1965] 1 WLR 1013, if sold as secondhand. Goods will be unmerchantable if they 'would not have been used by a reasonable man for any purpose for which goods which complied with the description under which those goods were sold would normally be used', *Cammell Laird v Manganese Bronze* [1934] AC 402 at 430; *Kendall v Lillico* [1969] 2 AC 31 at 77. If goods have many uses the fact that they may not be fit for the buyer's special purpose will not render them unmerchantable if they are fit for other uses. Such a buyer to obtain a remedy must satisfy the requirements of s. 14 (3) as to fitness for purpose, *Sumner Permain v Webb & Co* [1922] 1 KB 55. If part of the goods are unmerchantable all may be rejected, *Jackson v Rotax* [1910] 2 KB 937, also holding that minor defects may render goods unmerchantable even though they may be simply and cheaply corrected. It has been suggested that the new statutory definition may have altered this to the extent that when it is normal to expect goods, e.g. new cars, to have minor defects they will not now be unmerchantable if they are defective. If goods would normally be processed before use, e.g. pork cooked, they will not be unmerchantable if used without proper processing, *Heil v Hedges* [1951] 1 TLR 512. It has been held that when perishable goods, e.g. potatoes, are to be sent on a voyage or journey they will not be merchantable if not fit to 'endure the normal journey and be in merchantable condition on arrival'. *Mash & Murrell v Emanuel* [1961] 1 All ER 485; revsd. on facts [1962] 1 All ER 77. This has been limited to perishable goods, *Cordova v Victor Bros* [1966] 1 WLR 793, and other cases raise doubt as to whether merchantability includes any element of durability, *Oleificio Zucchi v Northern Sales* [1965] 2 Lloyd's Rep 496 at 518; *Crowther v Shannon* [1975] 1 WLR 30.

The term as to merchantable quality will not be implied in private sales since the seller must be selling 'in the course of a business'. By s. 14 (5) if a private seller sells through an agent acting in the course of a business the term will be implied unless the buyer either knows that the principal is a private seller or reasonable steps were taken to bring this to his notice before contracting. Even in business sales the term will not apply in respect of defects specifically drawn to the buyer's attention before the contract, or, when the buyer examines the goods before contracting, in respect of defects which 'that examination' ought to have revealed. Hence if the buyer makes only a cursory examination the term will still apply in respect of defects which that superficial examination would not have brought to light. Under the Unfair Contract Terms Act 1977†, s. 6 liability under s. 14 cannot be excluded or restricted by any contract term as against anyone dealing as a consumer and as against others an exclusion clause will only be effective so far as it is reasonable, but s. 26 allows exclusion in international supply contracts.

Mergers. The Monopolies and Mergers Act 1965 provided for the reference of mergers of companies to the Monopolies Commission and special provision was made for newspaper mergers. The law as amended is now embodied in Part V of the Fair Trading Act 1973 providing for reference to the Monopolies and Mergers Commission†.

If as a result of the merger of two or more enterprises either monpoly conditions (*see* MONOPOLIES) will prevail or be strengthened or the value of the assets taken over will exceed £15,000,000, the relevant Department may refer the matter to the Commission for investigation. The conditions must prevail in the United Kingdom or in a substantial part of the United Kingdom unlike monopoly references which, apart from export, may be limited to part of the United Kingdom. If it is found that the merger will be against the public interest the Commission must consider what action is needed and include recommendations in their report. The report must be made within a time limit not exceeding six months set by the Department with a possible extension of three months. If the Commission reports that a proposed merger is against the public interest the Department may inter alia order the merger not to be effected and the Secretary of State may require it to be delayed pending the report.

The transfer of a newspaper or newspaper assets to a proprietor whose papers would have, with the paper to be transferred, an average daily circulation of 500,000 copies is unlawful and void unless the Secretary of State consents. He must refer such a proposed transfer to the Commission within one month of an application for consent unless he is satisfied that the newspaper to be transferred has an average daily circulation of less than 25,000 copies or is satisfied that the paper is not economic as a going concern and either it is not to continue as a separate newspaper or that, if it is, the case is of urgency.

When a reference is made the Commission must report within three months (with a possible extension for a further three months) whether the transfer may be against the public interest 'having regard (amongst other things) to the need for accurate presentation of news and free expression of opinion'. For newspaper references the Secretary of State may appoint additional members to the Commission from a special panel.

Minor. *See* CONTRACTUAL CAPACITY.

Misrepresentation. A misleading statement of material fact made prior to a transacton, frequently a contract, and inducing the representee to act on it to his detriment. If the statement was made with knowledge of its falsity or recklessly, without caring whether it was true or false, it is the tort of deceit or fraud. Mere negligence does not suffice for this tort, *Derry v Peek* (1889) 14 App Cas 337. The victim may avoid the contract within a reasonable time, with or without suing for damages, or may affirm the contract and sue for damages. He can recover for all the loss directly caused by the misrepresentation, *Doyle v Olby* [1969] 2 QB 158. Prior to *Hedley Byrne v Heller* [1964] AC 465 all other misrepresentation was described as 'innocent', but that case allowed an action in tort for negligent misrepresentation when a special relation of reliance existed between the parties, this being available for both pre-contractual and other misrepresentations, *Esso v Mardon* [1976] QB 801. The Misrepresentation Act 1967 also provides remedies for both negligent and purely innocent pre-contractual representations so that fraudulent, negligent and innocent misrepresentations must now be distinguished.

Mere silence does not amount to misrepresentation except in contracts uberrimae fidei but a partial and misleading representation of true facts, (e.g. all good points without mentioning bad), will do so as will concealment of defects and failure to correct an initially true statement which has become untrue before being acted on. A 'puff' which a reasonable man would treat as mere advertising exaggeration will not be misrepresentation (simplex commendatio non obligat) nor will a statement of opinion which proves to be ill-founded unless the maker had better grounds than the other on which to found the opinion and he in effect misrepresents these, *Smith v Land & House Property Corpn* (1884) 28 Ch D 7. Nor is a statement of intention which is not fulfilled unless it can be shown that the misrepresentor did not form that intention, *Edgington v Fitzmaurice* (1885) 29 Ch D 459. Nor is a statement of general law, unless perhaps it amounts to a misrepresentation of opinion, but a statement of private right, e.g. ownership of particular property, is fact and may ground misrepresentation. The fact that the victim was given an opportunity to check the statement will not negate misrepresentation if he does not check but if he does not rely on it but on his own inquiries he cannot claim remedies, *Attwood v Small* (1838) 6 Cl & Fin 232.

Misrepresentation, unless it induces mistake in contract, renders a contract voidable not void.

Remedies for negligent misrepresentation are avoidance or re-scission of the contract and damages. As the Misrepresentation Act 1967 puts the burden of proof on the representor this may now be used in preference to *Hedley Byrne v Heller* for pre-contractual representations. Remedies for innocent misrepresentation are avoidance and action for an indemnity against obligations created by the contract. This is more limited than a claim for damages. The court has under the Act a discretion to award damages in lieu of rescission in negligent and innocent misrepresentation.

Rescission or avoidance will be barred if the representee affirms the contract, if full restitution of the subject matter is not possible, if third parties have acquired rights in the subject matter in good faith and for value, or, in non-fraudulent misrepresentation, after the lapse of time sufficient to discover the truth. Under s. 1 of the Act the fact that the misrepresentation has become a term of the contract or the fact that the contract has been performed are no longer bars.

Exemption and exclusion clauses designed to exclude liability for fraud are ineffective and under the Misrepresentation Act 1967, s. 3 (as amended by the Unfair Contract Terms Act 1977†) in the case of other misrepresentations such clauses are only effective to the extent that they satisfy the requirement of reasonableness in the latter Act, proof of which lies on the party seeking to rely on the clause. A clause denying the existence of any representation may take a statement outside these provisions, *Overbrooke Estates v Glencombe Properties* [1974] 3 All ER 511.

Mistake in Contract. For reasons of policy the courts allow only a limited range of mistakes to vitiate a contract. Such mistakes may be classified either as mistakes negativing consent or mistakes nullifying consent, or as mutual, unilateral and common mistakes, the first two negativing consent as preventing the parties reaching agreement and the third nullifying consent, as preventing a real agreement being effective.

Mutual mistake occurs when the parties are at cross-purposes, e.g. as in *Raffles v Wichelhaus* (1864) 2 H & C 906, each party having in mind a different ship of the same name, *Peerless*. In such cases the courts endeavour to ascertain 'the sense of the promise', what a reasonable man would have understood the parties to have agreed, and enforce that. Only if the confusion is so great, as in *Raffles v Wichelhaus* that no such 'sense' can be ascertained will the agreement be void. Unilateral mistake occurs where one party, to the knowledge of the other is mistaken as to the nature of the promise being made to him. Such mistake may relate to the terms of the promise, as in *Hartog v Colin & Shields* [1939] All ER 566 where an offer to sell goods at a price per pound was accepted though the prior negotiations in accordance with usage had been for sale at a price per piece, a piece being worth a third of a pound. It was held that the buyer must have realised that the seller was mistaken and the transaction was void. (*See also* NON EST FACTUM). Such mistake may also relate to the identity of a party. Here one party must to the knowledge of the other be confusing that other with a third existing person and have good reason for wishing to contract with that third person, *Boulton v Jones* (1857) 27 LJ Ex 117 (mistaken party wished to contract with former owner of business as having a set-off against him), *Cundy v Lindsay* (1878) 3 App Cas 459 (mistaken party wished to contract with firm of repute who had apparently ordered goods). If there is no existing third person, as where the party not mistaken purports to write on behalf of a substantial but non-existent company, there may be a voidable contract because of deceit but not a void contract because of mistake, *King's Norton Metal Co v Edridge, Merrett* (1897) 14 TLR 98. This is described as a mistake of attribute as distinct from a mistake of identity. When the parties are dealing face-to-face there is a very strong presumption that there is no mistake of identity even when the non-mistaken party adopts the identity of an existing third person, *Lewis v Averay* [1972] 1 QB 198. The presumption may be rebutted by proof of care in attempting to verify the purported identity. As unilateral mistake, when operative, may render a contract void this may have serious consequences for innocent third parties who will not acquire title to property the subject of the transaction. This explains the presumption against mistake face-to-face, the fact that a mistake as to attribute as distinct from confusion with a third person will not render a contract void and the severe limits on non est factum.

In common mistake there is no mistake as to the terms of the agreement but because of the failure of some common assumption, e.g. as to the existence, (res extincta), *Couturier v Hastie* (1856) 5 HLC 673 (cargo ceased to exist) *Strickland v Turner* (1852) 7 Ex 208 (sale of annuity on life of person already dead) or ownership, (res sua), *Cooper v Phibbs* (1867) LR 2 HL 149, of the subject matter or the physical possibility of the contractual purpose, *Sheik v Ochsner* [1957] AC 136, the agreement cannot take effect as a contract. In view of *Bell v Lever Bros* [1932] AC 161 (contract to discharge valueless voidable service agreements not void) it is doubtful if a mistake as to a quality, however important, of an existing subject matter will render a contract void. Sometimes a party may be taken to have guaranteed (perhaps by collateral contract) the existence of the subject matter and hence will be liable if it does not exist, *McRae v Commonwealth Disposals* (1951) 84 CLR 377. Mistake must be of fact or of private right, such as to the ownership of particular property, not of general law. Both at common law and in equity the types of mistake described will, when operative, render a contract void but some mistakes, insufficiently serious to render a contract void, may render it voidable in equity, *Solle v Butcher* [1950] 1 KB 671 (common mistake as to application of Rent Acts to flat), *Magee v Pennine Insurance* [1969] 2 QB 507 (common mistake as to validity of insurance on which compromise based) or affect the grant of equitable remedies. *Grist v Bailey* [1967] Ch 532, (common mistake as to application of Rent Acts to property contracted to be sold. Specific performance refused provided new contract made to sell property at appropriate price).

The equitable remedy of rectification may also be granted in respect of common clerical error in reducing an agreement or understanding into a written contract or in respect of unilateral clerical error when there has been sharp practice on the part of the party not mistaken.

Mitigation. *See* DAMAGES.

Money had and received. *See* QUASI–CONTRACT.

Moneylenders Acts 1900–1927. These, now repealed and replaced by the Consumer Credit Act 1974, defined a 'moneylender', provided for the licensing of and the imposition of restrictions on money lending, invalidated contracts not complying with these restrictions and provided for the re-opening of harsh and unconscionable transactions.

Money of account. In international contracts the currency in which the measure of liability is expressed. This may or may not be the money of payment in which the debtor actually discharges the debt. Since it is now possible to award damages in a foreign currency (*see* LEX FORI) the distinction between money of account and money of payment is less important than formerly.

Monopolies. Agreements between traders tending to distort competition and to create monopolies were at common law valid subject to a test of reasonableness. The Monopolies and Restrictive Practices (Inquiry and Control) Act 1948 established the Monopolies and Restrictive Practices Commission to investigate and report on such practices which might then be controlled by delegated legislation. The Commission's work was limited by the Restrictive Trade Practices Act 1956 but extended by the Monopolies and Mergers Act 1965 and further extended by the Fair Trading Act 1973. This renamed it the Monopolies and Mergers Commission† and now contains much of the law relating to the investigation and control of these economic situations apart from E.E.C. Competition Law. Either the Director-General of Fair Trading† or the Secretary of State or the Secretary of State jointly with other Ministers may make a monopoly reference to the Commission if it appears to them that a monopoly position exists in the supply of goods or services or in the export of goods either generally or to a particular market.

The Act specifies that such conditions prevail in the supply of goods when it appears that either at least one quarter of the relevant goods supplied in the United Kingdom or any part of it, are supplied by or to any one person (or by or to two or more persons if they are inter-connected bodies corporate or so act whether by agreement or not as to prevent, restrict or distort competition) or any agreements or arrangements (whether legally enforceable or not) result in goods of the type not being supplied in the United Kingdom or any part of it. In the supply of services, monopoly conditions prevail if it seems that either at least one quarter of the relevant services supplied in the United Kingdom is by or for any one person (or by or for two or more persons if they are interconnected bodies corporate or so act whether by agreement or not as to prevent, restrict, or distort competition), or any agreements or arrangements (whether legally enforceable or not) result in services of the type not being supplied in the United Kingdom or any part of it. There may be monopoly conditions in relation to exports if it happens that either one-quarter of the relevant goods produced in the United Kingdom are produced by one person or group of interconnected bodies corporate or if agreements affecting at least one quarter of the relevant goods produced in the United Kingdom prevent, restrict or distort either export or competition in regard to export from the United Kingdom or if agreements affecting at least one quarter of the relevant goods produced in the United Kingdom prevent, restrict or distort supply of goods of that type (whether from the United Kingdom or not) or have a similar effect on competition in respect of supply.

In deciding whether the relevant quarter is supplied or produced the Department and the Commission may apply such criteria (value, cost, price, etc.) as they think fit.

The Commission may be asked either to report merely as to whether monpoly conditions prevail and how they are maintained, or further, whether such conditions do or may be expected to operate against the public interest. References, which may be varied, may be confined to particular practices or to particular parts of the United Kingdom. The Commission may be required to report on the general effect on the public interest of monopoly practices or on the desirability of remedying mischief arising from them. In determining the public interest all relevant matters are to be taken into account, particularly the need for effective competition in the United Kingdom, the interests of consumers, purchasers and users of goods and services in this country in regard to price and variety, the reduction of costs, development of new techniques and products and the facilitating of the entry of new competitors into existing markets. Account is also to be taken of the balanced distribution of industry and employment within this country and the need for promoting competition abroad amongst producers of goods and services in this country.

Before any action can be taken on a report there must have been a reference to the Commission not limited to ascertaining the facts; the report must have been laid before Parliament, with or without omissions, and the report must find that monopoly conditions prevail contrary to the public interest. The Department may then make orders to remedy the mischief and prohibit the operation of the agreements. The Director-General may obtain undertakings to remedy or prevent the effects of monopoly.

An order may prohibit the withholding or threats to withhold supplies or services, the attaching of conditions to supply, price discrimination or other preferences, require the publication of prices or other information, regulate prices, forbid the acquisition of another business and require the division of any trade or business.

Contraventions do not result in criminal proceedings but the Crown or others can bring civil proceedings for an injunction or other relief. The Director-General is to keep under review any undertaking he receives, to consider whether it requires to be varied or superseded and, if it is not being fulfilled, to advise the Department.

Monopolies and Mergers Commission. A body which investigates and reports upon matters relating to trade competition subject to limits prescribed by statute, the matter being referred to it either by the appropriate Government department or by the Director General of Fair Trading†. The Commission was first constituted as the Monopolies and Restrictive Practices Commission by the Monopolies and Restrictive Practices (Inquiry and Control) Act 1948 to report on matters relating to the supply or processing of goods, buildings, or structures referred to it by the Board of Trade. Action might then be taken by delegated legislation on the report. The name was changed to the Monopolies Commission by the Restrictive Trade Practices Act 1956 which set up the Restrictive Practices Court† to adjudicate on restrictive practices relating to goods. Matters within the jurisdiction of the Court were withdrawn from the competence of the Commission, this being reflected in the change of name. The matters to be investigated by the Commission were extended by the Monopolies and Mergers Act 1965 to cover the supply of services and proposed mergers of companies that might lead to a monopoly situation. The possible scope of the Commission's investigations into monopolies and mergers was further extended by the Fair Trading Act 1973. This inter alia reduced the share of control or prospective control over a field of commercial activity giving grounds for inquiry from one-third to one-quarter. The Commission was renamed as the Monopolies and Mergers Commission and it was provided that merger references were to be made by the Secretary of State and monopoly references either by the Secretary of State or by the Director-General of Fair Trading, whose office was brought into being by the 1973 Act. The Director must assist the Commission with information and in other ways. The Director may also under the Competition Act 1980 refer to the Commission trading practices which distort competition.

This Commission can require the attendance of witnesses, administer oaths and require the production of documents and other information but not evidence which could not be required in ordinary civil proceedings. After investigating it submits a report which must be comprehensive and reasoned. Where the reference is not merely for fact finding the report must consider if and what action is needed to remedy any mischief it finds. The chairman has a casting vote, but a dissenter can require his dissent and reasons to be included in the report. The report must be laid before Parliament unless it appears to be contrary to the national interest to publish any part of it. The Commission must consider how far it is possible to exclude mention of the private affairs of an individual or the specific affairs of a body of persons when mention might seriously prejudice their interests.

A monopoly reference must include a time limit for reporting and if this is not observed it lapses but extensions may be allowed.

Mortgage (or charge). A form of real security where the borrower (mortgagor or chargor) normally retains possession of the property mortgaged but grants a proprietary interest to the lender (mortgagee or chargee). Where a mortgage or charge is granted by a company formalities and rules prescribed by the Companies Acts must be observed, especially in regard to registration, in addition to whatever procedures are necessary for the type of property being mortgaged. In the case of individuals and unincorporated bodies, mortgages of land are largely governed by Law of Property Act 1925 and associated legislation governing registration. Mortgages of things or choses in action are largely governed by the rules for assignment of contracts and mortgages of goods are regulated by the Bills of Sale Acts 1878–1882†.

Mortgages of ships. A registered ship or any share therein (*see* REGISTRATION OF BRITISH SHIPS and BRITISH SHIPOWNERS) may under the Merchant Shipping Act 1894, ss. 31–46 be mortgaged either by a direct mortgage with registration or by a mortgage under a mortgage certificate. The first type must be in the form prescribed and be entered by the registrar in the register. Priority of mortgages depends on order in the register. Transfers and discharge must also be registered. The mortgage does not transfer ownership in the vessel but, subject to the rights of prior mortgagees, confers a power of sale on non-payment of the debt. The mortgagee may take possession if money becomes due under the mortgage or the security is impaired. He is then entitled to accruing freight† but not to freight earned before he went into possession. Mortgage under a mortgage certificate is to be used when the ship is out of the country of her port of registry and is not to be used in the United Kingdom or in any British possession if the port of registry is located there. In applying for the certificate, the owner must specify who is to exercise the power, the maximum amount to be raised on mortgage, if this has been fixed, and the time and place where the power is to be exercised. Applications are made to the registrar at the port of registry who will enter these particulars on the register. When the mortgage is effected it must be registered by endorsement on the certificate by a British consular official.

Multiple Agreements. The Consumer Credit Act 1974, s. 18, provides that these arise either when part of an agreement falls within one category of agreement mentioned in the Act and part within another category or part falls within a mentioned category and part does not. Those parts within the Act will be regulated by their appropriate categories and parts within and parts outside the Act are to be treated as separate agreements. By s. 18 (6) the Act does not apply to a multiple agreement relating to the hire of goods when payment is made by rent for land (other than a rent charge), thus excluding from the Act the hiring of furniture in a furnished letting.

N

Negligence. In tort negligence may indicate the commission of some tort (other than the separate tort of negligence) through want of due care as when libel is committed by the careless publication of defamatory matter. In this sense negligence is contrasted with intention and breach of a strict duty as methods of committing torts and denotes a state of mind characterised by a lack of desire for the tortious consequences. Negligence may also indicate the separate tort of that name established by *Donoghue v Stevenson* [1932] AC 562. Here negligence denotes conduct creating an undue risk of harm which has resulted in harm to the plaintiff. The requisites of the tort are a legal duty of care between the parties, breach of that duty by failure of the defendant to attain the proper standard of care, which is that of the reasonable man in the circumstances, and damage or personal injury to the plaintiff which is not too remote a consequence of the breach. In determining the existence of a duty of care the court asks whether the plaintiff could be regarded as the defendant's 'neighbour', that is, should the defendant reasonably have foreseen harm to the plaintiff when directing his mind to the act or omissions called in question. The 'neighbour test' does not necessarily require geographical propinquity. The legal duty to take precautions against purely physical harm is now almost universal, some qualifications, e.g. in regard to premises, having been abrogated by legislation. For reasons of policy a number of other exceptions and qualifications to the 'neighbour duty' remain, e.g. in regard to economic loss, pure omissions, negligent misrepresentation, advocacy in legal proceedings. In determining whether there has been breach of duty the court will again ask whether the defendant could reasonably have foreseen harm to the plaintiff but even then this may not amount to breach if the likelihood was small, the utility of the act of the defendant was great or the cost of avoiding harm was great in comparison with the risk run. In determining whether the defendant's act or omissions has caused the plaintiff's loss the courts apply a 'but-for test', asking whether the loss would have occurred but for what the defendant did. Even if it is decided that the defendant did cause the loss he will not be liable in damages for such loss as is too remote a consequence of what he did. Since *The Wagon Mound* [1961] AC 388 the test for remoteness is whether the defendant could reasonably have foreseen the loss. The use of the test of foresight in each of the three chief components of the tort means that their limits are sometimes unclear in the cases and it was said in *Roe v Ministry of Health* [1954] 2 QB 66 that the three components are simply different ways of looking at the one question: 'Is the consequence fairly to be regarded as within the risk created by the negligence?'. The damages to be awarded to the plaintiff may be reduced because of his contributory negligence.

The doctrine of vicarious liability under which an employer ('master' in legal terminology) is liable in damages for torts committed by his employee ('servant' in legal terminology) in the course of his employment in practice operates to impose liability upon a person better able to satisfy a claim for damages and to insure against such claims. A plaintiff carries the burden of proving negligence but the discharge of this is often facilitated by res ipsa loquitur.

The test for negligence in determining whether a collecting banker is to be deprived of the protection of s. 4 of the Cheques Act 1957 and hence liable in conversion to the true owner of a cheque or other instrument which the banker has collected for a person not entitled to it depends on a special body of case law based on the practice of bankers.

Negotiable instrument. A document embodying an obligation to pay money (or, exceptionally, to deliver a security for money) which, either by mercantile custom or by statute may be transferred by the holder either by delivery† or by indorsement and delivery so that the transferee, taking it in good faith and for value (*see* CONSIDERATION), will be able to sue the person primarily liable on the instrument and others such as indorsers who may be under a guarantee liability in respect of that person, such transferee also being able to obtain a better title to the instrument that his transferor had. Negotiable instruments thus constitute important exceptions to the rules of privity of contract and nemo dat quod non habet. As negotiable instruments are contracts they require consideration but, by exception to the ordinary rules of contract, for many negotiable instruments such as bills of exchange, including cheques, and promissory notes, consideration will be presumed in favour of the holder and an antecedent debt or obligation may constitute consideration, thus forming an exception to the normal rules as to past consideration. A holder may also rely on consideration given by other parties to the instrument, this again departing from the general rule. (See the Bills of Exchange Act 1882, ss. 27 and 30). The chief forms of negotiable instrument are bills of exchange, including cheques, promissory notes, dividend warrants, interest warrants, share warrants, debenture warrants, scrip and bankers' drafts. Postal orders and money orders are not negotiable by their terms and share certificates and debenture certificates are not negotiable because transfer requires the completion of a separate document of transfer and entry on a register kept by the company. An I.O.U. is not negotiable but if it contains appropriate additional promissory words may amount to a promissory note. It is very doubtful whether travellers' cheques are negotiable. At first a mercantile custom to treat a type of instrument as negotiable will have to be proved, *Bechuanaland Exploration Co v London Trading Bank* [1898] 2 QB 658, but in later cases the court may dispense with proof and judicially notice the custom, *Edelstein v Schuler* [1902] 2 KB 144. A bill of lading may be transferable by delivery or by indorsement and delivery and the Bills of Lading Act 1855 qualifies the ordinary rules of privity of contract but a transferee in good faith and for value may only in two cases obtain a better title than his transferor had, over and above the cases in which an ordinary buyer of goods may do so. These two cases are that he may override a seller's lien and a right of stoppage in transitu. Hence bills of lading are said to be quasi-negotiable.

Negotiable instruments may be used for making payment at a distance without transporting coin as where a debtor drawer draws a bill of exchange ordering a drawee indebted to him (often a bank with which he has deposited funds) to make payment to his payee-creditor. These instruments may also be used to give additional security for the payment of a debt but this has been very severely restricted for agreements falling within its scope by the Consumer Credit Act 1974, ss. 123 and 125. In the case of accommodation bills they may be employed as a device for obtaining credit and the holder of a negotiable instrument which is not immediately payable may 'discount' it, that is, transfer it at some small discount from its face value, to a bank or financial house who will collect the proceeds from the party liable when the instrument matures. Thus merchants may advance credit to their debtors by drawing time instruments on them only payable after the lapse of a period of time and by discounting the bill enjoy the immediate benefit of almost all the sum advanced by way of credit.

In general a conditional instrument expressed to be payable only on the happening of an event which may or may not happen will not be negotiable. An instrument negotiable in a foreign country will only be negotiable in this country if it is treated as negotiable by mercantile custom here, *Gorgier v Mieville* (1824) 3 B & C 45; *Picker v London and County Banking Co* (1887) 18 QBD 515.

The words 'not negotiable' written on an ordinary bill of exchange may prevent all transfer of the instrument, *Hibernian Bank v Gysin & Hanson* [1939] 1 KB 483, but by the Bills of Exchange 1882, s. 81 when these words appear on a crossed cheque the instrument remains transferable but the transferee cannot obtain a better title than his transferor.

Negotiation credit. *See* BANKERS' COMMERCIAL CREDITS.

Negotiation of negotiable instruments. The Bills of Exchange Act 1882, s. 31 provides that a bill of exchange is negotiated when it is transferred from one person to another so as to constitute the transferee the holder of the bill. A bearer bill is negotiated by delivery and an order bill is negotiated by the indorsement of the holder completed by delivery. When the holder of an order bill transfers it for value without indorsing it, the transferee acquires such title as the transferor had in the instrument together with the right to demand the indorsement of the transferor. (By s. 89 these provisions apply to a promissory note.) The Cheques Act 1957, s. 2, however, provides that a banker who takes an unindorsed order cheque for value has the same rights as if the cheque had been indorsed and could, therefore, immediately take as a holder in due course.

Nemo dat quod non habet. 'Nobody gives what he has not got'. The maxim expresses the rule in Sale of Goods Act 1979, s. 21, where goods are sold by someone 'who is not their owner and who does not sell them under the authority or with the consent of the owner, the buyer acquires no better title to the goods than the seller had'. The principle has been applied in e.g. cases where there is a void contract because of mistake† of identity. A third party who takes goods which were the subject matter of the transaction does not acquire a good title against the original owner, *Cundy v Lindsay* [1878] 3 App Cas 459; *Ingram v Little* [1961] 1 QB 31. For the convenience of commerce there are numerous exceptions to the maxim, many embodied in the Act. Section 21 mentions the owner being precluded, as by estoppel, from denying the seller's authority to sell, sales under the Factors Acts† or similar legislation and sales under special powers of sale, whether statutory or common law or by order of court; s. 22 mentions market overt; s. 23 sale under a voidable title as when a transaction is not void for mistake of identity but is merely a voidable contract because of misrepresentation and has not been avoided before the goods have been sold to an innocent third party, *King's Norton Metal Co v Edridge, Merrett* [1897] 14 TLR 98; *Lewis v Averay* [1972] 1 QB 198. Section 24 provides that where a seller remains in possession after goods have been sold any sale, pledge or other disposition of the goods or documents of title for them by the seller or a mercantile agent acting for him to a person taking them in good faith is as valid as if authorised by the owner. The seller need not continue in possession as seller. Possession in another character suffices, *Pacific Motor Auctions v Motor Credits* [1965] AC 867; *Worcester Works v Cooden* [1972] 1 QB 210. The second buyer must take possession of the goods or documents to achieve protection. Section 25 provides that where a buyer obtains, with the seller's consent, possession of the goods or documents of title to them, the delivery or transfer of the goods or documents by the buyer or a mercantile agent acting for him under any sale, pledge or other disposition to a person taking in good faith has the same effect as if the person making the delivery or transfer were a mercantile agent in possession with the consent of the owner. Sections 24 and 25 reproduced in narrower language the Factors Act 1889, ss. 8 and 9. A hirer under hire-purchase who has merely an option to buy is not a buyer under this section, *Helby v Matthews* [1895] AC 471 but a buyer under a conditional contract of sale is, *Marten v Whale* [1917] 2 KB 480. Section 25 (2), however, excludes from it any 'conditional sale agreement' which is a consumer credit agreement within the Consumer Credit Act 1974. Section 25 operates even if the buyer obtains possession by crime or if an original has been withdrawn. In *Newtons of Wembley v Williams* [1965] 1 QB 560 it was held that the provision that the sale 'would have the same effect as if the person making the delivery or transfer (i.e. buyer in possession or his mercantile agent) were a mercantile agent . . .' meant that the buyer in possession or his agent must act in the ordinary course of business of a mercantile agent, e.g. sell on business premises during business hours. This limits the operation of s. 25. Negotiable instruments also form an important exception to nemo dat as did the Hire Purchase Act 1964, Part III in respect of cars (now re-enacted in the Consumer Credit Act 1974).

Non-commercial agreements. The Consumer Credit Act 1974, s. 189 provides that these are consumer credit agreements or consumer hire agreements which are not made by the creditor or owner in the course of a business carried on by him. Section 189 also provides that a person is not to be treated as carrying on a particular type of business merely because he occasionally enters into transactions of that type. Non-commercial agreements enjoy the same exemptions as small agreements, licences, standard or group†, are not required for making them since they are not part of a business, and the special rules in s. 75 imposing liability on a creditor in a debtor–creditor–supplier agreement for breaches by a supplier do not apply to them.

Non est factum. 'Not the deed'. A form of unilateral mistake in contract where one party presents to the other a document for signature knowing that the prospective signer is under a serious or substantial mistake as to the document thinking that it is radically different from what it is in fact. The document will be null and void. Non est factum will not normally be available to literate persons of full capacity but to the handicapped or those tricked into signing nor will it be available when the signer is careless, *Saunders v Anglia Building*

Society [1971] AC 1004. Non est factum is restricted lest third parties be prejudiced by the fact that documents are void. *See also* MISTAKE IN CONTRACT.

Notarial act of honour. A formality often used in acceptance for honour supra protest and required for payment for honour supra protest of bills of exchange and promissory notes. It involves a declaration before a notary public by the payer for honour or his agent, stating that payment of the instrument is for honour and indicating for whose honour payment is made. This declaration may be attached to the protest†. (See the Bills of Exchange Act 1882, s. 68 (3), (4).

Notice of dishonour of a bill of exchange or promissory note. When these are dishonoured by non-acceptance or dishonoured by non-payment the holder must give notice of dishonour, unless excused, to the drawer and indorsers in order to retain his right of recourse against them. If he does not they are discharged. If an indorser pays an instrument and becomes holder he in his turn must give notice to previous parties to retain their liability unless notice operating for them has already been given. Notice is not required to retain the liability of the acceptor (Bills of Exchange Act 1882, s. 52 (3)). Notice must be given by or for the holder or an indorser liable on the instrument. It may be given by an agent in his own name or that of a party liable even if that party is not his principal. When given by or for the holder it operates for the benefit of all later holders and all previous indorsers who have a right of recourse against the party to whom it was given and when given by or for an indorser it operates for the benefit of later parties. Notice may be written or by personal communication and in any way which identifies the instrument and the type of dishonour. Return of the instrument to drawer or indorser is enough. A written notice need not be signed and, if insufficient may be supplemented verbally. Notice may be given to an agent, to a personal representative of a dead party and either to a bankrupt party or his trustee. Where there are two or more drawers or indorsers who are not partners notice must be given to each unless one is authorised to act for all. Notice must be given within a reasonable time. Unless there are special circumstances it will not be reasonable unless it is given or sent off to reach the person to receive it on the day after dishonour when the parties live in the same place and, if they do not do so, it must be sent off on the day after dishonour or by the next convenient post if there is not one on that day. Where a dishonoured instrument is in the hands of an agent he may either give notice to the parties liable or give notice to his principal. In the latter case, the agent must give notice within the same time as if he were a holder and the principal has the same time as if the agent had been an independent holder. The principal may not add to his own time, time saved by the agent in giving notice to him, *Yeoman Credit v Gregory* [1963] 1 WLR 343. Where notice is properly addressed and posted it is deemed to have been given in spite of loss or delay in the post. Delay is excused by circumstances for which the party to give notice is not responsible but once these cease notice must be given. When a bill is dishonoured by non-acceptance and notice of dishonour is not given a holder in due course is not prejudiced. If such notice is properly given it shall not be necessary to give notice of dishonour by non-payment unless the bill has in the interval been accepted. Notice of dishonour is dispensed with when after reasonable diligence it cannot be given or does not reach the parties to be charged or by waiver, express or implied, before or after the time to give proper notice. Notice is not required to retain the liability of the drawer (1) where drawer and drawee are the same person, as in bankers' drafts; (2) where the drawee is a fictitious person or lacks capacity to contract (*see* CAPACITY IN RELATION TO BILLS OF EXCHANGE); (3) where the drawer is the person to whom the bill is presented for payment (e.g. when the drawee becomes insolvent); (4) where the drawee or acceptor is as between himself and the drawer under no obligation to accept or pay the bill (e.g. when a cheque is drawn on an account with insufficient funds); (5) where the drawer has countermanded payment. Notice is not required to retain the liability of an indorser (1) where he knew the drawee was a fictitious person or lacked capacity when he indorsed; (2) where the instrument is presented to the indorser for payment (e.g. when the indorser is the personal representative of a dead drawee); (3) where the instrument was accepted or made for his accommodation (*see* ACCOMMODATION BILL).

(See the Bills of Exchange Act 1882, ss. 48, 49, 50 and 89 applying the previous sections to a promissory note).

Noting. In relation to bills of exchange and promissory notes a step preliminary to protest†.

Not negotiable crossing. *See* CROSSED CHEQUE.

Novation. The replacement of one contract by another, often, but not necessarily, with some change of parties.

O

Offer and acceptance. The steps through which in almost all cases the parties reach that agreement basic to simple or parol contracts. The court looks for the objective or outward appearance of agreement, not for the parties' inner intent, *Smith v Hughes* (1871) LR 6 QB 597; *Tamplin v James* (1880) 15 Ch D 215. The offer, which may be made orally, in writing or by conduct must be a clear intimation that the offeror intends to be legally bound if the offeree will accept the offer. This must be distinguished from an invitation to treat, a step in preliminary negotiations. An offer may be made to a particular person or persons or the world at large, *Carlill v Carbolic Smoke Ball Co* [1893] 1 QB 256. An offer remains open for acceptance either for a period it specifies or if none, for a reasonable time or until revoked. It may be revoked even within a specified period of time during which it is to remain open unless it is either made by deed or there is a separate contract with consideration known as an option, to keep it open. If a specified period or, if none, a reasonable time elapses without acceptance the offer expires. Revocation must come to the notice of the offeree before he accepts, *Byrne v Van Tienhoven* (1880) 5 CPD 344, but not necessarily by notice from the offeror, *Dickinson v Dodds* (1876) 2 Ch D 463. A counter offer from the offeree destroys the original offer and, if the offeror rejects the counter offer, the offeree cannot claim to revive the original, *Hyde v Wrench* (1840) 3 Beav 334 but 'a mere enquiry' from the offeree will not have this effect, *Stevenson v McLean* (1880) 5 QBD 346. The death of the offeror automatically determines offers for contracts of a personal character, e.g. service, and notification of death will terminate other offers.

An acceptance must unconditionally accept the offer, not propose amending it, for if it does it will be a rejection and counter-offer. Acceptance requires knowledge of the offer, *R v Clarke* (1927) 40 CLR 227 but not necessarily intent to accept it as the prime motive, *Williams v Cawardine* (1833) 5 C & P 566. The offer may expressly or impliedly prescribe the method of acceptance. Subject to that, it may be by conduct, words or writing but the offeror may not prescribe that inaction or silence will be acceptance, *Felthouse v Bindley* (1862) 11 CBNS 869. It may be that the inactive offeree could hold the offeror bound in such a case. It is a question of construction whether a prescribed method only must be used, or whether any equally efficacious method may be employed, *Manchester Diocesan Council v Commercial & General Investments* [1969] 3 All ER 1593. An offer by a speedy method, e.g. telegram, impliedly requires a reply by as speedy a method, *Quenerduaine v Cole* (1883) 32 WR 185. An offer for an act, e.g. reward, may be accepted by doing the act without separate communication of intent, *Carlill v Carbolic Smoke Ball Co*, but otherwise acceptance must be communicated to the offeror. When instantaneous communication is used, e.g. face-to-face, telex, telephone, acceptance is effective when received by the offeror, *Entores v Miles Far East* [1955] 2 QB 327; *Brinkibon v Stahag Stahl* [1982] 1 All ER 293 but when the post is used it is effective when a letter is put into course of post, *Adams v Lindsell* (1818) 1 B & Ad 681, even if it is lost, *Household Fire Insurance Co v Grant* (1879) 4 Ex D 216, unless the offer excludes this rule, *Holwell v Hughes* [1974] 1 All ER 161. Offer and acceptance must not be vague, *Guthing v Lynn* (1831) 2 B & Ad 232, contain ambiguous terms, *Bishop & Baxter v Anglo-Eastern Trading* (1944) KB 12; *British Electrical v Patley Pressings* [1953] 1 All ER 94, nor explicitly require further agreement between the parties, *May & Butcher v R* [1934] 2 KB 17n ('at price to be agreed'). If parties do not explicitly indicate that further agreement is needed the court would imply that the price or other term was to be reasonable and uphold the contract, *Hillas v Arcos* (1932) 147 LT 503. If the parties partially perform an incomplete agreement they may by their conduct resolve the unsettled terms and it will be enforced as a contract, *British Bank for Foreign Trade v Novinex* [1949] 1 KB 623. Meaningless words will be ignored and the rest enforced, *Nicolene v Simmonds* [1953] 1 QB 543. Agreement may be spelt out from a course of conduct or prolonged correspondence, *Brogden v Metropolitan Rly* (1877) 2 AC 666. If tenders are invited for the periodical supply of goods as and when required the tender will be a standing offer to be accepted as and when goods are ordered and any earlier 'acceptance' of the tender is merely notification that the existence of the offer is recognised, *G.N.R. v Witham* (1873) LR 9 CP 16. An agreement which may appear to be insufficient for a contract may be made good by implications of reasonableness as to the intent of the parties, by implying terms from local or trade custom†, by implying terms to give 'business efficacy' under *The Moorcock*† (1889) 41 PD 64, and in contracts in certain commercial categories, e.g. sale of goods, partnership, by reference to the provisions of relevant statutes. Cross-offers do not amount to offer and acceptance, *Tinn v Hoffman* (1873) 29 LT 271. Acceptance may be retrospective in effect, *Trollope & Colls v Atomic Power* [1962] 3 All ER 1035. If an offer is made for an act taking time to perform acceptance occurs and revocation of the offer is no longer possible when performance of the act is begun, *Daulia v Four Millbank Nominees*

[1978] Ch 231. If an offer or acceptance is garbled in transmission because of circumstances for which the relevant party is not responsible no contract results, *Henkel v Pape* (1870) LR 6 Ex 7. The Uniform Law on the Formation of Contracts for the International Sale of Goods provides rules in regard to revocation, post and other matters which differ from the rules above. *See* UNIFORM LAWS ON INTERNATIONAL SALES ACT 1967.

    See CONSIDERATION for the point that an offer must request or stipulate a return as 'the price of the promise'.

Off hire clause. *See* TIME CHARTERPARTY.

Official Receiver. He is an official appointed by the Department of Trade but is also an officer of the court to which he is attached. When a receiving order is made against a debtor it is the duty of the Official Receiver to receive the debtor's property until the appointment of a trustee in bankruptcy. Official Receivers are assigned to districts and deputies may be appointed. The duties of the Official Receiver relate both to the conduct of the debtor and his estate. The Official Receiver must investigate and report to the court and the Department of Trade on the debtor's conduct, stating whether any offences have been committed or if there has been conduct which might affect discharge. He must also take part in the public examination and assist in the prosecution of a fraudulent debtor. In regard to property the Official Receiver must see that a proper statement of affairs is prepared; pending the appointment of a trustee he must act as interim receiver and, if he does not appoint a special manager he must act as manager of the estate; he must summon and preside at the first meeting of creditors and issue forms of proxy; he must advertise the receiving order, the date of the first meeting of creditors and of the public examination of the debtor; he must report to the creditors on any proposal of the debtor's for liquidating his affairs; he must make applications in connection with new forms of discharge of the bankrupt under the Insolvency Act 1976; and he must act as trustee during any vacancy in the office of trustee in bankruptcy.

    (See the Bankruptcy Act 1914, ss. 70–75).

Omnis ratihabitio retrotrahitur ac priori mandato aequiparitur. 'Every ratification is drawn back in time and is equated to a prior mandate.' This expresses the principle that ratification of an unauthorised act relates back in time and is treated as if there had been prior authority from the principal for the originally unauthorised act.

On approval. *See* PASSING OF PROPERTY IN SALE OF GOODS.

Open cheque. One which is not a crossed cheque.

Order bill or promissory note. The Bills of Exchange Act 1882, s. 8 (2) provides that a bill of exchange or promissory note may be payable either to bearer or to order, that is to a payee to whom the drawer of a bill of exchange 'orders' payment to be made or who is specifically indicated by the maker of a promissory note. Such a payee may by indorsement order that an indorsee be entitled on the instrument and he in turn may negotiate the instrument to a further indorsee and so on, each indorsement being tantamount to a new drawing of the instrument. Thus an 'order' instrument is payable to a named payee or indorsee or whoever that payee or indorsee may by appropriate indorsement 'order' the drawee of a bill or the maker of a note to regard as entitled to it. Section 8 (4) provides that an instrument is payable to order when it is in terms so payable or when it is expressed to be payable to a particular person and does not contain words prohibiting transfer or indicating an intention that it should not be transferable. When a bill is expressed to be payable to the order of a particular person and not to him or to his order, it is nonetheless payable to him or his order as he chooses.

Ostensible authority of an agent. A synonym for apparent authority of an agent.

Overdue negotiable instrument. *See* MATURITY.

P

Paris Convention on Industrial Property. *See* INTELLECTUAL PROPERTY, INTERNATIONAL PROTECTION.

Parol contract. A synonym for simple contract. *See* CONTRACT.

Parol evidence rule. This requires that when a transaction, such as a contract, has been reduced to writing no evidence as to its terms other than the writing itself should be admissible. It is subject to numerous exceptions and qualifications. Thus extrinsic evidence may be given that an apparently complete and valid transaction is merely part of a larger agreement, that there is a collateral contract to be taken with it, that there is some later agreement waiving, varying or rescinding the transaction (*see* VARIATION AND WAIVER OF CONTRACT; DISCHARGE OF CONTRACT BY AGREEMENT); that the transaction is invalid because of some vitiating factor (*see* ILLEGALITY IN CONTRACT; MISTAKE IN CONTRACT; RECTIFICATION; MISREPRESENTATION; PUBLIC POLICY; UNDUE INFLUENCE; DURESS; CONTRACTUAL CAPACITY); that it is discharged by supervening impossibility (*see* FRUSTRATION); that some local or trade custom† applies to it; to identify the subject matter or persons to whom it relates; to translate it; to explain latent or perhaps patent ambiguities but not to supply meaning for total blanks or meaningless expressions.

Particular average. This is a term of maritime law for damage done to the ship or property which is not suffered for the general good. In that respect it is contrasted with general average†.

Particular lien. *See* POSSESSORY OR COMMON LAW LIEN.

Party to a bill of exchange or promissory note. The Bills of Exchange Act 1882, s. 23 provides that no person is liable as drawer, acceptor or indorser who has not signed as such and where a person signs in a trade or assumed name he is as liable as if he had signed in his proper name. The signing of the name of a partnership is equivalent to signing by all the partners. By s. 21 delivery† in addition to signature† is essential to make the liabilities of parties complete and irrevocable. By s. 56 where a person signs otherwise than as a drawer or acceptor he incurs the liabilities of an indorser and may be known as a quasi-indorser. By s. 58 a transferor by delivery is not liable on the instrument he transfers but may be liable on warranties to his immediate transferee for value. By s. 65 when there is an acceptance for honour the acceptor for honour incurs liability as defined in s. 66.

Since by s. 53 a bill does not of itself in England operate as an assignment of funds in the hands of the drawee, a drawee who does not accept does not incur liability. By s. 28 an accommodation party who has not received value but has signed as drawer, acceptor or indorser to lend his name to another may be liable to a holder for value, whether or not he knew the party was an accommodation party. (*See* ACCOMMODATION BILL and CONSIDERATION FOR A BILL OF EXCHANGE). By s. 89 (2) in applying the provisions of the Act for bills to a promissory note the maker of a promissory note is deemed to correspond with the acceptor of a bill and the first indorser of a note to the drawer of an accepted bill payable to drawer's order.

By s. 16 the drawer of a bill and any indorser may insert a stipulation (usually sans recours or 'without recourse') negativing or limiting his liability on the right of recourse to the holder.

Passing off. The tort of conducting business or selling goods in a way calculated to lead others to suppose that they are the business or goods of another. Damage need not be proved. There may be damages or an account of profits and an injunction if there is fraud and an injunction if there is no fraud. The tort may be committed by using another's trade name or a name so similar that confusion is likely, *Reddaway v Banham* [1896] AC 199. A trade name must be acquired by usage and very much greater protection is given to a personal or invented name than to a descriptive name. A person may carry on business in his own name although it is similar to another's name if he does so honestly but may not sell goods, however honestly, under his own name if it resembles that of another without distinguishing them, *Parker-Knoll v Knoll International* [1962] RPC 265. A person must not 'garnish' or alter or abbreviate his name so as to increase its resemblance to that of a competitor, *Short's Ltd v Short* (1914) 31 RPC 294. Traders from an area may protect their interest in a common name for their goods. *Bollinger v Costa Brava* [1960] Ch 262 (champagne); *Vine Products v Mackenzie* [1969] RPC 1 (sherry); *Walker v Ost* [1970] 2 All ER 106 (Scotch); *Erven Warninck v Townend* [1979] AC 731. Resemblance in the distinctive appearance of goods may suffice for the tort, *White Hudson v Asian Organisation* [1964] 1 WLR 1466. Improper use of another's trade mark may also be enough as s. 2 of the Trade Marks Act 1938 preserves the common law of passing off. Selling the plaintiff's defective or secondhand goods as goods of normal standard may be passing off, *Wilts United Dairies v Thomas Robinson* [1958] RPC 94. If the parties are not in competition in similar business there will be no passing off, *McCulloch v May* [1947] 2 All ER 845; *Wombles v Wombles Skips* [1975] FSR 488. If damage is proved remedies may be granted if there is likelihood of confusion between the businesses of the parties even if all the elements of passing off, e.g. direct competition, are not present, *Borthwick v Evening Post* (1888) 37 Ch D 449. The limits of these torts analogous to passing off are not yet fixed but there must be definite damage, usually to goodwill, and not mere vexation, e.g. from the adoption of a similar address, *Walter v Ashton* [1902] 2 Ch 282; *Street v Union Bank* (1885) 30 Ch D 156; *Day v Brownrigg* (1878) 10 Ch D 294. The Companies Act 1981, Part II contains rules for company and business names.

Passing of property in sale of goods. The Sale of Goods Act 1979, s. 2 (1) makes the transfer of property† in goods† by the seller to the buyer central to sale. Section 61 (1) says 'property' means the general property, that is, ownership as contrasted with the 'special property' of a bailee or other with a limited interest. Section 16 provides property is not to pass from seller to buyer until the goods are ascertained. (*See* UNASCERTAINED GOODS). Subject to that s. 17 says the passing is a matter of intention of the parties to be discovered from all the circumstances; s. 18 then provides five rules for determining intention when there is no contrary indication. Rule 1 says that when there is an unconditional contract for the sale of specific goods in a deliverable state property passes to the buyer when the contract is made and it is immaterial that payment or delivery (*see* DELIVERY IN SALE OF GOODS) or both be postponed. 'Unconditional' here means the contract is not subject to a condition precedent or subsequent. Rule 2 provides that when there is a contract for the sale of specific goods and the seller is bound to do something to the goods to put them into a deliverable state property does not pass until it is done and the buyer notified. Rule 3 provides that when there is a contract for the sale of specific goods in a deliverable state but the seller is bound to weigh, measure, test or do something else in reference to the goods to ascertain the price the property does not pass until it is done and the buyer is notified. Rule 4 provides that where goods are delivered to the buyer on approval or on sale or return or other similar terms the property in the goods passes to the buyer (a) when he signifies approval or acceptance to the seller or does any other act adopting the transaction, or (b) if he does not signify approval or acceptance but merely keeps the goods without express rejection, then if a time has been fixed for returning the goods, at the end of that time, and if there is no fixed time, at the end of a reasonable time. If the buyer on sale or return pledges or sells the goods to a third party, this will be an 'act adopting the transaction', property will pass and the third party be protected, *Kirkham v Attenborough* [1897] 1 QB 201. If the original seller expressly stipulates that property is not to pass until the buyer on sale or return has paid for the goods this shows a contrary intention excluding r. 5 (a) and property will not pass, *Weiner v Gill* [1906] 2 KB 574. In such a case the apparent buyer on sale or return may be found to be a mercantile agent and if the requirements of the Factors Acts† are satisfied the third party will get a good title under them, *Weiner v Harris* [1910] 1 KB 285. As to retention, if the buyer on sale or return voluntarily transferred the goods to a third party who loses them property passes, *Genn v Winkel* (1912) 107 LT 434, but if the goods are held by a third party (as by a sheriff on execution) for whom the buyer is not responsible, property does not pass, *Re Ferrier* [1944] Ch 295. Rule 5 (1) provides that where there is a contract for the sale of unascertained or future goods by description (*see* CORRESPONDENCE WITH DESCRIPTION IN SALE OF GOODS) and goods of that description and in a deliverable state are unconditionally appropriated to the contract, either by the seller with the assent of the buyer or by the buyer with the seller's assent, the property passes. The assent may be express or implied and prior or subsequent to the appropriation. Rule 5 (2) illustrates appropriation. It provides that when under the contract the seller delivers goods to the buyer or to a carrier or other bailee (whether named by the buyer or not) for transmission to the buyer and does not reserve the right of disposal, he is taken to have unconditionally appropriated goods to the contract. An appropriation will not be unconditional if the buyer is only to have the goods on payment. When an unidentified part of a bulk is to be sold there is no appropriation until separation. When goods ordered are posted there is appropriation, *Badische Anilin Fabrik v Basle Chemical Works* [1898] AC 200. Where bicycles had been manufactured to buyer's orders, packed and marked with buyer's name for despatch it was held there was no appropriation, *inter alia* because appropriation always involved actual or constructive delivery and is usually the final act of the seller. Here shipment remained to be done, *Carlos Federspiel v Twigg* [1975] 1 Lloyd's Rep 240. Section 19 deals with the effect of reservation of a right of disposal by the seller. Where specific goods or appropriated goods are sold the seller may either in the contract or the appropriation reserve the disposal of the goods until conditions are fulfilled and then, even though the goods have been delivered to the buyer or to a carrier or a bailee for transmission to the buyer, property does not pass until the conditions are fulfilled. Where the goods are shipped and by the bill of lading are made deliverable to the order of the seller or his agent the seller is prima facie taken to have reserved the right of disposal. Where the seller draws a bill of exchange on the buyer for the price and sends both the bill of lading and the bill of exchange to the buyer to secure acceptance or payment of the bill of exchange (*see* ACCEPTANCE OF BILL OF EXCHANGE; PAYMENT OF BILL OF EXCHANGE) the buyer is bound to return the bill of lading if he does not honour the bill of exchange and if he wrongfully retains the bill of lading property in the goods does not pass to him. The buyer is, however, a buyer in possession under s. 25 (1) and if he sells to a bona fide third party, that party will obtain a good title by exception to nemo dat quod non habet, *Cahn v Pockett's Bristol Channel Co* [1899] 1 QB 643. Section 20 sets out one of the most important consequences of the passing of property. Unless otherwise agreed the goods are at the seller's risk† until property passes and then at the buyer's, whether delivery has been made or not. If any party is at fault in delaying delivery he is responsible for any loss which otherwise might not have occurred, but this does not affect the duties of a party who is a bailee of the goods for the other. Also once property has passed the seller can sue for the price not merely damages, s. 49. If the seller becomes bankrupt (*see* BANKRUPTCY) or if a company goes into liquidation, the buyer's right to claim the goods as distinct from a dividend may depend on property having passed to him as may the buyer's ability to give a good title to a sub-buyer, who will not have to rely on an exception to nemo dat quod non habet. Passing of property does not give the buyer or those claiming under him a right to claim possession of the goods as that depends on payment or grant of credit, s. 28. Despite s. 18 it has been said 'in modern times very little is needed to give rise to the inference that the property in specific goods is to pass only on delivery or payment', *Ward v Bignall* [1967] 1 QB 534 at 545.

Past consideration. *See* CONSIDERATION.

Patent. The grant of a monopoly in the exploitation of an invention for a limited number of years in return for full disclosure. The Crown's common law right to make such grants was preserved by the Statute of Monopolies 1623 in respect of 'any manner of new manufacture'. Under the Patents Act 1977 there are now four distinct fields of law in this topic: (i) the old domestic law for patents granted before the 1977 Act came into force, which are governed by the Patents Act 1949 as amended; (ii) the 'new domestic law' chiefly found in Part I of the 1977 Act; (iii) European patents (U.K.) regulated by Part II of the 1977 Act and the European Patent Convention 1973; (iv) Community patents also regulated by Part II and the Community Patent Convention 1975. A 'new domestic application' may be for a purely United Kingdom patent or may be an international application under ss. 89 and 90 of the 1977 Act and the Patent Co-operation Treaty 1970.

A patent may be granted for an invention which is new, involves an inventive step and is capable of industrial application. It will be new, or possess 'novelty' if it does not form part of 'the state of the art'. This in general comprises all matter available to the public before the priority date, normally the date of the application. If the invention is a substance for the treatment or diagnosis of humans or animals the fact that the substance is part of the art will not deprive it of novelty if its use is not part. An inventive step will be present if the invention is not obvious to anyone skilled in the art. Industrial application is present if the invention can be made or used in any kind of industry including agriculture. A method of treatment or diagnosis for humans or animals is not regarded as capable of industrial application but a substance for use in such a process may be capable of industrial application.

A discovery, scientific theory, mathematical method, literary, dramatic, musical, artistic work, any other aesthetic creation, any scheme, rule, method for performing a mental act, playing a game, or doing business, a computer programme and the presentation of information are not inventions and cannot be patented. An invention involving such matters can be patented except in regard to the excluded matter. Many of these excluded matters could be protected as registered designs or copyright if in suitable form or under the law of confidence. Patents may not be granted for inventions which would encourage offensive immoral or anti-social behaviour nor for any variety of animal or plant nor for any biological process other than a micro-biological process. Plants may be protected under the plant breeders† legislation.

The extent to which the Patents Act 1949 governs 'existing patents' (those granted under it) is regulated by s. 127 and Schedules 1–4 of the 1977 Act. 'Old existing patents' granted more than eleven years before the commencement of the 1977 Act continue to last for sixteen years with a possible extension to twenty years on proof of insufficient profit. New 'existing patents' are given the new duration of twenty years and the 'new domestic law' of infringement applies to all infringement begun after the commencement of the 1977 Act. Many grounds of invalidity, e.g. lack of novelty and obviousness, are common to both systems but there is one, wrongful amendment by adding matter not in the specification when filed, which is peculiar to the new and some such as inutility, non-disclosure of best method and ambiguity, which are peculiar to the old. Some existing patents are 'patents of addition' for improvements to earlier patents. No new 'patents of addition' can be created.

Since 1978 state immunity no longer fully applies to patent proceedings.

Patent agents. They act for others in applying for patents. They must reside in or have a place of business in the United Kingdom and must be registered. They do not commit offences under the Solicitors Act 1974 merely in carrying on proceedings before the comptroller of patents or appeals under the Patents Acts. A person must not act for gain in applying for a European patent unless they are on the European list and European patent attorneys do not commit offences under the Solicitors Acts merely by so describing themselves.

Patent, application for. Every application for a patent must be in prescribed form, be filed at the Patent Office and contain a request for a patent, a specification describing the invention, a claim or claims and an abstract. The specification must disclose the invention sufficiently completely for it to be performed by anyone skilled in the art. The claims must describe clearly and concisely the matter for which protection is sought, must be supported by the description and must relate to one invention or several forming one inventive concept. The abstract is to give technical information, its publication is not part of the art and the comptroller may reframe it. Rules may prevent an applicant from restricting the availability of a micro-organism required for the performance of an invention. An application may be amended or withdrawn before grant but a withdrawal may not be revoked.

Subject to security considerations, the comptroller will after a prescribed period publish an application unless it has already failed, omitting disparaging, offensive, immoral or anti-social matter. The comptroller will, on request, refer the application for searches to determine whether it complies with the Act. Third parties may make written observations on applications. The comptroller may restrict the publication of information prejudicial to the defence of the realm or public safety. United Kingdom residents are forbidden to apply for a patent abroad unless they have applied for a patent in the United Kingdom and within six weeks no restrictive security directions have been given. If a decision that the application complies with the Act has not been given within the prescribed period the application is treated as refused, appeal lying to the patents court established by the 1977 Act within the Chancery Division. After grant the comptroller must publish in the journal a notice, the specification, the names of the proprietor and inventor and other particulars. The term of the patent begins with the publication of the notice and lasts for twenty years, subject to renewal at intervals to be prescribed. Lapsed patents may be restored within one year of lapse, the specification may be amended after grant and the proprietor may surrender a patent by notice to the comptroller. No one may impugn a patent on the ground that it lacks unity in that it contains several inventions not forming one inventive concept.

An application for a patent is personal property and may be transferred and mortgaged.

Patent Co-operation Treaty. *See* INTELLECTUAL PROPERTY, INTERNATIONAL PROTECTION and next entry.

Patents, European, Community and international applications. The Patents Act 1977 provides that a European Patent (U.K.) is in general treated as if it had been granted under domestic law and gives the same rights and remedies. Amendments and revocations are to be treated as if made under the Act. The authentic text is to be in the language in which proceedings were conducted in the European Patent Office, and there is special provision for translations. In certain circumstances an application for a European Patent (U.K.) may be treated as an application for a domestic patent. The jurisdiction of the court and the comptroller to determine questions of right is subject to conditions as to residence, location of business or employment and agreement to accept or exclude jurisdiction which in turn may be subject to the proper law. Proceedings may be stayed in United Kingdom courts when they have been commenced in the courts of another contracting state and, subject to conditions final decisions of competent authorities in other contracting states may be accorded recognition.

The 1977 Act provides that all rights, liabilities and restrictions arising from the Community Patent Convention are to have the force of law in the United Kingdom and the Secretary of State may make regulations to give effect to this. There are complex provisions as to residence for the purpose of jurisdiction.

An international application for a patent under the Patent Co-operation Treaty is to be treated for many purposes as if it were an application for a domestic patent. This ceases to be so if either the application or the United Kingdom designation is withdrawn except by the error of the Patent Office or other treaty institution or when the application is received late by the International Bureau through no fault of the applicant. Countries may be declared 'Convention countries' by Order in Council. (*See* INTELLECTUAL PROPERTY, INTERNATIONAL PROTECTION).

Patents, infringement of. Infringement occurs when any person in the United Kingdom without the consent of the proprietor makes, disposes of, offers to dispose of, keeps for disposal, uses or imports a patented production. There need be no element of copying. It also occurs when anyone uses or offers for use a patented process when he knows or reasonably should know that use would be infringement. It is also infringement to offer to supply in the United Kingdom to an unauthorised person any of the essential means for working an invention when the supplier knows or should know that these means are suitable and intended for putting the invention into effect in the United Kingdom. There will be no infringement if what is done is either done privately, or for experiment or in the extemporaneous preparation of a prescribed medicine for an individual or is for the needs of a ship, aircraft, hovercraft or vehicle temporarily or accidentally within the United Kingdom, these means of transport belonging to some country other than the United Kingdom which is a party to the 1883 Paris Convention for the Protection of Industrial Property, or is the use of an aircraft exempted from seizure for patent claims by the Civil Aviation Act 1949 when the aircraft has lawfully entered the United Kingdom.

Civil proceedings for infringement may be brought in the High Court or by agreement before the comptroller. They may result in an injunction, an order to deliver up or destroy offending articles, damages, an account of profits and a declaration. Damages are not to be awarded or an account ordered against a defendant who neither knew nor ought to have known that he was infringing. The fact that the word 'patented' appears on an article does not give sufficient notice unless the patent number also appears. When a person makes serious preparations to do an otherwise infringing act before the priority date (filing of application) he may continue to do it and transmit his right. The court or comptroller may certify that a patent was found valid in contested proceedings and in any subsequent proceedings a person relying on validity will be entitled to heavier costs. A co-owner or exclusive licensee may sue but an unregistered proprietor is not entitled to damages or an account unless he registers within six months or shows that it was not practicable to do so. When an application has been published the applicant may sue. Where a person makes groundless threats of infringement proceedings the person threatened may claim an injunction, a declaration and damages. Notifying the existence of a patent does not amount to a threat nor will action lie when the alleged infringement is said to consist in making or importing a product for disposal or of using a process. Where a person has applied in writing to a patent proprietor for an acknowledgment of non-infringement for proposed action and has received no reply the court or comptroller can make a declaration.

Patents, Licences. Licences to work an invention may be granted. Transactions must be in writing. A register of patents is to be kept at the Patents Office to record transactions relating to patents. As between claimants to a patent or licence the later is entitled as against an earlier whose transaction is unregistered or for which no notified application has been made. Restrictive conditions which purport to require a licensee or a person supplied with a patented article to acquire other things from the licensor or supplier or to prevent them being acquired elsewhere or which prohibit the use of other products or processes are generally void. Supply contracts and licences relating to expired contracts may be determined by three months written notice.

At any time after the grant of a patent the proprietor may ask the comptroller to enter on the register that licences are to be as of right. Thereafter any person shall be entitled to a licence to work the invention on agreed terms or, failing that, terms settled by the comptroller. At any time after three years from the grant of a patent anyone may apply to the comptroller for a licence or for an entry for licences as of right and a Government department may apply for a licence to a specified person. The grounds for applying for such compulsory licences are that the patent is not being adequately exploited in this country. The comptroller in exercising his powers must take account of a wide range of circumstances but must so exercise these powers as to ensure that the patent is worked commercially to the fullest extent reasonably practicable in the United Kingdom, that the proprietor or inventor is reasonably remunerated and that anyone working or developing a patent in the United Kingdom is not unfairly prejudiced. If monopolies or mergers involve patents relief may be granted by the comptroller entering that licences are to be as of right. Any Government department may use or authorise, without the consent of the proprietor, the use of any patented invention for the service of the Crown and there are special provisions for Crown use in a period of emergency.

Patent, ownership of. A patent may be granted to the inventor, joint inventors, any one entitled to the whole property in the invention or to successors in title. The inventor means the actual devisor and he is entitled to be mentioned in every patent or published application. Entitlement may be determined before or after grant by the comptroller of patents. An invention made by an employee will belong to the employer if it was made in the course of normal duties or of special duties likely to result in the invention or there was a special obligation to advance the employers' undertaking. Other inventions belong to the employee. When an invention of outstanding benefit belongs to an employer the employee may be compensated. Subject to any obligation of confidentiality, an employee cannot by contract diminish his patent rights.

Patent, revocation of. The court or the comptroller may on application revoke a patent either unconditionally or, where it is only partially invalid, subject to its not being amended within a limited time. Grounds for such revocation are that the invention was not patentable, that the patent was not granted to the person or persons entitled, that the specification did not disclose the invention sufficiently clearly and completely, that the matter disclosed in the specification extends beyond that disclosed in the application and that the protection of the patent was extended by an amendment which should not have been allowed. These are the grounds on which the validity of a patent can be challenged. The comptroller may on his own initiative revoke a patent when it appears that it formed part of the state of the art or when a patent under domestic law and a

European patent exist in respect of the same invention he may revoke the domestic patent. In any revocation or infringement proceedings the comptroller may allow the specification to be amended but not so as to include added matter.

Pawn. *See* PLEDGE.

Payee of bill of exchange or promissory note. The payee is the person designated to receive payment of such an instrument. The Bills of Exchange Act 1882, s. 7 provides that where an instrument is not payable to bearer the payee must be named or indicated with reasonable certainty. There may be two or more joint payees or alternative payees or an instrument may be made payable to the holder of an office. If the payee is a fictitious or non-existing person the instrument is payable to bearer. The effect of this is that a forged or unauthorised signature purporting to be the indorsement of the payee can be ignored and prior parties such as the drawer and acceptor held liable by the holder. A negotiable instrument may not have an 'impersonal' payee as in the case of instruments analogous to cheques with words such as 'cash' or 'wages' in the position of the payee's name. Such instruments may be valid mandates to a banker or other drawee to make a payment but are not negotiable, *North and South Insurance Corpn v National Provincial Bank* [1936] 1 KB 328, *Cole v Milsome* [1951] 1 All ER 311, *Orbit Mining Co v Westminster Bank* [1963] 1 QB 794. If, however, the instrument was drawn in the form 'Pay wages or bearer' it would be valid as a bearer instrument, *Grant v Vaughan* (1764) 3 Burr 1516.

Paying banker. The drawee banker of a cheque. The relationship of banker and customer is fundamentally one of debtor and creditor upon which a number of special terms have been superimposed. *Joachimson v Swiss Bank Corporation* [1921] 3 KB 110. One is that the banker must pay a cheque when presented if he has funds of the drawer available and the cheque is correctly drawn. Otherwise the banker will be liable in contract for wrongfully dishonouring the cheque. Non-traders will recover only nominal damages unless they prove special damage, *Gibbons v Westminster Bank* [1939] 2 KB 882. The banker may also be liable in defamation, *Jayson v Midland Bank* [1968] 1 Lloyd's Rep 409. The banker normally cannot debit the drawer's account if the drawer's signature is forged (*see* FORGED AND UNAUTHORISED SIGNATURES ON BILLS OF EXCHANGE), unless the drawer is prevented by estoppel from raising the forgery as where he has represented it to be genuine or knowingly remained silent in breach of duty, *Greenwood v Martins Bank* [1933] AC 51; *Brown v Westminster Bank* [1964] 2 Lloyd's Rep 187. The drawer does, however, owe a duty so to draw his cheques as not to facilitate forgery and if the customer is in breach the banker will be able to debit the amount of a forged cheque to the account, *London Joint Stock Bank v Macmillan* [1918] AC 777. A banker who pays a cheque does not impliedly represent that the drawer's signature is genuine so as to be estopped from recovering the amount if it is forged, *National Westminister Bank v Barclays Bank* [1975] QB 654. In the case of companies, other corporations and organisations the banker may be authorised to pay only cheques carrying specified signatures. If he pays other cheques he will not be entitled to debit them. He also owes a duty of care to his customer so that if he knows or ought to know that a cheque carrying authorised signatures has been drawn for an improper purpose he will be liable if he pays it, *Selangor United Rubber Co v Cradock* [1968] 1 WLR 1555. If a banker mistakenly credits an account which is drawn on by the customer the banker will not be estopped from recovering the money if the customer knew of the mistake and was not misled into changing his position, *United Overseas Bank v Jiwani* [1976] 1 WLR 964 but will be if the customer did not know and was misled, *Holt v Markham* [1923] 1 KB 504.

By the Bills of Exchange Act 1882, s. 53 a cheque is not in England an assignment of the drawer's funds in the bank so the banker is not liable to the payee as assignee. Cheques are never in practice accepted so that the banker is never liable as acceptor to the payee, *Bank of Baroda v Punjab National Bank* [1944] AC 176. The drawer is the party liable to the payee or other holder; the banker is only liable on his contract with his customer. It is the practice of bankers not to pay 'stale' cheques, i.e. those which appear to have been in circulation for more than six months, without the drawer's confirmation. By the Bills of Exchange Act 1882, s. 75 the duty and authority of a banker to pay a cheque are determined by countermand, i.e. 'stopping', and notice of the customer's death. A countermand must be unambiguous, *Westminster Bank v Hilton* (1926) 43 TLR 124, and sent to the branch where the account is kept, *London Provincial v Buzard* (1918) 35 TLR 142. If a banker mistakenly pays a cheque after a countermand he cannot debit the customer but may recover the sum from the collecting bank, *Barclays Bank v Simms* [1980] QB 677. Authority is also terminated by notice of the presentation of a bankruptcy petition against a customer, by the making of a receiving order against him and by a garnishee order.

A paying banker has received statutory protection against liability for paying on forged, defective or absent indorsements. The Stamp Act 1853, s. 19 protects a banker who pays 'drafts payable to order on demand and indorsed by payee'. It does not explicitly require good faith on the part of the banker but this must be taken to be implied. The section may now give protection in respect of forged indorsements on bankers' drafts. It once applied to indorsements on cheques but it was said in *Carpenters Co v British Mutual Banking Co* [1938] 1 KB

511 that it had been impliedly repealed in respect of them by the Bills of Exchange Act 1882, s. 60, which protects from liability a banker paying a cheque in good faith and in the ordinary course of business when the indorsement has been forged. This applies to open and crossed cheques. Section 80 provides that a banker who in good faith and without negligence pays a crossed cheque in accordance with the crossing is to be regarded as being in the same position as if he had paid the true owner. In regard to cheques this may duplicate protection given by s. 60 but since the crossed cheques sections are extended by the Cheques Act 1957, s. 5 to certain analogous instruments mentioned in s. 4 it may have independent operation in respect of these. The Bills of Exchange Act 1882, s. 79 (2) provides that if a crossing has been obliterated or imperceptibly altered a banker who in good faith and without negligence pays the instrument in accordance with its appearance does not incur liability. The Cheques Act 1957, s. 1 protects a banker who pays in good faith and in the ordinary course of business cheques, mandates to pay which are not bills of exchange (e.g. 'cheques' with impersonal payees) and bankers' drafts when they are not indorsed or irregularly indorsed. This is in pursuance of the policy of the Act to eliminate the former practice of requiring a payee to indorse a cheque before paying it into his account. Since a forgery is a nullity it may be that an instrument carrying a forged indorsement can be treated as unindorsed. Section 1 then duplicates the protection given by the Stamp Act 1853, s. 19 and the Bills of Exchange Act 1882, s. 60. If a forged indorsement is not tantamount to no indorsement then these latter sections still give independent protection. The Committee of London Clearing Bankers resolved in 1957 to continue to require endorsement of order cheques paid in cash over the counter. If a banker fails to obtain a regular indorsement in such a case or in a case where indorsement was necessary for the negotiation of the instrument, e.g. when it was presented not by the payee but by an indorsee from him, the banker would not be protected by s. 1 as he would have failed to act 'in the ordinary course of business'.

Payment credit. *See* BANKERS' COMMERCIAL CREDITS.

Payment for honour supra protest. When a bill of exchange or promissory note has been dishonoured by non-payment, whether or not it is overdue (*see* MATURITY), any person, whether or not already liable on it, (cf. acceptance for honour which is only open to persons not already liable and for non-overdue bills) may intervene and pay it for the honour of any person liable on it or for whom it has been drawn. The instrument must be protested for non-payment with the additional formality of a notarial act of honour which may be added to the protest. If there is no notarial act, the payment is merely voluntary

205

and the payer is not entitled to the rights of a payer for honour, i.e. on paying the holder the amount of the instrument and notarial expenses to receive the instrument and the protest and succeed to the rights and duties of the holder as regards the party for whom the payment for honour is made and all parties liable to that party. Any indorsers subsequent to the party for whose honour payment is made are discharged by the payment. Whilst a holder is free to reject acceptance for honour, if he rejects payment for honour he loses his right of recourse against any party who would have been discharged by the payment.

(See the Bills of Exchange Act 1882, s. 68).

Payment in due course of a negotiable instrument. This is a form of discharge of a negotiable instrument. The Bills of Exchange Act 1882, s. 59 provides that such a payment must be made by or on behalf of the drawee or acceptor of a bill of exchange. By s. 89 similar payment by the maker of a promissory note will have the same effect. Such payment must be at or after maturity† to the holder and must be made in good faith and without notice of any defect in his title to the instrument.

When a bill payable to or to the order of a third party is paid by the drawer, the drawer may enforce payment against the acceptor but may not re-issue the bill but if a bill is paid by an indorser or where a bill payable to drawer's order is paid by the drawer the payer is remitted to his former rights against the acceptor and parties previous to himself and may strike out his own and later indorsements and negotiation of the bill is again permitted. When an accommodation bill is paid in due course by the party accommodated the bill is discharged. The Act does not define 'payment' and it is not a legal term of art but since a bill or note must order or promise the payment of money and an acceptance undertakes the payment of money, payment should primarily be in money but it seems that any consideration that would satisfy the rule in *Foakes v Beer* (1884) 9 App Cas 605 (i.e. any act or thing other than a smaller sum paid in the same circumstances as the original debt or by negotiable instrument) would suffice. Payment of the same amount by negotiable instrument is payment in due course, *Meyer v Sze Hai Tong* [1913] AC 847.

Statutory provisions for the protection of a paying banker from liability in conversion also include instances of payment in due course. Section 60 of the 1882 Act in effect provides that if a banker in good faith and in the ordinary course of business pays a cheque on the strength of a forged indorsement he is deemed to have paid in due course. The Cheques Act 1957, s. 1 (1) in pursuance of the policy of that Act to reduce the need for indorsements similarly provides that where a banker in good faith and in the ordinary course of business pays a cheque drawn on him which is not indorsed or irregularly indorsed he does not merely by so doing incur any liability and is deemed to have paid in due course. If a forged indorsement as a total nullity is tantamount to the absence of an indorsement this section covers the same ground as s. 60 of the 1882 Act. Though the Acts do not expressly so provide, the better view is that if the cheque had actually or constructively reached the payee before being paid by the banker the drawer is discharged. Protection to a banker making payment on a forged indorsement on a bankers' draft or an interest or dividend warrant is given by the Stamp Act 1853, s. 19 and it seems clear that such payment similarly discharges. The Cheques Act 1957, s. 1 (2) provides that where a banker in good faith and in the ordinary course of business pays an analogous instrument or a bankers' draft he does not incur liability merely because the indorsement is absent or irregular and it is expressly provided that the instrument is discharged. The Bills of Exchange Act 1882, s. 80 further provides that where a crossed cheque is paid by a banker in good faith and without negligence in accordance with the crossing the banker and, if the cheque came into the hands of the payee, the drawer, shall be in the same position as if payment had been made to the true owner, thus amounting to discharge. The Cheques Act 1957, s. 5 applies the crossed cheque provisions of the Bills of Exchange Act 1882 to bankers' drafts and analogous instruments, so s. 80 governs these also. The protection given to bankers in respect of payment on forged indorsements does not extend to the payment by bankers on behalf of their customers of ordinary bills of exchange drawn on the customer.

By s. 89 these provisions apply with necessary modifications to a promissory note.

Penalty. *See* DAMAGES.

Performing Right Tribunal. Certain organisations, known as 'licensing bodies', negotiate or grant licences for the use of copyright material. These 'licensing bodies' include the B.B.C., I.T.A. and the Performing Right Society. Applicants for licences are usually the managers of places of entertainment.

The Copyright Act 1956 established the Performing Right Tribunal, consisting of a legally qualified chairman and two to four other members, to determine disputes between 'licensing bodies' and applicants for licences other than for films. The Tribunal may either adjudicate on 'licence schemes' set up by the 'licensing bodies' to regulate the granting of licences or on individual applications, whether or not made under a scheme. Acts authorised by an order of the Tribunal, whether on the reference of a scheme or on an individual application will not be an infringement of copyright if the conditions are complied with. The Copyright (Amendment) Act 1971 provides for the reference back and review by the Tribunal of proceedings, whether or not taken under a scheme. Any party to proceedings may request the Tribunal to refer a point of law to the High Court or Court of Session.

Personal credit agreement. The Consumer Credit Act 1974, s. 8 provides that this is an agreement by which a creditor provides an individual debtor with credit of any amount. Since such agreements form an element in the definition of consumer credit agreements it follows from the restriction of 'the debtor' to natural persons, partnerships or other unincorporated bodies, resulting from the definition of 'individual'† in s. 189 that a company or other corporate body cannot be a party as a debtor to a consumer credit agreement.

Personal security is guarantee or suretyship which operates by way of contract and, unlike real security, does not give the creditor rights to property of the debtor but merely claims against those who have agreed to be sureties for him.

Plant breeders rights. The Plant Varieties and Seeds Act 1964 was passed to give special protection to the breeders of new plants and seeds since patents and trademarks did not achieve this. Breeders rights may last for periods of fifteen to twenty-five years. The Act is administered by a Controller with appeal to a Plant Variety Rights Tribunal. See also the Agriculture (Miscellaneous Provisions) Act 1968 for variety characteristics suitable for protection. Since 1978 state immunity no longer fully applies to proceedings relating to plant breeders' rights.

Pledge or Pawn. A form of real security under which the creditor is given possession (not ownership, as in mortgage) of the security. It is a form of bailment created when the borrower (pledgor) delivers goods or documents of title to goods to the pledgee (lender) who must take reasonable care of the goods and not use them unless they will not deteriorate in use and then use is at his peril. On the pledgor's default the pledgee has a power of sale at either the agreed time or, if none, after reasonable notice. Any balance on sale over the amount of the debt goes to the pledgor. Pawnbrokers, who conduct a business of advancing money, were once governed by the Pawnbrokers Acts 1872–1960 but now by the Consumer Credit Act 1974, ss. 114–121, governing formalities such as the giving of a pawn-receipt, and copies of documents, requiring that rights of redemption be exercisable within six months and specifying the procedure on redemption, rendering it an offence unreasonably to refuse to allow redemption, providing for the consequences of failure to redeem and regulating the realisation of the pawn. These provisions do not apply to non-commercial agreements or pledges of documents of title. The extortionate credit bargain procedure is available to the pledgor.

Possessory or common law lien. A form of real security under which the person entitled to the lien may retain possession of goods until some debt due to him has been paid by the person whose chattels are subject to the lien. If it is a particular lien only goods giving rise to the debt may be retained but if it is a general lien goods may be held for any claims the holder may have against the owner. Liens may arise by contract, by statute or by custom. Examples are those of the innkeeper (Hotel Proprietors' Act 1956), the carrier, the repairer of goods and the unpaid seller of goods. The law does not favour general liens but some professions have established customs entailing such liens. They include bankers, solicitors and stockbrokers. A lien arising from custom may be excluded by contract. There will be no lien if the possession is wrongful, or the goods have been deposited for a particular purpose inconsistent with the lien or for mere storage or keep. Normally a lien is merely a right to retain, not to sell or re-sell, but there are many exceptions by statute, e.g. unpaid seller, and generally an application may be made to the court for an order to sell if the goods are perishable or some other good reason can be shown.

A lien is lost by surrender or abandonment of possession (but not by re-delivery for a limited purpose to the owner), on payment or tender of the debt, by the making of an excessive demand by the holder and by the taking of some other security for the debt inconsistent with the lien.

Power of attorney. *See* ACTUAL AUTHORITY.

Preliminary point of law. *See* ARBITRATION: APPEAL ON LAW AND PRELIMINARY POINT OF LAW.

Premature payment. The Consumer Credit Act 1974, s. 94 gives the debtor under a regulated agreement which is a consumer credit agreement the right to make early payment at any time on notice to the creditor. Section 95 provides that regulations may provide for a rebate of charges for credit, s. 96 provides that on the discharge of the debt any linked transaction other than a debt already payable is discharged and s. 97 requires the creditor to supply information to the debtor.

Presentment for acceptance. It is always advisable for the holder of a bill of exchange (other than a cheque) to present it to the drawee for acceptance because if it is dishonoured by non-acceptance the holder has an immediate right of action against other parties to the bill, such as the drawer and indorsers, even though the bill has not matured. (Bills of Exchange Act 1882, s. 43 (2))

Where a bill is payable after sight† presentment for acceptance is necessary to fix the start of the period and hence the date when the instrument matures. Again where a bill expressly requires present-ment or is payable at a place other than the residence or place of business of the drawee presentment for acceptance is necessary before presentment for payment but in the latter case if the holder has not got reasonable time to present for acceptance before presenting for payment delay caused by presenting for acceptance is excused and does not release the drawer and indorser from their guarantee liability. In no other case is presentment for acceptance necessary to render a party liable on the bill. Where a bill payable after sight is negotiated the holder must either present it for acceptance or negotiate it within a reasonable time. This is to prevent uncertain liabilities hanging over a party for too long and if it is not done the drawer and indorsers are released. Reasonable time depends on the nature of the bill, usage of trade and the facts of the case.

Presentment must be made by or on behalf of the holder at a reasonable hour on a business day to the drawee or a person authorised to accept or refuse acceptance for the drawee. When a bill is addressed to two or more drawees who are not partners the bill must be presented to all unless one has authority to accept for all. When the drawee is dead presentment may be made to his personal representa-tive and if he is bankrupt it may be made to his trustee. Where authorised by agreement or usage presentment through the post office is sufficient. Presentment is excused and the bill may be treated as dishonoured by non-acceptance where the drawee is dead, bankrupt, a fictitious person or a person not having capacity to contract by bill or where after reasonable diligence presentment cannot be effected or where, though presentment is irregular, acceptance is refused on some other ground. The fact that the holder believes that the bill would be dishonoured does not excuse him making presentment.

(See the Bills of Exchange Act 1882, ss. 39, 40 and 41). Presentment for acceptance does not apply to a promissory note (s. 89).

Presentment for payment of a bill of exchange or promissory note. The Bills of Exchange Act 1882, s. 45 provides that, subject to the provisions of the Act, e.g. as to excuses in s. 46 or cheques in s. 74, a bill of exchange must be duly presented for payment and if it is not so presented the drawer and indorsers are discharged from liability. By s. 89 these provisions apply to a promissory note. When an instrument is not payable on demand it must be presented on the day when it falls due. When payable on demand it must be presented within a reasonable time after issue to render the drawer liable and within a reasonable time after indorsement to render the indorser liable. Presentment must be made by the holder or his agent authorised to receive payment at a reasonable hour, on a business day (*see* FIXED OR DETERMINABLE FUTURE TIME FOR BILLS OF EXCHANGE AND PROMISSORY

NOTES), at a 'proper place' to the payer or someone authorised to make or refuse payment on his behalf. The 'proper place' is either that indicated in the bill or the address of the drawee or acceptor in the bill or, where these are not given, the drawee's or acceptor's business address or ordinary residence if these are known. If none of these are available the instrument may be presented wherever the drawee or acceptor can be found or to the last known business address or residence. Where presentment is made at a proper place and after the exercise of reasonable diligence no person authorised to pay or refuse payment can be found no further presentment is necessary. If a bill is drawn upon two or more persons who are not partners and no place of payment is specified presentment must be made to all. Where the drawee or acceptor is dead and no place of payment is specified, presentment must be made to a personal representative, if there is one and he can be found with reasonable diligence. Where authorised by agreement or usage presentment may be made through the post. By custom, however, banks will not pay by cash remittance through the post cheques presented through the post, except those drawn by the customer on his own account. In the case of other cheques the customer should either pay them into his own account or else, if they are not crossed cheques, cash may be taken over the counter. By s. 46 delay in making presentment for payment is excused when it is beyond the control of the holder and not caused by his default, misconduct or negligence but when the cause of delay ceases presentment must be made with reasonable diligence. Presentment for payment is dispensed with when after the exercise of reasonable diligence it cannot be effected. The fact that the holder believes payment will be refused does not excuse presentment but it is excused where the drawee is a fictitious person or where presentment is expressly or impliedly waived. The drawer will remain liable even if there is no presentment for payment if the acceptor or drawee is not bound to accept or pay the bill and the drawer has no reason to believe that the bill would be paid if presented. This could arise in the case of an accommodation bill† where the drawee or acceptor merely lent a name to the drawer. Although the drawer's liability will remain even if there is no presentment it is still necessary to present to preserve the liability of indorsers. There is a similar provision for a case where a bill was made to accommodate an indorser. His liability will remain despite non-presentment. Section 74 makes special provision for cheques. As these are not accepted by banks the drawer remains the party primarily liable and is not absolutely automatically discharged by delay in presentment for payment, as are drawers of ordinary bills. The drawer of a cheque is only discharged by delay if during the interval the bank fails and can only pay the cheque in part. The drawer is discharged as to the unpaid balance. This is of little practical importance since the disappearance of the small private banks of the eighteenth and nineteenth centuries.

Personal chattels. In the English classification of property† as the subject of ownership most interests in land other than leases are denominated real property or realty; other forms of property are called personal property or personalty. This is further subdivided into chattels real, comprising leases, and chattels personal. This latter category is subdivided into things (or choses) in action, that is, intangible property to which rights can be asserted by taking legal action, e.g. book debts, patents, copyright, etc. and things (or choses) in possession, that is, tangible moveables over which control can be asserted by taking possession. This last category includes goods and money.

Presumed authority arising from cohabitation. A husband may give his wife actual authority to act as his agent or apparent authority or confirm her unauthorised acts by ratification. All the normal modes of agency are possible though legislation in 1970 abolished the possibility of a deserted wife acting as an agent of necessity in making contracts binding her husband. From the fact of cohabitation (which will include a mistress as well as a wife and exclude a wife when there is no household, as when the spouses are living in a hotel) the courts will presume that a husband gives his wife actual authority to purchase necessaries suitable to his ostensible standard of living. The presumption can be rebutted by showing that the woman was already well supplied with the goods in question, that the husband had forbidden her to buy on credit or that she had sufficient money for her to buy for cash. As it is a question of presumed actual authority these nullifications of authority need not be known or apparent to the third party and authority is also excluded if the trader gave credit to the wife alone or if he was warned not to give credit to her.

Price. In sale of goods a 'money consideration'; Sale of Goods Act 1979, s. 2 (1). The money must be treated as currency. A coin treated as a curio will be goods, *Moss v Hancock* [1899] 2 QB 111. If goods are exchanged for goods the transaction is barter† but not, it seems if goods and money or goods or money are the consideration. By s. 8 the price may be fixed by the contract or in a way agreed in the contract or by the course of dealing beween the parties. If not so fixed, the buyer must pay a reasonable price. Where goods are to be sold at the valuation of a third party and he cannot or does not act the agreement is avoided but if any goods have been delivered and appropriated by the buyer he must pay a reasonable price. If one party prevents the valuer acting the other party may sue for damages. By s. 10 stipulations as to time of payment are not of the essence of a contract (are warranties rather than conditions) unless a different intention appears from the terms of the contract. By s. 49 where the property† in goods has passed to the buyer and he wrongfully neglects or refuses to pay for them the seller has an action for the price, as he also has, whether or not the property has passed to the buyer or the goods have been appropriated to the contract, when the price is payable on a day certain irrespective of delivery† and the buyer again wrongfully neglects or refuses to pay.

Private carrier. The private carrier, whether of goods or passengers, unlike the common carrier†, reserves the right to select and reject prospective customers as he wishes. One who carries as a casual or incidental undertaking is also a private carrier, *Belfast Ropework Co v Bushell* [1918] 1 KB 210. At common law a private carrier is only liable for negligence. It has frequently been sought to exclude this liability by exclusion clauses and notices but such terms in contracts of carriage and notices are now subject to the Unfair Contract Terms Act 1977†. British Rail carries goods subject to its General Conditions for the Carriage of Goods which provide terms differing as the carriage is at owners' or at Board's risk with special terms for livestock and fuel. Most road hauliers are now private carriers, carrying subject to the Road Haulage Associations' Conditions of Carriage which expressly state that they are not common carriers and in general resemble the railway conditions.

There are a number of Acts designed to give effect to conventions regulating the international carriage of passengers and goods. These often restrict the power of the parties to contract freely.

The Carriage of Goods by Road Act 1965† gives statutory force to the Convention on the Contract for the International Carriage of Goods by Road (CMR). Two major conventions apply to international rail carriage – the International Convention concerning the Carriage of Passengers and Luggage by Rail (CIV) and the International Convention concerning the Carriage of Goods by Rail (CIM). The Carriage by Railway Act 1972† describes these as the Railway Passenger Convention and the Railway Freight Convention and is primarily designed to give effect to a convention additional to CIV – the Convention Relating to the Liability of the Railway for Death or Personal Injury to Passengers and recognises somewhat indirectly the two major conventions.

The Carriage of Passengers by Road Act 1974† is to give effect to the Convention on the Contract for the International Carriage of Passengers and Luggage by Road. The Carriage by Air and Road Act 1979 is chiefly to give effect to amendments made by the Montreal Protocols to the Warsaw Convention on Carriage by Air (*see* CARRIAGE BY AIR: CONVENTIONS AND LEGISLATION) but also provides for revision of the Conventions scheduled to the Carriage of Goods by Road Act 1965 and the Carriage of Passengers by Road Act 1974 and replaces references in those Conventions to gold francs as a measure of limitation of liability by references to special drawing rights.

Private International Law. A synonyn for conflict of laws (q.v.).

Privity of contract. The basic rule is that a person who is not a party to a contract cannot take either rights or liabilities on it. This is associated with the concept of contract as a bargain and the rule that consideration must move from the promisee. These rules proved inconvenient in commerce and hence were subjected to many common law and statutory exceptions and qualifications. Major common law exceptions arise in agency, assignment of contracts, negotiable instruments, bankers' commercial credits, and covenants running with land. Assignment and negotiable instruments have been modified and re-stated in legislation. Statutory exceptions occur in insurance and resale price maintenance.

It seems that privity might be circumvented by one party to a contract holding the promises made to him in trust for a third party beneficiary but this device was deprived of efficacy by the courts insisting on strict proof of a trust, *Re Schebsman* [1944] Ch 83.

The collateral contract has similarly been employed to allow a stevedore the benefit of exemption or exclusion clauses in a contract of carriage between a shipowner and the owner of goods, the owner being taken to have made a contract collateral to the contract of carriage, in which collateral contract he is treated as having offered the stevedore the benefit of exclusion or exemption clauses in the contract of carriage if the stevedore will unload the cargo, *New Zealand Shipping v Satterthwaite* [1975] AC 154. This is not affected by the stevedore having already contracted with the shipowner to unload since a promise to perform a contract with a third party may be valid consideration.

The collateral contract has also been used to obtain a positive undertaking as to quality or fitness from a third party as when A guarantees his product to B if B will enter into a further contract with C requiring C to use the product, *Shanklin Pier v Detel Products* [1951] 2 KB 854.

Privity may also be defeated in some cases by one contracting party applying to the court to stay proceedings which the other is taking against a third party contrary to the terms of the contract, *Snelling v John G. Snelling* [1973] QB 87. In *Gore v Van der Lann* [1967] 2 QB 31 it was said that there must be a definite promise not to sue the third party and the contractual party applying for the stay must have an interest in the observance of the promise.

It was once thought that the Law of Property Act 1925, s. 56 (1) which provided that 'a person may take . . . the benefit of any condition, right of entry, covenant or agreement over or respecting land or other property, although he may not be named as a party to the conveyance or other instrument' might provide a wide exception to privity since a contractual promise is a thing in action and a form of property. A wide interpretation applying to all contracts in writing was rejected in *Beswick v Beswick* [1968] AC 58 but the scope of the subsection is uncertain. It may be confined to cases where the document purports to covenant with or grant to the third party or to deeds.

Privity may also be circumvented by novation. Here one party, in consideration of the discharge of an existing contract and the release of the other party agrees to accept a new party to a fresh contract on similar terms to the old.

The existence of a contract brings third parties under an obligation in tort not to induce one of the parties to break it or to interfere deliberately with its performance, *Lumley v Gye* (1853) 2 E & B 216. Whilst this tort is not confined to interference with contracts of employment it has been closely connected with industrial disputes and here legislation has conferred important immunities.

Promissory estoppel. This operates when a party to a contract or other transaction, e.g. a lease, makes a promise to the other party which is intended to be legally binding, intended to be acted upon and is acted upon by the other party, the promise being to forego strict compliance with legal rights. If the promisor attempts to resile he will only be able to do so if he gives the other party adequate notice to resume the former position. Promissory estoppel thus gives at least temporary efficacy to promises made without consideration and not by deed or specialty. It cannot operate as discharge of contract by agreement, which would wholly release the other party, since that requires consideration. This form of estoppel is a development of equity (and was once called equitable estoppel), differing from estoppel at common law because, following *Jorden v Money* (1854) 5 HLC 185, the latter requires an assertion of present fact, thus excluding a promise, and requires that the representee should act on the assertion to his detriment. This last may not be necessary in promissory estoppel since it does not appear to have been present in *Central London Property Trust v Hightrees House* [1947] KB 130 where Denning J, in reviving old authority, laid the foundation of the modern law in declaring that head landlords who promised to forego full rent for a period when property was under-occupied would not be allowed to resile. In *Ajayi v Briscoe* [1964] 3 All ER 556 mere change of position was mentioned as also in *Alan v El Nasr* [1972] 2 QB 189, *Brikom v Carr* [1979] QB 467 (in each case by Lord Denning) and in *Societe Italo-Belge v Palm and Vegetable Oils* [1982] 1 All ER 19. Resultant inaction is sufficient change, *Hughes v Metropolitan Railway* (1877) 2 App Cas 439. That case, *Tool Metal v Tungsten Electric* [1955] 2 All ER 657 and *Ajayi v Briscoe* are authority for promissory estoppel being suspensory, the promisor being able to resume his rights on notice (unless it is impossible for the promisee to be restored to the former position), but it may be that for periodic payments, such as rent or royalties, resumption will only be for the future. Promissory estoppel operates as a defence for the promisee, not as a cause of action, *Combe v Combe* [1951] 2 KB 215 though it could be used as an ancillary to a plaintiff's case. It may be that the promisee must show that he acted equitably, not obtaining the promise by undue pressure or threats, *D & C Builders v Rees* [1966] 2 QB 617. Promissory estoppel is closely related to variation and waiver of contract. *See* DISCHARGE OF CONTRACT BY AGREEMENT.

Promissory note. The Bills of Exchange Act 1882, s. 83 defines this as 'an unconditional promise in writing made by one person to another signed by the maker engaging to pay on demand or at a fixed or determinable future time a sum certain in money to or to the order of a specified person or bearer'. Section 89 applies most of the law relating to bills of exchange with necessary modifications to promissory notes. In applying these provisions to notes the maker corresponds to the acceptor and the first indorser of a note corresponds to the drawer of an accepted bill payable to drawer's order.

Provisions relating to presentment for acceptance, acceptance, acceptance supra protest, bills in a set and protest (if a foreign note is dishonoured) (*see* INLAND AND FOREIGN BILLS AND NOTES) do not apply to notes, (s. 89). There must be a promise of payment, not a mere acknowledgment of indebtedness as in an I.O.U., *Gould v Coombs* (1845) 1 CB 543, *Brooks v Elkins* (1836) 2 M & W 74 and it has been held that a document promising payment of money together with terms of employment is not a promissory note, *Dickie v Singh* (1974) SLT (Notes) 3 though the Act provides, s. 83 (3), that a note is not invalid merely because it also promises collateral security with authority to sell or dispose of it. But in *Mason v Lack* (1929) 140 LT 696 an instrument which could not be a bill of exchange since it did not carry the name of a drawer or of a drawee but only a form of acceptance was held valid as a note. An instrument in the form of a note payable to the maker's order is not a note until it is indorsed by the maker since until then he is not promising to pay anyone and any note is inchoate and incomplete until delivery to the payee or bearer.

When a demand note has been indorsed it must be presented for payment within a reasonable time of the indorsement. If not the indorser is discharged. What is a reasonable time depends on the nature of the note, usage of trade and the facts of the case. A demand note is not deemed to be overdue for the purpose of affecting the holder with notice of defects of title merely because a reasonable time for presenting for payment has elapsed since issue. This differs from the corresponding rule for demand bills, s. 36. The reason is that notes may be continuing securities outstanding for much longer periods than bills before any reasonable suspicion of defect need arise.

Prompt. In c.i.f. contracts the date on which the seller hands over the shipping documents in return for payment of the price.

Proof of Debts (Bankruptcy). A proof is a written claim by a creditor to participate in the distribution of property amongst creditors in a bankruptcy. It should be made as soon as possible after the receiving order and should be sent to the trustee in bankruptcy or the Official Receiver if he is acting in the case. Since the Insolvency Act 1976 it need only be verified by affidavit when the trustee or the Official Receiver so require. It must deduct all trade discounts and certain cash discounts. It must state whether the creditor is secured. If a security is not declared it may be forfeited (*see* DISTRIBUTION OF PROPERTY). Proof may be made by an agent. A creditor may prove up to the discharge of the bankrupt but delay in proving may limit the creditor's rights against the estate under the Bankruptcy Act 1914, s. 65.

A trustee must within twenty-eight days admit or reject a proof or require further evidence. The official receiver acting as trustee has fourteen days from the latest date in his notice of intention to declare a dividend in which to decide. If a trustee rejects a proof he must send written notice to the creditor. The court has power to review any decision and may expunge or reduce a proof admitted by the trustee on the trustee's own application, as well as that of a creditor or the debtor. The trustee cannot recover payments from a creditor whose proof has been expunged or reduced, but in the latter case the creditor cannot receive further dividend without allowing for overpayment.

A creditor may prove for all debts and liabilities, present or future, certain or contingent, to which the debtor is subject at the date of the receiving order or to which he may become liable before his discharge because of any obligation incurred before the date of the receiving order. A contingent claim must be estimated by the trustee. If no estimate is possible the court may declare the debt not provable. Demands in the nature of unliquidated damages not arising from a contract, promise or breach of trust are not provable. Thus claims for damages in tort are not provable if they have not been liquidated except when the tortfeasor-debtor is dead when the estate will be subject to administration in bankruptcy. Other debts not provable are those contracted by the debtor after the creditor had notice of an available act of bankruptcy, those contracted after the receiving order and those the value of which cannot fairly be estimated.

(See the Bankruptcy Act 1914, ss. 30–36 and the Bankruptcy (Amendment) Act 1926, s. 2.)

Proper Law. When a conflict of laws case involves a contract with a foreign element, as when the contract has been made in one country to be performed in another, the court must find the system or systems of law applicable to it. There is a presumption in favour of a single system but different parts of the contract may be governed by different systems, *Kahler v Midland Bank* [1950] AC 24. The court will seek the express or implied intention of the parties. They may have designated a system in a 'choice of law clause' and effect will be given to this provided it is 'bona fide and legal', *Vita Food Products v Unus Shipping* [1939] AC 277. An implied choice may be found when the parties agree that disputes should go to the courts of or to arbitration in a designated country, but this may be rebutted by other factors, *Tzortzis v Monark Line A/B* [1968] 1 WLR 406; *Compagnie d'Armement Maritime SA v Compagnie Tunisienne de Navigation SA* [1971] AC 572. When the language of the contract does not assist, the general rule is that the court will apply the law of the country with which the contract has 'closest and most real connection'. A wide variety of factors may be taken into consideration in ascertaining this. These were once described as presumptions but this usage is not now favoured, *Coast Lines v Hudig & Veder* [1972] 2 QB 34. They include the place of formation (lex loci contractus), of performance, (lex loci solutionis), residence or place of business of the parties and nature and subject matter of the transaction. A conveyance of immovables (land) is governed by the law of its location (lex situs) but a different proper law of a contract to convey may be chosen provided this does not conflict with the lex situs. Where the proper law is the law of a part of the United Kingdom solely because the parties have chosen it and otherwise would be the law of another country many provisions of the Unfair Contract Terms Act 1977† preventing exclusion of liability will not apply to it (s. 27). If, however, a contract selects the law of another country to evade the Act or one of the parties, resident in the United Kingdom, dealt as a consumer the Act still applies (s. 26). It does not, however, apply to 'international supply contracts' for the sale of or transfer of possession or ownership in goods where the places of business of the parties or, if none, their habitual residences are in different states and at the time of the conclusion of the contract the goods were in transit or about to be in transit from one state to another or offer and acceptance were effected in different states or the goods are to be delivered in a state other than that where the contract was formed. The Channel Islands and the Isle of Man are 'different states' from the United Kingdom for this purpose.

If a contract is illegal by its proper law English courts will not enforce it, *Kahler v Midland Bank* [1950] AC 24. Nor it seems will they enforce it if it is legal by the proper law though illegal by the law of the place of performance. This is certainly so if the proper law is English law, *Ralli Bros v Compania Naviera Sota y Aznar* [1920] 2 KB 287 but it seems a contract may be enforced if legal by the proper law though illegal by the law of place of formation, *Re Missouri SS Co* (1889) 42 Ch D 321. Whatever the position under the proper law, English courts will not enforce a contract which infringes justice, morality and public policy as accepted by English courts, e.g. a contract which prejudices the relations of this country with another state, *Regazzoni v Sethia* [1958] AC 301.

The proper law governs the essential or substantial validity of a contract, i.e. interpretation, nature and effect of the obligations, performance and discharge otherwise than by performance. Matters of evidence, procedure and remedies are governed by the lex fori, the local law of the court.

For bills of exchange and promissory notes the Bills of Exchange Act 1882, s. 72 provides special conflict rules which differ from ordinary contract rules in referring most questions, not to the proper law, but to the law of the place where the contract is made or an act is done or to be done. Foreign stamp law can usually be ignored. (*See* CONFLICT OF LAWS FOR BILLS OF EXCHANGE).

Property. In commercial law this may carry its ordinary meaning of the subject matter of ownership, e.g. in bankruptcy referring to the property of the debtor divisible amongst creditors. But elsewhere as in sale of goods it may be used as a synonym for ownership and lesser rights in goods. The Sale of Goods Act 1979, s. 2 (1) makes transfer of property central to sale. Section 61 (1) provides that 'property' means the general property in goods, and not merely a special property. 'General property' is tantamount to ownership; bailees who have possession and not ownership and others with limited interests are said to have a 'special property' as their interest.

Property divisible amongst creditors (Bankruptcy). Subject to certain exceptions, all property belonging to a debtor at the commencement of the bankruptcy vests on adjudication in the trustee in bankruptcy and is available for distribution to creditors. Certain categories of property not belonging to the debtor but which are either in his reputed ownership or were the subject of certain types of settlements voidable in bankruptcy or were used to give a fraudulent preference or were disposed of after the commencement of the bankruptcy are also available for distribution. So, too, is all property that may be acquired by or devolve upon the bankrupt before discharge of the bankrupt.

The commencement of the bankruptcy is the date of the act of bankruptcy upon which the receiving order was made or, if there was more than one, then the date of the earliest act within three months prior to the presentation of the petition. The bankruptcy and the title of the trustee relate back to that act. The category of property belonging to the debtor includes payments made to creditors after that date unless they are protected transactions and some rights of action in contract and tort. A right of action in contract or tort involving injury only to the person, reputation or feelings of the bankrupt will not pass to the trustee but such a right of action involving injury only to his property will pass and a right of action involving injury both to the person and property of the bankrupt will be split. A right of action for wrongful dismissal before adjudication will pass but not one for dismissal after that event. The trustee may assign choses in action, including a right to sue, to the bankrupt on proper terms. The trustee also takes choses in action subject to equities and thus, except where statute otherwise provides, gets no better title than the bankrupt.

Property not available for creditors includes tools of the bankrupt's trade and necessary clothing and bedding for himself, his wife and children to the value of £250 and property held by the bankrupt on trust for others if it can be distinguished from the rest of his property. Special rules apply to execution creditors of the bankrupt and protected transactions.

Subject to s. 47 which validates all transactions entered into with a bankrupt bona fide and for value after adjudication, unless the trustee intervenes before completion, almost all property acquired by or devolving on the bankrupt before discharge vests in the trustee but the trustee is not entitled to so much of the bankrupt's earnings as is necessary to support him and his family. Under ss. 50 and 51 the trustee has only restricted rights to the income of a clergyman, service officer, civil servant or any fixed salary or income, including pensions and maintenance. In all except the first case an order of the court is required, and in the case of officers and civil servants, assent from the appropriate department also before the trustee can take the whole or part of the income. Income does not include the prospective or contingent earnings of professional men and these are not to be set aside for creditors.

The trustee further may exercise all powers such as powers of appointment in respect of property which the bankrupt might have exercised for his own benefit and is entitled to all goods which, at the commencement of the bankruptcy, were within the possession and control of the bankrupt in his trade or business in such circumstances that he was the reputed owner of them. Choses in action, other than book debts, are not within this. Reputation of ownership may be excluded by proof of a well-known custom to hold the goods of others

exemption order may be made if it appears that in default of a system of maintained minimum resale prices

(a) the quality or variety of the goods would be substantially reduced to the detriment of the public;
(b) the number of retail establishments for sale of the goods would be substantially reduced to the detriment of the public;
(c) retail prices of the goods would in general and in the long run be increased to the detriment of the public;
(d) the goods would be retailed under conditions likely to endanger health in consequence of their misuse by the public;
(e) necessary services actually provided at or after the sale of the goods would cease or be reduced to the detriment of the public;

and in any case that the resulting detriment to the public as consumers or users of the goods in question would outweigh any detriment to them as such resulting from the maintenance of minimum resale prices.

When exemption is granted individual enforcement against persons not in privity of contract with the price maintainer continues to apply. An exempt resale price condition can be enforced against any person not a party to the sale from the supplier as if he had been a party provided that he had notice of the condition but this does not apply against a person who did not buy the goods for resale in the course of business or against one who derives title from such a person. Nor does it apply to sales by an order of court or by way of execution or distress or subsequent sales. Nor does it allow the enforcement of restrictions declared by the Restrictive Practices Court to be contrary to the public interest. An injunction granted to enforce price maintenance can extend to any goods of the supplier and not merely goods of the same description.

Rescission of contract. The exercise by a party to a contract of his right to avoid it. When a party rescinds for misrepresentation, mistake or want of consent the contract is treated as never having come into existence, whereas when a party elects to treat a contract as discharged by breach the termination operates for the future, not retrospectively, *Johnson v Agnew* [1980] AC 367, 373. (*See* VOIDABLE CONTRACT).

Reservation of title clause. *See* ROMALPA CLAUSE.

Res extincta. 'A thing which has ceased to exist'. Used in mistake in contract to describe a contractual subject which no longer exists.

Res ipsa loquitur. 'The matter speaks for itself.' A principle of evidence rather than of substantive law. A plaintiff in an action for negligence bears the burden of proving negligence but if the agency causing the harm is within the knowledge and control of the defendant and the event is of a type which does not normally occur without negligence on someone's part (e.g. objects falling from buildings on passers-by,

Scott v London & St Katherine's Docks Co (1865), 3 H & C 596; *Byrne v Boadle* (1863) 2 H & C 722), the court may on proof of this find for the plaintiff unless the defendant either shows how the event occurred without negligence on his part or, without showing how the event occurred, shows there was no negligence on his part, *Walsh v Holst* [1958] 1 WLR 800 or, perhaps, advances some reasonable explanation of how it might have occurred without negligence on his part, *Ludgate v Lovett* [1969] 1 WLR 1016. Cf *Moore v Fox* [1956] 1 QB 596 and *Turner v Mansfield Corpn* (1975) 119 SJ 629.

Res magis valeat quam pereat. In its full form verba ita sunt intelligenda ut res magis valeat quam pereat. Words are so to be understood that a matter stands valid rather than fails. A principle of construction or interpretation under which a court should, in case of doubt, seek to uphold a transaction, e.g. a contract rather than hold it invalid. See its application to alleged vagueness in contractual terms in *Hillas v Arcos* (1932) 147 LT 503 at 514.

Res perit domino. 'Loss of goods falls upon the owner'. The maxim embodies the basic rule in the Sale of Goods Act 1979, s. 20 that risk† accompanies property† and passes with it. The rule may be and often is displaced by the contract, e.g. in c.i.f. contracts.

Respondentia bond. A security for a loan binding the cargo of a ship. Now obsolete, but some of the cases are relevant for agency of necessity.

Res sua. 'His own property'. Used in mistake in contract of a case where a mistaken party agrees to buy what is his own property.

Restitution. Alternative title for quasi-contract and may also cover certain associated heads of liability.

Restricted-use credit. *See* CREDIT.

Restrictive indorsement. *See* INDORSEMENT OF A NEGOTIABLE INSTRUMENT.

Restrictive Practices Court. This court was established by the Restrictive Trade Practices Act 1956 to determine in the light of criteria provided by the Act whether certain agreements relating to trade were contrary to the public interest and to be declared void. These were known as Restrictive Trade Practices. The jurisdiction of the court was extended to Resale Price Maintenance in 1964, to information agreements in 1968 and to agreements relating to services in 1973. Most of its jurisdiction is now governed by the Restrictive Trade Practices Acts 1976 and 1977 and the Resale Prices Act 1976 though it has jurisdiction under Part III of the Fair Trading Act 1973 over proceedings relating to unfair trading practices brought by the Director-General of Fair Trading†. The structure, composition and procedure of the court are now principally governed by the Restrictive Practices Court Act 1976.

The court consists of five judges and not more than ten other members. Three of the judges are nominated from the High Court by the Lord Chancellor, one from the Court of Session by the Lord President and one from the Supreme Court of Northern Ireland by the Lord Chief Justice of Northern Ireland. In the case of temporary absence or inability to act other judges may be nominated. The other members are appointed by the Crown on the nomination of the Lord Chancellor. They must be persons with knowledge of or experience in industry, commerce or public affairs. Their appointment is for not less than three years and is renewable. They may resign at any time and may be removed for misbehaviour, inability or conflict of interest. The numbers of the court may be increased. The court may sit anywhere in the United Kingdon but its central office is in London. It may sit as a single court or in divisions and either in public or in private. For a hearing there must be a presiding judge and at least two other members except that for a hearing involving only issues of law a judge alone may sit. The judge or judges determine issues of law; otherwise decisions are by a majority of all members, the presiding judge having a casting vote. He delivers the judgment. The Lord Chancellor may make rules of procedure covering in particular persons to be made respondents, the place of sitting and evidence which may be required or admitted. In regard to the attendance and examination of witnesses, production and inspection of documents and the enforcement of its orders, the court has all the powers of the High Court or Court of Session.

The court proceeds as far as possible on documentary evidence, the proofs of witnesses and memoranda being exchanged and submitted to the court before the hearing.

The decision of the court on questions of fact is final (except in regard to proceedings under Part III of the Fair Trading Act 1973) but an appeal lies to the Court of Appeal or Court of Session on questions of law.

Restrictive Trade Practices (Goods). This covers agreements relating to goods which fall within the jurisdiction of the Restrictive Practices Court†. When the court was established by the Restrictive Trade Practices Act 1956 only agreements relating to goods were covered; information agreements were added in 1968 and agreements relating to services by the Fair Trading Act 1973, (*see* RESTRICTIVE TRADE PRACTICES (SERVICES)). The law is now almost entirely embodied in the Restrictive Trade Practices Acts 1976 and 1977 and the Restrictive Practices Court Act 1976.

The general scheme of the 1976 Act in relation to goods is that a wide variety of agreements and arrangements, described in detail in the Act, embodying restrictions as to prices, quantities, descriptions and processing of goods and the parties to be dealt with in regard to the goods must be registered with the Director-General of Fair Trading†. He is given extensive powers to enforce this obligation. It is then for the Director to take the agreements before the Court and for it to determine in the light of criteria prescribed in the Act whether the agreement may stand valid. There is a presumption that all restrictions are contrary to the public interest and void but this may be rebutted if it can be shown that the agreement manifests one or more of eight advantages specified in the Act. This is sometimes described as 'entering a gateway'. In addition it must be shown that any such advantage outweighs any detriment to the public or others not parties to the agreement resulting from the existence of the restriction. There are very similar provisions as to registration, presentation to the Court and the determination of the public interest by the court in relation to restrictions on services and information agreements relating to restrictions both on goods and services come within the scope of the Act.

In regard to goods, subject to certain exceptions, all agreements, whether intended to be legally enforceable or not, must be registered with the Director-General of Fair Trading if (1) they are made between two or more persons carrying on business in the United Kingdom in the production or supply of goods or in the application to goods of any process of manufacture; and (2) restrictions are accepted by two or more parties in respect of:

(a) the prices to be charged, quoted or paid for goods supplied, offered or acquired, or for the application of any process of manufacture to goods.

(b) the prices to be recommended or suggested as the prices to be charged on re-sale;

(c) the terms and conditions on which goods are to be supplied or acquired or any process is to be applied to goods;

(d) the quantities or descriptions of goods to be produced, supplied or acquired;

(e) the process of manufacture to be applied to any goods or the quantities or descriptions of goods to which any such process is to be applied; or

(f) the persons or classes of person, to, or from whom, or the area or places in or from which, goods are to be supplied or acquired, or any such process applied.

The Secretary of State may by statutory instrument apply the registration provisions of the 1976 Act to any class of 'information agreement'. This is an agreement for furnishing information on prices charged or to be recommended, terms of supply, costs, quantities or descriptions of goods, processes of manufacture or persons or places supplied.

In determining whether agreements are registrable the 1976 Act provides that certain restrictions are to be disregarded under s. 9 and certain agreements are excepted from registration under s. 28. The most important exceptions and exemptions are:

(1) In agreements for the supply of goods or for the application of any process of manufacture, terms relating exclusively to the goods supplied are to be disregarded. This does not apply where two or more suppliers or processors or two or more customers accept restrictions, unless this is done in pursuance of a registered agreement or is exempt from registration.

(2) An agreement for the supply of goods or information between two persons neither of whom is a trade association is exempt from registration if no other person is a party and the only restriction accepted or provision for the furnishing of information is:

   (a) by the party supplying the goods, in respect of the supply of goods of the same description to other persons; or

   (b) by the party acquiring the goods, in respect of the sale or acquisition for sale of other goods of the same description.

Other disregarded restrictions and excepted agreements include terms as to complying with British Standards or as to conditions of employment, agreements made under certain statutes or relating to patents, registered designs and trade marks, agreements for the exchange of information as to processes and agreements relating solely to exports or trade outside the United Kingdom.

The Secretary of State may make an order exempting from registration certain agreements of importance to the national economy and any of a number of Ministers may make an order exempting from registration agreements designed to prevent or restrict price increases or to secure reductions in prices. It seems that the Act has no application to agreements conferring rights or interests on the Crown which might be affected by registration.

An agreement which has become registrable remains so despite variation or determination and particulars of these must be given to the Director. The Restrictive Practices Court may declare whether an agreement is registrable or not and may order the rectification of the register. The Director-General may give notice to persons or trade associations whom he thinks may be parties to a registrable agreement requiring them to say whether they are parties and if so to register particulars. After giving this notice he may apply to the Restrictive Practices Court for an order for examination on oath. If particulars of a registrable agreement are not duly furnished, the agreement is void in respect of all relevant restrictions accepted under it and it is unlawful for any party to it carrying on business in the United Kingdom to enforce it in respect of such restrictions and the

Restrictive Practices Court, on the Director-General's application, may make an order restraining a party from enforcing the agreement in respect of any relevant restriction.

The Court declares, on the application of the Director-General, whether the restrictions which render an agreement registrable are contrary to the public interest and so void. The Court may make an order restraining the parties from observing or enforcing a void agreement or entering into a similar one. Applications for discharge of an order require leave which will only be granted if there has been a change of circumstances. The Director-General has a discretion to decline to proceed in regard to a determined agreement. The Director may also request the Secretary of State to discharge him from taking proceedings when the restrictions are 'not of such significance as to call for investigation by the Court'. The Director may also refrain from proceedings having regard to any directly applicable E.E.C. provision and any authorisation or exemption granted in connection with it (*see* E.E.C. COMPETITION LAW). The 1976 Act applies to an agreement even though it may be rendered void or authorised by a directly applicable E.E.C. provision but the Court may either decline, postpone or exercise its jurisdiction having regard to such a directly applicable provision and any authorisation or exemption granted under it.

There is a presumption that any restriction is contrary to the public interest and to rebut it the Court must be satisfied of one or more of the following circumstances:

(a) that it is reasonably necessary to protect the public against injury:
(b) that the removal of the restriction would deny to the public as purchasers, consumers or users of goods other substantial benefits;
(c) that it is reasonably necessary to counteract restrictive action by any one person not a party to the agreement;
(d) that it is reasonably necessary to enable the parties to negotiate fair terms with a monopolistic supplier or customer;
(e) that its removal would be likely to have a serious and persistently adverse effect on the general level of employment in an area;
(f) that export business might be substantially affected;
(g) that the restriction is reasonably required to maintain another restriction which is found not to be contrary to public policy;
(h) that the restriction does not restrict or discourage competition to any material degree and is not likely to do so.

After the court is satisfied that the restriction can be brought within one or more of these 'gateways' it must further be satisfied that the restriction is not unreasonable, having regard to the balance between these 'gateway' circumstances and any detriment resulting from the restriction. This is the 'tailpiece'.

Restrictive Trade Practices (Services). The Fair Trading Act 1973 first brought restrictions relating to services and information agreements relating to services within the restrictive practices legislation and they are now covered in Part III of the Restrictive Trade Practices Act 1976. 'Services' do not include a manufacturing process applied to goods or services under an employment contract but do include engagements, whether professional or not, which are undertaken for gain or reward but not for the production and supply of goods. The Secretary of State may by statutory instrument order that the Act shall apply to agreements and information agreements relating to restrictions on or information about charges for, terms and conditions of supply, extent and scale of supply, form and manner of supply of services and the persons or classes of person to be supplied with services. Most commercial service agreements have been brought within the Act, but many professional services are exempt by the First Schedule and the Third Schedule exempts others. In a service supply association, agreements will be regarded as made between the members. No account is to be taken of a term which relates exclusively to services supplied under the agreement containing the term nor of terms agreeing to observe standards set by the British Standards Institution or some other body approved by the Secretary of State. As with goods, restrictive agreements and information agreements relating to services are presumed to be contrary to the public interest unless the Restrictive Practices Court find that they satisfy a set of criteria in the form of 'gateways' and a 'tailpiece' which reproduce those prescribed for goods. (*See* RESTRICTIVE TRADE PRACTICES (GOODS). The Restrictive Trade Practices Act 1977 is designed to ensure that agreements between banks and financial institutions for the provision of loans and credit are exempt from registration so long as the restrictions accepted under them are directed to the maintenance of the security. Information agreements are similarly exempt.

Return Order. The Consumer Credit Act 1974, s. 133 provides that in proceedings involving a regulated agreement the court may make such an order for the return of goods to the creditor if it appears just to do so.

Revocable Credit. *See* BANKERS' COMMERCIAL CREDITS.

Revolving Credit. *See* BANKERS' COMMERCIAL CREDITS.

Right of recourse. The drawer of a bill of exchange or cheque and the indorsers of any negotiable instrument use these as substitutes for money hence if the parties from whom payment is primarily expected, that is the drawee or acceptor of a bill, the drawee bank in the case of a cheque or the maker of a promissory note, dishonour by non-acceptance or dishonour by non-payment the instruments in question the holder, provided that he takes or is excused certain formal

giving notice of dishonour may call upon the drawer or
sers to act as, in effect, guarantors of those from whom payment
primarily expected. This is the right of recourse. By the Bills of
Exchange Act 1882, s. 16 the drawer or any indorser may insert an
express stipulation negativing or limiting his own liability to the
holder and thus exclude the right of recourse. The usual forms are
'without recourse' or 'sans recours'. Equally he may waive some or all
of the holder's duties, such as giving notice of dishonour. Subject to
this, by s. 57 (1) the holder may sue any party liable on an instrument.
This includes the acceptor, drawer and indorsers. Each is individually
liable for the whole amount of the instrument but the drawer if
compelled to pay may sue the acceptor and an indorser who is
compelled to pay may sue the acceptor, the drawer and any prior
indorser. The drawer and indorsers are jointly and severally liable to
the holder for the acceptance and payment of the instrument,
Rouquette v Overmann (1875) LR 10 QB 525 at 537.

Risk in sale of goods. When goods† are at the risk of a party to a
contract of sale he remains liable under the contract even though the
goods may have accidentally deteriorated or perished. If the risk is
with the seller he will be liable for non-delivery and the buyer will not
be liable for the price†; if the risk has passed to the buyer he will be
liable for the price or for damages for non-acceptance. The facts of
such a case may resemble those giving rise to frustration but in the
latter event the parties are (subject to the Law Reform (Frustrated
Contracts) Act 1943) discharged from their obligations of delivery
and payment.

The Sale of Goods Act 1979, s. 20 (1) provides that unless otherwise
agreed, goods remain at the sellers' risk until the property† in them
is transferred to the buyer, whereupon they are at the buyers' risk,
whether delivery has been made or not. (*See* PASSING OF PROPERTY IN
SALE OF GOODS). Section 20 makes it clear that risk relates to accidental
loss or harm, for it also provides that where delivery has been delayed
through the fault of either party the goods are at the risk of the party at
fault as regards any loss which might otherwise not have happened
and, moreover, nothing in the section is to affect the duties or liability
of a party acting as bailee for the other, the chief duty of a bailee being
to exercise reasonable care. Hence if a buyer is late in taking delivery
the seller must take due care of the goods. Property and risk are often
separated as in c.i.f. contracts. It is possible for risk to pass in respect of
an unascertained portion of an ascertained bulk even though property
did not pass, *Sterns v Vickers* [1923] 1 KB 78. Section 33 provides that
when the seller agrees to deliver goods at his own risk at a place other
than that of sale, the buyer must (unless otherwise agreed) take any
risk of deterioration necessarily incident to the transit. It may be that

the seller will be liable if he supplies goods not properly fit to endure the journey and the loss occurs because of this. (*See* DELIVERY IN SALE OF GOODS). Also *Mash & Murrell v Emanuel* [1961] 1 All ER 485 (rvsd. on facts [1962] 1 All ER 77); *Kemp v Tolland* [1956] 2 Lloyd's Rep 681 but *Cordova v Victor* [1966] 1 WLR 793; *Oleificio Zucchi v Northern Sales* [1965] 2 Lloyd's Rep 496, *Crowther v Shannon* [1975] 1 WLR 30. In most contracts for the sale of specific goods property and risk pass to the buyer when the contract is made under s. 18, Rule 1. When this does not operate the seller will escape liability and the contract is discharged by s. 7 which provides that when there is an agreement to sell specific goods which subsequently perish without fault of either party the contract is avoided. This is frustration. A contract to sell purely generic goods cannot be frustrated by destruction because a type of goods never perishes (genus numquam perit) but a contract to sell generic goods from a defined source basic to the contract, e.g. crops from specified land, may be frustrated by failure of the source, *Howell v Coupland* (1876) LR 1 QBD 258; *Sainsbury v Street* [1972] 1 WLR 834.

Romalpa Clause. A clause taking its name from *Aluminium Industrie v Romalpa Aluminium* [1976] 2 All ER 552 where it was held that a supplier of goods to a manufacturer could validly reserve title in the goods and trace the proceeds of their sale so that on the insolvency of the manufacturer the supplier could claim the amount of the proceeds in preference to secured creditors of the manufacturer. *Re Bond Worth* [1980] Ch 228 (retention of equitable title amounted to a charge requiring registration) and *Borden v Scottish Timber Products* [1979] 3 All ER 961 (reservation ineffective when goods are wholly changed in character), indicate limits to the efficacy of clauses of this type, which may need registration as company charges. (*See* TRACING).

Running-account credit. *See* CREDIT.

S

Safe Port. *See* TIME CHARTERPARTY.

Sale by Description. *See* CORRESPONDENCE WITH DESCRIPTION IN SALE OF GOODS.

Sale by Sample. The Sale of Goods Act 1979, s. 15 provides that a contract of sale is one of sale by sample when there is an express or implied term to that effect in the contract. This means that the fact that a sample has been shown in the negotiations leading to the contract does not of itself make it a sale by sample, *Gardiner v Gray* (1815) 4 Camp 144. In a contract of sale by sample there are implied conditions that the bulk will correspond with sample in quality, that the buyer will have a reasonable opportunity of comparing bulk with sample and that the goods† will be free from any defect rendering them unmerchantable which would not be apparent on reasonable examination of the sample. 'Merchantable'† is here to carry the same meaning as in s. 14 of the Act. When by trade usage only visual correspondence between bulk and sample is required the buyer cannot complain if there are important but non-apparent differences, *Hookway v Isaacs* [1954] 1 Lloyd's Rep 491; *Steel & Busks v Bleecker Bik* [1956] 1 Lloyd's Rep 228. The requirement of correspondence will not be satisfied if the bulk requires a simple process to make it correspond with sample, *Ruben v Faire* [1949] 1 KB 254 at 260. When there is a sale both by description and sample by s. 13 the goods must correspond with both, (*see* CORRESPONDENCE WITH DESCRIPTION IN SALE OF GOODS). Under the Unfair Contract Terms Act 1977†, s. 6 liability under both s. 13 and s. 15 of the Sale of Goods Act cannot be excluded or restricted by any contract term as against anyone dealing as a consumer and as against others an exclusion clause will only be effective so far as it is reasonable, but s. 26 allows exclusion in international supply contracts. The Sale of Goods Act 1979, s. 15, unlike the terms as to merchantable quality and fitness for purpose implied by s. 14, is not limited to sales 'in the course of a business' and hence may apply to private sales.

Sale of Goods. A contract of sale of goods is a contract by which the seller transfers or agrees to transfer the property in goods for a money consideration called the price, Sale of Goods Act 1979, s. 2 (1). The law of sale of goods was codified in the Sale of Goods Act 1893. The Act of 1979 repeals the Act of 1893 (except for s. 26 dealing with writs of execution), re-enacts its provisions and consolidates other legislation amending the 1893 Act. A contract of sale may be absolute or conditional and may be made between part owners. Where the property in goods is transferred from seller to buyer the contract is called a sale but where the transfer of property is postponed or is subject to some condition to be fulfilled the contract is called an agreement to sell. Capacity to buy and sell is regulated by the general law relating to capacity to contract. Minors, the mentally incompetent and drunks must pay a reasonable price for necessaries sold and delivered to them. The contract may be made orally, in writing, partly orally and partly in writing or may be implied from conduct. The Act provides for various categories of goods which may be the subject matter of the contract, for the consequences of goods perishing, the ascertainment of the price, the terms of the contract, stipulations as to time, conditions and warranties, sales by description and sample, terms as to merchantable quality and fitness for purpose, transfer of property, passing of risk, transfer of title and sales by non-owners, duties of buyer and seller in regard to performance, especially in regard to delivery, the rights of the unpaid seller against the goods, lien, stoppage in transit and a right of re-sale, the seller's action for the price and for damages, the buyers' action for damages, specific performance and remedies for breach of warranty. Exclusion of implied terms is allowed subject to the Unfair Contract Terms Act 1977. Special provision is made for auction sales. It is also provided that the rules of common law, including the law merchant, except in so far as they are inconsistent with the Act, and in particular the law of principal and agent, fraud, misrepresentation, duress, and other invalidating causes apply to contracts of sale of goods. It was held, however, that a codifying Act such as the 1893 Act should first be construed without reference to pre-Act case law kept in being by such a provision and that recourse should only be had to that case law when the Act was ambiguous or to clarify a technical term or on a point not covered by the Act, *Bank of England v Vagliano* [1891] AC 107 at 144–5. (*See* AUCTION SALE; BARTER; C.I.F. CONTRACTS; CORRESPONDENCE WITH DESCRIPTION IN SALE OF GOODS; DELIVERY IN SALE OF GOODS; EX SHIP CONTRACTS; F.A.S. CONTRACTS; FITNESS FOR PURPOSE; F.O.B. CONTRACTS; F.O.R. CONTRACTS; GOODS; MARKET OVERT; MERCHANTABLE QUALITY; NEMO DAT QUOD NON HABET; PASSING OF PROPERTY IN SALE OF GOODS; PRICE; PROPERTY; RISK IN SALE OF GOODS; SALE BY SAMPLE; SPECIAL POWERS OF SALE; TITLE IN SALE OF GOODS; UNIFORM LAWS ON INTERNATIONAL SALES ACT 1967; WRITS OF EXECUTION IN SALE OF GOODS; WORK AND MATERIALS; UNPAID SELLER).

Sale or return. *See* PASSING OF PROPERTY IN SALE OF GOODS.

Salvage. A reward for saving or assisting in saving a ship, apparel (equipment) and cargo, freight†, or the lives of those on board ship from shipwreck, capture or similar peril, see *Wells v Gas Float Whitton* [1897] AC 337 at 344. The right to salvage may, but need not, arise from contract. The salvor must show that his services were voluntary as not arising from a pre-existing contract. Members of a ship's crew may earn salvage in respect of their own vessel, but only if it has been finally abandoned, *The Albionic* [1942] P 81, and a tug may salve its tow only if circumstances justified her in abandoning it, *The Leon Blum* [1915] P 290. There must be peril and some skill and enterprise shown. The services must normally be beneficial. 'No cure, no pay' is of the essence of non-contractual salvage but may be excluded by contract. The owner of a ship effecting salvage services may claim salvage even though the vessel salved was put in peril by another of that owner's vessels, *The Beaverford v The Kafiristan* [1938] AC 136, but there is now no rule that a successful salvor is free from liability in damages for negligence. He is not merely subject to reduction of the salvage award, *The Tojo Maru* [1972] AC 242. The Crown is now liable and entitled in salvage, Crown Proceedings Act 1947 s. 8. At common law there was no claim for life salvage unless property was also saved but under the Merchant Shipping Act 1894, s. 544 life salvage may be claimed and if property also salved is insufficient to pay the award this may be paid from the Mercantile Marine Fund. The salvor has a maritime lien extending to ship, freight and cargo on the property salved, ranking above all other liens previously attached to the property. The salvage award is usually assessed by the court but the parties may agree a sum before the services were rendered. The court may re-open the contract if it is inequitable, *The Medina* (1877) 2 PD 5. The salvage money is divided between the owners, master, officers and crew of the salving vessel. Except in the case of a seaman on a ship engaged in salvage service, a seaman cannot agree to abandon his rights to salvage. Salvors guilty of or privy to theft forfeit all claims and those who by negligence allow it to occur may have awards reduced. Under the Unfair Contract Terms Act 1977† it is not possible by a contract term or notice to exclude liability in negligence for death or personal injury in a salvage or towage contract but many other provisions of the Act do not extend to such contracts except in favour of a person dealing as a consumer.

Sample. *See* SALE BY SAMPLE.

Sans recours. A formula used by the drawer of a bill of exchange or an indorser to negative their liability under the right of recourse. See the Bills of Exchange Act 1882, s. 16.

Scott v Avery Clause. *See* SUBMISSION TO ARBITRATION.

Scrip and Letters of Allotment. These are documents issued as a preliminary to the issue of a share warrant, share certificate or a security for stock. Scrip gave an option to become a full holder and when in bearer form transferable by delivery was a form of negotiable instrument, *Rumball v Metropolitan Bank* (1877) 2 QBD 194; *Goodwin v Robarts* (1876) 1 App Cas 476. Scrip giving merely an option has in practice been replaced by letters of allotment which make the holder a full shareholder unless he 'renounces' in favour of another. Such letters of allotment are not treated by mercantile custom as a form of negotiable instrument.

Seaworthy. Under both a time charterparty and a voyage charterparty a shipowner is under an absolute implied obligation at common law to provide a seaworthy vessel at the commencement of the charter and at the commencement of separate stages of a voyage which is to be by stages, *The Vortigern* [1899] P 140. The obligation is an 'innominate' term, neither a condition nor a warranty and the effect of a breach as entitling the charterer to repudiate and claim damages or merely to claim damages will depend on the nature of the breach which in fact occurs, *Hong Kong Fir Shipping Co v Kawasaki Kisen Kaisen* [1962] 2 QB 26. Under the Hague Rules†, scheduled to the Carriage of Goods by Sea Act 1971, which are embodied in almost all bills of lading, the carrier is obliged to use due diligence before and at the beginning of the voyage to make the ship seaworthy. 'Seaworthy' means that the ship is fit to encounter the ordinary perils of navigation and that the ship, its furniture and equipment are fit to carry the cargo, *Steel v State Line* (1878) 3 App Cas 72. Seaworthiness is to be assessed in relation to the voyage the ship is to undertake and the cargo to be carried, *Burges v Wickham* (1863) 3 B & S 669; *Stanton v Richardson* (1874) LR 9 CP 390; affd. (1875) 45 LJQB 78. One test whether a defect renders a ship unseaworthy is whether a prudent owner would have remedied it before putting to sea, *McFadden v Blue Star Line* [1905] 1 KB 697 at 706. Defects rendering a ship unseaworthy need not be in the structure and propelling machinery of the ship. An inadequate or unqualified crew, *Hong Kong Fir v Kawasaki Kisen Kaisha* [1962] 2 QB 26; *Standard Oil v Clan Line* [1924] AC 100, inadequate refrigeration for a perishable cargo, *The Cargo in the Maori King v Hughes* [1895] 2 QB 550 and inadequate loading tackle, *Hang Fung v Mullion* [1966] 1 Lloyd's Rep 511, may all have this effect. Bad stowage will amount to unseaworthiness only if it endangers the ship as distinct from the cargo, *Elder Dempster v Paterson Zochonis* [1924] AC 522.

Secret profit. *See* AGENT, DUTIES OF AN AGENT, BRIBE.

Servant. *See* AGENT and VICARIOUS LIABILITY.

Settlements voidable in bankruptcy. The trustee in bankruptcy is entitled to certain property which the bankrupt may have settled on others. If the settlement was made fraudulently it may be set aside under s. 172 of the Law of Property Act 1925. This is not limited to bankruptcy and prescribes no time limits. Unlike analogous provisions of the Bankruptcy Act 1914 it can be used when a deceased debtor's estate is subject to administration in bankruptcy. A voluntary conveyance is voidable if it will necessarily defeat creditors, even though no fraudulent intent can be proved. A conveyance for valuable or good consideration (this latter meaning family affection) can be avoided if it is proved that the grantor was intentionally fraudulent and the grantee was aware of this.

Under the Bankruptcy Act 1914, s. 42 (1) if a voluntary settlement is not fraudulent and more than ten years have elapsed since it was made it is unimpeachable. If less than ten but more than two years have elapsed then it is voidable (so held in *Re Carter and Kenderdine's Contract* [1897] 1 Ch 776 though the Act says 'void') by the trustee unless those claiming under it can show that the settlor was solvent at the making of the settlement without the aid of the property settled and that the settlor's interest in the property passed to the trustee of the settlement on its execution. If the settlement was made within two years of the commencement of the bankruptcy it is voidable without these qualifications. Settlements not within s. 42 (1) include settlements made before or in consideration of marriage and settlements in favour of a bona fide purchaser or incumbrancer for valuable consideration. This latter means a fair commercial return, replacing the property settled, *Re Windle* [1975] 1 WLR 1628.

Although s. 42 (4) says 'settlement' includes 'any conveyance or transfer of property' it appears from the cases that there must be an intention that the property should be retained for an indefinite period. *Re Tankard* [1899] 2 QB 57; *Re Plummer* [1900] 2 QB 790. Since these settlements are voidable a bona fide transferee for value of the settled property will get a good title before the commencement of the bankruptcy. Thereafter he must rely on ss. 45 and 47.

(*See* PROTECTED TRANSACTIONS IN BANKRUPTCY).

If avoided, a settlement is set aside only so far as necessary to pay debts and costs and the trustees of the settlement may prove as deferred debtors in the distribution† of property amongst creditors.

A covenant or contract made in consideration of the settlor's marriage for the future payment of money for the benefit of the spouse or children or for the future settlement on them of property in which at the marriage the settlor had no interest is void against the settlor's trustee in bankruptcy unless the covenant or contract has been executed before the commencement of the bankruptcy. Also payments or transfers under a covenant to make future payments or transfers will be void unless they were either made two years before the commencement of the bankruptcy or when the settlor was able to pay his debts without the money paid or property transferred or were made under a covenant to pay or transfer money or property expected to come to the settlor from a person named and were made within three months of the settlor obtaining possession of it.

Section 42 does not apply when a deceased debtor's estate is subject to administration in bankruptcy but the Law of Property Act, s. 172 may apply in such a case.

Share certificate. *See* SHARE WARRANT and NEGOTIABLE INSTRUMENT.

Share warrant. Under the Companies Act 1948, s. 83 a company, if authorised by its articles, may in respect of fully paid up shares, issue warrants certifying that the bearer is entitled to the shares specified. Transfer is by delivery and, unlike a share certificate, no separate document of transfer is required nor are the holders of warrants registered. Coupons are normally attached to a warrant to be detached and returned to the company in exchange for a payment of dividend when it advertises that a dividend is available. Share warrants are a form of negotiable instrument, *Webb, Hale & Co v Alexandria Water Co* (1905) 21 TLR 572. (*See* DELIVERY OF A BILL OF EXCHANGE OR PROMISSORY NOTE.)

Ship. Defined in the Merchant Shipping Act 1894, s. 742 as including 'every description of vessel used in navigation not propelled by oars'. 'Vessel' is there defined as including 'any ship or boat, or any other description of vessel used in navigation'. Merchant Shipping (Liability of Shipowners and Others) Act 1958, s. 4 provides that Part VIII of the 1894 Act which deals with limitation† of a shipowner's liability 'shall apply to any structure, whether completed or in the course of completion, launched and intended for use in navigation as a ship or part of a ship' and the word 'ship' in the 1894 Act Part VIII and the 1958 Act is to be so interpreted. The Merchant Shipping Act 1921, s. 1 provided that Part I of the 1894 Act applying to registration of British ships and Part VIII were to apply as if 'ship' included 'every description of lighter, barge or like vessel used in navigation in Great Britain, however propelled' unless these vessels are exclusively used in non-tidal and non-harbour waters. A navigational buoy is not a ship, *The Gas Float Whitton No. 2* [1897] AC 337, nor is a landing stage, *The Craighall* [1910] P 207.

Shipowner's lien. The shipowner has a lien upon the goods he carries until he received payment of freight†. The lien ceases on delivery of the goods but extends to all property consigned on the same voyage by the person from whom freight is due. Delivery of part does not defeat the lien on the remainder of the goods. At common law the lien does not apply to advance freight, dead freight or freight payable after delivery. Liens for these may be created by express agreement. It may be inconvenient to retain the goods on board hence the Merchant Shipping Act 1894, ss. 492–501 makes provision for such goods to be landed, for the maintenance of the lien and for the sale of the goods after ninety days (or earlier if perishable), to satisfy dues, expenses and freight. The shipowner also has a possessory lien for general average contributions and for the expenses of protecting goods.

Shipping documents. *See* C.I.F. CONTRACTS. They normally include a bill of lading, insurance policy and invoice.

Ship's master. At one time the master had extensive powers as an agent of necessity to sell his ship and raise money on the security of it and its cargo by means of respondentia and bottomry bonds. Though the general principles in these authorities may still be applicable to other agents of necessity they will rarely now apply to a master since he will almost always be able to communicate with his owners or their agents and inability to inform them was a pre-requisite of his acting as an agent of necessity. This also applies to a master contracting for necessaries for his ship. Formerly the master would also sign a bill of lading but this is now normally done by a loading broker, *Heskell v Continental Express Ltd* [1950] 1 All ER 1033, 1037. The master's responsibilities are nowadays largely confined to the navigation and management of the ship and he does not have the wider commercial functions mentioned in older cases.

Ship's papers. Those usually carried are the certificate of registry, the crew agreement relating to employment of the crew, any charterparty or bill of lading, the bill of health, invoices relating to the cargo and the official log book. Certain customs and consular officials have powers to require production of these, e.g. under s. 723 of the Merchant Shipping Act 1894.

Sight. A bill of exchange or promissory note may be drawn payable at a period after sight, that is after it has been exhibited to the drawee in the case of a bill or to the maker of a promissory note. In the case of a bill 'sight' must appear either by acceptance or by protest† for non-acceptance, *Campbell v French* (1795) 6 TR 200, but as a promissory note cannot be accepted 'sight' there means mere exhibition to the maker to fix the commencement of the period, *Sturdy v Henderson* (1821) 4 B & Ald 592. A bill cannot be drawn payable at a period after acceptance and, if a document is so drawn, 'acceptance' will not be read as synonymous with 'sight', *Korea Exchange Bank v Debenhams* [1979] 1 Lloyd's Rep 548.

If a bill is drawn payable 'at sight' this is equivalent to 'on demand'; the Bills of Exchange Act 1882, s. 10.

Signature to a bill of exchange or promissory note. The Bills of Exchange Act 1882, s. 91 provides that a person may sign by his agent and that a corporation such as a company may either sign by agent or use its seal. Section 23 provides that no person is liable as drawer, acceptor or indorser who has not signed as such and where a person signs in a trade or assumed name he is liable as if he had signed in his proper name. Also the signing of the name of a partnership is equivalent to the signing of the names of all the partners. By s. 21 delivery in addition to signature is essential to make the liability of parties complete and irrevocable. By s. 24 a forged or unauthorised signature on a bill of exchange or promissory note is wholly inoperative unless the party whose signature it purports to be is precluded, as by estoppel, from denying it is his. By s. 25 a 'procuration signature', one which expressly indicates it is made by an agent (e.g. *per pro*) gives notice that the agent has only limited authority and the principal is only bound if the agent acts within those limits. Section 26 provides that where a person clearly signs 'as agent' or in a representative capacity he is not personally liable but the mere addition of words describing him as an agent or as filling a representative capacity (and *not as signing as* agent or *as a representative*) is not enough to exempt from personal liability. In determining whether a signature is that of the principal or agent by whom it is written, the construction most favourable to validity is to be adopted. By s. 17 a simple signature suffices for an acceptance and by s. 32 such a signature suffices for an indorsement in blank. By s. 56 where a person signs otherwise than as a drawer or acceptor he incurs the liabilities of an indorser and may be known as a quasi-indorser.

By s. 89 these provisions apply with modifications to a promissory note.

Simple contract. *See* CONTRACT.

Simplex commendatio non obligat. ('Mere praise does not involve legal obligation'). This maxim means that language which a reasonable person would disregard as mere advertising eulogy will not involve the consequences of misrepresentation, *Dimmock v Hallett* (1866) 2 Ch App 1. Stricter standards may now be applied, *Erven Warnink v Townend* [1979] AC 731. The Trade Descriptions Act 1968 imposes criminal liability for false advertising but does not affect the contractual position, (*see* TRADE DESCRIPTIONS).

Slander of Title. *See* TRADE LIBEL.

Small Agreements. The Consumer Credit Act 1974, s. 17 provides that these are consumer credit or consumer hire agreements involving less than £30 other than hire purchase or conditional sale and unsecured or secured only by guarantee or indemnity. These are relieved by s. 74 of most of the requirements as to formalities and by s. 78 of the duty to supply statements of accounts. Section 17 provides that it is not possible to obtain these benefits by splitting a non-small agreement into separate agreements within the limit.

Sovereign Immunity. *See* STATE IMMUNITY.

Special agent. *See* AGENT.

Special crossing. *See* CROSSED CHEQUE.

Special damage. Actual harm to some interest of a plaintiff which is an essential part of his cause of action in certain torts such as negligence.

Special damages. Damages in respect of loss which the law does not presume to have occured if a plaintiff succeeds in his claim but which he must specifically plead. *See* REMEDIES OF THE BUYER IN SALE OF GOODS; REMEDIES OF THE SELLER IN SALE OF GOODS and the Sale of Goods Act 1979, s. 54.

Special drawing rights. These, as defined by the International Monetary Fund, are now used as a stable measure of the value of currencies in place of the gold franc in provisions limiting the liability of carriers. The Carriage by Air and Road Act 1979 provides in s. 4 for the replacement of references to gold francs in the Carriage of Goods by Road Act 1965† and the Carriage of Passengers by Road Act 1974† by references to special drawing rights and the amended Warsaw Convention on Carriage by Air which is scheduled to the 1979 Act also contains references in Articles 22 and 22A to special drawing rights. Section 5 of the 1979 Act provides for the conversion of special drawing rights into sterling. The Merchant Shipping Act 1981 replaces references to gold francs in the limitation provisions of the Merchant Shipping Acts (*see* SHIPOWNER'S LIMITATION OF LIABILITY) and the Carriage of Goods by Sea Act 1971 by references to special drawing rights and s. 3 provides for their conversion into sterling, the sterling value for any day to be that fixed by the International Monetary Fund for the day or the value last fixed by the Fund, a Treasury certificate to be conclusive evidence. Special drawing rights originated as a form of financial reserve holding in 1969 and their value is fixed from time to time by the Fund in relation to a 'basket' of currencies.

Special indorsement. *See* INDORSEMENT OF A NEGOTIABLE INSTRUMENT.

Specialty. A synonym for deed.

Special Manager (Bankruptcy). This appointment is made by the Official Receiver, whether he is acting as such after a receiving order or as interim receiver after presentation of a bankruptcy petition against a debtor. The Official Receiver may make the appointment on the application of a creditor if he is satisfied that the debtor's estate or business or the interests of creditors generally require it. The manager must give security to the Department of Trade and his remuneration is fixed by the creditors or, if they fail to do so, by the Department. He may be removed by the Official Receiver and must be removed if the creditors pass a special resolution to that effect. He assists the Official Receiver in the management of the debtor's business.

Special powers of sale. The Sale of Goods Act 1979, s. 21 mentions these powers, whether statutory or common law, and sale by order of the court among exceptions to nemo dat quod non habet. Statutory powers include sales of unredeemed pledges under the Consumer Credit Act 1974, ss. 114–122; sales under the Innkeepers' Act 1878, under the Torts (Interference with Goods) Act 1977, s. 12, replacing the Disposal of Uncollected Goods Act 1952, and sales by a Sheriff under a writ of execution under the Bankruptcy and Deeds of Arrangement Act 1913. Under the Sale of Goods Act 1979, s. 48 an unpaid seller may re-sell the goods. An important common law power is that of an agent of necessity. The court has powers under the Rules of the Supreme Court to order the sale of perishables, goods whose value is falling and other goods for which there is good reason for sale.

Specific goods. The Sale of Goods Act 1979, s. 61 (1) defines these as 'goods identified and agreed on at the time a contract of sale is made'. The classification of goods† as specific is important for ss. 6 and 7 of the Act dealing with the avoidance of contracts on the perishing of goods, ss. 17 to 19 dealing with the passing of property, s. 29 (2) dealing with delivery in sale of goods, s. 52 dealing with specific performance (*see* REMEDIES OF THE BUYER IN SALE OF GOODS) and the Law Reform (Frustrated Contracts) Act 1943, s. 2 (5) (c) which excludes from the general provisions of that Act 'any contract to which s. 7 of the Sale of Goods Act [1979] applies, or any other contract for the sale or sale and delivery of specific goods where the contract is frustrated by reason of the fact that the goods have perished'.

Specific Performance. An order of the court directing the defendant to carry out the terms of a contract as agreed. It is an equitable remedy (*see* EQUITY) and so discretionary. Thus it will not be granted unless damages are not an adequate remedy, nor will it be granted for ordinary items of commerce for which substitutes could readily be purchased, *Cud (Cudee) v Rutter* (1720) 1 P Wms 570, but normally only for subject matter of unique or special character. Every piece of land is regarded as unique for this purpose so this remedy is specially important in land law. A contract of employment will not be specifically enforced and this cannot be circumvented by the use of an injunction. As a matter of discretion, *Price v Strange* [1978] Ch 337, the court may not grant the remedy if there is lack of mutuality between the parties, that is, the remedy would not be equally available to either of them. Thus specific performance will not be granted for an infant since it would not be granted against him. *Flight v Bolland* (1828) 4 Russ 298; *Lumley v Ravenscroft* [1895] 1 QB 683, (*see* CONTRACTUAL CAPACITY, also REMEDIES OF THE BUYER IN SALE OF GOODS).

Stamp duties for bills of exchange and promissory notes. Such instruments once had to be drawn on paper carrying a revenue stamp. This was ad valorem for most bills of exchange and promissory notes but at a flat rate for demand bills including cheques. A general flat rate for stamping was introduced by the Finance Act 1961 and the Finance Act 1970 abolished stamp duty as from 1 February 1971. The Bills of Exchange Act 1882, s. 20 (1) dealing with inchoate instruments, in its original form referred to stamped paper but these references have been repealed by the Finance Act 1970. By the Bills of Exchange Act 1882, s. 72 (1) when an instrument is issued outside the United Kingdom it will not be invalid merely because it is not stamped in accordance with the law of the place of issue.

Standard form contracts. This refers to the use by contracting parties of documents containing contractual terms which with necessary adaptation, can be used for a large number of contracts. In *Schroeder Music Publishing Co v Macauley* [1974] 3 All ER 616 Lord Diplock pointed out that there are two main types – a first and unobjectionable type of long standing setting out the terms on which mercantile transactions of frequent occurrence take effect and which save the necessity of re-negotiation and a second, more recent and more objectionable type resulting from 'the concentration of particular kinds of business in relatively few hands'. As these were not freely negotiated by the other party they often contained oppressive exemption and exclusion clauses. The courts endeavoured to control these by the contra proferentem rule, the requirement of notice in ticket cases† and clauses, and fundamental breach. They are now subject to the Unfair Contract Terms Act 1977†, which in s. 3 makes special provision for contracts on one party's 'written standard terms of business' (s. 17 for Scotland speaks of 'standard form contract'). These are not defined. See *McCrone v Boots Farm Sales Ltd* [1981] SLT 103. In commercial contracts standard terms may be imported into a contact when the parties have had a consistent course of dealing in which they have been used in contracts even though in the instant case the ordinary requirements of notice are not satisfied, *Spurling v Bradshaw* [1956] 2 All ER 121; *Hardwick Game Farm v Suffolk Agricultural Assoc* [1969] 2 AC 31; *British Crane Hire v Ipswich Plant Hire* [1975] QB 303 (trade custom), but this cannot be done if the course of dealing was not consistent, *McCutcheon v David MacBrayne* [1964] 1 All ER 430 and will be more difficult in consumer transactions or if dealings have been infrequent, *Hollier v Rambler Motors* [1972] 2 QB 71.

Standard Licence. The Consumer Credit Act 1974, s. 22 provides that this is one of the two forms of licence required for the carrying on of consumer credit or consumer hire business by anyone other than a local authority or a body corporate authorised by statute to carry on the business. A standard licence is issued to a named person or partnership or unincorporated body by the Director-General of Fair Trading† authorising the carrying on of specified business for a prescribed period. Licences are in practice issued for different categories of business. Whilst debtor–creditor agreements may not be canvassed off business premises, debtor–creditor–supplier agreements may be so canvassed to the extent permitted by the licence. There is no right to a licence, s. 25 requiring an applicant to satisfy the Director-General that he is a fit person and the name under which he proposes to trade is not misleading or undesirable. Sections 27–37 deal with the issue, renewal, variation, suspension and revocation of licences and the keeping of a register. By s. 39 unlicensed trading is an offence and by s. 40 any regulated agreement made by an unlicensed trader is unenforceable unless the Director-General makes a validating order. The other form of licence is a group licence.

State immunity. It was once the general rule that foreign States and their government corporations were immune from suit in United Kingdom courts unless they submitted to the jurisdiction. The State Immunity Act 1978, ss. 1–14 reaffirms the general rule but subjects it to many exceptions in addition to submission. States are now not immune in respect of the following matters: some commercial transactions and contracts to be performed in the United Kingdom; contracts of employment with individuals made or to be performed in the United Kingdom; actions for personal injury or property damage caused in the United Kingdom; actions relating to the use, possession or ownership of property in the United Kingdom; proceedings relating to patents, copyright, trade marks, registered designs and plant breeders' rights† applied for or alleged to be infringed in the United Kingdom; proceedings relating to a state's membership of a corporate or unincorporate body or a partnership; proceedings relating to arbitration when the state has made a written submission to arbitration; proceedings relating to state ships used for commercial purposes; claims for V.A.T., customs and excise duty, agricultural levies and rates. The term 'state' covers the Head of State in his public capacity, its government and any of its departments. State corporations, termed 'separate entities' are only immune when acting in exercise of sovereign authority and when the state itself so acting would have been immune. The property of a central bank or monetary authority is immune from enforcement process whether or not it is a 'separate entity'. Section 16 provides that the Act is not to affect diplomatic and consular immunity. Immunity is also retained in respect of the employment of diplomatic and consular staff, diplomatic mission property, taxation other than those taxes specifically mentioned, and criminal proceedings. The 1978 Act also does not apply to foreign armed forces in this country. Section 18 provides for the recognition in United Kingdom courts of judgments given under similar legislation against the United Kingdom in countries which are parties to the European Convention on State Immunity.

Statement of affairs (Bankruptcy). A receiving order must be served on a debtor and contains a notice that he must attend upon the Official Receiver for an interview at which he will be instructed to prepare a Statement of Affairs. This must give full particulars of assets, debts, creditors and securities held by them and any other information the Official Receiver may require. Under the Bankruptcy Rules 1952, r. 329 the Official Receiver may require trading and profit and loss accounts and a cash and goods account for any period not exceeding two years before the receiving order and the court may require them for a longer period. If the debtor fails to submit a statement without reasonable excuse an adjudication may be made on the application of the Official Receiver or any creditor.

A statement must be verified by affidavit and made within three days of an order made on a debtor's petition and seven days of an order on a creditor's petition, though the court may extend these limits. (See the Bankruptcy Act 1914, s. 14).

Stoppage in transit (or transitu). *See* UNPAID SELLER.

Subject to equities. In the case of a negotiable instrument this means subject to the defects of title of a prior holder. If a transferee does not take an instrument for value in good faith, takes one that is not apparently complete and regular on the face of it or has notice of a defect in the transferor's title or takes one that is overdue (*see* MATURITY) he will not acquire the status of a holder in due course and so be able to acquire a better title than his transferor had. Assignments of choses in action are always subject to equities.

Submission to arbitration. An agreement to submit to arbitration, known as a submission, may be oral but the 1950 Act only applies to written submissions. These frequently take the form of arbitration clauses in commercial contracts.

If, despite a submission to arbitration, a party takes ordinary legal proceedings, the court in its discretion may on the application of the other party, before he has delivered any pleadings, stay the proceedings. Good grounds must be shown to oppose a stay, e.g. fraud or partiality. The parties may by a *Scott v Avery* clause make a reference to arbitration a condition precedent to an action. They may also provide that if an arbitrator is not appointed within a specified time, a claim will be deemed to be waived, in which case it cannot be enforced by action or arbitration. When a party denies the existence or validity of a contract, e.g. as illegal, he may not set up an arbitration clause as a defence but it is otherwise if he admits the existence of the contract, but merely denies liability under it. It may be difficult to distinguish a valuation from an arbitration but the Arbitration Act does not apply to a valuation and a valuer is not entitled to any judicial immunity which may be enjoyed by an arbitrator. A submission may be amended by agreement between the parties but not by the arbitrator. It may be rectified by the court but even the court cannot enlarge the time for making an award. In the absence of an express contrary intention, the authority of an arbitrator is irrevocable except with leave of the court which will only be given in exceptional circumstances. The court may then make a new appointment. An arbitration clause may be enforced by or against the assignee of an assignable contract and may be enforced by or against a trustee in bankruptcy if he adopts the contract. If he does not the court may yet, on application, order a question to be determined by arbitration. On the effect of delay see *Bremer Vulkan v South India* [1981] 1 All ER 289; *Japan Line v Himoff* [1983] 1 Lloyd's Rep 29.

Subrogation. This refers to a situation where one party is allowed 'to step into the shoes of another' and enforce claims originally vested in that other. Thus an insurer, having paid the insured, will be subrogated to any claims the insured may have had against third parties and the lender of a void loan to an infant or minor which is used to pay off debts for necessaries binding on the infant may be subrogated to the rights of the supplier of necessaries against the infant. (*See* CONTRACTUAL CAPACITY).

Sum certain in money for bills of exchange and promissory notes. By the Bills of Exchange Act 1882, s. 9 a sum is certain for the purposes of the definition of a bill of exchange (including a cheque) and a promissory note (ss. 3, 73, 83) even though it may be required to be paid with interest, by stated instalments, by stated instalments with a provision that upon default in any instalment the whole shall become due or according to an indicated rate of exchange or according to a rate of exchange to be ascertained as indicated by the bill. If there is a conflict between the sums expressed in words and figures on bill, the sum in words is payable. Where a bill is stated to be payable with interest, unless the bill provides otherwise, interest runs from the date of the bill and if it is undated then from its issue.

Summary administration (Bankruptcy). In bankruptcy this is employed when the debtor's estate is not likely to exceed £4000. On making the receiving order, the court can order summary administration. The Official Receiver will act as trustee in bankruptcy. The Bankruptcy Rules provide for a simplified procedure, with limited advertising and normally only one dividend. Costs are on a reduced scale. (See the Bankruptcy Act 1914, s. 129; Bankruptcy Rules 1952, r. 298; Insolvency Act 1976, s. 1).

Supply of Goods and Services Act 1982. This is partly designed to secure the implication in contracts analagous to sale of goods, such as contracts of barter or for work and materials, of terms as to title, correspondence with description, fitness for purpose, merchantable quality and sample similar to those implied in sale of goods by the Sale of Goods Act 1979. For contracts of hire it implies terms relating to the bailor's right to transfer possession and, as to the goods hired, correspondence with description, merchantability and fitness for purpose and terms where hire is by sample. All such terms may, subject to the Unfair Contract Terms Act 1977† be expressly or impliedly excluded or varied. Part II of the 1982 Act implies in contracts for services (which do not include contracts of service [employment] or apprenticeship) terms as to reasonable care and skill, performance within an agreed or reasonable time and as to a reasonable charge or consideration when this is not otherwise determined. Again, subject to the Unfair Contract Terms Act 1977 all such terms may be expressly or impliedly excluded.

Suretyship. *See* GUARANTEE.

Synallagmatic contract. One consisting of promises exchanged between more than two parties, thus being akin to a bilateral contract and contrasted with a unilateral contract where a promise is given for an act. See *United Dominions Trust v Eagle Aircraft* [1968] 1 All ER 104 at 108.

T

Tailpiece. *See* RESALE PRICE MAINTENANCE and RESTRICTIVE TRADE PRACTICES.

Tender. *See* DISCHARGE OF CONTRACT BY PERFORMANCE (meaning proffer of performance) and OFFER AND ACCEPTANCE (meaning standing offer to supply goods at an indicated price).

The Moorcock. Under the rule in *The Moorcock* (1889) 14 PD 64 a court may imply a term or terms to give 'business efficacy' to a contract but not merely because such a term would be reasonable. Such implication is to be contrasted with implications arising from the language used by the parties, from statute, and from custom.

Things (or Choses) in action. A sub-category of personal chattels comprising intangible property such as patents, copyright, trade marks, debts and the like over which rights can only be asserted by the bringing of an action and not by the taking of possession as in the case of things (or choses) in possession, comprising money and goods.

Threats action (Patent). *See* TRADE LIBEL.

Through Bill of Lading. A document covering the carriage of goods by stages, only one or some of which will be carriage by sea as covered by an ordinary bill of lading. Through bills or combined transport documents are now frequently found in connection with roll on – roll off and container traffic. Despite some doubt based on old mercantile custom, the better opinion seems to be that such documents are bills of lading for modern legal purposes. The Carriage of Goods by Sea Act 1971 and the Hague Rules† apply not only to bills of lading strictly but also to 'any similar document of title' and hence would appear to apply to the sea carriage stages covered by through bills and combined transport documents.

Ticket Cases. In these a party has sought to incorporate exemption and exclusion clauses in a contract by means of a notice displayed or unsigned ticket delivered on formation of the contract. (*See* OFFER AND ACCEPTANCE). This in part depends on whether the viewer of the notice or the recipient of the paper would regard it as being contractual and not as a mere voucher or receipt. If the latter it will not import terms into the contract, *Chapleton v Barry UDC* [1940] 1 KB 532. Whether a notice or writing is to be regarded as contractual depends on current commercial practice. If it can be regarded as contractual it will incorporate the terms if reasonable steps were taken to bring them or a source where they may be found to the attention of members of the class of persons with whom the profferor of the terms ordinarily deals. If this is done prior to the formation of the contract the terms will be incorporated even though the recipient or viewer does not acquire actual knowledge of them and despite some unusual disability, e.g. illiteracy, preventing knowledge, unless the profferor knew of the disability and failed to take further suitable means to give information of the terms, *Thompson v L.M.S.* [1930] 1 KB 41, *Grier v Kujawa* [1970] 1 Lloyd's Rep 364. Whilst it is not absolutely necessary to print on the face of a ticket words, such as 'For conditions see back' this is the usual method and if words such as these are absent or obscured this may prevent the terms being incorporated. *Sugar v L.M.S.* [1941] 1 All ER 172. The more unusual or abnormal a term the more conspicuous must be the notice, *Thornton v Shoe Lane Parking* [1971] 2 QB 163.

If the notification comes after the contract has been formed the notice or document will not be incorporated, *Olley v Marlborough Court* [1949] 1 KB 532. Such a delayed notice or ticket may be operative if the parties agree to adopt it (*see* VARIATION AND WAIVER OF CONTRACT) or if it embodies terms which would in any event have been implied in the contract on formation either by custom and usage or by course of dealing, *British Crane Hire v Ipswich* [1974] 1 All ER 1059; *Spurling v Bradshaw* [1956] 2 All ER 121.

When a contract is signed there is no need for reasonable notice and the party signing will be bound unless non est factum, misrepresentation, rectification or some other vitiating or discharging element is present.

Time charterparty. A form of charterparty under which the charterer hires a ship for a specified period of time, the control and management of the crew and vessel remaining with the shipowner. At common law a number of terms will be implied into such contracts. These may be varied or excluded subject to the Unfair Contract Terms Act 1977 which has only limited application to charterparties except in favour of a person dealing as a consumer. As in a voyage charterparty a term will be implied that the ship is seaworthy, at the port of delivery and the owners usually undertake to maintain her during the charter. The charterer impliedly agrees not to ship dangerous goods and only to nominate 'safe ports'. A port is not safe if ordinary skill and care would not prevent danger and is not safe if, though safe within its limits, an ordinary prudent and skilful master could not reach it in safety, *The Polyglory* [1977] 2 Lloyd's Rep 353. The charter may provide for cancellation if hire is not paid punctually, *Mardorf Peach v Attica Sea Carriers* [1977] AC 850, and also include an 'off hire' clause relieving the charterer from the payment of hire for periods when the ship is not available for use, as when drydocked or lost or missing. The charterparty may further deal with the obligation of the master to sign bills of lading and the relationship of such bills to the charterparty. Where the charterer is an agent obtaining a cargo from a third party the charterparty will contain a 'cesser clause' under which the charterer's liability for freight is to cease as soon as the cargo is loaded and the shipowner is given a lien over the cargo for freight†, deadfreight and demurrage. It will then usually contain an 'employment and indemnity' clause requiring the charterers to indemnify the shipowners against any liability in which the charterers may have involved them, particularly in regard to bills of lading. There may also be a 'redelivery clause', covering the charterer's obligation to return the vessel at the end of the charterparty and providing for the fact that the vessel may then be on a voyage that prevents immediate redelivery.

Time orders. The Consumer Credit Act 1974, s. 129 allows the court to make such an order either on an application for an enforcement order or on application by the debtor or hirer after service on him of a default notice or analogous notice or when it considers it just to do so. The court must order one or both of the following courses: payment by the debtor or hirer or surety of any sum owed or any security at times the court considers reasonable having regard to their means; the remedying of any breach other than non-payment within a period specified by the court. Where an offer to pay by instalments is made and accepted the court may give effect to it without hearing evidence of means. When a time order is in force the creditor or owner cannot take any further action except with leave of the court and the order may be varied on the application of any person interested. The court may impose conditions on the order or include terms it considers just.

Title in sale of goods. The Sale of Goods Act 1893, s. 12 implied in contracts of sale of goods a condition that the seller would have a right to sell the goods and warranties as to quiet enjoyment and freedom from encumbrances. This was substantially amended by the Supply of Goods (Implied Terms) Act 1973, and these amendments are now embodied in Sale of Goods Act 1979, s. 12. This provides that in a contract of sale there is normally an implied condition that the seller has a right to sell the goods or will have such a right when the property† is to pass. There are also implied warranties that there are no undisclosed charges or encumbrances and that the buyer will enjoy quiet possession except in so far as it may be disturbed by owners of disclosed charges. The condition and warranties will not be implied if the seller makes it clear that he only intends to transfer such property, if any, as he or a third person may have but in such a case he must disclose to the buyer all encumbrances known to him, and there is a warranty against disturbance by the seller, a third party whose title may have been sold and those claiming under them.

The seller may be in breach of the condition as to title even though he is the owner of the goods if some third party is entitled to restrain the sale, e.g. because the goods infringe his trade mark, *Niblett v Confectioners' Materials* [1921] 3 KB 387. If the condition is broken there is a total failure of consideration, the buyer can recover the price in full without any allowance for use and the term is not reduced to a warranty by s. 11 (4), *Rowland v Divall* [1923] 2 KB 500. A claim for breach of the condition as to title will be barred by limitation six years after the contract but the warranties are continuing and time will run in favour of the seller only from the actual disturbance of the buyer.

The Unfair Contract Terms Act 1977† forbids all exclusion or restriction of the Sale of Goods Act 1979, s. 12, (except in so far as a seller is allowed to sell whatever title he or a third party may have). Section 26 of the 1977 Act does allow exclusion in international supply contracts. *See also* NEMO DAT QUOD NON HABET.

Tort. A civil wrong which may arise independently of any contract between the parties, always remediable by an action for unliquidated damages and sometimes by an injunction or by self-help. Examples of torts of importance in commerce are negligence, interference with goods, deceit, passing off, injurious falsehood or trade libel.

Torts (Interference with Goods) Act 1977. *See* CONVERSION, BAILMENT and INTERFERENCE WITH GOODS.

Tracing. A process in equity which enables a person with a claim to property† in one form e.g. goods, to assert a claim to some other form of property into which the original property has been transformed, e.g. money, resulting from the sale of goods.

Trade Descriptions Acts 1968–1972. These, which replace the Merchandise Marks Acts 1887–1953, impose criminal liability for misleading statements in supplying goods or services. For goods the 1968 Act s. 1 provides that it is an offence for anyone in the course of a trade or business to apply a false trade description to goods or to supply or offer to supply such goods. Intent or recklessness need not be proved but ss. 24 and 25 contain defences. 'Trade description' covers any 'direct or indirect indication of quantity, size, method of manufacture, production or processing, composition, fitness for purpose, strength, performance or other physical characteristics, testing and its results, approval, place where, date when or person by whom the manufacturing, production or processing was effected and other history, including previous ownership or use' (s. 2). There is provision for exemption for export goods and certain other categories (s. 32). A false trade description must be false 'to a material degree' (s. 3). Any disclaimer must be sufficiently conspicuous and clear as to neutralise the description. An oral description suffices and any description need not be applied by a party to any contract. 'Applies' covers not merely marking or juxtaposing with the goods but any use which is in any way likely to be taken to refer to the goods, (s. 4). When a class of goods is described by advertisement the description covers all goods of the class, whether or not in existence at the time of the advertisement, (s. 5). 'Offering to supply' includes possessing goods for supply, (s. 6). Orders may be made that goods be marked, accompanied by information or that information regarding them be advertised (ss. 8, 9, 10). There are separate offences of falsely representing royal approval or award or that goods or services are of a kind supplied to any person (ss. 12, 13) and two offences of false pricing, the first being the giving of any indication that the price of goods is equal to or less than a price recommended by the manufacturer or one at which the supplier himself offered them, an indication that the goods were previously offered being taken to mean that they were offered by him for a continuous period of twenty-eight days in the last six months, and the second offence being any indication that goods are being offered at a price less than that at which they are in fact being offered, (s. 11).

In regard to services it is an offence in the course of a trade or business knowingly or recklessly to make a false statement as to the provision of, or nature of any services, accommodation or facilities or the time or place at which or persons by whom they are to be provided or their amenities, examination or approval (s. 14).

The import of goods with false indication of origin is prohibited and the import of goods bearing infringing trade marks is restricted (ss. 16. 17). When an offence under the Act is committed by any body corporate with the knowledge or consent of or through the neglect of any officer or purported officer they may be prosecuted as may a person who is an accessory in the United Kingdom to acts abroad which would be offences under s. 1 if they were committed here (ss. 20, 21). Where an offence by one person is due to the act or default of another, either or both may be prosecuted (s. 23). It is a general defence under the Act when it can be shown by the defendant that the offence was due to a mistake, or to reliance on information given him or to the act or default of another or an accident or some other cause beyond his control and that he took all reasonable precautions and exercised all due diligence to avoid an offence either by himself or by any person under his control. Seven days notice must normally be given identifying a person whose act, default or false information is alleged under this defence. In an offence of supplying or offering to supply goods when the false description was applied by someone other than the supplier, it is a defence for the supplier to prove that he did not know and could not reasonably have discovered that the goods did not conform to the description or that it had been applied to them (s. 24). When an offence is alleged to have been committed by publishing an advertisement it is a defence for the advertiser to show that he is in the business of publishing advertisements, that he received the advertisement in the ordinary course of business and did not know or suspect that it would amount to an offence (s. 25). There are special exemptions for market research experiments (s. 37). There are special time limits for prosecutions, three years or one year from discovery, whichever is the earlier, and duties of enforcement are laid on local authorities but private prosecution remains possible (s. 26), and the authorities are given powers to make test purchases (s. 27), and to enter premises and inspect and seize goods and documents (s. 28). The fact that an offence has been committed under the Act does not itself render any contract for the supply of goods void or unenforceable. (*See* ILLEGALITY IN CONTRACT).

Trade Libel also known as Injurious Falsehood or Slander of Goods or Slander of Title. The tort is committed when a defendant makes a false and malicious representation to a third party disparaging the plaintiff's property or business but not necessarily defaming the plaintiff's personal character. The representation may be made in writing orally or by conduct e.g. by selling defective goods made by the plaintiff as if they were normal, *Wilts United Dairies v Thomas Robinson* [1958] RPC 94. It may reflect on the plaintiff's right to property or the quality of his goods or more generally on his property or business e.g. by alleging that a house he is selling is haunted, *Barrett v Associated Newspapers* (1907) 23 TLR 666, by stating specifically that the defendant's business is more successful than the plaintiff's, *Lyne v Nicholls* (1906) 23 TLR 86, or that the plaintiff has retired or ceased to trade, *Ratcliffe v Evans* [1892] 2 QB 524; *Joyce v Motor Surveys* [1948] Ch 252, or that he is continuing in an employment which has ceased, *Shapiro v La Morta* (1923) 130 LT 622, but it is not enough to allege that the defendant's product is the best available without any specific reference to the plaintiff's rival product, *White v Mellin* [1895] AC 154. There it was said that malice required either an intent to injure or knowledge of falsity but it seems that recklessness, making the representation without caring if it was true or false, will also suffice for malice, *Shapiro v La Morta.*

At common law special damage in the sense of pecuniary loss had to be proved but general loss of custom suffices when the nature of the business or the representation makes more detailed proof impossible. By the Defamation Act 1952, s. 3 (1) it is no longer necessary to prove special damage if the words are calculated to cause pecuniary damage to the plaintiff, are published in writing or other permanent form or are in respect of any office, profession, calling, trade or business held or carried on by him at the time of publication.

If the plaintiff's title to property is wrongly impugned but the elements of injurious falsehood e.g. malice, are not present he may obtain a declaration of his right, *Loudon v Ryder* [1953] Ch 423. By the Patents Act 1977, s. 70 a person threatened without good cause with infringement proceedings may claim an injunction, a declaration and damages.

Trade Marks. The Trade Marks Act 1938, s. 68 states that 'mark' includes a device, brand, heading, label, ticket, or any combination of these and 'trade mark' means, except in relation to a certification trade mark, 'a mark used or proposed to be used in relation to goods for the purpose of indicating or so as to indicate, a connection in the course of trade between the goods and some person having the right either as proprietor or registered user to use the mark, whether with or without any indication of the identity of that person.'

Entry of a trade mark on the register kept under the Act allows the registered proprietor to sue for trade mark infringement arising from the unauthorised use of the mark or a deceptively similar mark for goods of the type for which the mark was registered. Registration may be in Part A or Part B, more extensive protection being given to Part A.

For Part A a mark must consist of at least one of the following (i) the name of a company, individual or firm represented in a special manner; (ii) the signature of the applicant for registration or a predecessor in his business; (iii) an invented word or invented words; (iv) a word or words not referring directly to the quality or character of the goods and not being in its ordinary meaning a geographical name or a surname; (v) any other distinctive mark but a name, signature or word other than those in (i)–(iv) is not registrable except on proof of distinctiveness. A colour scheme may be a trade mark, *Smith, Kline and French v Sterling-Winthrop* [1975] 2 All ER 578, but a trade mark may not be registered in respect of a repairing process, *Aristoc v Rysta* [1945] AC 68. Registration in Part A gives an exclusive right to use the mark and after seven years is presumed to be valid unless it was obtained by fraud or the mark is scandalous, deceptive or contrary to law.

A trade mark may be registered in Part B when it is capable of distinguishing, either generally or subject to registered limitations, goods of the type for which it is registered and with which the proprietor of the mark is or may be connected in the course of trade from goods with which there is no such connection.

Unlike a Part A mark, a Part B mark need not be distinctive when first used but may become distinctive in use. It may then be registered in Part A. A mark may be registered in both Part A and Part B. The presumption of validity after seven years use does not apply to Part B. The Act states in s. 5 (1) that subject to s. 5 (2) registration in Part B gives the same protection as in Part A. Section 5 (2) provides that no relief will be given for infringement of a Part B mark, except for infringement by breach of contractual restrictions under s. 6, if the infringer proves that his use is not likely to confuse or mislead.

Trade Mark Infringement. Valid registration in Part A of the Trade Marks Act 1938 gives the proprietor the exclusive right to the use of the trade mark and this is infringed by any unauthorised use of the mark or one deceptively similar to it in the course of trade in relation to the relevant goods. 'Use' means printed or visual, not spoken use, but the latter might amount to passing off. Infringement must take place within the realm. The importing of infringing goods is infringement and the Trade Descriptions Act 1968, s. 17 (adding s. 64A to the 1938 Act) allows written notice to be given to the Customs requiring them to seize infringing goods. There will be no infringement when the mark was applied by the proprietor and not removed by him or he consented to its use. This may be important when goods are reconditioned or form components of a larger whole. In the case of accessories the goods to which they are subsidiary may be described by trade marks, provided that this does not mislead in any way. The proprietor of a mark may by written contract with the owner or purchaser of goods impose restrictions on marked goods and breach of these constitutes infringement. The restrictions bind anyone who takes the goods with notice, unless they took from or under someone who took for value in good faith without notice. The vested rights of one who used a similar mark before the registration of the plaintiff's mark are saved as also is the right of a person to the bona fide use of his own name, address or the description and quality of his goods.

The proprietor of a mark need not be a manufacturer. He may be e.g. an importer, distributor or finisher of the goods. On joint application with the proprietor, another person may be registered as a registered user of a mark. Joint registration is only possible when all the joint proprietors are connected with all the goods. Associated trade marks, which are only assignable and transmissible as a whole, are registered when a proprietor has identical or similar marks for classes of goods. He may also have a series of marks for similar goods or may divide a mark, using the parts as separate marks. A proprietor, but not a registered user, may transmit or assign his right to a trade mark but if it is to be assigned apart from the goodwill of a business the Registrar may direct advertisements. Registration may be subject to the disclaiming of parts of a trade mark. A mark which is deceptive, confusing, contrary to law or morality or any scandalous design cannot be registered. Where a well known trade mark, consisting of an invented word or words, is registered for any goods, a defensive trade mark may be registered (even though it is not to be used) to prevent the first mark being used for different types of goods if such use would be taken as indicating a trade connection between these different types of goods and the proprietor of the mark.

Registration is initially for seven years and thereafter for successive periods of fourteen years. If a mark has not been used for five years, then in the absence of special circumstances, a person aggrieved may apply to have it removed.

Trade marks and passing off are related fields of law. The Trade Marks Act 1938, s. 2 in providing that no action may be taken for the infringement of an unregistered mark expressly saves the law of passing off. Passing off may also give a remedy for the spoken as distinct from the visual misuse of a trade mark. For passing off the plaintiff must prove not merely wrongful use of his device but also that he has an established goodwill in it but this is not required in an action for infringement of a registered mark. Thus such a mark will protect a new business or type of goods and proof of infringement is simpler and cheaper than proof of passing off but passing off will protect against misleading forms of indicating a trade connection other than the use of a mark, such as confusing similarity of appearance or get up of goods.

The Unfair Contract Terms Act 1977† has only limited application to any contract in so far as it relates to the creation, transfer or termination of any right in a trade mark.

Since 1978 state immunity has not fully applied to trademarks actions.

Trading Standards Officers. Local Government officials who enforce consumer protection legislation.

Transferor by delivery of a bill of exchange or promissory note. A holder who effects a negotiation of a bearer instrument by delivery and who incurs no liability on the instrument itself. The Bills of Exchange Act 1882, s. 58 provides that the transferor is taken to warrant to his immediate transferee for value (*see* CONSIDERATION FOR A BILL OF EXCHANGE) that the instrument is what it purports to be, that he has a right to transfer it, and that at the time of transfer he was unaware of any fact rendering it valueless.

Transfer order. The Consumer Credit Act 1974, s. 133 provides that in proceedings involving a regulated agreement the court may make such an order transferring the creditor's title in part of the goods to the debtor and the return to the creditor of the remainder.

Traveller's Cheques. These are instruments by which a traveller may obtain cash from a bank of which he is not a customer. The documents take a variety of forms some of which resemble a promissory note in that the issuing bank promises to reimburse anyone providing cash for the traveller's cheques, others of which resemble a bill of exchange or cheque in that the issuing bank orders payment to be made to the person presenting the traveller's cheques. It is normally the case that on purchase the holder of the traveller's cheque is required to sign each cheque in the presence of an official of the issuing bank or institution and the traveller's cheques state payment is not to be made unless the holder provides a further counter-signature. Hence a traveller's cheque is a conditional instrument and cannot be either a bill of exchange or cheque, which require an unconditional order, or a promissory note which requires an unconditional promise. It has been argued that mercantile custom may have rendered travellers' cheques negotiable independently of the other categories of negotiable instrument but as yet there are no authorities in point in this country.

Trespass to goods. One of the torts now grouped together as wrongful interference with goods. Trespass to goods is any direct interference with the possession of goods which does not necessarily imply a denial of the plaintiff's title to them, such as moving goods without his permission, *Fouldes v Willoughby* (1841) 8 M & W 540. If the interference implies a denial of title the tort will co-exist with conversion. Any unauthorised touching or carrying off of another's goods will constitute this tort, the better view being that it is actionable per se and the plaintiff need not show actual loss. The plaintiff must have had possession except that a trustee may sue for trespass to goods in the possession of a beneficiary and the title of executors and administrators relates back to the death so that they can sue for trespasses between the death and the grant of probate or letters of administration. When there is a bailment at will either bailor or bailee may sue but when there is a bailment for a term (fixed period) only the bailee may do so. The bailor will have an action in case for any harm to the reversion. A plaintiff must prove that the defendant was either intentional or negligent, *Fowler v Lanning* [1959] 1 QB 426 and it may be that since *Letang v Cooper* [1965] 1 QB 232 intention must be proved, negligent interference being left to the tort of negligence where harm must be proved. Inevitable accident is a defence when there is no intent to interfere, *N.C.B. v Evans* [1951] 2 KB 861, but not mistake where there is intent to interfere but error as to justification, *Kirk v Gregory* (1876) 1 Ex D 55. Other defences are that the act was done in defence of person or property or in exercise of a legal right, as in levying distress. A finder does not commit trespass by taking lost property into his care.

The Torts (Interference with Goods) Act 1977 (ss. 3–10) as to form of judgment when goods are detained, interlocutory relief, extinction of title on satisfaction of damages, allowance for improvement of goods, double liability, competing claims, concurrent actions and co-owners may all apply to trespass as well as to conversion. By s. 11 contributory negligence is not a defence to intentional trespass to goods. By s. 8 it is now always a defence to show that some third party has a better title than the plaintiff.

Trover. A synonym for conversion. *See* CONVERSION.

Trustee in bankruptcy. His chief duty is to realise the estate of the bankrupt to best advantage and to distribute it as speedily as possible amongst the creditors. More persons than one may be appointed by the creditors, or appointments may be made of persons to hold office in succession. From the adjudication until the appointment of a trustee and during any vacancy the Official Receiver is trustee. The property of the bankrupt vests in the trustee and on resignation and new appointment it passes from trustee to trustee without any need for a conveyance; the certificate of appointment is evidence of ownership.

The trustee may be appointed by the creditors at any of their meetings after it has been resolved that there should be an adjudication of the debtor, or the appointment may be made by the Committee of Inspection if the creditors have resolved to leave the choice to it, or the appointment may be made by the Department of Trade if the creditors do not appoint within four weeks of adjudication or seven days of the failure of negotiations for a composition or scheme or within three weeks of a vacancy. The trustee appointed by the Department ceases to hold office if the creditors later choose a trustee. The trustee may, but need not be, a creditor himself. The Official Receiver may not be a trustee except when there is a vacancy or when the estate is unlikely to exceed £4000 when there may be summary administration or when there is administration in bankruptcy of the estate of a deceased debtor.

The appointment of a trustee is not complete until the Department of Trade has given a certificate of appointment. This will only be given when the trustee has given security, fixed by the Department, for the due performance of his duties. The Department may refuse the certificate if the proposed trustee was not elected in good faith or is unfit to act, as when he has previously been removed from a trusteeship for misconduct or neglect, or if he is subject to conflicts of interest. Refusal of a certificate may be reviewed in the High Court. The appointment must be advertised in the *London Gazette* and a local newspaper.

The trustee will cease to hold office if he resigns, is removed, has a receiving order made against him or is released. To resign he should call a meeting of creditors, giving seven days notice of it to the Official

Receiver. The meeting may accept or reject the resignation. He may be removed by the Department of Trade for misconduct, failure to perform his duties, if the trusteeship is being needlessly protracted without probable advantage, if because of illness or absence he is unable to perform his duties, if because of his connection with the estate, the bankrupt or a creditor, he might find difficulty in acting impartially or where in any other matter he has been removed from office because of misconduct. If the creditors by ordinary resolution disapprove of the removal he or they may appeal to the High Court. When the estate has been fully realised or a trustee has resigned or been removed he may apply to the Department of Trade for release. This will only be granted after full investigation and notice to the debtor and creditors. It frees the trustee with regard to all matters done in his official capacity but is revocable on proof of fraud or concealment. Appeal against refusal lies to the High Court.

The trustee may be supervised by a committee of inspection†. This will audit his books and for the exercise of certain of his powers he will require the approval of the committee or, if there is none, then of the Department of Trade.

The trustee may sell all or any part of the bankrupt's property by public or private sale and transfer it to purchasers; he is not personally liable for selling goods which are on the debtor's premises or in his possession if he does so without negligence and without notice that they belong to third parties. The trustee may also give receipts discharging the person paying, prove for and draw dividends to which the bankrupt is entitled and exercise any power given him by the Bankruptcy Act 1914 and execute instruments to carry it out. He may transfer choses in action, stock, shares in ships and company stock and shares just as the bankrupt could have done. He must, as soon as may be, take possession of the deeds, books and documents of the bankrupt and of all parts of his property capable of manual delivery. Choses in action are deemed to be assigned to the trustee. This is the realisation of property divisible amongst creditors, which may include property comprised in voidable settlements or used by the debtor to make a fraudulent preference. The trustee may make a disclaimer† of onerous property and must investigate, admit or reject proof of debts. He must then 'with all convenient speed' arrange for distribution of property amongst creditors in the form of dividends.

The trustee is under extensive obligations to account. On request he must furnish any creditor with a list of creditors showing the amounts of their debts and if required by one-sixth of the creditors he must furnish a statement of accounts down to the date of the notice. He must always keep a record book and a cash book and a trading account book if he is carrying the debtor's business. The books are audited by the committee of inspection, when there is one, and by the Department of Trade. The committee must see all books and vouchers at least once every three months and can call for them at any time. Subject to the Insolvency Act 1976, s. 26 the Department of Trade may audit every six months from the receiving order to the trustee's release and at least once a year the trustee must submit a statement to the Department showing the proceedings up to the date of the statement. The trustee must not pay any money he receives as trustee into his private bank account and if he retains for more than ten days a sum exceeding £100 without authority from the Department he may be liable to penalties. The money should be paid into the Insolvency Services Account at the Bank of England.

Sometimes money handled by the trustee may be left at a local bank. A debtor's account is usually kept open for seven days after the first meeting of creditors and the funds of the estate may be kept at a local bank if the trustee, on the application of the committee of inspection, obtains permission from the Department of Trade or, if there is no committee, obtains such permission for special reasons. The trustee's remuneration is settled by the creditors, or by the committee of inspection, if the creditors so resolve. It should be a commission or percentage partly on the amount realised after deducting securities and partly on the amount distributed in dividends. The Department of Trade will settle it if a fourth in number of value of the creditors dissent or when the bankrupt satisfies the Department that the amount is unreasonably large or when the trustee was appointed by the Department of Trade.

The trustee must not make any arrangement to be remunerated by the bankrupt or by a solicitor or any person employed about the bankruptcy nor may he arrange to share his earnings with them. Nor may he arrange to share his earnings with creditors. The trustee must not indirectly or directly purchase the estate or make any profit out of it other than his remuneration.

If the bankrupt or the creditors or any other person is aggrieved by any act or decision of the trustee he may apply to the court which may make such order as it thinks just. The bankrupt can only apply if there might be a surplus nor in the absence of fraud can he interfere with the trustee's routine administration or question the exercise of his discretion. (See the Bankruptcy Act 1914, ss. 19, 20, 37, 48–69, 76–95, 116, 117, 143, 161 and the Insolvency Act 1976).

Trust letter. *See* BANKERS' COMMERCIAL CREDITS.

Trust receipt. *See* BANKERS' COMMERCIAL CREDITS.

Truth in lending. A term applied to requirements in consumer credit business that notices and advertisements should indicate the true rate of interest and other charges for obtaining credit. The Consumer

Truth in lending

Credit Act 1974, s. 20 provides that the Secretary of State shall make regulations prescribing what items shall enter into the total charge for credit and how that is to be calculated.

U

Uberrimae Fidei Contracts. *See* MISREPRESENTATION. The most important examples of these in commercial law are contracts of insurance and the obligation of utmost good faith (*uberrima fides*) means that mere non-disclosure of, as distinct from misrepresentation of, material facts which are known or ought to be known to him on the part of the party on whom the obligation rests will render the contract voidable. In practice by the use of basis clauses in policies insurers have rendered these voidable even for non-disclosure of facts which could not have been known to the insured.

U.C.P. *See* BANKERS' COMMERCIAL CREDITS.

Ultra Vires Act. 'Beyond the powers act.' *See* CONTRACTUAL CAPACITY.

Umpire. *See* ARBITRATOR.

Unascertained goods. This term is not defined in the Sale of Goods Act 1979 but seems to apply where the goods are indicated by description. only or are an unsevered part of a larger bulk. They become ascertained by subsequent appropriation to the contract (*see* C.I.F CONTRACTS, 'notice of appropriation') or by severance from the bulk. It seems this may take place by exhaustion of the bulk, leaving only the quantity for the relevant contract, *Wait & James v Midland Bank* (1926) 31 Com Cas 172. The terms 'ascertained' and 'unascertained goods' appear in the Sale of Goods Act 1979, ss. 16–18 and (by implication) 19 (1) dealing with passing of property in sale of goods and s. 52 (1) dealing with specific performance. (*See* REMEDIES OF THE BUYER IN SALE OF GOODS). When a complete bulk shipment is covered by contracts physical allocation may not be necessary to ascertain the goods for a single contract, ascertainment taking place at shipment, and appropriation may not be necessary when the goods are ascertained by exhaustion, *Karlshamms Oljefabriker v Eastport, The Eilafi* [1982] 1 All ER 208.

Unconfirmed Credit. *See* BANKERS' COMMERCIAL CREDITS.

Undisclosed principal. When an agent either identifies or discloses the existence of his principal, the latter alone is normally liable and entitled on the transaction concluded by the agent, but if the agent does not disclose the existence of his principal when he concludes a contract then in general either the principal or the agent may sue the third party who in turn may sue either the principal or the agent when the principal's existence is disclosed. If the principal sues he does so subject to any right of set-off which the third party may have acquired against the agent before he knew of the principal's existence, *George v Clagett* (1797) 7 TR 359, but the set-off can only be claimed if the third party believes the agent to be a principal, not if he was uncertain or indifferent on the matter, *Cooke v Eshelby* (1887) 12 App Cas 271. The contract may exclude intervention by the principal when the agent uses language indicating he alone is a party, *Humble v Hunter* (1848) 12 QB 310 (owner). If the agent is described in terms which are equivocal the principal may intervene, *Fred Drughorn v Rederiakstiebolaget Transatlantic* [1919] AC 203 (charterer); *Danziger v Thompson* [1944] KB 654, (tenant); *Epps v Rothnie* [1945] KB 562 (landlord); Intervention will also be excluded if the contract was intended to be made by the third party with the agent, and no one else, *Greer v Downs* [1927] 2 KB 28; *Said v Butt* [1920] 3 KB 497. The third party must elect to sue either principal or agent. Commencing proceedings against one would not necessarily be a final election, but recovering judgment would be, *Clarkson Booker v Andjel* [1964] 2 QB 775. If the judgment is unsatisfied and set aside on its merits a further action can be brought but not if it is set aside by consent. If the third party settles with the agent before he knows of the principal's existence he will be discharged, *Coates v Lewes* (1808) 1 Camp 444. *Armstrong v Stokes* (1872) LR 7 QB 598 suggests that if the principal settles with the agent before disclosure this discharges the principal as against the third party but this is contrary to *Heald v Kenworthy* (1855) 10 Ex 739 and was rejected in *Irvine v Watson* (1880) 5 QBD 414.

Undue influence. This renders voidable at the option of the party influenced any contract procured by the improper use of influence by one party over the other. In many relationships, e.g. solicitor and client, doctor and patient, trustee and beneficiary, parent and child, perhaps fiance and fiancee but not husband and wife, influence will be presumed and the apparently stronger party must disprove it, e.g. by showing that the other had fully informed independent legal advice, *Inche Noriah v Omar* [1929] AC 127, but outside these the burden of proof is reversed and the apparently weaker party must prove influence, *Smith v Kay* (1859) 7 HLC 750; *Howes v Bishop* [1909] 2 KB 390. Judgments in some recent cases, e.g. Lord Denning in *Lloyds Bank v Bundy* [1975] QB 326; *Pau On v Lau Yui* [1979] 3 All ER 65; *North Ocean v Hyundai* [1979] QB 705 suggest possible expansion of this concept to situations of substantial inequality of bargaining power or economic duress.

Unenforceable contract. This term is applied to contracts which are in other respects valid simple contracts but which have not been evidenced by a note or memorandum in writing in accordance with the Statute of Frauds 1677, s. 4 (guarantees: contracts to answer for the debt, default or miscarriage of another) or the Law of Property Act 1925, s. 40 (contracts for the sale or other disposition of land or any interest therein). *See* FORM IN CONTRACT.

Unfair Contract Terms Act 1977. This applies to exemption and exclusion clauses, which are widely defined in s. 13 as including terms restricting or rendering onerous the enforcement of liability or any right or remedy or excluding or restricting rules of evidence or procedure. The Act is additional to other methods of defeating such clauses. Some it nullifies, others may operate if they are reasonable but the Act in general only applies to clauses restricting 'business liability' arising from the running of a business or use of business premises. 'Business' includes professions, Government departments and local or public authorities. Many contracts are outside the Act, (see ss. 26, 27, 29 and Sch. 1), including international supply contracts, insurance, contracts relating to land, patents, trade marks, copyrights, registered designs and the formation, dissolution and structure of a company. A written submission to arbitration is not an exemption clause and the Act does not apply to any term incorporated in a contract by statute under an international agreement or which has been approved by a competent public authority. Whilst liability for death or injury negligently caused may not be excluded in carriage of goods by sea, salvage or towage, other restrictions on exclusion clauses in such contracts only operate when one party is 'dealing as a consumer'. By s. 12 this means he must not contract or profess to contract in the course of a business whilst the other party does and, additionally in sale of goods, the goods† must be such as are ordinarily supplied for private use and consumption. In auction sale and sale by competitive tender buyers do not 'deal as consumers' and hence reasonable exemption clauses may always operate. Employees, but not employers, may rely on clauses exempting from liability for negligently caused death or injury. The Act does not apply if the proper law is English merely by the parties' choice but does apply if a foreign proper law has been chosen to evade it or one of the parties, resident in the United Kingdom, dealt as a consumer and the essential steps of contract formation took place here.

Subject to these limits the Act renders ineffective all attempted exclusion, whether reasonable or not, of liability in the following cases:

(1) by contract term or notice for negligence causing death or injury; (s.2).

(2) by term or notice in a guarantee for loss or damage caused by defective consumer goods in consumer use resulting from negligence in their manufacture or distribution; (s. 5).

(3) by contract term for breach of the term as to title in sale of goods,

hire purchase (though the primary legislation allows restriction and title can be excluded in analogous contracts when reasonable). In sale and hire purchase this extends to private as well as business transactions; (s. 6).

(4) by contract term for breach of the other statutory implied terms in sale of goods, hire purchase and analagous contracts when the other party is dealing as a consumer. Although in sale and hire purchase this is extended to private transactions it will not operate there since one party cannot then deal as a consumer. Hence reasonable exemption clauses will operate; (ss. 6 and 7).

(5) by contract term for any liability arising under the Consumer Protection Act 1961, s. 3; (s. 30).

Again subject to its limits, the Unfair Contract Terms Act 1977 requires any effective exclusion of liability to satisfy its test of reasonableness in the following cases:

(1) by contract term or notice for negligence causing damage other than death or injury; (s. 2).

(2) by contract term for breach of contract when one party is dealing as a consumer or on the other's standard written terms, nor can the other claim to render no performance or one different from that expected unless the term is reasonable; (s. 3).

(3) by contract term for breach of the statutory implied terms (other than that as to title) in sale of goods, hire purchase and analagous contracts when no party is dealing as a consumer; (ss. 6 and 7).

(4) by contract term for misrepresentation prior to contract; (s. 8).

A party dealing as a consumer is not bound by an unreasonable indemnity clause (s. 6). A reasonable exemption or indemnity clause when valid remains so even if the contract has been terminated by breach or by a party electing to treat it as repudiated and the affirmation of a contract after breach does not dispense with any requirement of reasonableness (s. 9). Evasion of the Act by putting exemption clauses in a separate secondary contract is prevented (s. 10). The burden of proof of 'reasonableness' is on the party alleging it and it is to be assessed by what was known or ought to have been known at the time of the contract (s. 11). Guidelines are provided for sale and hire purchase but may perhaps be used for other contracts. The court should consider the bargaining position of the parties, whether the customer received any inducement to agree to the term, whether he knew or ought to have known of it, whether compliance with any condition in it was practicable when the contract was made and whether goods were prepared to the special order of the customer. (Sch. 2).

Uniform Laws on International Sales Act 1967. This gives effect to two Conventions designed to achieve some uniformity in this field of law, Sch. 1 containing the law on sales, Sch. 2 the law for the formation of such contracts. The two Uniform laws are part of English law and available whenever the transaction is governed by English law, but apply only when the parties have expressly so chosen. The parties may elect to apply the laws to domestic transactions, but only so far as this does not conflict with mandatory provisions of English Law. The Act came into force in 1972 but appears to be little used. The Law on Sale deals with delivery, conformity of goods with the contract, handing over of documents, undertakings as to title, contracts of carriage and insurance, payment of the price, avoidance of the contract, damages and risk. It does not deal with validity of the contract or any usage, the passing of property, effects of frustration or failure to obtain export–import licences nor does it provide detailed regulation for c.i.f., f.o.b. and ex ship contracts. The Law on Formation deals with offer and acceptance, providing that silence shall not constitute acceptance, that no formalities are required, that an offer must be definite, communicated, may be expressed to be irrevocable, but otherwise may lapse if the revocation is communicated at or before the offer or after that if this is done in good faith and fair dealing. Acceptance may be by conduct. If it is materially qualified it will be a counter-offer. It must be communicated with the time fixed or within a reasonable time or, in the case of an oral offer, immediately, unless time for reflection is required. Delay in acceptance may be waived by the offeror, or may be ignored if it would have been in time but for failure in the means of transmission. Acceptance may be revoked by a communication before or at the same time as the communication of the acceptance. Usage may be employed in interpreting both Laws.

Unilateral contract. One consisting of a promise for an act and contrasted with bilateral and synallagmatic contracts where promises are given in consideration of promises.

Universal Copyright Convention. *See* INTELLECTUAL PROPERTY, INTERNATIONAL PROTECTION.

Unjust enrichment. Alternative title for quasi-contract (q.v.).

Unliquidated damages. Damages which are not fixed or calculable before an action but must be assessed by the court or arbitrator.

Unpaid seller. The Sale of Goods Act 1979, s. 38 provides that a seller is unpaid when the whole of the price† has not been paid or tendered or when a bill of exchange or other negotiable instrument has been received in conditional payment and been dishonoured. 'Seller' includes anyone in the position of a seller, such as an agent of the seller to whom a bill of lading has been endorsed or an agent who has paid or is responsible for the price. The seller has remedies of lien, stoppage in transit and resale against the goods and actions for the price and damages (ss. 39–50). The first three remedies can be used when the buyer has acquired property in but not possession of goods which the seller has come under an obligation to deliver in performance of the contract. If property has not passed (*see* PASSING OF PROPERTY) the seller has rights over the goods at least as extensive as the three remedies, s. 39 (2). One pre-condition of lien and stoppage is insolvency of the buyer. 'Insolvency' here means that he has ceased to pay his debts in the ordinary course of business, whether or not he has committed an act of bankruptcy, s. 61 (4). Lien is a right to retain possession of the goods for the price and arises either where the contract has no term as to credit, or where the time allowed for credit has expired or where the buyer is insolvent. It may be exercised even if the seller holds as bailee for the buyer and even over such goods as may remain after part delivery to the buyer, unless such delivery shows an intention to waive the lien (ss. 41–42). The lien is lost when the goods are delivered to a carrier to take to the buyer without the seller reserving a right of disposal, or when the buyer or his agent lawfully obtains possession of them or when it is waived (s. 43). By s. 44 if the buyer becomes insolvent the unpaid seller is given a right of stoppage in transit whilst the goods are held by an intermediary in transit to the buyer. Transit is defined in s. 45 and methods of effecting stoppage in s. 46. Stoppage is now of diminished importance since modern methods of payment such as bankers' commercial credits eliminate the need for it. By s. 47 lien or stoppage are not affected by any sub-sale by the buyer unless the seller has assented to it and the assent must show waiver of the lien, *Mordaunt v British Oil & Cake Mills* [1910] 2 KB 502: *Mount v Jay* [1960] 1 QB 159. But if a document of title has been transferred to anyone as buyer or owner of the goods and he transfers the document to another taking in good faith and for value then if the second transaction is a sale the original seller's rights of lien and stoppage are defeated and if it is a pledge they can only be exercised subject to it. By s. 48 a sale is not rescinded merely by the seller exercising rights of lien or stoppage but if he improperly re-sells a bona fide second buyer gets a good title by exception to nemo dat quod non habet. But if the goods are perishable or if the unpaid seller gives the buyer notice that he intends to re-sell and the buyer does not pay or tender the price within a reasonable time the seller is entitled to re-sell the goods and sue the buyer for any loss. Re-sale rescinds the sale, *Ward v Bignall* [1967] 1 QB 534, as does re-sale under an express term in the contract. The seller may include a reservation of title clause in the contract which may entitle him to recover the goods or proceeds of sale if the buyer does not pay, *Aluminium Industries v Romalpa* [1976] 1 WLR 676. This is not governed by the Act.

By s. 49 if property has passed to the buyer and he wrongfully fails to pay or if payment is required on a day certain, irrespective of property passing, the unpaid seller may sue for the price, without falling under an obligation of mitigation. By s. 50 the unpaid seller may sue for damages a buyer who wrongfully fails to accept the goods. (*See* ACCEPTANCE IN SALE OF GOODS). If property has passed or there is a fixed payment day and also non-acceptance the seller may choose whether to sue for price or damages. The measure of damages is the estimated loss directly and naturally resulting in the ordinary course of events from the breach (cf. first rule in *Hadley v Baxendale*: Damages). If there is an available market for the goods the measure is prima facie the difference between the contract price and the current or market price at the time for acceptance or, if no time was fixed, the time of refusal to accept. 'Market' here seems to mean a level of trade, not a place or institution. This is also the measure for anticipatory breach. If the trial comes before the date for acceptance the court must estimate the market price for that date. Where the price falls between repudiation and the date for acceptance if the seller accepts the repudiation he should re-sell to mitigate loss. If he does not accept he need not thus mitigate but damages are in either case measured against the market price for the acceptance date, *Garnac Grain v Faure & Fairclough* [1968] AC 1130. If there is no market because the goods are unique the measure may be loss of profit, *Re Vic Mill* [1913] 1 Ch 465. By s. 37 if the seller is ready to deliver but the buyer does not take delivery within a reasonable time of being asked, the buyer is liable to the seller for any loss caused by this failure and for a reasonable charge for care of the goods. Under s. 54 the seller may also recover special damages and interest.

Unrestricted-use credit. *See* CREDIT.

Unsolicited Goods and Services Act 1971. *See* CONVERSION and BAILMENT.

Usual authority of an agent. This may be used in any one of three meanings. It may be a form of implied actual authority derived from the normal powers of a position or appointment held by the agent; it may be a form of apparent authority when the appearance of authority is derived from some position or appointment held by an agent, as when the principal has placed some secret limit upon what would otherwise be the agent's authority, or when an agent's authority has been terminated by the principal but notice of this has not been given to third parties and it may give rise to the anomalous situation exemplified in the case of *Watteau v Fenwick* [1893] 1 QB 346 where a principal was held liable on a contract for the purchase of cigars by the agent, a manager of a public house, despite the fact that there was no actual authority, because the principal had forbidden such a purchase, and no apparent authority since, far from there being any holding out, the third party was ignorant of the principal's existence. It was, however, usual for such purchases to be made by such managers. It has been suggested that the best explanation of such a case is that the principal is liable for having created or permitted, not an appearance of agency, but of ownership.

V

Variation and waiver of contract. *See* DISCHARGE OF CONTRACT BY AGREEMENT, PROMISSORY ESTOPPEL.

Vicarious liability. Under this head of tort an employer ('master') is held liable for the torts committed by his employee ('servant') in the course of his employment. The servant is in fact jointly liable with the master and if the employer is held vicariously liable he may in his turn sue the servant on an implied term in the contract of employment for an indemnity but after an employers' insurer had thus sued in *Lister v Romford Ice and Cold Storage Co* [1957] AC 555 insurers agreed not to enforce this indemnity liability and a countervailing term excluding it in an industrial context was implied in *Morris v Ford Motor Co* [1973] QB 792.

For vicarious liability a servant used to be defined as an employee for whom the employer could not only define the aim of the work but also its detailed execution, but this test was unrealistic in many modern circumstances. Hence it has been replaced or supplemented by the 'scope of organisation' test under which a servant is an employee who is part of the master's permanent organisation as contrasted with one who is hired for a specific task, *Stevenson, Jordan & Harrison v Macdonald & Evans* [1952] 1 TLR 101. The master is liable for all torts within the scope or course of the servant's employment, that is, incidental to what he is employed to do even if the tort is fraudulent or a crime, *Lloyd v Grace, Smith & Co* [1912] AC 716; *Morris v Martin* [1966] 1 QB 716. The master may be liable for conduct outside working hours, *Poland v Parr* [1927] 1 KB 236 or which he has forbidden, *Limpus v L.G.O.* (1862) 1 H & C 526 unless the prohibition shows the conduct is outside the scope of employment, *C.P.R. v Lockhart* [1942] AC 591.

If the work of an employee is not under the employers' detailed control or if he is not part of the master's permanent organisation the employee is known as an independent contractor. The employer is then not liable on the basis of torts being committed within the course of employment, but only if the tort committed by the independent contractor is instrumental in breaking a duty incumbent on the employer, e.g. not to create a nuisance, not to create dangers on the highway, not to cause damage by the use of fire. The employer is not liable for collateral negligence on the part of the contractor, that is harm from conduct not within the specific risks underlying in the employer's special duties which ground liability for independent contractors, *Padbury v Holliday & Greenwood* (1912) 28 TLR 494, though if the contractor had been a servant the conduct might have been within the course of employment thus involving vicarious liability. (*See* AGENT). In exceptional cases there may be vicarious liability in criminal law.

Voidable Contract. A contract which, because of some vitiating factor such as misrepresentation, one of the parties may choose to rescind, thus avoiding the contract for the future, or may choose to affirm, thus rendering the contract wholly valid. If a third party acquires in good faith and for value an interest in the subject matter of such a contract before he has been notified of rescission his interest stands good.

Void contract. An agreement in appearance a contract but which, because of some serious vitiating factor such as mistake or illegality, is in law devoid of contractual effect and hence may not e.g. result in the passing of property† in sale of goods. Though devoid of contractual effect a void contract may have some legal effect, e.g. it may be a crime, and the rights of parties to a void contract to recover money or property transferred under it vary with different grounds of nullity.

Voyage Charterparty. A form of charterparty under which the charterer hires a ship for a voyage or voyages, the control and management of the crew and vessel remaining with the shipowner. At common law a number of terms will be implied into such contracts. These may be varied or excluded subject to the Unfair Contract Terms Act 1977† which has only limited application to charterparties, except in favour of a person dealing as a consumer. The major implied terms are that the ship is seaworthy† at the time of sailing from the port of loading, that the voyage will be commenced and carried out without unreasonable delay and that there shall be no unwarranted deviation from the route. The common law term as to seaworthiness is absolute in that the shipowner must provide a ship which at the outset of the voyage is fit to carry the cargo on the agreed route. Defects arising later will not amount to a breach of this obligation unless the voyage is by stages, in which case the ship must be seaworthy at the commencement of each stage, *The Vortigern* [1899] P 140. If no route is specified the ship should follow either the shortest geographical route or the usual route, *Reardon Smith Line v Black Sea & Baltic Lines Insurance Co* [1939] AC 562. Deviation is often permitted by an express term but apart from that is permissible for the safety of the ship and crew even though the emergency resulted from a culpable act on the part of the master, *Kish v Taylor* [1912] AC 604, and also to save life but not property, *Scaramanga v Stamp* (1880) 5 CPD 295, though the Hague Rules† allow deviation to save property.

Voluntary unwarranted deviation renders the charterparty voidable by the charterer and, if loss or damage to cargo occurs, the shipowner cannot rely on excepted perils terms, *Morrison v Shaw, Savill & Co* [1916] 2 KB 783. Damages may also be claimed.

The terms as to unseaworthiness and delay are 'innominate', that is, neither conditions nor warranties, so that whether they entitle the charterer to repudiate and claim damages or merely to claim damages will depend on the character of any breach that in fact occurs, *Hong Kong Fir Shipping Co Ltd v Kawasaki Kisen Kaisha* [1962] 2 QB 26. The charterer is under an implied obligation not to ship goods which involve the risk of danger or delay to the ship, *Mitchell Cotts v Steel Bros* [1916] 2 KB 610. Merchant Shipping Act 1894, ss. 446–450.

A voyage charterparty will usually contain a term as to the 'preliminary voyage' to bring the vessel to the loading port together with a 'cancelling clause', allowing for the cancellation of the charterparty if the ship does not arrive by a specified date or within a reasonable time. The charterer will usually be required to load 'a full and complete cargo' and to pay dead freight for any cargo space not filled. The charterparty will normally specify a number of 'laydays' or 'laytime' for loading and unloading cargo. These normally start to run when the ship is an 'arrived ship', i.e. has reached the commercial area of the port in question and is at the charterer's disposal even though no berth may be available for her, *Oldendorff v Tradex, The Johanna Oldendorff* [1974] AC 479, *The Maratha Envoy* [1978] AC 1. 'Demurrage' as agreed damages, will be payable, generally per day, for time taken in loading and unloading beyond the laytime and the same term is also applied to unliquidated damages payable for unreasonable delay by the charterer when no laytime is specified but in neither case will the charterer have to pay if the delay is the fault of the shipowner. The charterparty may also contain war clauses, strike clauses and ice clauses covering loss, damage or delay or re-routing from those causes. A 'cesser' clause may be included to cover the case when the charterer is acting as an agent for a third party in obtaining the cargo. This will provide that the charterer's liability for freight is to cease as soon as the cargo is loaded and gives the shipowner a lien over the cargo for freight†, dead freight† and demurrage.

W

Wagering contracts. 'A wagering contract is one by which two persons, professing to hold opposite views touching the issue of a future uncertain event, mutually agree that, dependent upon the determination of that event, one shall win from the other, and that other shall pay or hand over to him, a sum of money or other stake; neither of the contracting parties having any other interest in that contract than the sum or stake he will so win or lose, there being no other real consideration for the making of such contract by either of the parties.' *Carlill v Carbolic Smoke Ball Co* [1892] 2 QB 484 at 490, per Hawkins J.

A wager may be on a present or past event when there is uncertainty in the parties' knowledge. Each party must stand to win or lose, *Ellesmere v Wallace* [1929] 2 Ch 1, hence many betting transactions, e.g. bets placed with the totalisator, are not in law wagers. There can only be two parties. Certain commercial agreements such as insurance without an insurable interest, stock exchange contracts to pay differences without taking delivery of shares and apparent sale of goods where the price is contingent on an uncertain event may in law be wagers, *Brogden v Marriott* (1836) 3 Bing NC 88; *Rourke v Short* (1856) 5 E & B 904.

The Gaming Act 1845, s. 18 provides that all gaming or wagering contracts shall be null and void and that no action shall be brought to recover any money or valuable thing alleged to have been won or which has been deposited in the hands of any person to abide the event on which a wager was made. Thus, not only is the wager void but so too is any agreement to circumvent this as when a loser promises to pay the winner the amount of the wager in return for a non-wagering consideration, e.g. not being reported as a defaulter, *Hill v William Hill* [1949] AC 430. A person may recover from a stakeholder his own stake before it has been paid to the other, s. 18 merely barring the recovery of an opponent's stake. Prizes for lawful games may be recovered but not when the event is in fact a wager, *Diggle v Higgs* (1877) 2 Ex D 422. No game is now of itself illegal but gaming may be if it infringes the complex requirements of Gaming Act 1968. As wagers are void, not illegal, a bookmaker's partnership is not illegal, *Jeffrey v Bamford* [1921] 2 KB 351. Under the Gaming Act 1892 an agent, employed to make wagers cannot claim an indemnity (*see*

INDEMNITY OF AN AGENT) for money he has paid to the winner nor can a principal sue an agent for failing to make a bet, *Cohen v Kittell* (1889) 22 QBD 680, but if an agent receives winnings his principal may sue him for these, *De Mattos v Benjamin* (1894) 63 LJQB 248. By the Gaming Act 1968, s. 16 (4) a cheque given for cash or tokens on registered gaming premises is enforceable between the parties. Otherwise negotiable instruments given in settlement of any wager are not enforceable between the original parties. If cheques are given in settlement of gaming wagers by the Gaming Act 1835 they are deemed to have been given for an illegal consideration and may be enforced by a later holder if he can prove that value was subsequently given in good faith; if cheques are given in settlement of non-gaming wagers the Gaming Act 1845 renders the consideration void but consideration will be presumed in favour of a subsequent holder. (*See* CONSIDERATION FOR NEGOTIABLE INSTRUMENTS). *Woolf v Hamilton* [1898] 2 QB 337; *Fitch v Jones* (1855) 5 E & B 238.

Money lent for illegal gaming is not recoverable but *C.T.H. v Ward* [1965] 2 QB 63 suggests it is otherwise if it is for legal gaming. The Gaming Act 1968 makes validating provision for loans and cheques for gaming lawful within the Act. Loans for gaming abroad are recoverable if recoverable in the foreign country. If money is advanced by payment directly to the winner it cannot later be recovered from the loser nor if it is advanced to the loser whilst imposing on him an obligation to use it to settle wagers, *Macdonald v Green* [1951] 1 KB 594, but may be recovered if advanced without such an obligation, *Re O'Shea, Ex p Lancaster* [1911] 2 KB 981.

Waiver of tort. *See* QUASI-CONTRACT.

Warranty. In sale of goods and contract generally a term less important than a condition. See the Sale of Goods Act 1979, ss. 11 (3), 53 and 61 (1). Breach of warranty is remediable by damages (in sale of goods by reduction of the price) and not by repudiation, which is available for breach of condition. Whether the parties describe a term as a warranty or condition is not conclusive as to its status, *Schuler v Wickman* [1974] AC 235. In modern insurance law, and in older cases the word 'warranty' may be used of terms breach of which gives rise to a right to repudiate. See the Marine Insurance Act, 1906, s. 33 (3). The word 'warranted' may also be used as a synonym for 'guaranteed', whatever the status of the term embodying the guarantee. *See also* WARRANTY OF AUTHORITY.

Warranty of authority. A person who professes to act as an agent is taken impliedly to undertake to the third party that he possesses the authority that he claims to have. If it transpires that this is not so the third party, if he suffers loss, may sue the professed agent for breach of warranty of authority, the consideration given by the third party for the agent's undertaking being the entry into the transaction on the footing of the assertion of authority, *Collen v Wright* (1857) 8 E & B 647. Good faith will not be a defence to the agent, even if an authority he once possessed has ended without his knowledge, *Yonge v Toynbee* [1910] 1 KB 215, except that Powers of Attorney Act 1971, s. 5 (1) provides that the donee of a power of attorney is not liable if he acts when the power has, unknown to him, been revoked. The warranty is not limited to cases where the purported agent professes to contract, *Starkey v Bank of England* [1903] AC 114. The assertion by the professed agent must be one of fact, not law, *Rashdall v Ford* (1866) LR 2 Eq 750.

Warsaw Convention. *See* CARRIAGE BY AIR: CONVENTIONS AND LEGISLATION.

Work and materials. A contract analagous to sale of goods but where 'the substance of the contract . . . is that skill and labour have to be exercised for the production of [an] article . . . and it is only ancillary to that that there will pass from [one party] to his client or customer some materials in addition to the skill involved . . .' per Greene LJ in *Robinson v Graves* [1935] 1 KB 579 (painting a portrait). Prior to the Law Reform (Enforcement of Contracts) Act 1954 when contracts for the sale of goods of the value of £10 or upwards required special evidence it was important to distinguish contracts for work and materials since they did not require this evidence. The distinction is now less important. Terms similar to those implied in contracts of sale of goods by the Sale of Goods Act 1979 are implied in contracts for work and materials by the Supply of Goods and Services Act 1982. The reproduction of an ordinary article of commerce e.g. a fur coat, (as distinct from an article of unique or special character, e.g. the portrait in *Robinson v Graves*) will be sale of goods, *Marcel Furriers v Tapper* [1953] 1 WLR 49.

Writs of execution in sale of goods. The Supreme Court Act 1981, s. 138 provides that a writ of fieri facias or other writ of execution to enforce a judgment shall bind the execution debtor's property in the goods when the writ is delivered to the Sheriff to be executed but the writ will not defeat anyone who in good faith and for value acquires title to the goods without notice that any writ had been delivered to the Sheriff and remained unexecuted. Once the Sheriff has executed the writ by seizing the goods even a party acting in good faith and for value cannot acquire a title free from the Sheriff's claim and this even though the Sheriff may have allowed the debtor temporary possession of the goods, *Lloyds and Scottish Finance v Modern Cars & Caravans* [1966] 1 QB 764. A writ of execution is effective even against a trustee in bankruptcy except that when the execution is not completed by the date of the receiving order the trustee takes priority over the execution creditor. Similar rules apply to County Court process.

Y

York–Antwerp Rules. *See* GENERAL AVERAGE.